Y0-DCI-997

Special Edition of
COMING OUT OF THE ICE
Prepared especially for

D. James Kennedy, Ph.D.
and Coral Ridge Ministries

Rev.

NOTE: Certain language has been removed from this
book at the request of Dr. Kennedy. An "*" centered in a blank space will indicate that exple-
tives have been deleted.

Rev.

"Herman's tale is awful and heartening—awful that anyone should have undergone such things, and heartening that he did and endured. This book is sure to take its place alongside Solzhenitsyn and Koestler's DARKNESS AT NOON."
William F. Buckley, Jr.

Vyatlag was a frozen-over graveyard   *A. Solzhenitsyn*

A modern classic   *Smith-Richardson Foundation*

It's a tremendous story of courage and love.
Frank Konigsberg (producer)

Never have I read a book so important. Every American should read it   *Charlie Huff*

The mightiest men in history should humble themselves in the shadow of your deeds.   *Dennis M. Rilley*

Every reader of your book is your brother or sister. ICE is second to none except the bible.   *Norman Sayles*

Your book is noble. The best. I hope America proves itself worthy of you and your family. I salute you in humility.
Mrs. R. S. Gorski

I am blind so I identify myself with other people's feelings. Help America Understand.   *Rev. Harold J. Wright*

COMING OUT

an unexpected life

illustrations by Mary Ellen Dohrs

FREEDOM PRESS Ltd.   OKLAHOMA CITY,   OKLAHOMA _____

NOTE: Certain language has been removed from this
      book.   An "*" cen-
      tered in a blank space will indicate that exple-
      tives have been deleted.

OF THE ICE

by Victor Herman

COMING OUT OF THE ICE
A FREEDOM PRESS BOOK

PRINTING HISTORY

Harcourt Brace Javanovich Edition Published 1979

Freedom Press Edition/October 1983

2nd printing . . . . November 1983
3rd printing . . . . November 1983
4th printing . . . . January 1984
5th printing . . . . January 1984
6th printing . . . . March 1984

Copyright © 1979 by Victor Herman

All rights reserved. No part of this publication may be reproduced or transmitted in any form or by any means, electronic or mechanical, including photocopy, recording, or any information storage and retrieval system, without permission in writing from the publisher.

FREEDOM PRESS, Ltd.
5823 Mosteller Drive, Oklahoma City, OK 73112
(405) 843-1561

Printed in the United States of America

Library of Congress Cataloging in Publication Data

Herman, Victor.
  Coming out of the ice.

  1. Herman, Victor. 2. Americans in Russia—Biography. 3. Political prisoners—Russia—Biography.
I. Title.
DK34.A45H47   947.08 [B]   78–14075
ISBN 0-915031-02-7

I dedicate this book to the people of the United States
and the people of the Soviet Union, to the woman who
came to me in the one and will come again to me in the other,
my Siberian wife Galina, and to the daughters that are ours,
Svetlana and Janna.

My debts are many and great and cannot be redeemed. They are especially considerable to David, Harry, Shael, and Helen Herman, to Rebecca and Jack Kemsley, to Bob Greenstein, to Gayle Benderoff. There is another person whose connection with this book is absolute, but because he asks that his name not be cited, I will enter the initials of his son, A. A. L., and state the wish of the father that the boy one day read herein, to know the heart of a man.

V.H.

SPECIAL ACKNOWLEDGEMENTS

To those daring people who, realizing the plight of COMING OUT OF THE ICE, aware of obvious efforts of the Russian Secret Service to suppress its printing and distribution and still came to my help—those founders of FREEDOM PRESS, Jerry Womack, Ed Kopp and Ron Laytner—my grateful thanks.

Victor Herman, Southfield, Michigan 1983

The real names of many people mentioned in this book who are still living have been changed to preserve their privacy.

PROLOGUE

Who chooses for you? Or chose?

My father chose for me—and because I loved him with all it was in me to love with, I let him.

He had an idea, my father. What he had was a dream, and this dream chose *him*. All his life it held him in its hand.

He went where it took him—and he took me with him. To Russia. In 1931. From here, from where I write this, from Detroit, to Russia.

No, he did not *take* me—I followed.

My father? Sam Herman? I would follow him anywhere.

I was a boy. I was sixteen. I am sixty-three now. Even now, a man sixty-three, I would do it still.

I loved that man. It did not matter what his dream was—or where it made me follow. Going where your father goes? I say it is what a son is—and that was *my* dream, to be a son to Sam Herman.

He's dead now. But his dream died long before he did. They killed it for him.

They killed his son for him too—but my father never knew how much. The Russians took me away from my father, and they murdered the years of my youth. They took me away for eighteen years when I was little more than a boy, and when they let me go my father was dead.

There was no boy left in me when they let me go—but even then they did not really let me go. I lived forty-five years in Russia. How do I tell you about that time?

Was it nothing but time as life gives it to you to live?

Who gave me a year in Cell 39? Who delivered me into the vaults of *Spets Korpus?* Who called me forth into the *Lagers* of the north—and into the hole in the frost north of Yeniseysk? Who gave me the year under snow? And gave it also to my wife and my child?

Who summoned me for eighteen years? Who beckoned and said, Victor Herman, eat rat?

It was not my father that did that.

I followed him.

You follow, and it is a life, and that's that.

It was a life like smoke, like *LUCKIES* written in the sky. And then it was a deadfall from sky to earth. That pilot nodded and pointed—*down.*

I jumped. It was the longest fall.

They cheered. They said, look, the Lindbergh of Russia!

I ate an apple all the way down.

My father went and I followed. I was the Lindbergh of Russia and then in Russia I was an American and a slave. You follow, and the going gives you a life—and whatever it is, there is nothing more to say about it than that. Except to tell what happened—except to read the smoke before it is gone.

I used to look into the sky when I was a boy. I saw a plane writing *LUCKIES.* One time when I was a boy they printed *LUCKIES* over the sky of Detroit. I watched that plane make that word and I kept on looking and looking. But in time the air turned, and the letters were gone—just smoke that signified nothing.

My life is like that now—almost all lost smoke. One day my daughters will look, and the thing that it signified will be gone.

I make this record for them, then—words that won't blow away. And I make it for anyone who will look.

A man lived—oh . . . a life.

He began as a son, a boy willing to follow. An American. A dreamer like his father. One summer afternoon in Detroit that boy looked into the sky and saw an airplane write *LUCKIES.* He thought he was the only one who saw. He thought, it's writing for *me,* that airplane.

It is how a boy thinks.

I was forty-five years in Russia and now I am in a room in Detroit. I sit at a table as I write this. There is a window. The table stands against the window. But I cannot see the sky from where I sit. I don't want to.

It is on this page.

Look! Look up!

I am writing this for my daughters. I am writing this for everyone.

Will *you* be the only one who sees?

PART 1

THE BOY WHO WENT OUT: FROM IRONWOOD STREET TO SPETS KORPUS

ONE

It is like two potatoes, my life. What has happened to me, that I live at all, is like a second potato found in the snow, crazily revealed there, dropped warm and heavy from a birch, resting there on the lid of the snow.

That is how it is, my life—from a tree, frozen and barren, a baked potato falls. Look! A potato has grown on a birch tree.

There in Siberia, north of Yeniseysk, in the chop-out, in the hole I chopped in the snow, I told my daughter a fairy tale. I told her the one I knew. My mother and father, they did not tell me fairy tales, not any. But I knew one, and I told what I knew, and Galina told the ones that she knew, and together, my wife and I, we kept on telling that baby stories to keep the cold back and the hunger too.

My wife and I, we took that child against us and held her very hard and told and told whatever we knew. When that baby was cold, we told about Cinderella. When that baby was hungry, we told about Cinderella. But that baby was always cold and always hungry—and we always told about Cinderella and then about Cinderella all over again.

My baby, my firstborn, my Svetlana, lived in that chop-out one year. My baby lived one year in that cold.

When she could talk, Sveta would say, "Story, Papa," and fix me with her eyes. But she did not have to say it for me to know now was when I had to take her against me and begin again.

Once upon a time there was a beautiful girl . . .

I could tell. When the cold in her was too much and the hunger in her was blazing, dear * , I could always tell.

Once upon a time there was a beautiful girl and her name was Cinderella . . .

But then it did not work anymore, and I could tell that too.

It was then I thought to tell about America. I had not wanted to think about America. But I began.

Once upon a time there was a place called America . . .

"Tell America, Papa," my child would say when she could talk.

I told about Detroit.

In America there is a beautiful city and it is called Detroit. There are buildings there and houses and people with fine clothes, and it is always very warm there. There in Detroit the people are always warm and they eat all the time, and you cannot believe all the wonderful food there is to eat . . .

"Two potatoes, Papa?"

She said that every time, my child. Two potatoes.

"Two potatoes, sweetheart? Oh my, they eat wonderful things —ice cream and cake and cookies and roast beef and all sorts of chops and . . ."

"Two potatoes, Papa?"

She would fix me with her eyes, eyes that are very blue, like mine.

Two potatoes. Oh, dear * .

"Yes, my sweetheart, *two* potatoes. In the beautiful city of Detroit, everyone has a second potato."

There in the chop-out in Siberia, my wife and child held hard against me, I would say, "Yes, my sweetheart, two potatoes."

It was unimaginable. It was the outer limit of magic, as far as a fairy tale dare go. Two potatoes. What could be more fantastic?

So, you see, it is the same thing again for me now, searching for words to set my story down, to tell the crazy thing my life has been. Talking to you is like talking to Sveta there in the chop-out, like saying yes, yes, *two* potatoes—because that child could not imagine anything more.

Say that my life is like that, then—a second potato, wondrous and hideous, a thing that fell from a tree onto the wide and furious snow.

My father was a laborer, a Socialist, a unionist. My mother was these things too.

They lived in Detroit, and I was born there, and when I was sixteen years old I went with them to Russia, and that was in 1931. In 1976 I returned to the United States, to the city of my birth.

I was an American in the Soviet Union for forty-five years.

I was a hero in the Soviet Union, and then I was a prisoner and a slave in the Soviet Union, and through all this I was an American, a boy from Detroit who went where his parents took him and who paid what his father's dream cost.

My father is dead now, and so is my mother. They are dead and buried in Gorky. But you cannot see the grave sites. A factory covers them now.

My brother Leo is dead too, hanged, and by his own hand. He also lies buried in Russia. But my sister Miriam lives, and so does my sister Rebecca—Miriam *there,* Rebecca here—and Galina, my wife, there too. And my daughters, *they* live—Svetlana and Janna.

And *I* live—I, Victor Herman, still live.

Oh, I remember when they tapped the message. I will always remember when they tapped the message. It was tapped from cell to cell. *Victor Herman is dead.*

And I lived to tap back *I am Victor Herman.*

But Red Loon is dead—and so many whose names I will never remember or never know.

How many died and how did they die? It is like *three* potatoes. And how they *lived* is like four.

Listen: I am Victor Herman, and this is what my life has been.

TWO ————————————————————————————————

My firstborn was four months old when her mother carried her north and found me there dug into the snow. It was hard, what that child had. But it was hard before her too. My father was Sam, Samuel, born in the Ukraine in 1886, and my mother was Rose, Rose Rukhamin, also born in the Ukraine, two years after.

These people were Jews, and the living was hard. They were Jews, and there were pogroms, and the living was very hard. My father labored—carpentry—and he read. This led to that, and in time he was a member of a radical organization. He ran errands for them, these people, a group of Jewish revolutionaries—they called themselves Social Democrats, and they worked for the first Russian Revolution. This was 1904, 1905, in there. My father carried guns. He took them from here to there. I suppose you would call him a gunrunner—but he was afraid of them, of guns. Anyway, he would get the guns from Army units and carry whatever he got to the revolutionaries, to these radicals he knew. I don't know how he would get those guns. Did he steal? Perhaps he stole. He was a kid, really—and his job was delivery. He would get the guns, put them in a wagon, cover them all over with straw, and make his delivery to someone in charge.

In time the Czarist police caught him and put him in jail. But that was okay—already, before that, he had been in prison. But then they caught him again. It was for doing more than running errands. It was for organizing a meeting of revolutionaries. They put him in prison again, and this time they sentenced him to be hanged. He was just a kid, really, and he says he didn't care. He told me this when I was a kid, that he didn't care about hanging or shooting or anything that brought death. But the revolutionaries got him out, worked out some kind of escape for him—thirty rubles, a false passport, passage into Switzerland.

He carried a letter introducing him, and Sam Herman moved up, made his way up the ranks. He believed in everything, and he was fearless. They sent him to Germany and to Italy and at last they sent him to England, and there he set up rallies in Hyde Park. But in 1909 he came to the United States, and not long after my mother came, and they got married in New York—and then Rose and Sam moved out to Detroit, here, to the beautiful American city where I am telling all this—and Sam started organizing the auto workers. What he was doing here was trying to build up trade unions—Red unions they called them in those days.

It was underground work, secret work. I guess you could say it was dangerous work.

I was born into that—into the family and times I am trying to tell you about.

Sam Herman had, all told, three years of schooling—and it was primary school and in Russia. He was what I said, a laborer chiefly, not a big man, but powerful in the arms. And his principles, they were powerful too. He held them as he held his family, the five of us, tightly, because they were his and he believed in them.

Anyway, he came to Detroit. Detroit was where the workers

were, and my father came here to unite them. It was the way he understood things—fairness and the good life for all. It was Sam Herman's idea of Socialism. It was a simple idea. Sam Herman, my father, was a simple man, and he was dogged in his convictions.

And so he came to Detroit to work—in the auto industry as a carpenter and among the men as a unionist.

I knew right from the start what my father stood for. He'd come home torn and bloody from a fight, and sure, like any father, he'd try to hide his bleeding from his children, but we found out—and found out why. Rebecca, my older sister, and Leo, my older brother, and me, we'd see our mother holding Sam's head over the kitchen sink, leaning down to him, her small hands bathing water on his face, and we found out why—and heard them whispering, and in time the words we heard came to mean things. What did we know, really? But when it's your father, what *don't* you really know?

You know everything.

And when I was seven, Sam took Rebecca and me to Finnish Hall, a meeting, workers, Socialists—and we joined the Pioneers that night. It was 1922.

I never thought we were different, us Herman kids. I just thought this was America, my home, and everybody was like us—even Henry Ford. There was Mr. Ford and Mrs. Ford and Mr. Herman and Mrs. Herman and all the kids I always played with, and we were just Americans. As for the people who beat up my father almost once every week, I don't know what I thought they were, but I guess I didn't think they were real Americans.

Leo was born in 1911, Rebecca in 1913, and then I came, two years after—and then Miriam, Rose Miriam actually, ten years after me. Did I ever think we were different? That we led a life that wasn't just like what America wanted?

I did not. I never knew a thing like that until I was well into my forties—and if that seems remarkable to you, what will you think when I tell you that I did not have sexual relations with a woman until I was thirty-four?

Sex? Girls? Women?

Three potatoes. When you know what my life was like, you will know why I say that. Sex! It was unimaginable.

Why should the Herman kids feel different? Like ours, the other kids' fathers worked at Fisher Body or at Wadsworth or at

Ford's. Like ours, their fathers came home bloody. We all went to Pioneers together and to the workers' camp and sang the same songs about fairness and the good life for all. What I did all the kids did—and it was play for us, putting up posters and stickers on trees, and signs on telephone poles and anywhere else we could find.

Later on, when I was about thirteen, I guess, I could see that play was getting more like work, that it was serious. They gave me jobs to do, the Socialists—running errands mainly. In fact my job was delivery—just like my father's before me. I used to run stacks of pamphlets and films from here to there, and when I got my license, when I was fourteen, they let me use a car and I drove those things around—delivering. I'd go alone, driving all over Detroit, delivering—and I got to see there were people out there who would beat me up if they caught me. It was an adventure—and, like any boy, I liked it.

Leo never helped. I don't know why. Leo, he just didn't care about any of these things—and Miriam was just a baby then. Rebecca, she helped. We were close, Rebecca and I. Odd, that among the four of us kids, Rebecca was the one who stayed behind, the one who did not go to Russia when we went.

Leo was handsome, and he knew it. I, Victor, was tough, and I knew that too. I ran a lot—and later on I boxed. And I could fight. And I *would* fight if I had to—I'd go after anyone in sight if I had to. I did all the sports—and the rougher they were, the more I liked them. I was good at these things. I was strong and agile and I liked to use myself. Whatever it was, I could do it—and *would* do it—and it was endless, this energy in me. I can remember, when I was nine, ten, how surprised I was if some other kid said let's quit, if anyone said he was tired. Me, I ran—and I didn't stop. I just never got tired—what did that *mean?*

I was born on Henry Street and from there we went to Ferry Street. Later on we moved to Ironwood. But I had my first fight on Ironwood and it was because we were Jews. The Goldmanns, our next-door neighbors, they threw rocks in our windows, and somehow I found out that was why—because we were Jews. But I remember now how I found out, because I remember that my dad went out in the yard and scolded them and they called back *Dirty Jews!* The Goldmann boys were waiting for me when I went out too, following my father Sam. They smacked me with pieces of a fence, Michael and Stephen. Michael was Leo's age, but Leo stayed inside.

I fought them.

Then their two cousins came, Joseph and Philip. So there were four of them. First I beat them one by one. I had to do that almost every day. Then it got so I could take on all four of them together. I could beat the * out of those boys, all four at once. And the way boys are, we were all great friends after that.

I was a tough kid—and after that there were lots of fights.

I guess I thought my father approved. My mother was always complaining about it, but my father never said a word. I'd come home with my nose or something broken, and that night my mother would tell my dad. But he never came to me about it, and I got the idea it was okay with him.

I went on fighting.

By now I couldn't stop—because the word had got around, and there were kids who wanted to try me, kids at school and from neighborhoods that were far away. And then there were the little kids who would come to me and ask me to fight for them, and it got so that every day after school I'd have to walk some kid home.

It's funny. Some of the kids I used to walk home are rich men now, fellows who are pretty well off here in Detroit. But they won't talk to me. They don't want any part of me. No one really wants much to do with me now—except Rebecca, who's here in Detroit, old now, pensioned off from her job at GM, and my cousin Dave, who used to live with us in the old days and then went to New Orleans.

But my daughters are with me—and Galina is coming. I have that thought every hour, and I will not stop believing it: *Galina is coming.* If she could follow me north through the snow, if she could make that distance with an infant in her arms and keep on going into the frozen wilderness beyond Yeniseysk, what could stop her now?

Not anything.

THREE

It was sports, for me it was all sports—and fighting and doing my deliveries. People I see in Detroit now, people who knew me then, they all say they were afraid of me—but I never thought so at the time. But that's not why these people are afraid of me now. They just don't want any part of it, what's aged me. They don't want to hear about it, and my daughters don't, and no one really does, and I don't, either. No one wants a part of this. You can go so far as to tell about two potatoes, but three? *Four?*

I'm trying to make you see the kind of boy I was—a neighborhood tough, maybe, but not a bad kid. A dreamer, mostly— and quiet. I didn't have much of an idea of what I wanted to be. I had nothing in mind exactly. I was pretty much that way about everything—everything and anything was okay. Skywriting was the one thing I remember that got all the way to me. It must have been 1927 when I saw it, saw that thing happening in the sky. It was the first time I saw it, and I liked it. I thought, well, that's what I want to do—write in the sky like that. I remember just how it was, the letters chalked up there against the blue sheet the sky was that day—*LUCKIES.* I suppose that was the life I picked out for myself—if I ever really picked any. Somehow I was going to get to write in the sky.

Which raises another thing about me that's worth giving you a picture of. My eyes. They're like that, like sky. I mean, they're strange, like clear sky, light blue and sort of uninterrupted. People notice it—and I think it upsets them, or maybe it distracts them. They're not usual eyes—and maybe I should be glad they're not.

I often wonder how I got through. I often wonder what it is in me that made me so I got through and all those others didn't, how could I have lived to return here, home, safe, fed, and warm, to say *I am Victor Herman* in English, the same man who back then said it in code, in Russian and in code, tapping out the letters with a hard piece of soap, tapping on that wall *I am Victor Herman.*

It was like writing *LUCKIES* on the sky. Let them all over everywhere go to * . Look! Over here. *I am Victor Herman.*

My eyes, they may have helped. They may have been a part of what got me through. I don't know. It is my quiet, too, I sometimes think. And I am strong. I have never been afraid—not afraid to work or afraid to fight. It is, I think, because I do not think about fear. Nor do I think of death.

I never thought: *Now I will die.* I never thought: *I will stop now because I cannot go one step more.* I never thought of those things. What I thought of was what was put in front of me. Here, do this! And I did it—whatever it was. If it must be done, then I would do it—and that was all that was in my mind, the doing—this after that and then another thing, until whatever it was, was done.

Is that how I got through? I don't know. I only know that it is how I am.

Speed was another thing. I did things fast and I liked to go fast. When I was eleven, I stole Leo's car and drove all around. I really went pretty fast. And I ran. I was good at all the short runs in track. Like when I stole Leo's car and brought it home, he came after me. I'd never seen him angry like this, so angry he did not think what he would do if he caught me. I was eleven and he was fifteen, and even so I knew I could beat him up and he knew it, too. But I just ran and he ran after me and then I'd stop to let him catch up. And when he did, I'd start up running again and then stop again —until it made no sense anymore and I just stood there, waiting. I didn't hit him or anything when he got to me. I just took him by the arms so he wouldn't hit me—and I turned him around and walked him home, holding him like that.

Things started changing in 1929. My dad was blacklisted that year. You know what that means. It means no work. He'd been at Fisher Body then—hanging doors—but he got blacklisted, and that was that—he couldn't get work. But about a year later he started doing something with Ford's—not working there, actually, but hanging around. I didn't know what it was all about at the start. I was fifteen, and I was doing my deliveries for the Socialists and keeping at my sports—and still fighting. I was busy with this and that, but I knew that my father was all of a sudden at Ford's a lot, doing something or other there. Off he went in the morning and there he was at night, and suddenly there was plenty of food on the table, and that was after a year when there had been hardly any at all. And there was another new thing too. My father was going off to Ford's, but he wasn't putting on his work clothes. All my life all I ever saw was my dad doing work you put on work clothes to do. But now he wasn't—and by and by all the kids noticed that, and little by little he told us what was what.

There were Russians at Ford's and he was helping the Americans talk to the Russians and the Russians talk to the Americans. He said he was helping with "negotiations," but maybe it was only interpreting that he was doing. After all, he could speak Russian as good as anybody, and his English must have been more than fair. Oh, it must have been—because he must have been like me with languages, easy with whatever he hears, a quick learner when it comes to that. I know my dad was fast in German and Yiddish and Polish and Finnish. And of course he had his Russian and his English.

Not many people know about it, even today, so many years after it happened. What I mean is how Ford's did business back then with the Russians. It didn't matter what the politics were; it only mattered where the marketplace was. Henry Ford was all for it; he thought it was a great idea—yet Ford's mainly kept the notion pretty much to themselves. But they were doing business, and the idea with Ford's was mostly to sell jigs and dies and patterns and a whole lot of old machinery. Ford's was already set up to sell the Model T in Russia even before the Revolution in 1917, and now, in 1930, the idea was to provision a motor plant in Gorky so that the Soviets could produce the Model A. The Five Year Plan got going in 1928, and this was right in the middle of it, and the Russians were here to buy what they needed, and Ford's was selling. My father helped it happen.

I never saw him happier.

He saw it that he was doing something for the good of the world. Making Russia strong meant making Socialism work, and that was for the good of everyone everywhere—because didn't that mean there would be more fairness for everyone and the good life for all?

He never used to tell us much about his work, Sam. But now he was talking, talking more and more. He was like a kid with this thing, all excited about a dream coming true. He told us more about it every day, and then he told us Henry Ford himself, that famous worker and famous American, was coming to our house! I guess we all knew it was a miracle, but we were workers and Americans too. It even seemed, this miracle, an ordinary thing.

Henry Ford came and he sat with my father in the front room and my mother served him tea and the two men talked and then Henry Ford said good-bye to all of us and stepped into his car and drove away.

Only Leo gaped. He said, "Did you see? A chauffeur?"

But the rest of us tried not to notice. Henry Ford was an American and a worker, just like us. What did chauffeurs mean? They got in the way of an American truth. We were all just the people, and this was the United States. What difference, a chauffeur? Better not to notice.

All that evening my father talked of Mr. Ford, how greatly he admired that great American man.

No, Sam Herman's Socialism did not make him hate the rich. The rich were all right. They were fine. They were the way *everyone* should be—and *could* be. That was Sam Herman's Socialism.

It's a Socialism I have no quarrel with.

But I have no quarrel with anyone or anything anymore. I never did, really. Even those that jailed me and those that beat me and those that tortured and starved and froze me—who? the man who took a scissors and cut off the tips of my toes and sent me out into the snow to fell trees?—not even with him, with no one, with not even the ones who did worse to me by far—I have a quarrel with no one. Not anymore.

You could see that my father was proud that Mr. Ford had sat with him in the front room and they had talked the way any two men would. They talked and drank their tea and said good-bye—and it was really a miracle, how ordinary and wonderful that all was.

I was very proud for my father—and proud for myself when the miracle, it was announced, would reveal itself for a second time. A few days later my father told us all at the supper table—he, Sam Herman, the revolutionary, a man who had been three times in prison and once so-and-so many steps from the hangman's noose, he would go the next day to the house of Henry Ford. These men had things to talk about. They would take tea and talk. And I, the family roughneck—did he wink when he said that?—this rascal Vickie, who does such a job with the driving of a car, I, his son Victor, would accompany him.

"A reward," my father said, "for the roughneck who drives as if the devil sits beside him." And this time he did wink.

But I knew it was because I was my father's favorite. Leo was handsome and did well in school, but I was my father's boy—it was no secret.

What bound me to him that way? Was it my silence? The power that was in my arms also? Perhaps it was my daring—but I sometimes think it was my eyes. I think he was amazed at my eyes. How could he be the father of a fellow with eyes like this, so strange?

Anyhow, Leo left the table, angry. But I could tell Rebecca was happy for me—and my mother, yes. She busied herself with cutting Miriam's meat. But I could see the pleasure in her face.

He kept on talking all the way through dessert, my father did— what a wonderful man Henry Ford was, of all the capitalists the fellow with the most brains! Well, Edison too. There was a smart one, that Edison. They don't come any smarter than Edison and Ford. Why, if all the capitalists had the vision of these two, hah, what a world it would be for all men!

So, the roughneck was to visit at the house of Mr. Ford. But isn't *that* what America is? And more wonderful still, no more would I go to the golf course to caddy after school and on weekends —because Mr. Ford had fixed it. The wonderful Mr. Ford had talked to his man Swenson, and this Swenson, a top man at Ford's, he would make a job for the roughneck.

It happened, that job. All that summer of 1931 I operated a pickup truck for Ford's—making deliveries. The visit happened too, the visit to the house of Henry Ford.

The house of Henry Ford? It did not impress me all that much. I suppose I was that sort of boy. Should anything like that impress me? I was an American, just like him—and we all did American things, listened to the radio and drove our cars and liked to eat an ice-cream cone. Who in Detroit didn't love Vernors, our famous ginger ale? Didn't Mr. Ford and all his family drink Vernors and love it like everyone else?

And then one day my father came home and said, who wants to go?

"Go where?" Leo said.

"Where else?" my father said. "To Russia—to work at the Ford's auto plant. To make the machines run and to build a great future for all men."

My mother was not happy at this. Nor was Leo. Leo was

twenty and was having a good time. What, leave his girl friends? No, Leo was staying put. And Rebecca, by now she was married— to a cop's son named Bob Laing. Could a cop's son go to Russia? So Rebecca was not going—and was my father really serious? Russia? To make cars? Did they have Vernors in Russia? And Jack Benny?

All I saw was an adventure. Who cares about Vernors and Jack Benny when adventure crooks a finger at you? Russia! There would be bears there—lions and tigers leaping from tree to tree!

"Go?" my mother said. "What do you mean, Sam, *go?*"

"For three years," my father said. "We give three years of our lives to build a great Socialist world. What does it cost us, three measly years?"

"Am I to leave Leo here, Sam? Is this what you think? And Becky? Is this what you want?" But my mother seemed more teasing than anything else. Did she take this man seriously? It was a joke. My father was playing a joke.

But my father did not play jokes. That was one thing there never was in Sam Herman—jokes.

There in Dearborn, on either side of that house Henry Ford lived in, were woods like a forest—with reindeer walking in them. Oh, I knew what they were—from the pictures every child sees. And he let me go out into them, those woods—Henry Ford said, "Let the boy look around." And I went out and saw the reindeer walking.

Imagine what I could do in Russia—with wolves and bears and all the forests that must grow everywhere there!

I think now on the irony of that. Those woods of Henry Ford's—and my idea of the fabulous forests to come.

Trees! Infinite trees! Mysterious forests full of every kind of adventure!

How could I know, a boy of sixteen, what trees would come to mean to me? How could I ever have guessed what a forest could do to you, the malevolence of wood?

I saw forests as playgrounds. How could I know what really lay in store in them, the weight of birch and pine? How could I know that in the years ahead I would labor as a slave, and that a slave might do this and that, but to be a slave in the woods? All those years in the camps, after all those years in prison, nothing, no labor, was more greatly feared. Did they send you to the forests with an ax and a saw? Then they sent you there to die in shadows. Here, they said, you go to the woods. And the terror in you was immense, a colossal falling into fear.

Eighteen went out that morning from Subcamp 8. Three were women—or at least I thought they were. Eighteen went out into the snows before the dawn came up, and when it broke you could see the railroad wagons. Through the pale light and the mist that rose up, up there on the rise where the tracks were laid, you could see the wagon they assigned to you, and on either side, off about sixty yards from yours, two wagons that were just like it. Sixty-tonners, that's what they were—massive steel things that held that much.

Load!

Load it all, till every inch is taken!

Cut a tree, saw a tree, and load it all from top to bottom. You! *Zk!* Prisoner! Prisoner Herman! Yourself! Do it!

And to each of us, the eighteen, two guards were assigned—and they had their guns and their German dog.

You! Prisoner! *Zk!* Yourself! Sixty tons in the snow—and the woodline, the verge, way off back there, back down the rise and all the way behind you.

How could I know when I walked in Henry Ford's woods that summer day in Dearborn what a forest can sometimes mean? What the forest could do to you when it got its chance?

Eighteen went out that winter before dawn. Were three of them really women? There is no way of ever being sure. Eighteen went out, and only I came back.

But not all of me came back. Something, I left something behind. I think it was disbelief.

Not ever again would I not believe. It will happen—whatever *can* happen *will*.

FOUR ————————————————————————

It went on for weeks like that, mealtimes, nothing but talk about Russia—would we go, would we not go, what it would be like if we did. Leo finally came around—if we would go, *he* would go—and I suppose I sort of sneered at that, knowing it was really that he was scared to stay behind. Does this seem ungenerous of me, speaking this way of the dead? I don't think so. The dead deserve no special privileges. Besides, there are none left over. When it comes to special privileges, they all get used up on the living, and *still* there's not enough to go around.

Sam was no talker, but you'd never know it from how he was acting now—Russia this and Russia that. We could expect things to be different, all right—but not all that much. After all, didn't my mother put Russian food before us? So what could be so different?

Yes, *what!*

Oh, dear father, did you sit beside me in Cell 39 to take my ball of porridge with me?

And did you step lively with me along the runway in Camp 231, wolfing down the cereal, the merest spoonful but still a job to get down because you had to do it running?

Run, my father, but not too fast! Because I saw a man get there too fast and another man bite off the fast man's lips for the last smear of cereal on them!

And did you, dear dead father, partake of rat with me those six crazed months when I had meat?

I ate *cat,* father. I ate *dog,* and maybe even men.

No, the dead deserve no special privileges. Death may be all the privilege they need.

But Sam Herman was talking that summer of 1931, and it was to me that he mainly did it. He disclosed all his hopes to me, the dream our sacrifice would secure. I guess he'd confided in me before, ever since the time I was shot, but not anything like he talked to me now. And I was glad he did, and glad he was happy—and mostly glad he had something to do. Most of the fathers didn't then. But my dad had work and I had work, and things were moving along pretty good. I'd show up for work at Gate 2 of the River Rouge plant, and Frank, my boss there, he'd say check with the Ruski fellas in the building there—and there was a two-story brick building right inside Gate 2, and I found out it was where the *Autostroy* company was working out of—getting the stuff they needed and recruiting men.

Anyway, there'd always be a Russian or two in there who was looking for someone to teach him how to drive, and I guess Frank might have gotten the word handed down to turn over the job to the Herman kid. It'd be a couple of hours just driving around, and I'd get a couple of bucks for it. I liked it, teaching driving—and it was mostly with sign language that I did it—but more and more I caught on to a little Russian, and it wasn't all that hard, considering. Rose and Sam would speak any language under the sun but Russian—in front of us kids, I mean—but now and then they let down and I guess I had a good enough feeling for it before I started those driving lessons.

Anyway, there was that morning that Frank called me over.

"Got a Ruski engineer that wants to take a little spin?" I said.

Frank said no, said he'd heard it around that I was going to Cass Tech and that was a pretty good high school for a dumb kid like me, right?

I said I wasn't so dumb and just stood there. He was a nice enough guy, but he liked to tease.

Then he said he'd heard it around that I was a pretty fair hand with my dukes, and I said I was okay, sure.

"Word also is," Frank said, "you were shot once. That true?"

"It was a while back," I said. "It wasn't anything." I just stood there wondering what the * this was all about, and he just stood there too.

"So?" I said. "You want to dance?"

That Frank was a pretty good kidder himself. He just laughed.

"No sirree, Vic," he said, "you're a shade too ugly to interest me much. I'm just jawing, is all—thinking maybe you're looking to set yourself up as an automobile mechanic."

"I guess I've thought of it," I said.

"Now, that's just what I was thinking," he said, and put his hand on my shoulder and kind of drew me to him. "You see, kid," he said, talking in a manner that was meant to show me how confidential this all was, "if what you really want to do is set yourself up as a first-class mechanic, the way to do it really fast is you go to Russia, hear? No telling how fast a fella could advance himself over there among all them people. What the ✳ do *they* know? ✳ ✳ it, boy, you've seen it for yourself. ✳ Russians can't even drive a ✳ car! You take a tip from old Frank, boy, and you go along to over there with the rest that's going, you hear?"

I didn't know why he was pressing me that way. Maybe he just wanted to be helpful, and this was his way of doing it. Maybe not. But Frank kept pushing.

"Now, boy," he said, turning me around to face the *Autostroy* shack, "I'm here to help you get yourself a *contract!* Why, you'll get yourself into the shops over there and no telling how far and fast you'll advance yourself. Over here it might take you *years* to do what over there you can make of yourself in no time at all. Kid, let me tell you something, you'll come back here from that U.S.S.R. and you'll step right into a top job, I'm here to tell you. Now what do you say?"

I just said, yeah, sure, sounds good. Well, I knew my dad was talking the same—I mean, in that general direction. Sam Herman put it a different way, though—he talked ideals, making a better world, all that. This man Frank, he was talking good old American sense to me. But I guess it didn't matter what anyone said to me on the subject, because the truth was I'd go anywhere my dad went—and if he was going where adventure waited, so much the better.

So I just walked on into the *Autostroy* building and said to the Ford's guy that was sitting in there to go ahead and sign me up. "Put me down for three years," I said, thinking to tell my dad how I'd gone and acted like a man for myself.

The Ford's man in there, he said right off, "You got it, Herman."

So it was really happening!

I turned around and walked out of there, and I don't know all I was thinking at the time, but I sure remember thinking about wild bears.

Everybody knew I'd been shot about a year before that. All the kids at Cass knew and the kids around Ironwood. People weren't surprised. I'd been in lots of scrapes, and it probably seemed the natural thing that I'd get hurt bad one of those days. But how it happened had nothing to do with all that. It was just an accident.

It was bad. The bullet went right through my liver—and back in those days that was bad. I remember hearing *mortal wound*.

It happened when I was over at Rebecca's house, a friend and me. She'd moved, was living with the Laings then. Alan was the friend, Alan Aberbach. He calls himself Avery now—Dr. Avery— he's a dentist here in Detroit. Anyway, we went over to see Becky, Al and I, and Bob was there, and he just wanted us to have a good time, so he pulled out about five revolvers, and Al's going *bang bang bang* all over the place, trying out all five of them, and one of them, one of those big ugly Smith and Wesson .38's, just went off.

Anyway, that's what it was. *Bang.*

What I know about it is they couldn't stop the bleeding—so there was this talk about a special operation, and they went ahead and did it. They gave me a couple of shots—spinals, I guess—and I got numb—and when I noticed the big reflector over the table, I noticed what was in it—and it was where that *mortal wound* was.

I watched the whole thing.

I saw him cut me open, saw him take stuff out, snip stuff off— I saw all of it. It took about three hours, that operation. I watched it all. And there was another one after that. Even longer—and I watched it too.

They kept me there in Receiving for a pretty long while, and when they sent me home it was to stay in bed for three months, and when they got me home they put me to bed and my mother said, just sleep, and that she was going out to get the things the doctor told her to, and I got up and got dressed as soon as she walked out.

I had to move in a crouch. I was really bent over. But I took our dog for a walk, and I never went back to bed. I took him three blocks and back and I just stayed up after that. My mother and father let me. My dad said, it's Vickie's nature and let nature take its course. He was right. There wasn't anything special about me. Your nature isn't special. If that's your nature, that's what it is— and there's no sense in pointing to it and saying it's special.

But I had it, that kind of nature.

Is it why I'm here today?

The raid came not long after that, the raid on Camp Farming-ton, the workers' camp. It came between the time I got shot and when my father started setting up things between *Autostroy* and Ford's.

My dad took me to Camp Farmington quite a lot around that period, that interval between the shooting and when he went back to work without his work clothes. He might have had in mind to help me get really strong again, but I think, too, it was that he wanted me to see him with all the big shots that were there, that were in and out of Camp Farmington.

These were people like William Foster, Michael Gold, Elizabeth Flynn, John Reed, Louisa Bryant—these were some of the big shots I remember. And Sam Herman was getting to be one too. He had his pictures taken with all of them, but it was just a camp to me—a place to run and play ball and be under the trees.

That's just what I was doing when it happened. We all heard the trucks before we saw them. They came in toward the dorms and buildings and more or less tried to fan out. There were a lot of cars too—cops everywhere, and deputies. They were all armed.

I'd never seen anything like it before—all those uniformed men with arms at the ready. It was a sight, there in that kind of park setting. But there they came with their uniforms and their guns, and I remember thinking, now *these* can't be the bad guys, so what's going on?

A lot of men were arrested, and they kept all the men they arrested in Pontiac, my dad and Leo included—and there was a trial, there in Pontiac. It lasted two weeks, the trial. Teaching children Communism, that was the main charge. But it was over in two weeks, and they were all acquitted.

There wasn't any violence attached to the thing, but it made a large impression on me, all those officers with guns and a mass roundup. What I saw was all those officers coming out of all those cars and trucks, uniformed men and therefore men that were powerfully illustrative of a boy's idea of authority, the government, America—and here they were, rounding people up, the good guys going after the good guys. I really couldn't understand it at the time —and I distinctly remember being worried about it, really upset, yet knowing that it was something I didn't think I could discuss with my dad.

I wanted that man to be proud of me. I wanted him to see in me the very thing that *he* was.

It's true. I'd have done anything for him, followed him into any kind of fight that he thought was right. Isn't that what a son is?

But I kissed him good-bye one morning in Russia, and we never saw each other again. We went into our separate prisons. Mine was where you died from what they did to you. But his wasn't. My father's prison was where you died from what you did to yourself.

Sam Herman was alive from that morning in 1938 when I kissed him good-bye to when he died in 1953. In all that time I never saw him. And then he was dead, and there was no seeing him.

I loved him very much.

FIVE _____

It still wasn't real to me, going, actually going off to someplace foreign, until we started packing up—and even then it wasn't real to me. I knew I was going—and I was saying good-bye to my friends—but it was just three years, and then we'd be coming back. Besides, it wasn't like we were really leaving Detroit, because Becky was staying and that meant our family would still be here in a way, and after a while we would all be back. Dad gave Becky and Bob our house—so that knowing the place would be occupied, that our family was still in it, meant that all we were doing was taking a long vacation.

I was coming back—and when I came back, I'd be different, changed into something larger. I'd be an engineer or a journeyman mechanic—I'd be something different and important.

But Sam kept getting more and more specific about the hardships we'd have to handle when we got over there. Things would be pretty bad, he said—maybe worse than even he expected. He'd heard the food situation was critical, nationwide rationing, and that in some places there was nothing to ration. Who knew? We might even see people starving.

Starving? What could that possibly mean to a sixteen-year-old American boy? In the worst of times, and God knows we had just been through some that were close to that, who did we ever see starve?

As for my mother, she kept her mouth shut. For the time being, Mama had nothing more to say on the subject. She would go where her husband went, period. Like it or not, his destiny was hers.

Did she like it? I didn't think so. And later on, I did not even have to guess at that.

And then, as it got down to the wire, Sam kept reminding us all that we didn't really have to go. That *he* had to—because he had to make it work, help in bulwarking the first workers' country. But it was okay if we wanted to stay behind—even Mama—because, after all, it would, sure, mean a separation of three years, but we'd all be safe in America and three years would pass in no time at all: he'd have done his duty and we'd all be together again. How bad could that be, a three-year separation?

But what in the world could be worse than a three-year separation?

What, indeed!

All right. We were going, then. No two ways about it. We hugged my father and kissed him and went back to our packing. Papa said, "Next stop, Nizhni-Novgorod," and he smiled grandly.

It was the first time Miriam and I and Leo had actually heard the name of our destination. I don't think even Mama had heard it before.

Then Sam really called it out as if he were a streetcar conductor—"Next stop, Nizhni-Novgorod!" and we all took up the howl.

"Here we come, Neezie-Novgrot!" Leo yelled.

"Look out, Niz-Noovie!" I screamed. "The Herman boys are coming!"

"Niddle-Not, Niddle-Not," Miriam started chanting.

Maybe all that carrying on was a kid's way of covering up. Maybe, now that we were really doing it, it was all beginning to look a little different to us. What kind of place *was* that, with a name so crazy? But of course they would have to have lions and tigers in a place like that—yet what *else* would they have? It sounded like dragons had their dwellings there.

Is there something scarier in the name Gorky? Which is what the Russians changed Nizhni-Novgorod to not long after. Who knows? Maybe some of us might have asked out at the last minute if Gorky was the name of the place we were going to have to go to. I was a kid who'd never even been outside the state of Michigan, a kid whose idea of a place name ran on the order of Dearborn and Detroit, and I was on my way to Nizhni-Novgorod! I was awfully worked up—and I remember being more than a little annoyed that I had to share my special status with so many other kids. No fewer than about three hundred Michigan families, mostly all Detroiters, were scheduled to end up in—let's call it—Gorky. It hardly seemed fair, considering the courage I thought I alone had.

Like any life, the events that make it up seem to fall into clusters—so that, in hindsight, one can perceive the motion of his life in terms of states of varying rates of speed, in stages. I suspect this is a trick the mind plays on memory, or vice versa—but in any case, the degree of speed in my life seems to have picked up noticeably the day we left Detroit for the ship we would board in New York.

We took the train out of Detroit on the 23rd of September, 1931. Did my father know he would never return? Did my mother? Did Miriam? And as for me, *now,* now that I *have* returned, did I really believe I ever would? That morning, leaving Detroit, I took no special notice of this or that, the things of my home, of my city, things particularly Middle Western American. Years later, I was to take more notice of things Russian, the sights and sounds of the city of Gorky, as I sat in the back of that car on my way to NKVD headquarters. When the train pulled out of Detroit that morning, it was all too thrilling to see anything very sharply. The train ride, the prospect of New York, the ship, an ocean voyage, the colorful picture I kept painting of the bizarre land that lay waiting for me— it all made me blind. I was favored with a window seat, and I sat there watching the fields slip and somersault by, and I was in a dream.

I don't think I came out of my trance until we got to Buffalo, crossing that bridge where you can get a good look at Niagara Falls. It was nighttime, and the Falls were all illuminated by special lights—and the sight was so stupendous to me, I can't think of a thing that equaled it in my memory of New York. But I never really got to see anything much there. All I remember was the subway ride up to the Bronx where we were going to stay with some friends of my folks until it was time to go to the ship. That was on the 24th, and on the 25th we sat around all day in that apartment with nothing to do but think about the next day. And it arrived, right on time, the 26th of September, and standing on the deck of the *Leviathan,* more startled by its size and the enormous distance from where I stood all the way down to the water, more startled by *that* than I was by what was actually happening, I watched the dock move away from me as if *it,* the wharf and all those waving people on it, had been crazily cut adrift.

No! I did *not* feel I was leaving America. No American really does. You feel it is a terrain that spreads out over your heart, and there is really no leaving it ever.

That's not a thought a sixteen-year-old boy has. That's not a thing any American of any age ever bothers to raise to the level of thought. Not until you're an American who can't get back.

It took five days to get to England. I wish it had taken five thousand.

SIX _____

We sailed third class. But there was almost no part of the ship I didn't get a look at. I'd never before seen anything so massive—and, where the first-class passengers did their eating and dancing and card playing and the rest, so grand. This was really something to astonish, the *Leviathan.* To me it was like being on the back of some sort of fabulous serpent that was angrily consuming the sea.

The next morning the ship's photographer had pictures posted here and there—to show the height of the waves. Nobody in our class came out for breakfast. They rang the bell, and I'm not ex- aggerating when I tell you that I was the only one who showed up. Papa, Mama, Leo, Miriam, they were sick as dogs—Mama the worst. I guess I didn't feel all that great myself, but I felt okay enough to prefer anything to the fog of vomit that overlay the place where we slept. A nurse came around giving everyone something to take, but I left for my bacon and eggs just as she showed up.

It was the same at lunch. Only me and an old man in the dining room—and all those uniformed waiters. I'd never been any- place like it nor been waited on by strangers—unless you counted the nurses that took care of me in the hospital.

Piccolino those waiters called me, those waiters who were for the most part Italian. "Bravo, Piccolino!" a couple of them called to me those first few meals, when I showed up pretty much by myself. I'm short. Like my dad. I don't know exactly how short I was at sixteen, but I remember that in relation to the other fellows I was certainly on the short side. But also like my dad, I'm unusually strong, stronger than he was—and I never minded being kidded about my height. To me, it made my remarkable strength all that much more remarkable.

Piccolino. I could tell it was something small. But I didn't know what. I could tell that whatever it meant, it was a way of honoring me for my fortitude. Good! My courage was apparent to all. I was on my way to becoming somebody great. I didn't know how or what, but I figured it was going to happen.

I loved that ship. It got so that I began to think about never getting off it. Maybe *that's* what I should be, I began to think—a ship's engineer or something.

We put up at the Queensway Hotel in London, and my dad met with some people there. It was a dull week for me—my mother and father wouldn't let me go anywhere. But I wish that week had been five thousand weeks.

The *Siberia*. That was its name, the name of the ship we boarded for Russia. The *Siberia*. It was a Russian vessel and not much to get excited about after the *Leviathan*. But that was its name, the *Siberia*—and what could that name have meant to me? I knew *Leviathan* meant something big. What did I think *Siberia* meant?

There were seventy-two families in our group—the ones that had started from Detroit and gotten this far to the *Siberia*. The rest of the three hundred had already gone or were soon to go to Gorky. Did the others sail on the *Siberia*?

Was the name an omen? How *could* it have been? Who could ever imagine? If by some magic the future were unfurled in front of your eyes, and it was a thing beyond imagining, you would say how can I believe that when I cannot even *imagine* that? Three potatoes, four potatoes, five.

The *Siberia*.

I began to learn the language. I got Mama to teach me the Russian alphabet, ten letters more than English has, but I was fast at this.

My mother taught me, and then my father taught me—and it

got so I could read the signs around the ship, and before I knew it, I was making out pretty well. I got along with the food too. I've never been fussy about things like that, what I ate, what I wore.

Leo chased girls on the ship—and I chased around after sailors to try out my Russian on. Papa's spirits were heartier now, and you could see he was getting excited about setting foot on his homeland again. But my mother looked grimmer every mile the *Siberia* covered. She kept Miriam close to her, and more and more she occupied herself with staring.

We made Leningrad in five days.

The weather didn't improve things. It was one of those indecisive days that have always seemed to me more depressing than something conclusively lousy. The fog horns had waked me early, and when I went out on deck the grayness of everything almost knocked me flat. You could hardly make out one dismal thing from another, it was all so uniformly somber.

The *Siberia* lumbered on into what seemed to be the heart of the city. For a time there it looked as if we were going to plow right into the whole works—and in fact it turned out that the dock was right on the main street, Nevsky Prospect. When my dad joined me at the rail, he pointed across the way, to a building of no special description.

"We stay there until we're mustered out to Gorky. That's a hotel."

"You're kidding," I said. "That's a hotel?"

But what did I know about hotels? I was trying to sound worldly, and it was a mistake—because it was an awful-looking place, and I think my dad felt personally responsible for that, and guilty. Beginning with that childish remark, I imagine my father blaming himself for everything that went wrong, for every hardship and misery, large and small—and surely he kept right on at it into the vastly more grave events that were to befall us all, the entire Gorky contingent.

And as for the guilt he must have charged to his account when it came to the fortunes of his own son? How does a father reckon up accounts when *he* buys and his *child* pays? But does not every parent make choices for himself that prove decisive in the life of his child? Isn't this what history is?

Oh, Papa, you died and I lived. And you did not live long enough to know that in the end it was all okay, that *I got back.*

You did not live long enough to hear me say there is no debt between us, that there never was—that if there *was* owing, it was I who
always owed you—because you showed me what a man can be, true
to what he loves.

SEVEN ————————————————————————————

Everything crawled along, the business of luggage and papers and
who's who and which line to get in. I did not know that the sluggish
pace of things and the widening confusion there at the Leningrad
dock were just the curtain drawing back to reveal a vast land of
more of the same and worse by far.

It was hours after we tied up in the harbor that we finally got
sorted out and were allowed to leave the ship. It was only October,
but spectacular snowflakes began floating by just as we stepped out
onto the gangplank. I was suddenly aware of the cold, very aware
of it. Crazy, but I just hadn't noticed it there on the deck. My
mother was carrying Miriam and had her wrapped inside her coat,
and my dad grabbed me from behind as I went down the gangplank ahead of him, and he hugged me hard. Leo was farther ahead,
and as soon as he stepped to the dock he dropped his valise and
started dancing around and slapping his arms.

We all stood there on the dock, collected around Sam, all of
us huffing and blowing and laughing at the wonder of it, so cold.
Sam took stock, to see that all of us and all our belongings were off
the ship, and then he led us toward the hotel. It was just a little way
from where we were, but it gave me time to see a few things.

There were people all bundled up and lying all over the street.
I'd never seen anything like it, these sort of storybook cobblestoned
streets and people all swaddled in layers of rags lying out there.

I poked Sam and pointed.

"Sleeping," he said and pulled me along. "They're drunk and
they're sleeping. You see that sign—*Pivo?* Means *beer.* They're
drunk and they have no place to sleep, so they sleep in the street.
It's not so bad—in Leningrad there is a kind of heating system that
runs under Nevsky Prospect. They lie down like that, they're warm."

Me, I was freezing. "Papa," I said, "I'm dying from the cold," and I laughed to show I wasn't.

Sam gave me a little shove forward and then ushered the rest of the family along. "You'll get used to it," he called. "This is not cold."

"That's right, kid," Leo called, "like Jolson says, you ain't seen nothin' yet," and then he started clowning around and got down on one knee and stretched out his arms and waggled his head like Jolson.

"Move!" Sam shouted and snatched at Leo and jerked him along.

My dad was jumpy—he stayed jumpy all the time we were held in Leningrad while the okay was coming through to depart for Gorky. He was in a bad state when he barked at Leo, but he was in a much worse state when we got inside the hotel. Officials were arrayed there right inside the door, and in no time at all they'd opened all our bags and thrown everything out on the floor. Dad smiled and smiled and shifted from foot to foot—and every so often he'd reach a hand to my mother and pat her—but then he finally exploded.

My Russian was a long way from good enough to get all that he said, but I could make out the general drift—that we came to the Soviet Union as friends, as workers, and this was no way to treat us.

Sam Herman got not one word of reply for his pains. They picked through everything we had with us, those officers—and they did not trouble themselves to give one word of explanation or apology or greeting.

"Oh, well," Sam said in English, "they mean no harm—it is how things have to be done here. We'll all get used to it—it doesn't matter—no harm done," and he drew a smile onto his face and reached over and took Miriam from Mama and lowered her onto his shoulders and jogged up and down with her. "No harm, no harm," he said in a sort of singsong, awkwardly smiling.

One of the officers took a handful of things with him over to a window—a blouse and a scarf of my mother's and a knitted cap Mama had made for Miriam. He held each item up to the light and turned it all around and fingered it.

My mother started crying, and that got Miriam to crying too— and Sam just accelerated his jogging and his singsong: "No harm, no harm, no harm." And then he switched to repeating a phrase in Russian. It meant *no harm*. I will never forget the sound that I

heard—and the anguish that I felt for my father's having to make it
—that singsong in Russian, to let the oppressors know that the
oppressed were not complaining: "No harm, no harm, no harm. . . ."

Was *this* Socialism? Is this what my father had come home
torn and bleeding for?

We were all put in one room—on the second floor. As soon as
we got there, my mother let go. She wanted to go home, she said,
immediately. We had made a mistake, done something insane—the
only reasonable thing to do was to correct it immediately—go tell
whomever we had to that we were leaving, turning around, going
home—it was all a mistake, a mistake!

Sam stood by the window, nodding. Leo sat on the bed next
to Rose, alternately patting her and patting Miriam, who sat struggling to get free from her mother's lap.

I walked around the room, looking things over—one bed?

She kept at it, my mother did, insisting, then pleading, and
through all of it my father simply nodded and stared out the
window to the street below, and when she seemed finished with
this, Sam turned around and faced her. But he said nothing.

"So?" my mother said. "Speak to me, Sam! So?"

He sat next to her on the bed, his shoulders slumped forward,
his hands gripped together between his knees.

"So, Sam? You have a tongue?"

"It will be better," he said at last. "You have to expect these
things. After all, to these people we are foreigners, and they are
fearful and therefore suspicious. It is a new country, my darling.
It takes time to make a new idea work. We must be patient."

"It is crazy, Sam!" my mother said, pulling away from the arm
he tried to let fall over her shoulders. "It has nothing to do with
politics. This is a bad place, and if you love me and the children,
you will get us out of here this very instant."

"I signed a contract," my father said. "I gave my word. In
Nizhni-Novgorod, we will decide. Wait until Nizhni-Novgorod."

Miriam set up her chanting as soon as she heard that. "Niddle-
Not, Niddle-Not, piddle-pot, piddle-pot. . . ."

My mother said, "That is your final word?"

"That is my final word," my father said.

This scene would be rehearsed scores of times before my
mother died—in the Soviet Union. The words would be different,

but they always meant the same thing—Sam saying things would change, get better, were temporary, Rose saying that he had no right to sacrifice her and the children to his blind conviction, his empty hopes.

I know this line of reasoning drove a spike into my father's heart. He knew Mama was right. How could he not? But how could he abandon the battlefield on which his idea of a better world was being tested? If not in Russia, then *where?*

But it was all useless and beside the point. Our destinies must have been determined by that Czarist hangman's noose long, long ago in the Ukraine. My father had escaped the gallows. But thereafter his mind was a prisoner to the freedom he sought.

We stayed two months in the *Sovtorgflot*—that's the hotel in Leningrad—the Soviet Trade Fleet, to put it in English. It got me used to many things. We learned to live in that one room together and to make do with the food—a terrible fish soup with oil floating on the top. And Mother had to boil all our drinking water on a hot plate some hotel official gave her. It took forever, and it tasted rotten even so.

And we all got used to Sam's increasing distance from us, and the return of his characteristic silence. He was kept busy those two months, acting as some kind of dispatcher for all the Americans that were moving through Leningrad to different factory installations. They would arrive, be quartered at the *Sovtorgflot,* get instructions from Sam about where they were supposed to go, and then, like us, wait around and wait around until some Soviet official said it was okay to go.

I knew from the kids that some were going to Stalingrad and some to Kharkov. There were tractor factories in both places. Some were going to Kemerova, where their dads would work in a mine, a coal mine. A few kids were going to a place where they were building an electrostation, but I don't know where that was, and there was one kid, exactly my age, who was on his uncle's contract, and he was going to a place where they were going to start to make airplanes.

Who wouldn't rather be an airplane mechanic over an auto mechanic? I was crestfallen.

My passion for skywriting had never left me. Leave me? Not in a million years! How I'd ever get to *be* one I had not the vaguest notion, but that was what I wanted, and nothing less would ever do.

I wonder if that American boy, the boy who was going off with his uncle, lived to learn of the triumph I had. I am sure he could tell how much I envied him. Did he live to envy me when I was celebrated as a hero of the skies? Did he see in a newspaper somewhere that they gave me medals? That they hailed me as the "Lindbergh of Russia"? Did that boy die somewhere in the Soviet Union before the Lindbergh of Russia was proclaimed? Or had he gone back with his uncle to safety in America—and read about me there?

But he probably never knew my name.

Why not? I never knew his.

EIGHT _____

We were loaded into cattle cars—all the Americans who were headed for Gorky. I did not care about the cattle cars—I was that eager to get moving—it did not matter into what. My mother tried to be cheerful—but you could see there was nothing under it but a huge sadness.

Our clothing was entirely unsuitable. The warmest things we had were hardly enough for what the weather was. We were cold that whole trip—and that is what I remember best about it, the cold, its getting worse and worse even as we went southeast, first to Moscow, and then due east on to Gorky—to Nizhni-Novgorod.

My mother cried—the cold, the cattle car.

And at one point she screamed out "Sam!" and that was all she said—and my father's shoulders fell forward into a posture that was to become typical of him, more and more the way you saw him. He said nothing—simply shrugged—and then let his broad shoulders fall forward and set his face into an expression that was rigid, impassive.

He was resigned. What was there to do?

Bear it—whatever it is, bear it—whatever comes, keep going forward! This was the message my father's monumental silence conveyed to me. It was a lesson I took to heart.

I believe I saw it as a man's way—and I wanted to be a man, to be like *him*—forbearing, resolute—if need be, resigned.

No, I remember something else now—in the course of that

long train ride to Gorky. Mother screamed a second time, and this time it was not a single outcry.

It was the rocks. Between Moscow and Gorky—just after Moscow—rocks started banging against the outside of the cattle car. We didn't know if it was rocks or what—but that's what it sounded like. And who was throwing them? What was going on? Sam seemed scared—we looked to him, all of us frightened, and he seemed frightened too. Everybody else in the car was looking at Papa—I guess because they figured he was some kind of official. But he had no explanation—and nothing comforting to say. He kept to his stony silence, reached over and took Miriam from Mama and did a little jig with her as that banging got worse. And then it subsided and only started up briefly once again, about a half hour later.

It was at one of our stops to let people out to relieve themselves in the snow that Papa found out for us what that banging was all about. Mother wouldn't leave the cattle car—and Leo wouldn't. It was too cold out there and they would just hold it as long as they could, and she wouldn't let Miriam go with Papa and me. To me it didn't seem it could be any colder out there than it was inside that cattle car—and, besides, where Sam went, I went. In any case, Papa talked to a trainman, and when we were off a ways and urinating together he told me it was the *Kulaks*—peasants who used to have a little more than other peasants, but who had been collectivized.

"What's collectivized?" I said.

"Well," he said, "it's where everybody starts off equal. You take what everybody has and spread it around evenly, so that everybody has the same. Those *Kulaks* are peasants who had more than the rest—a horse, a cow, something—and they don't like being collectivized."

"Why should they?" I said, realizing now that my feet were freezing, that whatever my father was saying, it wouldn't make any sense to me—I was too cold to pay any real attention.

"It's for the good of all the people, for the eventual good. In a revolution, some people suffer—but it's temporary. You suffer to make a better world for your son. You understand, *boychik?*"

"Sure," I said. "But what are they throwing rocks at *us* for?"

"I don't know," Papa said. "They are angry. They probably throw rocks at everything."

We buttoned up and stepped gingerly through the snow, up the rise and back to the tracks.

"Do not tell your mother," my father said as he neared the opening of the cattle car.

I did not ask him why. I just did as he said.

Not long after I learned that *Kulak* means "fist," a label earned by these richer peasants because they tried to hold what they had —their land, their animals, their grain, whatever they had. Perhaps to those *Kulaks* our string of cattle cars looked like something with authority. Or maybe they thought the cows that were taken from them were inside those cars—or, anyhow, somebody's cattle was. What a curious gesture—if that's what they thought in their innocence. But it makes sense to me, even so—even if that's what it was, why they threw rocks. I cannot explain it, but I have the feeling that in the terms I have come to see the mad conduct of men, throwing rocks at a cow that was taken from you makes absolutely perfect sense.

It is even a little eloquent.

The trip to Gorky took two days. It was broken only by the stopover in Moscow, where we waited in the station for about an hour. There were troops everywhere. In the States, I had never seen one soldier, not one. But in Leningrad there were plenty of them, and in Moscow plenty more. But, then again, you could not be entirely sure that what you were looking at was indeed a soldier. Because most of the people who were *not* soldiers nevertheless wore something military. That's because that's what most of the clothing was—and virtually everyone would have on some item of military clothing. The people were in rags and the troops were in rags, and it was often difficult to distinguish between the two, which people were in fact civilian and which were not.

I think that's important—I think it's important to bear that in mind—in order that you have a sense of the U.S.S.R. at that time. The high visibility of things military—even if it was only civilians dressed in soldier's garb because they had nothing else to dress in —colored everything you saw.

It is quite wonderful, the adaptability of youth. I more and more was not surprised by whatever I saw—people in long queues waiting for food, people in exotic confabulations of rags, in every sort of custom-made ingenuity to keep the cold out—beggars everywhere, soldiers or men who appeared to be soldiers, officials wherever you turned who demanded to check this, check that, and who eyed you as if you were first of all their sworn assassin and least of all a murderer of bureaucracy.

Nothing shocked me after a time—how quickly a boy gets used to things, to anything, and how lucky for him that he does. And I did. Oh, I quickly got over my boy's anticipation of bears and lions and tigers. How could anything as colorful as those animals live in a land as drab as this?

Only people could.

NINE _____

I figured out who were soldiers. The difference was more apparent in Gorky—or perhaps it was that I was beginning to see, to observe rather than just look. If they were soldiers, they had guns. Simple as that. They were armed.

But the civilians were all armed with string bags—sometimes three or four string bags—because who knew when and where a queue would set up for some food or something else that was suddenly being sold? So the people always carried them—"nets" they called them, and we learned to carry them too. It was all a question of luck—because you might happen on a queue anywhere, anytime. There was never any telling when there'd be a rush in some direction, and you learned to run with the crowd and not to bother to ask what it was they were selling until you had a place in line. It could be potatoes or cabbage or, once in a blue moon, soap. You got in line and you got whatever it was, no matter how long it took to get it, because who knew if you would ever get another chance? You carried your money and your three or four nets and you kept your eyes open for a queue forming up, for the person in front of you suddenly to quicken his pace in a new direction. And at night you came home and, just like the Russians, everyone in the family, even Miriam after a year or so, emptied his day's bonanzas there on the one table, and Mama sorted through it all, testing.

You had your meal.

We could see the auto plant in the distance, could see the sign that said _Ford_. That got changed to _Molotov Auto Works_ a while later. The American Village was situated two miles away from the factory—a settlement of one- and two-story buildings made out of wood, plywood, and mud. The walls were doubled for warmth, but they were pretty flimsy anyhow—with all the cracks and spaces stuffed with manure for insulation. Come that first summer, we were to discover what came creeping and flying out of that manure once it had warmed into a breeding site for vermin. But with the clothing we had and in the kind of December you get north of the 55th parallel, most of us broke into a run when we saw those squat, unpainted wooden structures set out like sleeping geometric giants on the wide and killing snow.

It was good to be running again—although I felt bad leaving Mama behind, and Papa laboring along with Miriam on his shoulders. But Leo ran with me, and suddenly nothing mattered but to be running again, doing what I was good at. It made me feel at home, myself, centered within myself. It was as if home for me was the physical action *in* me, always ready to be made evident by the doing of something I could do very well—at Cass Tech High School, in the streets of Detroit, in the snowfields outside of Nizhni-Novgorod. It did not matter where I was, so long as I could be inside myself—running, boxing, driving, *doing* something.

What did it matter, this Russia? I was Victor Herman, running, and running powerfully, leaving Leo far behind, and running with real speed now—through snow, through *Russian* snow.

The main building was called the Clubhouse, and it happened that we were assigned to a room right there, on the second floor. Again, we were quartered in one room, the five of us. There was only the one toilet in the whole place, the Clubhouse. I remember thinking that was going to be a large change from what we were used to. Large change! I think now of the communal cauldron in Cell 39, that unspeakable pool of human droppings, a stew that always cooked for ten days at a time.

But we were well off, us Hermans, considering that in some cases there were three or four families to a room. We could deliver three workers—Sam and Leo and me—and were accordingly rewarded with a lodging all for ourselves. There was no furniture there—just a room—and for sleeping material you had to be inventive, getting bedding anyhow you could get it.

We got situated as best we could. There wasn't much to get set up. There just wasn't anything much for me to do.

I didn't have any school—I was a worker now, and so far no one had given me any work to do. So the second day I went downstairs and picked up a pair of skis and some other American kids, and we all went out and skied all day.

If this was Russia, I could love it. I'd never had a chance to ski before. Boys like me didn't get to ski. But here you just took the skis you saw lying around, and out there you had all that open country to do it, with more snow than you ever believed could keep coming down.

But it was our third day there that something happened, the thing that, now that I look back on it, fixed the course of my life.

I had been skiing around for a couple of hours, there on the outskirts of the American Village, and I heard shots, gunshots, and I skied toward them, going over a rise until I saw a little stadium not far off. It was a rifle contest that was going on down there between two groups of men—one group shooting .22's and the other group Army rifles. But when I got close enough I could see that it was men shooting the Army rifles and boys about my age with the .22's. That was one of the things about life in the Soviet Union in those days—it was hard to decipher the age and the gender of the people you saw, so somber and similar was the clothing they bundled themselves into in the cold. It was easier to tell what caliber of shells were being shot off than the years or sex of who was doing it. You also found out pretty fast that shooting was a very big thing over there—most everybody did it, practiced all the time with whatever sort of firearm they let you use. Everybody was given to understand that this was an important thing, a way to protect the U.S.S.R. from all the capitalist nations they figured were getting ready to invade it. A citizen had to learn to shoot, and even if they did not give you a gun, they let you use one often enough, always bringing a batch of them out, old guns and lots of mismade shells, to practice at targets whenever there was time enough.

There were Americans there and Germans and Austrians and Finns—kids and men—and when I stood watching, one of the men called out, in German, "You want to shoot?" I didn't understand—but after a while, another man called out, this time in English, "You want to shoot?" and to make himself clear he held a rifle up in the air, offering.

I could see it was a .22 that he held up. But I came forward and pointed to the Army rifle that one of the men held. I'd done plenty of shooting—chiefly at Camp Farmington—even though my father didn't like it, despised guns. But I had made it my business to find out what they were and how to use them. I didn't exactly love guns—I *couldn't,* considering how I wanted to be just like my dad. But I didn't hate them, either. I thought they were okay—and I liked being good with them.

I'd never shot a military rifle before—nor had I ever shot in such conditions, the snow, the cold, all bundled up. But I couldn't wait to get my hands on that gun. I didn't even take off my skis until I'd shot enough rounds and so well that the men all wanted me to try it sitting down on the little bench they had and then try it prone. They gave me five rounds standing and all five rounds I shot bull's-eyes.

They couldn't believe it. Neither could I. I didn't know I was that good—and maybe I wasn't, maybe I was lucky. But I think what did it was their watching me, all of them, all those people—and the need to prove myself, to compete, to show off.

There was a lot of excited chatter about the performance I had made, and the same American fellow, the man who'd called me over, kept saying, "And he didn't even take off his *skis,* this ✱ ✱ kid!"

The men started carrying on about it, asking me questions in different languages, and I did not say anything but just tried to act nonchalant, as if I always did just what I'd done, could shoot five straight bull's-eyes whenever I wanted. With all the excitement, a man who had been squatting off to the side got up and came over. I don't know what his rank was, but he was some kind of Army commander, one of the many Red Army people that were attached to the Village.

He spoke to me in Russian, simple phrases, but by now I could handle myself.

"You can do this again?" he said.

I said, "Sure."

"Do it," he said. "Try."

This time they gave me ten shells.

If I had *not* done what I did then—if I had not tried so hard, or had not the gift to do it no matter *how* hard I tried, or if something had gone wrong, the gun, the bullets, or the cold finally overwhelming my aim, would it all have happened to me, anyway?

Who can know what might have made a difference? Or if any

difference *could* have been made? Who can know at what precise point or on the basis of which small gesture a life is decided, its chapters ordained?

I shot ten bull's-eyes. I, Victor Herman, did that.

And in the doing of it, it began to happen that I sealed my fate.

But I did it myself. I wanted to do it. I was a boy, and I wanted to show off.

TEN _____

I was never a wise guy when I was a boy, a smart aleck, a weisenheimer. My mother and father were too strict for that—and I was too quiet, maybe too sullen, for that sort of thing.

But I was cocky. I know that. And I could not help it. Self-assurance just followed from all the things I could do so well—box and fight and drive, and all the sports, and being indifferent to injury, to fear. And I could shoot—flawlessly, it turned out, with surpassing accuracy, as it turned out that December morning, there in that little stadium, among those huddled and staring men and boys, there in the magic Russian snow.

That was *it*—the snow, the knowing I was someplace new, in this bizarre land where everything that moved with life was gray, and it moved through a vast snowy silence that was white—I think *that* was why I could do it, could aim that rifle at whatever they said and fire a bullet that went to its mark.

It was uncanny—and I was no less amazed than were all the rest, those boys and men who stood there muttering to each other in disbelief. And the commander, or whatever he was, said, "How many bull's-eyes can you shoot?" I didn't know the Russian for the word "bullets," but I understood his meaning, so I said in English, "How many bullets do you have?" and the American man who had started all this by calling me over, he told the commander what I'd said—and the commander didn't smile, but turned away.

This was strange to me, something different. My cockiness did not earn me favor or amusement or even a kind of joshing in return.

That's the American way, and it was what I was used to—but I presently found out that Russians are humiliated when someone kids with them—and that the usual Russian expression is a frown, a scowl. They are a solemn people, just like the hard land they live in. To put it more as it actually is, they like to kid but not be kidded. To a Russian, to be kidded is to be insulted and humiliated.

I had been shooting at targets set off at three hundred meters, and I had executed fifteen bull's-eyes in a row. They gave me more shells, anyway—even though I had apparently lost the interest of the man in charge. I took off my skis and shot seated, shot prone, not even caring if they made me do it in the snow. But they had cleared a place and there was a kind of rush-work mat there, all greasy and black from use.

I went home that day like a boy reborn. I had wanted an adventure—and behold! Just as in a story, I was getting it.

That night, in the course of the evening meal downstairs in the Clubhouse, the commander came over to where we were seated.

He said to me, "Who is your father?"

I nodded toward Sam.

Then the man spoke to my father, who got up from where he was sitting and stood by his place listening. I could get what the man was saying, most of it—that I was an excellent shot, a marksman, and that the Soviet Federated Socialist Republic needed every boy and man who was an excellent shot, and therefore this boy must report for shooting practice every day.

My father was silent. He had his wooden spoon in his hand and he looked foolish and small standing there, and it was clear he was a little alarmed and uncomfortable and didn't know what to say. So he said nothing.

The commander took out a square of paper and a little green box.

"Your name!" he said to my father, and my father gave his name.

"The boy?" said the commander, and my father gave my name.

The commander laid the paper he had down on the table, a certificate I could see, and printed my name into a place on it, and then scribbled something further on down. He gave this to my father, and then to me he handed the little green box.

There was a medal inside, for marksmanship. And the certificate was the same sort of thing, an award.

"Post it in your room," the Russian said to my father, and then he said, "We will tell you when the boy is to come."

With that he turned away, and we finished our meal.

Leo was excited for me, and he kept saying so—but Sam said nothing, and moments after the Russian left, my mother got up with Miriam and went back to our room.

The next day, around two in the afternoon, Papa told me I was to go back to the stadium. But there was only that commander there when I got there. He gave me three different kinds of rifles, and he told me to shoot—to shoot all I liked, from whatever position I liked—and I did it. I shot.

It was incredible. I could do it again—I could hit perfectly, or at least near to perfectly, any mark I tried.

The man watched and watched, and then he stopped me and gave me another little green box—another medal.

I thought this was unbelievable, until later when I found out they always gave out medals in those days and it didn't take all that much to get one. But I was getting mine for something truly outstanding—and I knew it and kept right on being amazed at myself, at whatever was in me that was doing this extraordinary thing I could do. It didn't matter about the medals anymore: I wanted something that would declare I was a superman, the world's most astonishing boy.

I was stunned with the prospect of what I could do. I had, there, that day, shooting for the unresponsive Russian who stood watching me hit mark after mark, the flowering of a feeling that I was invincible, that a mantle of some kind of miraculous power had settled on my shoulders.

It is an easy thing for a boy, a quiet boy, a dreamer, to get an idea of this kind. But I had help—my natural skill and circumstance, the unique conditions that caught me in the prime of my boyhood. It was my downfall, beginning to think this, to hold this crazy perspective on myself. But *there* is the irony. For just as believing nothing could stop me was to prove my undoing, it was the same belief that saved me, that carried me out, still sane and intact, to the other side of what was to come.

The Greeks explain this simply—that the composition of a

man's virtues yields his vice. But that's what's demonstrated in their theater, what's put on as a lesson for those who watch. I've sometimes read that some thinkers question whether that Greek theater has much to do with life, whether that theater is just a model of what *should* happen but scarcely ever *does*.

But in my case the Greeks were right—my strengths sought and found my agony.

In the weeks ahead I was to be taken to a number of military installations in the Nizhni area, small encampments of troops here and there, never farther away than a day's journey—and I was asked to shoot for the soldiers, to show off my remarkable aim.

I would come home at night, back to our room in the Clubhouse, a little antic from all the attention I was getting, and Sam and Rose and Leo and Miriam would listen to the few words I would say and look at the new medal someone had pressed on me, always in a little colored box. Neither Mama nor Papa had much to say about any of this. They took it in stride, or *didn't* take it in stride but just kept quiet about it, and life went from one dizzying experience to the next. I was now a member of the shooting team that had been gotten up out of the residents in the American Village, and we were taken around to all sorts of places, on a fairly regular basis, to compete against military teams and civilian teams, teams of men from *Spartak* and *Dynamo*.

ELEVEN _____

Russians started taking me for a Russian—wherever I went—and I was going to lots of places, competing—not just in riflery, but also, especially as it got closer to the spring, in boxing and basketball. It was my coloring that did it, the hair and eyes, pale skin—and the way I had picked up the language so naturally, young enough to have no trouble with the accent.

I got to talking Russian *all* the time—even when I was with my family or with other Americans from the Village. But I was less and less *with* Americans—because of all the sports I kept competing in. More and more I was with one team or another from Gorky, playing ball and boxing against other teams that came from all over Russia, or we went to them. There was one thing the Russians took as seriously as getting food and keeping out of the way of someone in authority, and that was sports, *any* kind of sports, *every* kind of sports. Later on, especially when I got into sport flying and jumping, I saw the relation between all this constant competition and constant encouragement of those who competed and the development of a military mind and body. I mean, it wasn't exactly *sports* that was the point.

In any case, I got to *thinking* in Russian, and no longer did I bother to identify myself as an American. It was not that I felt any less American. It was just that, increasingly, what did that have to do with anything? Why bother? Besides, I guess I was proud of myself, of how readily I could pass myself off as a Russian boy, good and even better than they were at the things they were interested in, real Russian boys, and even men.

Even in this, in wanting to appear to be Russian, and in being so successful at it, I see myself as a sort of frantic competitor, eager to win the race, regardless of the course that was being run and what the runner might get for his trouble.

In fact, I *did* run—just as regularly as I had been doing the shooting—because track was my original success in school, my favorite sport at Cass—and since I saw how much the Russians rewarded me for excellence in boxing and riflery, why not let them see me take off at what I figured I was best at? And as the weather warmed somewhat, although even into May and June there was still snow on the ground that first year, I got a chance to show my stuff in all the field events.

All this time my dad and Leo were working at the plant, and sometimes I was in and out of there too, but mainly I was off doing my sports. I saw very little of them, my family, and hardly anything of Leo, who took to refusing to accompany me in the off-hours we might have spent together in the evenings. In the evenings I used to go out to the perimeter of the Village, cut trees, and chop wood, bring whatever I could manage home—because by now we were living in one of the smaller buildings and we had a stove. And I would ask Leo to go along with me, if not to help, then just for company, but he always found an excuse and after a while I stopped asking.

There was never too much wood to burn, no matter what the

season was, and by this time it was a habit with me to go out every night to cut trees, saw logs, split them, and drag load after load home. I saw it as building up my body, keeping my body strong—and if I have ever had a religion, that's it right there. Going into those woods at night was like prayer to me—to me it was just like that.

Besides, it had to be done—and I didn't want my father doing it. He worked all day while I played, and Leo wouldn't do it. But I was glad to—glad to feel good about what I was doing for my body and for my family at the same time. Because, to some extent, I was slightly ashamed about my shooting—and my boxing—maybe about *all* my sports—because I knew it wasn't for my family, that it didn't make things any different or any better for them.

We'd moved from the Clubhouse to right across the street, into a one-story building. We were still in one room, but Mama did all the cooking here and it was more like home, having more privacy. I think my dad perked up a little bit at first.

But Rose didn't. She just went from bad to worse. Nothing cheered her, nothing anyone could say or anyone could do—except, of course, to tell her that she was going home, that all of us were —to fix a date, and then do it.

She *did* have a date—the 1st of October, 1934. We all knew our three years would be up then—and Rose surely knew that too. Wasn't it grownups who were always telling you to be patient, to just bide your time and the future would come in its inevitable course, all of its own accord?

But my mother was sad, inconsolably sad—the heart had gone out of her—and even Miriam could tell. We all knew it.

She would cry. Not loudly, or very noticeably, but sometimes unceasingly, sort of muted and to herself—and it was terrible.

But Sam said nothing about it. Or if he did, I never heard him. He had given his word—three years—and he would keep it no matter what it cost.

And I was no help either. I liked it here—I was getting on and having fun—and I was getting a bigger and bigger reputation. I was someone who excelled—*in this country I excelled*. It occurred to me that maybe it was the Russian air that did it, that maybe there was some kind of magic in the air, or maybe it was my American tricks, my American style, that threw them all off and let me win.

What does a kid know? But he thinks these things. Not *thinks,* really. He *feels* them—and *that's* what I think I felt.

I would *see,* rather than hear, my mother cry—but one night I heard her sobbing to herself as she so often did now. She was facing the wall and sobbing. I heard her stop herself and then, uttering it quietly and quite calmly, as if she had been speaking calmly like this for minutes, she said, "I will never see my daughter again—I will never see my Becky."

It was true.

They gave us two rooms—in the same building. Maybe it was because of what Sam and Leo were doing at the auto plant or because of what I was doing on the playing field. But, at any rate, it made life a little better. Sam and Rose had a room to themselves now—and I had the idea that maybe this way they could begin to work things out between them, that in their solitude together Sam would speak up and make her understand, or that Mama would wear him down with a woman's sweetness and my father would give up and do as she wanted.

But it didn't help. It changed nothing. And *could* we have gone if Sam had relented? I think so—in those early years, before the trouble began, the purges, I think we still could have gotten out. Others did. I know that now—since coming home to the States, to Detroit, I know that others got out in time.

Didn't the Reuther brothers get out, Victor and Walter? Weren't they in the American Village with us—as late as 1935? And *they* got out, got back. And others did too—before the trouble started.

But we stayed—we stayed right on—and we were not the only ones. But by then my mother was dead.

Things got tougher faster. After a while it wasn't sports for me *all* the time or even *most* of the time. I was expected to keep to a shift in the plant now, first as a mechanic and thereafter as a worker in tool and die. Leo was in the drafting shop, and he went from that into the design shop—and my father was foreman in the body shop.

The plant was a shot-down version of the River Rouge plant, and for the most part it was a mess. Safety features were haphazard, things went wrong more often than not, and it was pretty much a matter of chaos.

And it was cold. Working around all that metal and doing work you couldn't do with gloves on, it was very hard for all concerned. You were up at dawn and on the job at eight—and some-times I'd cut some wood beforehand if the supply I'd brought in at night seemed shy of lasting the day for my mother. But whatever the weather was like and no matter how early we got to our shops, the Russians were always there ahead of us, already working away.

It was incredible. But most of them didn't know what they were doing—these were not mechanics or skilled laborers—these were peasants, untrained men and women and boys, who had all they could do to keep from getting themselves killed or maimed by the machinery. But the machinery wasn't the worst of it. It was the cold, cold iron and cold steel that your fingers could freeze to.

When they finished their shifts, they went to _school,_ the Rus-sians did. Whereas those of us in the American Village who worked alongside them—us Americans or Germans or Austrians or Finns, and even some Italians—we'd go back to our buildings or to the Clubhouse and sit down and have a meal—with whatever sort of heat there was to warm us after the factory—because there was never any heating in the factory, except what was generated by the machines and given off from the congestion of working people.

My schooling stopped when I left Detroit, my formal educa-tion. None of us in the American Village, none of the boys or girls of any nationality, were going to anything like a school. Like the men and women we worked with, we just went back to our places and did what we wanted to do and then went off to bed. And while we were sleeping, the Russians we'd just put in a day with were off somewhere in the cold, sitting in some place that was probably just as cold as the auto shops, and going to school.

The little kids, it was different with them—with Miriam. Miriam went to school, and she kept on going to school in the American Village and then in Gorky.

I was long gone by then—when Miriam was graduated from university and from medical school. I was someplace else when she became a pediatrician. I was someplace Miriam couldn't have dreamed of, a kid who had grown up pretty much in Russia. Maybe Sam knew something about the kind of place I was in—or could at least guess about it from things he must have heard. By then people must have gotten stories out, and the stories must have made their way back to Sam, but he would never have told Miriam.

But of course Miriam eventually knew. In the end, she must have known about most of it—or anyhow, enough of it. Because she changed the kind of medicine she practiced from pediatrics to pathology—and that's what she practices in the Soviet Union to this day. She's there to this day, in Gorky, examining the diseased tissue of the dying and the dead when what she wanted to do was to bring life into the world.

She told me why before I left for America, why she changed the work she did.

It was her way of kissing me across all the years that we were apart. I think that's what it was—and despair.

TWELVE ————————————————————

Even now, so long after that black time, my daughters Sveta and Janna asleep in their beds, my belly still tight from the meals they have put before me, I often wake up gasping for food. At three, four in the morning, the last meal in me not yet digested, I come jolting out of sleep—the hunger in me wild, an old insanity gone mad again.

It is my brain, not my belly, that wakes me.

I ate tree slugs those years when I was starving. I ate tree slugs and other things that meant meat to my belly, and the belly was fed but the brain's craving was not. It is a madness that still comes to me at night.

In the spring of 1932 what I could do on the track overtook the attention I had been getting for what I could do with a gun.

I was entered into a meet in Gorky—placed first in the 100-meter run and in the broad jump. I cannot remember what place I took in the high jump, but I was somewhere in the running. However I scored in the high jump, my overall performance put me well over the mark for a spot on the Russian team officially representing Gorky. *Officially*. It is precisely the word. Sports were very official. I trained early in the morning—before work.

It was around this time that I got two trips to Moscow—first for the plant, then for track.

About thirty vehicles had been assembled—cars and mainly Model AA trucks—and these must have been the first batch the Gorky plant had turned out, and as I understood it from Sam, the idea was to make a big thing of this in Moscow, to really put on a show—and Moscow wanted those vehicles *there,* to put on display, but the trouble was there weren't enough people who knew how to *drive* them. It's hard to imagine, but among all those workers there at the auto plant, there were not thirty men who knew how to drive. But maybe that's not so hard to imagine. How many of them would have owned a car?

As a matter of fact, there were only sixteen of us who could drive—a man named McCarthy, an American who ranked high at the Gorky plant, fourteen Russian engineers, all of whom I'd taught myself back there in the States, and me. And so only sixteen vehicles could go to Moscow, thirteen trucks and three cars.

I was assigned a truck.

I remember Sam was anxious about my going to Moscow. I don't know why, but he seemed nervous about it. He kept cautioning me to do as I was told, to keep my mouth shut and just do my job. He talked a little bit about how things were going to get better.

It is in this respect that my father and I were very different. I was always fixed in the present, as captured by the moment *now* as he was captivated by his prospect of the time to come. I suppose we learn to be captives of the time that is best for us—and if you are my dad's sort of man, an idealist, a thinker, the present is never a good place of residence.

He tore off some tickets for me from his food ration card— for the trip. But they proved unusable—only in the store in the American Village would they get you any food, and that was only bread.

He was worried about me. That was plain.

It was 320 miles to Moscow. I did it on no food. It was, this first experience, good practice—two days and two nights without anything.

The snow was heavy even then, in early spring—and there was nothing you could really call a road.

Not far outside of Gorky the military man who came with us kept hopping out and trotting ahead to chase the peasants out of their homes. He'd herd them ahead of us to the place he called a road, and they would have to trample the snow to make a way for us to pass. This went on all that distance from Gorky to Moscow, from village to village, that military man hopping out and trotting ahead, tumbling farmers and their families from sleep to clear a path for the sixteen black machines that went clattering through the dark.

What the things we drove must have looked like to those people, jerked out of their dreams to the nightmare that was our mad procession through the snow!

Thirteen trucks were in the lead, and three cars came behind— and one of the lighter vehicles would sometimes crumple sideways into a gulley—and the military man would holler and try to get those peasants to push the black thing out—but even in their fear of him, not one of them would go near it, would touch that car.

Three hundred twenty miles of this! But we stopped for nothing —except to push a car back in line—and two days and two nights was pretty good time.

We slept that night in one of the factories there—there in Moscow. I had thought we'd be rewarded, but we slept on the floor.

Most of that next day we just kept driving our cars and trucks around Moscow, showing them off to the people who everywhere crowded close to get a look at them. It was a thing to see, how those people carried on. There was hardly even any cheering, they were so moved by what they saw. They wept openly—it seems incredible to me now—men and women crying to see the things that Russia had produced.

Somewhere in Moscow we stopped for a time, and I got out and walked around a little bit, stretching myself, easing out the kinks. No matter how I positioned myself, there were people coming over and patting me on the back, saying all sorts of things to express their admiration. I was starting back to my truck when a woman—she was in her thirties, with astonishingly white skin and dark, dark eyes—snatched me by my sleeve and asked if I were American.

I answered in Russian, "What makes you think so?"

"The way you walk," she said in English. "You walk like an American."

"I didn't know Americans had a special walk," I said, still in Russian.

"Then you are an American," she said, again in English.

"All right," I said, in English now myself. "What of it?"

"Tell me why you do this. Why you help them, the Soviets? You help make the Soviets strong, then you keep us under their thumb. Tell me why you help them!"

She kept snatching at my sleeve—and I could see that she was really angry.

I said nothing. I pulled away from her and strolled back to my truck.

I didn't know what to make of it—all those other people overjoyed, and this woman in a rage, suggesting I'd done something wrong. And then I thought of those *Kulaks* hurling rocks at anything that passed—I thought of that customs man fingering my mother's things in the light through that bleak window.

I put it out of my mind. I was having a good time.

That evening we were to appear at a banquet in the Kremlin, and McCarthy made certain I appreciated what an honor this was, just getting into the Kremlin, a rare thing indeed.

In those days the Kremlin was virtually shut to all but the most trusted and important. It was fear, mainly. There is just no calculating the degree of paranoia that festered in the Soviet chieftains then. Like everything else at this time in Russian life, it was excessive, beyond all relation to reason. Anyhow, the Kremlin was more or less impenetrable then—but I was going in—we were going to be driving the cars and trucks right in.

Some distance from the Kremlin we were hailed down and boarded by Army men—they climbed into the backs of the trucks and into the cabs and took up all the passenger seats in the cars. It was * driving with three in the front of that truck, but those two troopers weren't budging for anything. And as we were loading all these troopers up, tanks appeared, four of them, and took up positions to the front, rear, and sides of us—and like that, in that formation, we drove into the Kremlin.

We got inside into a kind of courtyard and lined ourselves up and shut down, and two members of the Politbureau, Comrades Kaganovich and Ordzhonikidze, came out to meet us. They said leave the vehicles and come with us, and McCarthy said that if we were leaving the vehicles to sit for a while, we'd have to run the water out of the radiators or else it would freeze. So the two officials looked at each other and back at McCarthy, and then said, "Wait here." They went back into where they'd come from, and by now I was getting a look around, and it was a thing to see, all right, like a fortress out of a book about knights—and after about forty minutes, with those troopers watching every move we made, the two officials came back out again and said it was okay to do it, to take the water out. So we drained the radiators into the buckets that we carried, and when the water started coming out, it came out steaming—and as if they'd had a command, all those troopers surrounded us, and they looked very worried. But one of the Russian engineers that was driving with us said no, not to worry, nothing was going to explode, and everybody calmed down, and we went inside, all of us following those two officials.

The banquet was going to be in what they called the Big Hall—and the two officials took us right in, and the first thing you noticed was not all the showy stuff they had in there or the really dazzling plates of food and trays of bottles that covered all those tables—it wasn't any of that. It was the warmth. It was warm everywhere in there. I realized it was the first time I had been really all-over warm since the crossing on the *Leviathan*. Sure, when it was cold you could now and then get acceptably warm for a while back at the American Village. But not really warm all over. You got up close to the stove or a fire somewhere, and parts of you warmed up, and you probably weren't even aware that parts of you were still cold, so good it felt just to be warm *somewhere*. But the cold was really nagging at you all the time—some part of your body was always complaining. You just got so used to it after a while, you thought you were warm when you really weren't. And you didn't actually comprehend any of this until now, until you were in the Big Hall and realized all over again what warm really was. And it was not until this large difference in things had registered with me that I began to see the spectacle that was all around me—the giant paintings that were on the walls, everything gilded and glowing, and the statuary, and gilt wood carved everywhere, going all the way up and all around you, and the carpet beneath your feet, that thick. And even with all the people that were already in there, the place was hushed, dim, radiant—churchly and reverent.

But that didn't last long—not once the drinking got started.

There was a long table up front, and it was for the high Kremlin officials. The sixteen of us all sat at separate tables. There were many tables set up in the room, but the ones we were sitting at were a little bit higher than all those others because they had been jacked up a few inches, to raise us above the rest—to show us we were being honored or to show us off to the rest, or both. Maybe it was even to keep an eye on us. Could that really have been the case? We had, the number of us, as many waiters standing at attention all around us, and they were dressed in frock coats. I was hungry. I wanted to eat. Aside from tea, I had had nothing since leaving Gorky. And I am not a drinker—not even wine, and surely in those days drink was the last thing you'd get down me, an athlete, a boy with medals on his mind.

But there was a toast for the great leader Comrade Stalin, then a toast for the first car, a toast for the first truck, a toast for the second car, a toast for the second truck—and so on. And after this, other things were discovered suitable for toasting—the factory that had produced the vehicles, the men that had driven them here, first this man, then that man, and so on. Then the toasting was elevated to grander concerns, to the coming of industry, to the strengthening of the Soviet, to Comrade this and Comrade that, and finally again to Comrade Stalin.

The assembly was in an uproar at the mention of Stalin's name, and promptly thereafter word was passed around among the tables that Comrade Stalin might indeed put in an appearance, but that it was not certain, that one could only hope—and then, as if in an appeal to this possibility, a series of toasts was offered in his name, praising achievements as recently won as that very morning, extraordinary things, undreamt-of accomplishments!

I served myself a chunk of smoked sturgeon and wolfed it down. Was I really going to see the famous Joseph Stalin?

I had no clear notion what Stalin was or why the Russians got so worked up about him. I mean, I knew very well, of course, that he was their leader, but like all national leaders to me at that time, what could he be but a bore? Would he be any less boring than Coolidge? Than Hoover? How in the world could anyone with a job like that be one whit different from a Herbert Hoover or a Calvin Coolidge? And surely neither of those fellows was anything to get all excited about. But the people in the Big Hall were out of their minds with the widening rumor that Comrade Stalin might honor us by presenting himself at the banquet.

I was of course prepared by this time to go along with a lot of Russian craziness. But how could a boy of my age and interests make sense out of all this wildness over a politician? I put it down to the drunkenness that was fast spreading all around me. Never before had I seen so many people drunk in one place. It was a little unsettling, maybe scary, all that insobriety—especially to a boy who was contemptuous of the very idea of alcohol. And mind you, all this boisterous carrying on was unfolding in a setting that had already stunned me with its pomp and mystery. Yes, it was all a little frightening to me, what was going on in that big room. I was still worn out from the long, wild trip from Gorky and from the parading around Moscow in my truck all day, and I'd been stuffing myself silly with food. All that and what was erupting around me combined to make me feel very odd, as if I had wandered into some sort of funhouse at a carnival and everybody was in on the joke— except me.

And then something was disclosed to me that made everything even crazier—because I noticed, and I don't know *how* I noticed it what with all that was going on, but I noticed that only one of the waiters at each of the elevated tables was actually serving anybody anything, and that the others were just watching us, and that underneath their frock coats, in each case on the left side right around where a shoulder holster would place it, there was the clear outline of a pistol pushing out the cloth. It gave me a terrible start, and made me think which thing was I going to tell my father first—that I'd seen Stalin, or almost had? Or that I saw gunsels masquerading as waiters, bodyguards, real bodyguards?

I heard someone saying Molotov was there, Kaganovich was there, would Stalin not be there? And then someone else said that if Molotov was there and Kaganovich was there, we had already been honored enough! And then someone at the table behind me said, no, no, Comrade Stalin, it had just been quietly announced, would *not* be there—it was regrettable, but he was much too busy with state business to spare even a few moments in the Big Hall, but that he sent his warmest respects to the heroes of the Gorky plant and to all the other illustrious guests present—and this sort of thing went on and on. For thirty minutes or more the expectation went up, then the expectation went down, then up again—until everyone in that vast hall, drunk or sober, a wild enthusiast for Stalin or not interested in him at all, was whipped up into a pitch of nervous passion, first up, then down, then maybe, then no, then well, possibly, yes, possibly—and when all this had contrived to heighten the tension in that room to something just short of hysteria, someone suddenly rose at the head table, struck his goblet for silence, and declared that Comrade Stalin was able to steal a few seconds from some very important thing he was doing and that, yes, he would, for just a few seconds, join us and extend his greetings to all those who were present to celebrate this great moment in Soviet history.

It was pandemonium.

You could hardly see him for all that was going on, the commotion, the screaming.

It was quite a show.

I told Sam all about it. I told my mother too. But she didn't seem to pay much attention.

When Stalin made his little appearance and went on briefly to congratulate the great Socialist heroes, workers and heroes all, who operated the Gorky plant, he ended by exhorting everyone to try harder, produce more, give it all you've got. I almost had to laugh. Did the man have any notion what working in that plant was like? Work *harder?* Produce *more?*

The applause was sensational, and I applauded too, but all I was really thinking about was working harder for the track meet coming up in Moscow in the summer. If I was going to give anything my all, it was that. Yet by the time that track meet arrived, my mind was miles away, thousands of feet above the turf the meet was held on, nowhere near the stadium in which I ran and jumped with the best of them.

It happened this way. Something drew my attention elsewhere. Sam had told me to keep my mouth shut—but I didn't, not entirely—I opened it enough to set the stage for the next miraculous shift in my life. Miraculous? *Yes.* A new marvel was introduced onto the course I was traveling. But marvels can be monstrous, and if that is not at first sight evident, then give it time, for all it needs is time.

THIRTEEN ————————————————————

At last the proceedings seemed finished, and we were marched down to the first floor again and handed slips of paper showing where we were to be quartered for the night.

I was standing there, near the exit of the building we were in, looking at my slip of paper and wondering who was then going to tell me where the thing was that I was assigned to, when a young man walked briskly over and stationed himself in front of me.

The fellow was a *general*—and he couldn't have been much older than my dad—forty-one or -two, a little more. He just stood there in a very relaxed way and introduced himself. His whole manner was different from what I'd come across in Russian officials so far—none of that tremendous formality and reserve.

In what was really a very offhand manner, he said, "I am General Tukachevsky."

It was amazing. It was a name I knew right away, a name I'd heard more often than I'd heard Stalin, even. Sam used to talk about this Tukachevsky—not a name you'd easily forget once you'd heard it a couple of times.

"I've heard of you," I said. "Unless—I beg your pardon—it's your father I've heard of."

The fellow actually smiled—still another remarkable piece of behavior, given my fix on uniformed Soviets.

"It is I you have heard of," he said and just stood there smiling.

"You were a hero in the Civil War," I said. "My father told me."

I had almost said the *Russian* Civil War, but stopped myself in time. Did I want to lose this game I was playing with myself, this tremendous fun I was having at seeing how well I could get away with seeming a Russian?

"Of course your father told you of me," this young smiling man said. "Every good Soviet father tells his son of Tukachevsky." And he laughed. And then he abruptly stopped his laughter and said, "You did not drink the toasts. Why?"

And that alarmed me at first, but then I thought, just tell him the truth.

"Because I am an athlete," I said.

"And also because you are not a Russian?" he said.

Now I laughed. "That's right," I said. "I'm an American. But I like to see if I can get people to take me for a Russian." I smiled, hoping he would feel complimented by this.

He said, "Yes, very good. One of the Americans who have come here to help us build. Very good."

I think I amused him, something in my manner. In any event, we stood there like that for an uncomfortable moment, both smiling.

And then he asked me an utterly insane question, and I thought he was kidding me, or that he was so ill at ease over having gotten himself into a conversation with me, because I'm not much of a talker, at least not when it comes to the kind of talk you've got to make in a situation like this, that I'd made him so uncomfortable he'd say anything just to keep the conversation going or end it with a final stroke.

He said, "What kind of airplanes do you fly?"

I looked at the guy, bewildered. I thought, well, maybe it's my Russian.

I said, "I am an American, General."

He said, "I know. You speak Russian like an American. Of course you are an American. I know. Tell me, what kind of airplanes do you fly?"

I began to think he was a lunatic. I didn't know what to say to the man—and I figured maybe it would be best to sidestep it all.

I said, "Is my Russian that bad? I thought it was good."

He said, "It is good. But it is not that good. You sound like an American and you are an American. Now, answer me—what kind of airplanes do you fly?"

It was getting really hot there. How long could this go on?

"General," I said, "I don't fly airplanes."

And now, again, he laughed. He stood there looking at me and winking—and then he poked me in the arm, just the way a kid at home would do if he thought you were horsing around with him. I tried to laugh too, but I couldn't. I couldn't because I couldn't figure out what was funny. He was crazy. That was the only funny part of this. But I didn't think that would be a good thing to laugh about.

Finally, he calmed himself and he said, with terrific gravity, "Be serious with me. What kind of airplanes do you fly?"

I repeated that I did not fly airplanes.

At this he flew into a great excitement. "American," he said, "what do you mean you do not fly airplanes? Can you not drive a car? Did you not drive a car to Moscow?"

"Yes, I did," I said and waited for more.

"American," he said, "if one drives a car, one flies an airplane. Now, tell me, in America, what kind of airplanes do you fly?"

It went back and forth like this for three or four minutes. He was utterly disbelieving. What the man *did* believe was that the two things went together—those that could drive could fly—at least in the States they could—because he figured everybody in the States had both an automobile and an airplane.

I suppose it is hard to reckon with a man thinking that. Surely, it was hard for me—at the time. But at that time Russians, most Russians, at least very many Russians, entertained the most fantastic notions about the United States, what life there was like—what people had and how they lived and what they lived with. A week earlier, a Russian who was helping with the coaching of the track team, the Gorky team, told me that one day he would visit America because he wanted to see the skyscrapers. So we got to talking about the skyscrapers, and as we talked I began to realize that the fellow thought skyscrapers went from one coast to the other, that the entire U.S. was plastered with nothing but skyscrapers, every square foot. And here this general facing me, the famous Russian hero I'd heard my own father talk about, was absolutely certain that driving and flying were things everybody in America did, and that if you could do one you could do the other—and *did* do it, all the time.

At any rate, it took a while to straighten him out, and then, even then, I still wasn't positively sure he didn't think I was still kidding him. But whatever he really thought, his next question was a lulu. If anyone has ever asked me a question that my whole heart wanted to hear asked, this was it—*this was that question.*

"Would you like to go to flying school?" he said. "You can drive. You should fly. It will be easy to learn. You are an American. It will be easy to learn."

All I could do was nod. I nodded.

He said, "All right, American. I will arrange it."

He asked me what my name was and where I lived, and I

could barely speak. I gave him all that information twice and kept nodding as I did it.

"Very good," he said, and put out his hand to shake mine. "Very good, American. Consider it arranged. I will arrange it. General Tukachevsky himself will arrange it."

And he did.

I recall my saying, "Please write it down—my name and address—my name is Victor Herman, American Village outside of Gorky."

But he did not write it down. He just said, "Do not worry, American. I will not forget."

I was so crazy with excitement, I didn't know how to close this. I kept thanking him and thanking him—and tried once or twice to shake his hand again. And it was killing me to come up with something expressive of my feeling, and I said, "You can call me Comrade Herman," and Tukachevsky just grinned and replied, "Very good, Victor. Very good."

It was about four days later that I got back to my family, all the way home on the train reciting to myself the sentence that would make up the stories I had to tell.

So much of it was all so special—the bizarre journey to Moscow, the parading of the cars and trucks, the troopers and the tanks, the Kremlin, that vast hall where there was food of a wealth and kind I had never seen, the hysteria of the people in that place, Stalin showing up, my * , *Stalin,* and all the ornament and the rest of it, and how warm it was, and what happened afterwards—*Tukachevsky! Flying school!* My dream come true!

But what would that mean to Mama and Papa? Had I ever told them about seeing *LUCKIES* up there? About seeing myself up there too, writing on the sky?

No, I had never told my parents that. I was not the sort of boy to tell my parents much—and not a thing like that.

So I said nothing about that at first—and maybe it wouldn't really happen, anyway. Maybe the fellow really was a lunatic, as I had originally believed. Or he *would* forget—or something. Yet I *knew* it would happen—I just *knew* it would—because look what had already happened, amazing things, completely astonishing, completely unexpected things. After all, here I was in Russia, an American boy! If that could happen, what could *not* happen?

Yes, *what!*

At that age one is not embarrassed to address himself before his audience—to say, yes, Victor Herman, *what?* If two potatoes— then why not three, four?

Why not a bushel, Victor Herman, picked just for you?

Because a man could choke on so much—*that is why not!*

In any case, I told about Stalin instead—and they listened, my parents, but with no great interest that I could see. And that was all right with me—I had no great interest in it myself. There was the *Spartakiad* to get ready for, the track meet that was coming up. There were more medals to win, and there was a dream to begin preparing for—because maybe it wasn't going to be just a dream anymore.

LUCKIES. I went to sleep that night, that first night back in the American Village, spelling it over and over again, in smoke, in white smoke poured out over crystalline blue, my body turning with the motion as I rode the arcs and angles of those letters through the sky.

FOURTEEN ————————————————————

I was entered into the Vodopyanov school of aviation—in Gorky— an appointment that came through not long after my return from Moscow. I did not have to wait that long for Tukachevsky to make good his promise. He remembered, all right—my name and address.

Perhaps if he had only forgotten. . . .

But how can I say that—even now? His promise delivered a dream. What it delivered *with* that dream, so be it—that is all behind me now.

Rose and Sam and Leo—oh, yes, Leo—were struck dumb by it. But Miriam's delight was more to my taste. She ran around me making buzzing sounds and dive-bombing with her hands.

I cannot remember this perfectly, but I think I never told my family how all this came about—and I don't know why that was so, *if* it was so. Perhaps I thought its just happening out of the blue would amount to a bigger kick for them. Or perhaps I was being a little cruel—and show-offy, as if these things just happened to me and who knew why? Because I was so wonderful, obviously—that's why. Or maybe I did not want to give my dad the pleasure of knowing that I had met his honored Tukachevsky. I don't know. Perhaps I thought I was paying my father back for something.

Who can remember subtle motives so far in the past? One's inclination is to judge himself too harshly, perhaps—to give it all the polish of an adult's account of things. Perhaps it is better not to raise the question at all.

I attended school, Vodopyanov, named after a Russian flyer—I wore my uniform, the uniform of a flying cadet—me, an American, a Russian flying cadet, in *uniform*—and I continued to work a shift in the factory, still a tool-and-die maker, still in that shop. By now I think Leo had moved into the design shop, a more important post—and so that was good for us, for sustaining our affection for each other—because good things were happening to him too.

But my mother worsened—steadily, rapidly.

And my father kept to his even course—silent, unbending, always speaking, when he spoke, when he was made to, of the great future that was before us, that we, the Hermans, were bringing about.

He did not talk of sacrifice anymore. The very word would send my mother from the room—sobbing.

My shift in the tool-and-die shop had me on the job from eight until four, and then from there I went to Vodopyanov—and Leo went to chasing girls. He was getting serious about some of them, a couple of them. At least he said so. And Miriam had her school—so I guess the three of us were getting along okay. Okay? I was getting along great! But I tried to hide my excitement. It wasn't hard. I rarely reveal emotion—sadness makes me even quieter than I normally am, and only the sweetness of some gesture of human sympathy or giving makes me want to cry. Emotions are hardly ever visible in me—even though I feel them as thoroughly, I think, as anyone does. But how does one know? These things cannot be measured.

But I was very happy then.

By the winter of 1932 I was in the air, up where all my life seemed to be waiting for me, the airborne creature I always wanted to be, transfigured by the feeling that I would never come down.

I soloed that winter.

It is a time to think about, that winter—sometimes staying at that airfield until three in the morning and going right from there to the factory, to sleep on that biting floor of the shop I worked in —and be waked at dawn when the Russian workers started coming in, noisy in their happy agitation to be where the food was, a bit of bread, some awful soup.

I practiced in an aircraft called the U–2—a little biplane affair with a 100-horsepower motor. Getting that thing to fly into the air in winter, you cannot imagine what that took. Everything, given the temperatures, happened in slow motion—heating the oil, even having to preheat the benzine we used as fuel, getting everything heated up beforehand, the liquids, before you could put them in the engine, in the tank. And there were no starters on those little U–2's. You had to crank the prop and crank the prop—and it just didn't want to move in that cold—nothing wanted to move in that cold, people included—and it seemed to take, and maybe it did take, *hours* just to get that plane ready to go. But once it was going, it was a swell plane, reliable, a really good flying plane.

It was a three-year school—the study for your pilot's certificate took that long—but I did it in a year and a half. The will in me here was no less than it was on the track or in the ring or on the firing line—and I was so mad with energy at that time in my life, I even kept at those things too, still ran for the Gorky *Spartak,* still boxed for them, still now and then did some shooting in competition—and, I remember this now, still chopped wood for Rose until she died, still went out there most every day, though now I had to sneak the time, do it whenever I could lever it in, but, anyhow, still went out there to the birches and to the pines that surrounded the American Village and chopped and sawed and split the logs that I'd sawed, so that Rose would have kindling and enough wood of a heavier grade to carry her through a day, a night.

In that year and a half I was four times kicked out of that school—always for no reason given and always for a few days to a week, and then I would be reinstated, and eventually I found out why I'd been kicked out, although it was only from one of the other cadets, not from anyone in authority. And it was what I would have expected if I had not been such an innocent. It was because I was an American, and *What the devil,* somebody high up must have said to somebody else high up, *was an American doing in a Russian flying school?* But then I was always taken back in again—because, I could only surmise, somebody *else* high up had said to the other fellow high up, *because, Comrade, General Tukachevsky ordered* it!

Somewhere in here, around this time of in and out, I got my first idea of what the Secret Police was all about—or the Secret Service —the GPU, anyway. A few of the cadets let me know it was the GPU that was behind it. It began to be a sound I heard more and more—GPU, the way it sounds when it's said fast—and it always is—mainly muttered and said fast. But I always got back in, and I got to fly—and I got my certificate.

Flying was like the thing I thought it *would* be, just as I had imagined it, on the ground looking up to see *LUCKIES* stamped way up there over my head and guessing what it must have felt like to be the fellow that had stamped it there. It was like that for me, *flying*—it was what the word says.

You make a box your first solo—up to the altitude they tell you, left turn, fly, left turn again, fly some more, one more left turn and come down. It's a simple box flight, about half a mile to the sides, and land. Then the instructor comes out, makes a few suggestions, and up you go again to do it over—two boxes—and that was my first time up alone.

Samsonov, he was my instructor—a flyer during the Civil War. He said, "Up. Again. Up again, Citizen Herman," and I was on my way for the second box. It wasn't much, flying that sort of pattern, but it was terrific.

I had that feeling again only once—that feeling I'd had my first solo flight—and that was my first time with Galina.

Oh, I felt myself lofted into some kind of dizzying soaring when Svetlana came, and when Janna came—but their births were different from this other—amazing, exhilarating, but not like that completely dizzy thing Galina made me feel that first time in bed, that Samsonov made me feel when he let me go up, *and I did it*.

He liked me, Samsonov—no question about that. He let me show up at the airfield at all sorts of hours and take the U–2 up if I wanted—no special permission, no special thing about it—just take the plane and go if I liked.

I suppose he saw what it meant to me—as withdrawn as I could be, I could not conceal my delirium over that—I suppose he just liked to see a kid happy flying, and not that many were all that happy to go up back in those days—not really—not with the colossal labor it was to get a plane ready to go—and the cold up there once you were up.

Samsonov didn't stop me when I tried to do things—because the box flight couldn't keep me long—and I didn't let it, no matter what the regulations were, because how could they have anything to do with me, an American? And so I got to trying things up there, doing more and more difficult stuff, or just stuff that I thought was different—and sort of experimenting and playing around—and sometimes spinning and diving and flipping and all the rest when nobody was really supposed to be doing any of that. And before I knew it, I was flying the way I'd done everything else before that— trying to do it my own way—and trying hard to beat my perform- ance each time out—and getting, more and more, that confidence I get—and the more I got of that, the more I believed I could do with that little U–2, and would try it, would go up there and *try* it, some crazy stunt.

And Samsonov would say okay, now you know you shouldn't do that, but go ahead and do that, and it was after a time like a kind of father-and-son joking between us, him warning me to watch myself, me promising to do it, him knowing I wouldn't keep my promise, and, like a father, angry with me, but not really—really, instead, proud, just like a father too—until it kept up this way for long enough that I was really doing some things up there that scared him—but impressed him too—and when I saw that *he* was impressed, how could I *not* be impressed? And that just urged me on all the more.

And this led to fooling around with the plane, getting the machine to do more than it could, tinkering with it, adding this, adding that, trying to move this around this way and tool up that a little better, and just generally doing all the things I had learned to do with auto engines when you wanted them to go a little bit better than the other fellow's, and customizing the rest of the air- craft too, just the way I'd fooled around with cars back in Detroit. It was just something most boys around Detroit did, tinkered with those things.

It was this, the tinkering, the playing with it, because I couldn't leave it alone, couldn't just let it be and do it the way everybody else was doing it, it was this will to go out there and beat the *
out of what everybody else was doing, just that, that will, that

brought me to the point where others began noticing me too much.

I loved it, the attention. What harm had getting lots of attention ever been? It had gotten me medals, kids that admired me, the great feeling that at this and at this and at this, I, Victor Herman, was the best.

It would get me Cell 39. And much more besides.

It would get me eighteen years in ice.

FIFTEEN _____

I soared and Leo chased. I took my U–2 up and twisted it through a repertoire of dives and flips and rolls and spins, pressing the possibility of that machinery against the willing temper of the sky, and Leo took himself after women and girls of every description, and they were less willing than the sky.

Sex had hardly anything you'd call a playground in that place —there was just no time or space for it, and who was really interested? Not many. Most were too exhausted from their labor, too cold or too overworked or too tired or hungry—or too little attracted to the species of female that you'd find in evidence in the place.

But Leo found them. It must have been real work, that finding and following through. It was something to admire, his obsession with those labors. The girls, the women, you could tell they really weren't interested, not in the sexual part of it. If they went with you, one of the locals, it was probably for food or a bit of clothing or a better place to sleep. But Leo kept at it, and I kept myself for flying, unready to interest myself in anything other than the grand figure I thought I cut in the sky. Besides, I saw nothing in the great rough bundles that were, underneath perhaps, something female— I saw nothing there to capture my attention and draw it from my impulse every instant to race back out there to the airfield and go wheeling through the sky.

There was nothing light or soft in those Russian girls I saw— and they did not want there to be. What they wanted was to work as a man worked, to dig a hole if *he* dug one, or lift a load if that's what *he* did—to them, to those Russian girls and women you came across around Gorky then, the great thing was to *work*—and sex was just a way of getting a jot more comfort in their lives, a kind of trading, doubtless done grudgingly, for the extras that might be gotten for it.

They had all kinds of aircraft out there at the Vodopyanov field—old Farmans and Newports and Fokkers left over from the Civil War—and the Russian jobs, the U–1, the U–2, the R–1 and R–2, SHA–1, SHA–2, and the Ant—I flew all those machines and fooled around with them all—and the better I got at it, the better the school administration realized I was getting, and not long after I was awarded my certificate as a pilot, they said it was okay to quit my work at the factory and instead to come teach at Vodopya-nov—me, the fellow they had been kicking out all the time.

I'd go out there every morning, teach some classes, take up some cadets and let them watch me fly, and then get in some flying on my own, more and more of the tricky stuff I was trying out. Word went around the academy that I was a regular daredevil, and I liked that, liked being thought that. And I liked nothing more than flying.

Until I got into jumping—and I liked that even better—because there was no weight of machinery, no airplane that held you fast.

Jumping? It was like *being* the letters in *LUCKIES,* being the smoke they were made of—not just the instrument that inscribed them.

My mother died in 1933. She just died then—very fast.

She'd been more and more complaining—and then it centered on noise, her complaining. She said the noise from everything was terrific, that all she heard was noise. The stove made too much noise, and the fire made too much noise, and there was too much noise when people talked or coughed or walked across the floor.

She got bloody noses. She howled about the noise, would somebody just please be quiet, would everybody stop making all that *noise,* and she got bloody noses.

The doctor in the Village said, that's okay—who doesn't get a bloody nose?

They called me home from the flying field—*Cadet Herman, your mother fell down.*

I ran all the way, my flying overalls, the outfit I wore, not easy to make real speed in, and there was snow.

She was still on the floor when I got there, and Miriam was squatting there by her head. It was Leo that let me in, and my dad was standing right behind him, and I remember thinking it is January, 1933, and then thinking what a crazy thought that was to have, my mother lying on the floor.

"Where's the doctor?" I said, and they said not to worry, he'd been there, and it was all okay but just not to move her for a while, let her rest right there where she is.

I went next door. There was only one car in the Village, and it belonged to the young couple next door, Americans, Kalick, that was their name—and I said I needed their car and they said, go ahead and take it, but they wanted to know what I was going to do with it, and I told them, told them I had to go to Gorky, that my mother was sick and I had to get the doctor in Gorky, and they said, you can't, the snow, the car won't make it through the snow.

I told them to get in there, Leo and Sam, to get into the Kalicks' car, and I got a spade and chains and whatever I figured I could use, and it took forever getting those chains on—even with Sam and Leo helping, it took forever. But we got them on and we got there, and we had to dig our way, but we got there, twelve miles through the snow, and we brought the doctor back to the American Village.

She died, anyway.

She just died like that, fast, a stroke, a bleeding in her brain.

There was never much noise in that Village. It was really mostly always quiet in the American Village. But my mother heard a roaring, a ceaseless evil howling, and the only real noise to speak of was what the engines made, out there over the airfield, those little airplanes straining to get themselves higher in the sky.

SIXTEEN ——————————————————————————

My mother died when I was seventeen. She died in Russia—with her head screaming from the noise that came roaring off the wide, hushed snow. I was seventeen and my mother was forty-three.

She had one more year to go.

Her dying then, I can count the differences it made in the lives she left behind. In Leo's, Miriam's, and mine—but mainly mine.

Sam would have taken us home if she had lived—she would have made him do it when our time was up, made him take us back.

My mother was buried in the Russian earth she hated, and she never got home. She had only one more year of it to go, one more year of the Russia that killed her.

I found some hair of mine among her things, a curl of it she'd been keeping, the baby blond fineness folded into tissue paper and "Victor" marked in crayon on it. There was a tiny packet of each of us—a lock of Leo's, Becky's, Miriam's, and mine—the baby hair she'd been keeping—kept hidden and always with her from Ironwood Street all the way to Nizhni-Novgorod.

That's where she lies in her long death now. There is a factory over her, a thing they built much later.

Oh, the noise in my mother's head now.

Now Sam cried—he took up where Mama left off.

Those weeks right after, us seated at our meal, the four of us, eating in our silence, he'd sometimes raise his head and to no one or nothing, nothing arousing it at all, he'd say, "She did not live to see me keep my promise. I meant to keep my promise, and I would have," and then he would fix us each in turn with those hard blue eyes of his, and say, "Yes?" and each of us in turn would answer, "Yes, Papa, yes."

He married again—not all that long afterward—and when that one died, he married another.

"Excuse me," my father said to me the first time. "It is that I cannot live without a woman."

We excused him. He did not have to ask. But when this wife died, Sam Herman did not have Victor Herman to beg a pardon from when he picked himself another, a third, woman.

Oh, I would have excused him had I been there for him to ask. I wasn't. I was only twelve miles away. Not far at all, considering—just twelve miles from where I was to my father's bed, to his bed in the American Village, twelve miles from him to where I sat in the position—behind the muzzle and in the position.

My father died making love to that third one, to Olga. The second one, she was Gusta—that was the second one's name.

So much dying, and why not? Was life such a treat?

For me it was. I was so very happy then, even with Rose, even with my mother's being dead. For me, then, during those years flying, and then jumping, life was very good.

But for Leo it was hard. He married soon after my mother's death—an American girl. It didn't work out. She got pregnant and said she was going to get rid of it, and he told her not to, but she did it, anyway—and they were divorced. She was Elma, Leo's first wife.

I'd never taken her flying, but I took Leo and I took Sam. I would have taken Miriam, but Papa said no. I never took her—or my mother either.

Myself, I started getting up in the really fast ones, getting all the speed I could get. In the I–16, I could do a little better than 300 kilometers an hour, and later on we got an improvement on that one, and this second one would get right up there to 500 kilometers an hour.

Rose might have liked that. Maybe with speed like that we could have left behind all that noise that was chasing her.

So much dying now—and more to come—because Stalin was starting to clean things out.

Me, I didn't know—but it was starting. I was paying attention somewhere else—up there on that blue slate I was writing on. Sam knew more than I did, but even he didn't know all that much—about the cleaning out, getting rid of all those impurities that were poisoning the revolutionary air.

There was some thinning out going on in the Village, this one and that one not showing up anymore. But nobody much noticed. Did so-and-so go home, then? Oh, so so-and-so went home, eh?

I was hardly ever there. Who noticed? Why should you? People come and go. Besides, they let me go to a special store—and it was for more than just bread and potatoes. I got butter sometimes—and sometimes eggs and cream.

It was pretty good—and I liked having the extra stuff for Miriam. She hardly knew what those things were.

Who noticed the thinning out? I certainly didn't.

All I noticed was how I was getting those airplanes up there higher—and goosing a little more and then a little bit more speed out of them too. And when there just didn't seem to be much more to do with that, no higher I was going to go, and no faster, I started jumping.

All the way, all the way, all the way down.

I got to jumping in anything, trying anything—any weather, any terrain, and into the water too.

This was something really to make a mark in—because who jumped? Very few. To begin with, there weren't that many parachutes around, and the ones that were weren't very good. Who wanted to jump?

I did.

So I jumped, and it beat everything I'd ever done, all of it put together. One jump was worth a hundred of anything else I'd ever won a medal for.

But the best of it was before you opened your chute, the sailing, the soaring—just sort of flying all by yourself and really moving yourself around as you came tearing down from way up there. Just the way I used to try all those crazy figures in my U–2—that's what I was trying now—jumping, my arms out there sailing me around.

I jumped as if the air was made for walking.

What did I weigh then? One hundred thirty-five? Well, jumping, I didn't weigh an ounce. I'd be up there falling like nine hundred tons, but I did not weigh an ounce.

That's what it was like—and I couldn't get enough of it.

At *Spartak* they wouldn't let me stop all the rest of the sports I was in—but the minute I was finished, I was back jumping, back out there coming down.

And I really didn't want to box much anymore—all of a sudden, for some reason—my mother's dying?—I was getting to worry about my liver, the old gunshot wound, the bullet that had gone through there. I wasn't supposed to be boxing, not really, not after that—but I'd been doing it all those years, always holding myself and my guard to favor that side and that region.

I wanted to jump. That's all I wanted to do.

I hung around the flyers and the cadets and I stayed pretty much away from home. I just kept jumping whenever I could.

Contracts were starting to run out now—the people who'd come over around the same time we had. But I didn't know much about that—I wasn't around enough to notice. I was mainly with the Russians. That's where the jumping was.

Our time came up and it just went on by. I hardly even noticed. Nobody told us to return.

I think I was in Moscow at the time, at a special sport-flying school. It didn't interest me much—I'd already flown the racing planes they had there. Only jumping, that's all I wanted to do now. *Sportivnaya Aviatsia,* the school in Moscow, it was fun, all right, but not enough. Only jumping was enough now—and so I found a way to do enough of it in Moscow, to do enough of it wherever I was, and our time just came up and went by and I scarcely even noticed.

Sam was willing enough to stay. Or to put it as it really was, he was unwilling to go home until things got as good as he said they were going to get—and that was a long way from happening. So Sam was in no hurry to go—and he had a Russian wife now, and maybe, to him, life for him was where he was. Me, what did I care then? I was jumping—and getting recognition for it—so why be in any rush to go anywhere but where the jumping was? Besides, it was my mother we'd said we'd leave for when the three years were up—and what good would that do her now?

As for Leo, he'd stay where my dad was—that was Leo's way —and besides, he also had a Russian wife now, his second, Walter Reuther's old girl or old wife—I wasn't sure if there was a difference.

Everybody at *Sportivnaya Aviatsia* was a pretty fair flyer, all aviators of the first rank. We just taught each other whatever tricks we knew—speed flying, diving, going for height, and then I started showing some of them how to handle a chute, how to do the things I'd worked out fooling around back in Gorky. It was a thing I liked to do, and always have—teach. I've always liked to do that, show a person how to do the things I can.

But *they* showed *me* how to sit in the position, behind the muzzle.

I became a master at it.

It took practice—that's all.

I got a letter there in Moscow, from Sam. It was about his staying on. That was okay with me. I was staying too. So I'd go home next year—or the year after that. Home would always be there, and meanwhile the jumping was over here.

But I heard from Leo that a lot of the Americans weren't staying and that, besides, the U.S. government said no. We didn't have an embassy in Russia then, there was just a consulate in Moscow, and the consulate said no—if your contract was over, you had to go. But the Russians said you could stay as long as you wanted if you just got yourself a Soviet passport, and that way, whenever you wanted to leave, you'd just leave with a Soviet passport, as simple as that.

I wasn't taking anything—no Soviet anything.

But my father did. He was staying—and right from there on it was an easy step for him into citizenship. He took it, he made that step. I think it was because he was ashamed to go back.

Not that Sam wanted me to take anything. No, it was all the other way around. He kept telling me I *had* to go back, that I *must* go back—but there really wasn't all that much reason to say it. Of course I was going back. What else? Of course. And when you get back, Sam Herman always said to me, you go to Mr. Ford and you tell him you're my son and he will see to it that you have a good job and he will give you $18,000 for your education, so you just go to Mr. Ford and tell him you're my son.

Had my father worked out some kind of deal with Henry Ford? For $18,000? That was a stupendous sum in 1934, and was it agreed in 1931? He said it had been—that Mr. Ford would give it to him when he got back in 1934. But he wasn't getting back.

So it was $18,000 for me—when I got back.

But right now I was over here—still jumping—and it was 1934.

And then my dad did a crazy thing. The passport he had was a *family* passport, and he turned it in for a Russian one. It didn't make any sense, him doing that and at the same time not knowing what he was doing.

I wrote the consulate. I said the Russians have given me Russian citizenship, but I didn't ask for Russian citizenship. I am an American citizen. All I have and want is American citizenship. What do I do?

They wrote back and said I was underage and they were writing to my father, and they did. And Sam said to them, the boy should do what he wants to do, and I wanted to be an American citizen. My * , where did anyone ever get the idea I didn't? So the consulate said all I had to do was write them another letter saying that's what I wanted, and it wouldn't matter even though I was underage—everything would be okay. So that's what I did—and I didn't hear anything from them again.

Sportivnaya Aviatsia was set up near a village called Mikhielivansk, which is outside of Moscow, and that's where I was living at the time, in that village, in a log cabin. It was like being nowhere near Moscow, really—it was that primitive, except for the airplanes—and at night we'd see the Moscow sky light up, all that energy of things the city gave off, and where we were, in Mikhielivansk, there wasn't even any running water—and no toilets, inside or out—you just made a hole in the snow. Strange, seeing the Moscow sky light up like that at night, and you were where you were.

I don't know why, but looking up to see the Moscow lights like that at night while I was squatting there in the Mikhielivansk snow, I used to get the strangest feeling—as if I were on the moon looking at the earth as if some crazy cosmology had moved me to the wrong place.

SEVENTEEN _____

The jump was in 1934.

It was on the 6th of September. I'm talking about the world's record free-fall jump I made—on the 6th of September, 1934. Units came from all over the Soviet Union to show what they could do, to put on their specialty over Moscow.

I wrote a letter in advance of this, saying that *Sportivnaya Aviatsia* wanted to enter in three events—speed flying, figure flying, and deadfall parachuting, and I was going to do the last one. I even said in my letter I was going to break the world's record— and this was not any idle boast a kid might make, because I had already done it, several times.

Well, they really hadn't heard of that—deadfall parachuting. But there was a sort of informal world's record the flyers knew about, and I'd already done better than that, better than the American who had the record. I don't remember his name, that American, but it was generally agreed that his deadfall was the longest anyone on a wide scale had heard about. He'd done about 5,000 meters, about 16,000 feet—and I'd already done better than that just practicing.

The fellows that were working with me at *Sportivnaya* had a plane that could take me up to 24,000, and that was the altitude I was going to jump from. Anyway, the Ministry of Aviation said no —it was impossible, they would not allow it. But then they sent some men out to Mikhielivansk, and they said, show us. So I demonstrated a couple of high jumps, not that high, but high enough—and they went back and reported what they'd seen, and the okay came through—and then the Russians were all for it, really all for it. Just imagine! The Russians getting a world's record— and getting it away from Americans!

Did the Ministry of Aviation know what I was, an American? I don't think so.

Officially I was an American, and surely Russian officials somewhere must have known I was, but for the most part it seemed by now nobody was paying any attention. For the most part I was just like anybody else, and my name didn't seem to take any-one by surprise.

Tupolev, the man who recently worked out the Russian version of the Concorde, had designed the high-flying aircraft I was going to use—he and Sikorsky had been great buddies, both great aircraft designers. We'd retooled the thing a little, and it would do even a little better than anyone knew. We juiced up the fuel a little and twisted the screw, the prop, a little more than Tupolev had it twisted, and I figured, when it came to it, we could do a little better than 24,000.

The Russians announced it all over the place, and the airfield was jammed, military, spectators, reporters from all over coming to see who was this guy that said he could break some crazy record jumping out of a plane? I guess, as far as that goes, I was just hoping the American press would be there—I thought of Rebecca— and of all the kids back home, my teachers, Frank back there at the River Rouge plant, and all the fellows I had played ball with and run around town with, and the cops who'd arrested my dad, and those Goldmann boys and their cousins, and Mr. Henry Ford and whoever else in the whole wide world of America I wanted to know about me and about the thing I was going to do better than anybody ever had.

I was supposed to land in a place called Zviney Gorod, some military field—but the wind changed, so instead we took off from Zviney Gorod, and I was to come down on the field at Mikhieli-vansk—in other words, we had to switch it, switch the fields around at the last minute to account for the change in drift.

It took us two hours to get up there, Tadzhik and me. He was flying, Tadzhik, a really great pilot. He got me up there—and it took just shy of two hours to do it.

It was small, of course, that Tupolev plane, and there was no shouting back and forth with oxygen masks on. You didn't have any radios or anything like that in those days. You just had to signal when you were way up there where you needed oxygen, using your hands the best you could, or just your head, to try to talk back and forth.

That last mile or so getting up, it was where most of our time went. It was a hard climb from there on up.

We made it up to well over 24,000—about 500 feet higher than that. I don't know exactly the altitude I jumped from. It was up around there somewhere.

I just went when Tadzhik nodded. I just went when he nodded and pointed down.

I fell deadfall 142 seconds. I got myself out of there the best I could and let go and fell deadfall.

It was 142 seconds.

It was eternity—and over in no time at all.

I slapped Tadzhik on the shoulder to let him know I was ready to go. He nodded and pointed down—and then he geared out the engine to slow the wind on me, and I slapped him again and went.

He had to air-chute to let me get out—just hold the plane on the wings, sort of. That Tadzhik was a wonderful flyer. I got one foot out and then the other foot out, slapped Tadzhik on the shoulder again, and then I pushed myself out there and went down.

I fell for 142 seconds.

I didn't open the chute for all that time.

Then, at 1,200, 1,300, somewhere in there, I pulled the rip cord.

I had my hand on it all that time. I had the grip in the pocket of my coveralls and I had my hand on the grip inside that pocket. I didn't want that grip on the rip cord whipping around. I had it in my pocket.

The press made a big thing out of my eating that apple as I fell. It looked like a cocky thing to do—and I don't blame them for making a big thing out of it. But it wasn't the way it looked, not really.

There was an apple in there in that pocket where the rip-cord grip was. I felt an apple in there when I put my hand in. I don't even know how it got there. Had Tadzhik put it in? A treat for me? Where had Tadzhik gotten an apple? No one had apples. There weren't any apples that I knew of around Russia in those days. Who ever saw any apples?

But there was an apple in that pocket where the grip to the rip cord was.

I got it out of there and put it into my hand and then I ate the apple. What else was I going to do with it? Throw an apple away?

I never asked Tadzhik if he was the one who did it, the one who put the apple there. There was too much going on when I got down, and I just never asked Tadzhik about it.

I held the grip of that rip cord with one hand and ate the apple with the other, and the newspaper people said, look at the cocky kid, the high flyer, the high jumper, eating an apple as he deadfalls 200 miles an hour to the ground.

What else was I supposed to do with the apple? I just took my mask off and ate the apple.

Sure I ate it. It was an apple.

It was the first apple I'd had since Ironwood Street.

The papers called me "The Lindbergh of Russia," and of course in no time at all it got picked up that I wasn't any *Russian* Lindbergh but just another *American* Lindbergh. It got out all over everywhere in the foreign papers that I wasn't Russian—that Herman was an American, so what was all this Soviet talk that a Russian had made a world's record of some kind, because the fellow that did it was *not* a Russian—but some American kid, a kid out of Detroit!

The Lindbergh of Russia! I thought that was rich. The Lindbergh of anything was just fine with me, Victor Herman, the kid out of Detroit. Did everybody back there get to find out what I'd done? How about the Goldmann boys—and their cousins?

If it was attention I wanted, I got it—I got all the attention I could use—and then some attention I could have done without.

But for the time being, it was great—and I could not have felt better—about myself and the thing that I had done.

One hundred forty-two seconds of deadfall! It was eternity itself—and over in no time at all.

But it was soon to give way to a second deadfall—one that was much longer than 142 seconds, but one that was also an eternity, eternity itself—yet one that would not be over in no time at all, one that would not really *ever* be over at all. In due course I was to fall endlessly, to keep on falling forever, not just for eighteen years, but even now, today, as I write this.

Still, they wrote about the Lindbergh of Russia in the Detroit papers, and Rebecca must have read it there. Papa must have told her. But who would have pointed it out to the Goldmann boys and their cousins?

And how would Mama ever know?

Deadfall, that's what it was—my mother and I falling, but not falling together, both falling endlessly, but through different zones of time.

That jump I made, it was for her.

EIGHTEEN _____

Perhaps for everyone life is like that—a trade. Perhaps in everyone's life that is the rule that governs—this for that—and the *better* this is, the worse that is *sure* to be. But this is another Greek notion, and it is foolish to believe it, that everything must come out even in the end, that some sort of balance must be made.

Who could make it work like that? What could be in such control? What are there, billions living, billions of people? What could make it come out even in so many lives?

It is nonsense to believe such a thing—and yet when each life is examined, it sometimes does seem so, that something has imposed a balance of the happy and the sad, a perfect bargain, this for that.

Who knows about the life of another? What do I know about anyone's? And what does anyone know about mine, the infinite things I've felt and done? What do even *I* know about the life I say is mine?

But when I think about it, when I write the sentences that seem to say *This was what it was,* how is it that it also seems to come out so even, a kind of trading going on, this for that, here's something good, here's something bad, and the one is the precise match of the other, equal forces in opposition?

I do not know. But I have considered this thought—and think it not inconceivable that we do this thing ourselves in the living of our lives—get the *this* and then seek the *that* to make the two things together come out even.

It could be that this is so.

There was trouble over the jump.

In order to get credit for the jump, for the record that was made, documents had to be sent to FIFA, an agency in France that oversaw aviation matters, that granted credit, and so on. It was where all the official flying information was registered and kept— and so the documents had to be sent there, and after they were all made out, the business of citizenship came up. There was a blank that called for the petitioner's citizenship, and I filled it in—*U.S.A.*

That was where the trouble started.

I heard from the Communist Party. I heard from the Red Army. I heard from the NKVD.

What did I mean, *citizenship U.S.A.!*

This was unacceptable! It was a Russian who had accomplished this remarkable achievement! It was a Russian who had done this thing! It would be a Russian who was going to get worldwide attention—and that was that!

The Communist Party showed up at *Sportivnaya Aviatsia.*

They wanted to see the superintendent there! The Red Army sent its people—they *too* would speak with the superintendent! And the NKVD was not to be omitted. They also had a few people who would like to have a chat with the superintendent of the flyers who had dared to commit the unthinkable blunder of letting an American citizen do this thing that was covering the entire Soviet nation with shame! How dare this man contrive to embarrass the people of the Union of Soviet Socialist Republics before the entire world! That it was permitted that an *American* do this thing? From a *Soviet* aircraft? Operated by a *Soviet* flyer? To make a parachute jump onto *Soviet* soil? An *American?*

They called me in—officials—an assortment of them all— there into the office of the superintendent at *Sportivnaya Aviatsia.*

I would have to change the papers that were to be submitted to FIFA. I would write in the appropriate blank *citizenship U.S.S.R.!*

I said, "How can I do that? I am an American citizen." Then I said, "I will not do that. I am an American citizen."

They said I was not to worry about that—they quite understood. Of course, it was patently clear, I was of *course* an American citizen—but what is the harm? Write *U.S.S.R.* You are a guest in our country. We have been hospitable to you. Be friendly. Write *U.S.S.R.* What is the harm?

I thought of my father that day in the Soviet Trade Fleet Hotel. I thought of the man in uniform that stood by the window fingering my mother's things. I thought of her and the noise that would not go away from her head. I thought of my father's flat voice straining for a singsong, a cheery melody, as he jogged my sister Miriam on his shoulders: *No harm, no harm, no harm, no harm. . . .*

They studied me, those men that were there. One made as if to speak, and another interrupted, a man from the NKVD.

"He is a young man, this Herman, and he worries about these things, the telling of a fib when it is of no consequence at all. Please believe me, young man, it is nothing but the merest formality. It matters not in the slightest what letters you enter upon the blank of this paper. Of what earthly magnitude is it, the small difference between a mark that says U.S.A. and another that says U.S.S.R.? Put it out of your mind—just leave it to us. Write. Write *U.S.S.R.* and be off about your business. Everyone here knows perfectly well that you are an American citizen. What harm, my boy? Write. Enter the correction here." He pointed to a space on the paper that sat on the desk facing me.

No harm, no harm, no harm, no harm. . . .

Perhaps if he had not used that word "letters." Perhaps if it were not a question of actually *writing* something, marking something down in a blank space.

I thought of white smoke pouring from me to paint the clear blue behind me, something everyone below would look up and see. I thought of that morning all that time ago. It was late spring. I looked up and I saw *LUCKIES*.

I took the pen he gave me and I wrote *U.S.A.*

They tore up the papers while I stood there. I smiled and left the room.

About a week later the superintendent called me in. He said that the U.S. had claimed the record. But that it would not be entertained by FIFA as official because what happened had happened on *Russian* soil, *Russian* instruments had been used to make the measurements, *Russian* timekeepers had validated the records, and so on and so forth—the point being that all the official witnesses were Russian and these Russians would testify to no such thing.

"Now, Citizen Herman," he said, "will you write *U.S.S.R.?*"

I said, "No."

I said I didn't give a　*　about any of it—not the record or anything—what did I care about this FIFA! I had done what I had done—and I knew I had done it!

"I am an American," I said. "I will write that or nothing."

But he was in a spot—and I knew that too—and so when he asked for a favor, I was willing. Besides, he said I owed it to him, considering that he'd let me make the jump, and he said I owed it to the Russian people because they'd been such agreeable hosts—and that I owed it to my father because he was a good Communist—and that I just generally owed, period. What he wanted was that I train a Russian jumper to do the same thing. They would provide the plane, the jumper, and take care of everything—and that much I owed them, and what did I say?

I said I didn't mind—I was happy to teach anyone anything. Fine. It was okay with me.

I knew I wasn't going to get credit for what I'd done—except

I also knew that back home they'd already given me credit for it—
so what was the difference what the Russians did, whatever the
* they tried to claim? Where it mattered, back home, they'd always know otherwise.

I said sure, I'd train anybody they liked.

It wasn't hard to say that. I felt sorry for that man. I was by
now not so innocent as not to know that he had probably had a
whole lot of trouble on account of me—and if this would fix things
up for him—sure, I'd do it. It wouldn't change anything for me—
it wouldn't wipe out my mark—and if anyone anytime ever asked
me to show him how to do something I could do, would I say no?

"That's all right," I said. "I'll do it."

Evdokimov, that was the name of the man they gave me to
train. And I trained him. He was all right—I liked him, a pleasant
enough fellow in his way—and I taught him how to do it. He'd
already made about two hundred jumps—and so he had a feeling
for what you have to do. I trained that man to do just what I did,
and it did not make me unhappy to do it. And then he was ready
to try it—but when that time came, they let me know he was going
to try it from another plane—one they'd done some work on.

It could fly higher than the one I'd had. It could fly 300
feet higher. And that's the altitude they got it up to, with Evdokimov
in it, and that's where he jumped from—and they took him out
there with that better plane and he went up with it and came down
from 300 feet higher. We did it three times in secret—and he did
it three times every time from higher than I had had a chance to go.
And when he'd done that three times and they were sure he could
do it again, they got the instruments there and the timekeepers there
and witnesses, and Evdokimov came out of that plane from just
about 300 feet higher than I had.

And that's what got sent to FIFA.

Yes, I don't mind saying it. It is true. It hurt me, having
helped that Evdokimov beat my record—it really hurt me very
much.

It wasn't the credit so much. It was that *I* could have done it—
and that I showed him how.

It didn't seem fair.

But I was just beginning to find something out. This idea of
fairness I had, it had nothing to do with the country I was in. It's
hard to get an idea like that through your head when everything

that is in you is American. You just think that's the way it's supposed to be—with everybody everywhere. And that's the wrong
thing to think. Fairness? It is an idea that is as peculiar to America
as any corny thing you can think of—ham and eggs, Vernors
ginger ale, some guy writing *LUCKIES* in the Michigan sky.

I guess I was a little crazy at this point, I wanted to do that
thing so much.

I asked for an appointment with the superintendent and he
said okay, he'd see me, and when I got there, this time the NKVD
and the Party each had a man there too.

I said, let me try to do it again, in the same airplane—and I
promise you I'll go out from even higher—and no one will know
the difference, because you can just say it was Evdokimov that did
it, and I won't care. I just want to do it, and I tell you I can do it
from even higher than he did, and all you have to do is say Evdokimov did it, and you'll have a world's record that will be even
harder to top.

They listened to me. They listened very seriously, really considering it, I thought.

But they said no.

They said they couldn't take a chance—somebody someday
might find out.

The answer was no.

I went a little crazy over that.

But the answer was no.

Then I made another mistake. Or maybe it wasn't. Because it
was the first good warning that I got.

I started telling the other flyers around *Sportivnaya* about my
offer, my saying to them I would do another jump, an even better
one, but that all the credit could go to Evdokimov, and one of the
flyers took me aside after I told him that. I wish I could remember
that man's name—because it was he who gave me my first warning
—not that it really mattered any, but at least I owe him for that.

I wish I could remember his name—to set it down here.

He said, "You were crazy to suggest that."

We were standing outside one of the hangars, and the wind
was blowing, and I could barely hear him, and I said, I shouted,
"Why?"

"Because," he shouted back, and then he quickly lowered his

voice, "if they let you do it, then they would get rid of you afterwards—to make sure nobody ever found out."

I shouted back at him, "What do you mean, get rid of me? What are you talking about?"

"Do something to you. Fix it so you could not talk. Make you vanish. Kill you. Something." I had to strain to hear what he was saying, so low was his voice and the wind blowing like that.

"They'd do a thing like that?" I said. "You're kidding. They'd really do a thing like that?"

The other flyer, he didn't say anything to that. He just put his arm around my shoulder and moved me in another direction, taking me along with him.

"Come," he said, "let's walk."

I can't really say I understood at this point.

But for the first time I was beginning to think a little bit about what there was around me.

That woman in Moscow, the one with the white, white skin—what was it she had said to me?

I remembered—and I remembered her dark, dark eyes, and the mad look in them. She was in a rage about something, she'd said I'd done something *wrong*.

Why had that flyer lowered his voice that way, when you could hardly hear in the first place? Didn't he *know* I could hardly hear him with the wind blowing like that?

It was right around this time that something else happened, a second warning. Sam told me. Everyone in the American Village had been told while I was away, and when I got back to Gorky, Sam told me.

No more letters home—and no more letters *from* home. Anyone caught sending a letter out or getting one would have ten years in prison!

This could not be so! I said to my father that this could not be so.

He said it was.

But how could this be, how could anyone stand for it—wasn't someone doing something about this?

Papa said it was temporary, not to worry, no harm, no harm.

"What does it matter?" he said. "How important is a letter?

How often do you write a letter anyhow? Who is there? Becky? How often do you write to Becky—or she to you? It hardly has to do with us at all. Stop thinking about it. It is of no importance at all." That is what my father said.

He said that—and it sounded to me like something else that someone had said to me—and then I remembered what. I remembered the NKVD man talking that day in the superintendent's office—there at *Sportivnaya Aviatsia*.

It was my father's singsong all over again—the cringing sound I heard that day when we all looked up toward the bleak light showing through that window in the Leningrad hotel. We looked and saw that man fingering my mother's things—and my father said, "No harm, no harm, no harm. . . ."

I said, "But how can they stop you from hearing from your relatives? And letting them hear from you? I mean, what's wrong with a family talking to each other?"

He was very changed by this. He did not say anything for a long time. We were sitting at our little table, and he just looked down and clasped his fingers and held his hands between his knees as he sometimes used to do, and he did not look at me when he finally began to talk. He just looked down at his hands, to where they were between his knees, the fingers clasping there.

He said, "In the world that is coming, relations are counterrevolutionary. One's allegiance must be to the State. It must be the State first, and what stands in the way of that, whatever that is, that is counterrevolutionary. Do you understand?"

I said I'd heard that kind of talk and I'd read that kind of thing, but that everybody knew it was just something that was said and that nobody took all that stuff seriously. It was crap, I said, talk and crap.

"We will not discuss it further," my father said. "If you write a letter or accept a letter, you know the penalty. I told you. Did you hear me?"

I nodded. All right, I thought, big deal. My dad was right, anyway. I really wasn't a letter-writer. The fact was that in all that time I had not written many letters to Rebecca—or to anybody else in the States—and not even a postcard to any of the kids I knew. Nor had Becky actually written to me—her letters were to Papa, and if there was anything in them specifically for anyone in the rest of the family, she'd stop herself and say *This is for Leo* or *This is for Vickie* or *This is for Miriam*—and there was nothing to say to Mama anymore.

I tried to smile for my father. Why was it? I felt bad for him. I tried to smile and then I smiled easily, and I told him everything about the jump and how I did it and how it felt and why he should be very proud of me—and I just left out the rest of it, everything else that had happened.

He listened. He said he was very proud of me. He kept repeating it, how proud he was. He kept his hands down there, clasped. We sat and looked at each other for a while, me smiling, him sitting there, clasping his hands together.

And then he just said, "Please, Vickie. I beg you, son— please, no letters."

I nodded my head. I said, "Sure, Papa," and I stood up to go to bed, and I kissed him before I did.

NINETEEN _____

That kiss, I am glad I kissed my father then.

What was his agony—and would it not have been greater without that kiss I gave him?

A son can kill his father. It is easy. He has only not to kiss.

A son, he has only to wait for the right time, a moment when there is just enough agony, and then, that moment, to withhold his kiss.

That is how you kill a father if you are the man who is his son.

But I kissed mine—it was such a moment. I kissed my father to help him live.

I went back to my work, to teaching, and I went back to *Spartak,* of course, and I did everything I could. I used myself. It emptied my mind and heart of everything and filled myself up with something else instead, the feeling I had always had up there, turning myself through air. I thought of nothing up there—except the glorious thing I was doing—and sometimes, always sometimes, but not with sadness now, I thought of my mother, that she flew with me in her way.

But it was not like jumping. It was not as good. And not far from the time I knew this, knew it was not as good, word got to Gorky that in Moscow they were setting up a special school for jumpers, men who would do nothing but jumping, jumping dead-fall and every other way they could think of, going for height, and trying out maneuvers and all sorts of innovations.

I wrote the school—requesting permission to enter. I ended up writing five letters to them, and they either did not answer or said something else that was a runaround, nothing to do with what I had asked.

So I went there, to Moscow, to demand an explanation. What was going on? I wanted to know—was I not a great jumper? Did not everyone know that? Why should I be excluded from this wonderful new school?

I got nowhere. I went back to Gorky and wrote more letters. That was what I wanted now—I wanted a place in that school—and I would not hear a no. I just kept on at them, and when I got absolutely nowhere again, for a second time I secured leave and went back to Moscow to try. And this time I made my way through the thicket of all the petty officials who just looked the other way whenever I put the question to them. I got through all that to someone who'd talk.

His name was Aideman, a general, and I said to this Aideman, why is it I cannot be in the special school for jumpers? And why is it no one will tell me why? And he was very glad to see me—he was really quite glad—and he said that he had wanted to meet me, that he had of course heard about what I had done—no, he had not been there to see it, a great pity, indeed, but many had told him how brave and how skilled I was.

Yes, yes, I said, but about the school?

"But this is absurd," he said. "Everyone here understands you do not *wish* to go to the school—that as an American, you *refuse* to go to our school."

I said, "That is not so—I have been trying to achieve just the opposite."

"But this is impossible," Aideman said. "We all understand otherwise."

So this Aideman picked up the telephone and ordered it. He

just told them, and that was that—and he said it had all been some sort of wretched error and not to be dismayed, he had fixed it, it was all taken care of now. Did I want to be an instructor? It would be arranged. He would call back and arrange it. I said of course—that would please me very much—and again he made a telephone call, and it was arranged.

This Aideman was a Jew. I could sense it. And I did something I had never done before, and I asked him, I said, "Pardon me, General Aideman, but I must ask this. Are you a Jew?"

He said, "You are."

"Yes," I said. "I am."

"I know," he said. "I know that," he said. "It is known," he said.

How long after this was it that Aideman was shot? I do not know. But it was picking up speed, the thinning out, the purifying—what was later to be called the purge, the purges.

Why shoot these people and not shoot me?

Because I was an American?

I don't think so. They shot Americans too.

Aideman—and other names—but they are just names to you. What is the worth of listing?

The ones you had in your head were more familiar ones—Leo, Sam, Miriam—and your own.

And then later on, after Cell 39 and beyond, it meant nothing anymore—the names, the dead—not even the way they'd come and kill them, the little ceremony they had, in the leather uniforms, three of them, black leather with something like straps, buckled straps, two of them, run tight and crisscrossed over the torso, always in that shiny black leather, three of them, and a fourth man, an officer, always with a pistol out.

It meant nothing—when they came for you. Most died the other way, all by themselves, all of their own accord. Most died just from living—so it was pointless to fear the others, those four that might come. It was living you were afraid of—it was living one more day.

Aideman—who remembers much more than a name? And mostly not even that.

When I showed up at my new assignment, they said, no, it was all in error again, there was to be no post for me as an instructor.

Student, yes, but not instructor—and I said that did not matter—so long as I could jump.

Oh, you can jump, they said—and you can teach the other fellows what you know. That was fine, teach all you want.

It was all the same—so what did I care what my title was?

Highest Parachute Center—that's the English for the name of that school—it was in Moscow—or really just outside of it. It was at a place that Stalin used, whenever he wanted a breather, a sort of country home to take it easy at. The name of it was *Forel*—*Sanatori Forel*.

I was teaching and I was jumping and I was having a good time. And then, gradually at first, the classes started changing. It wasn't just high jumping anymore—or doing somersaults as you came down—or working your lines so that you landed here instead of there. Now it was something else they wanted everyone to learn—jump onto a moving train or jump onto tracks or jump onto the roof of this or that—factories and into refineries and things like that.

This was military jumping that they wanted.

It wasn't sport jumping anymore. It was getting ready for war. But war? Where was there a war?

I went home very rarely—only a couple of times during the period I'm telling about. Sam looked grim every time I showed up. Had I written a letter to anyone—or been fool enough to take one? Do I know what ten years means?

I would assure him. Not to worry, Papa—I only wrote letters to people who never answered them—and that even when I did, it was only to the administrators of schools.

Leo seemed to be getting on okay—not notably sad or anything like that—though quieter than he routinely was. He had his new wife Lucille, the one who had been Reuther's wife, Reuther's girl, Walter's.

He never talked of going home now. Had he taken Soviet citizenship?

He did not wish to discuss it.

So, of course, it was understood he had taken it—and he had a good woman, a Russian, this Lucille that he loved. So?

So!

He lived in House 35, Apartment 4, Leo and his wife, and my dad lived someplace else, and Miriam lived with him, of course, and there was not so much congestion in the American Village now, because the place was thinning out—and who knew how? It didn't *matter* if anyone knew how. But with the thinning that was going on, there was another kind of filling up in its place, and I noticed it each time I went back there—and that was more Secret Service in evidence around the Village, and more cops, more militia, more uniforms everywhere in that place—and lots of fear coming in to fill up all that extra room the thinning out made.

I had medals and I took to wearing them, more often than not. That made a difference—the medals. Put those on a uniform and things were pretty much nine times easier for you—and for whoever was with you, Miriam, Sam, anybody.

It came in a little green box, that first medal. Who would have thought then, that evening in the eating hall, in the flush of my first triumph, my first notice in such an alien place, the excitement of that triumph coming off me like heat, who would have thought that night the power a medal was going to give? I'd think about that time, when everything here was so new and fuzzy in my eyes and really very bewildering and at the same time thrilling. I had come here for adventure—that was what I had wanted— a boy who sought lions and tigers and the dream of taming bears. How remarkable, that boy's unknowing vision of mine, a notion of magic, so few short years ago. How remarkable, what I had childishly envisioned—viewed against this dreary expanse of the deprived and the brutal I all around me, every day, saw.

TWENTY _____

I continued at the Highest Parachute Center, my touch with matters in the American Village sustained now only by letters I would now and then get from my father and a very occasional letter from some young friend there. It was 1937 when the character of these letters underwent an abrupt change. Sam no longer sounded like Sam— and I got no letters at all from friends anymore.

But the letters from Sam were now not typical of him at all. Oh, he was not a man for words and never had a great deal to say —yet there was always a good dose of his heart in his talk, and even in letters you could guess the warmth of the man. But the letters that began coming were nothing like that—they seemed blooded of every hint of feeling—and neither did they convey the usual sort of news, some item or two about Miriam's progress in school or some anecdote about the comically confused system of production at the plant. There was nothing like this, nothing that would suggest anything more than a pencil was making the words that were always so laboriously printed in painfully ruled lines across the scraps of paper that he used.

My father talked about the weather—I mean, he actually spent sentences on the weather—a subject of virtually no note in Russia, at least where he lived in Russia, so slightly did it vary, the weather. And if he did not talk about the weather, then he talked about writing the letter he was writing.

These were letters about the changeless weather and the little time there was to write letters—and that was all they said, save the changeless closing: *Your father sends you all his love—so do Miriam and Gusta, also your brother Leo and his wife.*

Yet in each there would be a hint of something odd—quite unlike the sort of written thing I had come to expect from my dad. There was something in each that caught my attention—and it was not just the restraint that was in evidence—but something notably *wrong,* something disquieting in its wrongness—such as not saying "Lucille," but "wife."

I tried for a leave from the Center. Was my father seriously ill in some way and trying his best to keep the bad news from me? That would be like him. It was a thing my father would do—hide whatever had to be hidden so that his family would not worry on his account. And if that was it, then I should be getting home to him quickly. Home! That I should think of that place outside of Gorky as home! That place and not Ironwood!

I applied for a leave—it was on the 14th day of December that I applied, and I was refused. No leave—no permission granted to return to Gorky.

Reason?

None given.

No leave. Your place is here. You are needed here. Teach!

Never before this had my movements been interfered with. Surely it had always required passes and papers and all sorts of red tape to go from here to there—but if you were patient, the bureaucracy would eventually get around to giving you what you wanted, and in time you got the documents you needed to travel.

But now it was no—no permission, no reason.

A week later, to the day, I was called in to see the Commissar, a fellow of political power who is attached to the school. That was the only title we knew him by, Commissar Bikov—and it was generally understood he was a member of the Secret Service. If he really was, I don't know—but that is what we understood. Every school and factory had a fellow like this—and although they never declared themselves as persons connected to the Secret Service, everyone believed that was the source from which they derived their authority; and everyone also understood that no one, at a factory or at a school or at any other place like this, no one had greater authority than did the man or woman who was the Commissar there. Sometimes this person would be called the Commissar or sometimes he would be called the Personnel Manager or sometimes the Chief of Information, but whatever he was called, *we* called him the Commissar, and we had a pretty clear idea of how great his power was.

Yet few people, so far as anyone knew, ever had direct dealings with such a person—and no one, not anyone I knew, wanted to. It was not that one heard unpleasant things about such dealings —it was just that no one heard anything much, yet *there* the person was, an overseer of some kind, a mystery of sorts, and perhaps because of this, fearful.

Anyway, this Commissar at the school, this Bikov, called me in—he wanted to see me and to see me right away.

He did not offer me a chair when I presented myself. He showed none of the usual, if grudging, courtesies. He just began right in as soon as I was standing before him. And I stayed that way, standing rather stiffly, throughout our brief interview.

He said, "Cadet Herman, get out of here!" And then he cursed me.

I didn't understand. I thought I had perhaps offended him in the way I had entered the room. That I had perhaps committed some sort of discourtesy—in some inadvertent way irritated him— perhaps had come into the room too abruptly, too forcefully, something.

And then I smiled—thinking that this was a joke of some

kind, not unlikely in the range of Russian customs. That was it—a joke. I smiled to show my appreciation.

And he screamed, "Do not approach my desk! Do not take one step nearer!"

And then I saw the guard that was standing off to the rear and side—and at this, at this shriek that came out of Bikov, the guard took two steps in my direction and then planted himself, as if in defense of the man behind the desk.

Again this Bikov cursed me—and I stood there dumbfounded. What a joke this was! How completely bizarre, the Russian idea of playing with a fellow, pulling his leg. Shall I curse him in return? I thought. Is this the way to show that I am getting the joke and it is time to call it off?

"You will remove your uniform!" Bikov screamed. "You will do it instantly! And you will not take one step closer to me—not one step!"

I actually laughed. But not much.

"Remove my uniform? What for? Why should I remove my uniform?"

"You have been dismissed! You are to remove your uniform and leave this place at once! Now, remove your uniform or I will have it removed for you!"

The guard took another two steps toward me.

I said, "Please be serious—it is cold. All right, I've been dismissed—but why must I remove my uniform? It is too cold in here. How will I get back to my quarters?"

"Guard!" Bikov screamed—and the guard began to come at me.

I had done lots of fighting in the States—but I had never been in anything approaching a fight in the Soviet Union—boxing matches, for sport, in and out of the ring, plenty of them, but never had I allowed myself to continue the sort of street fighting that I'd had so much of back home.

I did not want to fight anybody. I was not angry, really. I was just surprised. And I was not in the least willing to undress in front of these men—nor suffer the chill that would follow from doing so. And how to get back to my quarters? It was the third week in December—the cold was bad enough in here, in Bikov's office, and intolerable out there, and there was the long distance back to my barracks.

As for the guard, what if I hit him? A fellow in uniform? I would not take that chance.

I stripped off my clothes and stood there in my boots and my long underwear, two suits of it, one over the other. I just took off my clothes and dropped them beside me on the floor and stood there waiting for whatever was next.

Bikov handed a piece of paper to the guard and then motioned the man to carry it to me. As he came toward me, I began to take his measure, figuring where I would hit first and then second and third if I changed my mind and decided to hit. It was like drawing diagrams on his belly and heart, and just the drawing of them seemed to elicit their delivery. I could feel my fists connecting with the rough texture of that man's uniform, mindful to drive them in where there were no buttons to bruise me.

But I did not hit.

I took the paper from him. There was very little on it: just the name of the school, my name and official status, and the word DISMISSED, and the date, all of this last printed over with some sort of rubber stamp.

"All right," I said and folded the paper and turned to leave, but before I made it to the door, Bikov screamed again. The man sounded completely insane, his rage uncontainable.

"You are an enemy, Herman! Your kind does not belong here! All enemies are being weeded out! Dismissed, Herman, dismissed!"

I wheeled around and faced the man. He was still seated at his desk—his face crimson with the strain of his screaming, the guard stepping toward me again as I turned.

"What the * are you talking about?" I said.

I had scarcely got the words out of my mouth when his reply flew back at me, as if he had anticipated my question and had already rehearsed his answer.

He shrieked in reply, "You will find out! You will find out! Now leave here! I say leave here this instant and I will not tell you again!"

I kept myself remarkably calm, now that I think back on it. The more enraged this man became, the more I felt myself in control of the responses I made to him.

I said, "I suppose I will have to see my father about this."

Was I threatening him with my father's Party affiliation? My father's friendship with Kaganovich's brother?

Bikov screamed, "See your father! It will do you no good!"

I said, "Then I will go higher. I will see General Aideman."

"Go!" Bikov screamed. "Go to the grave to see your friend Aideman—because Aideman is dead! That is what happens to enemies, Herman! Now get out of here! Guard!"

Aideman an enemy? An enemy of what? The man was a general, the head of the *Osoviakhim,* a sort of semimilitary civil defense organization, a very important man. And this man was dead? From what? From being an enemy?

And then I understood. If this was true, that the man who had arranged things for me, my benefactor, as it were, was dead, then his protection of my status died when he died.

All right, so no more school—it was not so important. I had gotten along without it. It was not the end of everything.

I stood in the doorway, shivering, trying to think of something to say.

I thought of it.

I screamed at this Bikov, "General Aideman was a great man! He was the best Russian I ever met! You, Commissar Bikov, are nothing at all! You are welcome to your uniform! I am an American! What do I need with your ridiculous uniform? I would sooner freeze to death than wear it."

And with that, I turned and walked out into the blazing cold. Apparently I had the leave I wanted. At least that much of it was good. But I had nothing to wear—just that one uniform that now lay on the floor of Bikov's office.

But between the cadets and the instructors, enough was collected to cover me from the cold—and I got on the first train from Moscow to Gorky—after a long, angry walk from the airbase to Moscow, from *Sanatori Forel* to the first train home.

TWENTY-ONE ————————————

Something had gone wrong. I don't mean just with me, with my losing the footing I had. I mean generally, all over the Soviet Union, something was suddenly wrong. No, not suddenly, not suddenly at all. Suddenly only insofar as *I* could see, because what had I seen to this point? Had I looked?

If I looked at a newspaper or listened to a radio, it was not for any of this. What did all this Russian stuff have to do with me? A basketball game, maybe a boxing match—had someone done well in the 100-meter dash? That was my world—that and flying and jumping—and who knew about anything else?

A man like Sam. He would know. This was *his* world, this sort of thing—yet with what quality of eyesight did he see it? Was his vision very good—or any good at all? Were there casts in my father's eyes? Did he look but see through a squint?

And me, my vision was worse by far.

But if something was wrong, then it was wrong for all those *others*—for all those people whose home this was. Me, I was just an American passing through—perhaps somewhat more slowly than I had originally expected—but still, just passing through. Sooner than later I'd be off and away and heading happily back home—increased by my command of a difficult language and a certificate that qualified me to fly.

What stories there'd be to tell—to all those kids I'd left behind. I might even make up a little something about lions and tigers—what harm could there be in that?

I was the Lindbergh of Russia—I, Victor Herman! Who knew? Perhaps there would even be a parade in my honor right down Michigan Avenue—with the Goldmann boys and their cousins looking enviously on.

The thing now was to get home—first to Sam and the American Village—and then *really* home, all the way home, to the city where they made the world's greatest ginger ale.

And Henry Ford would have $18,000 all stacked up and waiting for me! So who cared about having to take off a uniform that itched like ✻ anyway! Who cared about anything Russian! Did any of it have anything in the whole wide world to do with the Herman kid, of 6094 Ironwood Street, Detroit?

They arrested you and jailed you and beat you to make you sign, and if you did or you didn't, they took you to the basement and they kept you there until they called you out at night, and you stood by the door waiting for them to open it, and when they did there were four of them, one with the pistol and three in black, the straps crisscrossed over black leather chests and all of them in leather and black. Three had rifles and they only seemed so long because that's how the bayonets made them look, and the fourth had the heavy revolver, and he held it pointed down. They told you to walk and you went walking with them, the three all around you and the fourth behind—until they stopped you to push the rubber gag in your mouth and then started you up again and said to look nowhere but down. It was only at night that they called you out, and you stood there waiting and they opened the door and there were four of them, the three in leather and the fourth behind, clean-shaven and bristling with formality, his heavy revolver pointing down. They made you walk and then they stopped you and put the rubber thing in your mouth and said, do not look anywhere but down, and then they made you get down until you were down on your knees, and in a while they would do it, it depended how long, but not until they had the automobiles ready, the ones they fixed to backfire and backfire, for when he fired the bullet into your head, him, the one with the heavy revolver.

The train from Moscow to Gorky seemed malevolently slow, its pace a maddening crawl broken by long unexplained pauses as it made its sluggish way through the great banks of snow that walled up the tracks on either side. It was like sleepwalking between glistening white walls, your steps leading you along a corridor bleached of all color but the color of cold.

It was white, very white, and inside, in the clanking iron of your dream, the thing that carried you through that tunnel of cold, there was nothing but your voice talking to you in your sleep, and all around you bundles of other sleepers, except you couldn't be sure.

I dozed and waked and dozed again—and once I waked with the sweat pouring off me.

What!

"You are an enemy, Herman!"

And then I fell into a long thin sleep, and with the sweat freezing on me I froze in the dream I had of walking, just walking through field after field of warm, candy-colored snow.

Sam embraced me when he opened the door. I hugged him back and kissed him—and hoisted Miriam to my chest and kissed her too.

My father held my hand all the way to the little table we used—and Miriam went to the stove to make tea for us all, and when she had things under way, she pulled on her high felt boots, the sort of Russian galoshes almost everyone in the Village wore, got into her coat, and went to fetch Leo and Lucille.

It was not that my family, what was left of it, had not always made a great fuss when I returned after some absence, but this was something more—my father's hand still grasping mine as we sat across from one another at the table. And then it must have embarrassed him to discover he was still doing this, and he released my hand, and I wished he hadn't.

We sat in silence for a moment. Would he not talk until he had his tea? But then he said, "It is good that Miriam is not here. I have things to tell you, and she must not know."

I said, "Papa, I have a great many things to tell you," but he raised his hand and then moved one finger to his lips to hush me.

"It is not necessary," he repeated.

"Told to take my uniform off, told that I am some kind of enemy—you can't believe the things they told me!"

Again he raised his hand in a gesture of indifference, impatience?—anyway, a signal to stop—and again he pressed his finger to his lips.

"Miriam will not be long," he said. "Let me speak. You don't need to tell me anything—believe me, your father knows." He looked nervously toward the door and then at the kettle on the stove. Then he turned back to me, and began, and as he talked, I dropped my gaze and I studied his hands, the thick wrists that grew bluntly back from them, your first evidence of the astonishing power that was in this man's arms. He seemed to know I sought that part of him to look at, and he kept his hands in front of him, there on the table, visible for me, to have if that's what I needed, and it may seem a small thing, but to me it was not, my father's denying himself the habit he had when he was seated of lowering his hands between his knees and clasping them there. It may seem a small thing that that's what he did, kept his hands there where I could see them, but he did that—and now I remember it.

I watched his hands, his wrists, and he talked—and none of it was said with any great feeling. It did not need that.

"I ask you to leave here with your sister. I ask you to take Miriam and return to Moscow. You are to go straight to the American consulate there. You will tell them that you wish to go home immediately, and you will do whatever they tell you you must do so that it happens. You will place yourself entirely in their hands. I want you to promise me, Vickie, I want you to make me your most solemn promise—you will not leave that building until they send you and your sister home. Do I have your promise?"

I said, "Yes, Papa, of course I promise—of course. But what's wrong?"

"I have your promise," he said.

"Yes, Papa," I said. "I promise you anything. I will do exactly as you say. But what *is* it that is wrong?"

He simply said, "There are twenty of us left. Of all the Americans, only twenty left."

And I said, "Yes? What happened to all the rest? Why did they leave? What's going on that everybody left all of a sudden?"

"That is not it," he said before the door banged open and Miriam was there with Leo and his wife, the three of them bustling in from the wind and the cold.

I went to the Clubhouse after the four of us ate. But it had been shut down. I went looking through the Village for some of the kids who had been my friends. I found two. They said they had nothing to say—it was not good to talk, Harry and Veikko would not talk. Did I not know that the Clubhouse had been shut down for exactly that reason—no one was to assemble, there was to be no talk?

Yes, yes, but what are you going to do? I in one fashion or another asked both of them, and both just looked at me as if I had taken leave of my senses.

It was amazing!

It was one thing, how grownups behaved, all caution and watchfulness for the sake of their children or just plain old adult prudence. But kids—young men? It was simply not anything I had ever come across before—young people frightened in a way like this, unwilling even to talk. What in the world could have scared them so?

My father waited until Miriam was in bed and until he was absolutely certain she was asleep, and then he motioned me to the table and again we sat.

"You gave me your promise," he said, whispering.

"Yes."

"You will keep it?" he said.

"Yes, of course."

"Out of hundreds, twenty are here. The others all arrested, taken away—who knows where? If they come for me, your sister will be alone. You want that?"

"No, Papa—trust me, Papa," I said, trying to lean across to him to give every proof of my acknowledging the gravity of the thing he was putting to me.

"All right," he said, "I have your promise. You will do as I say and we will speak no more about it. It is not good to speak about it"—he nodded toward where Miriam's bed was, toward where she lay sleeping, and then he tipped his head toward the door—"not good," he said. "I will expect you to be a man. I know you are a man, Vickie. You will take care of this business like a man."

"Of course, Papa," I said, and then I said, "But what about Leo?"

"Enough," my father whispered and again raised his hand to silence me. "This business is between you and me, Vickie—I have your word."

"You have my word," I said—and because I wanted him to know it was a man's word that I had given, because I thought, and thought so foolishly, that this was a way to reassure him, to comfort him in his terrible concern, I did not kiss my father good night. Boyishly, like a man, I rose and said good night to my father and went to the pallet Miriam had made for me, and with that, with the promise of silence that was vowed between us, I went to bed.

That morning Sam hurried Miriam off to school before it was time for her to leave.

He wasted not a moment.

"Listen," he said, "I will be late for the shop, and this is no time to be late, so listen. If something happens, and I am not here —I mean, if I am suddenly gone, you are not to give it a second thought. Over and done with. You understand me? I want you to swear this to me right now—on your mother's grave, I am asking you to swear."

I nodded.

He said, "Say it—say 'I swear.' "

"I swear," I said.

"All right," he said, and he hugged me and left.

But no one was getting out. No one was going to get home. There was no way to do it, no way to do the things my father wanted. Perhaps there had been—a month, two months—who knows how long ago?

Now there was no going, no matter how much you wanted it. I could get back to the American Village, but I could not get out again—at least no farther than Gorky. Those who tried did not get very far—and it went much worse for you if you tried. They shot you there, right where you stood, the enemy they had said you were thus incontestably proved.

That's how the warnings were then—always that much too late. The letters from my dad that weather was bad and it was hard to write, if they were warnings, what good did they do? They brought me back to the Village, and that put me all those many miles farther from the one chance we had. The consulate was in Moscow —and Miriam was here—and I, her one means of getting *there,* I was *here* now too.

I wanted to take my father and shake him—and scream, "October first! Nineteen thirty-four!" Scream just that, nothing more—scream it in his face.

But I would not do that. I would be a man—a man like my father—and all my screaming would happen only in my head. Besides, it was not his doing. Was I not accountable for myself? Had I not had my time—but was willing to let it go by? Had I not preferred my jumping and my flying, the attention, to anything else? And why should it have been otherwise? What reason would I have had? And, in the end, there was Miriam and Papa and Leo—my family—and my family was *here!*

It made no difference, any of this. The facts were simple and clear. *Here* we were—Miriam and I—and there was no getting *there*—no use to send a message, no use to try to run, no use to go out there and stand in the middle of the Village and scream and scream for all I was worth. No use to any of it. There was no one, not anyone for hundreds of miles, who could help you if he heard.

There was snow out there—snow all the way to Moscow. It could be snow from pole to pole for all the difference that would make—and I, I could have the power to scream from one to the other, from the top of the earth to the bottom, but over all the distance that my voice carried, it would only be my mother that heard.

I was twenty-two years old.

Miriam was twelve.

TWENTY-TWO _____

Run? With a twelve-year-old girl?

And if you did run and got away and got all the way to Moscow and found some trick to get from there across the even more impossible distance *to* and then *into* the consulate, what was it you left behind? The lifeless bodies of your father and your brother?

Trapped!

It was an idea that had never occurred to me in all my days. *People* could be trapped? *I* could be trapped? That I and those I loved could be caught and not get away, it was an idea that took some getting used to.

Even then, with all the testimony recorded, still the facts did not seem real.

A week or so passed. My father and I, we did not talk—what was there that needed to be said? He restored himself to his silence, and it was even stonier than before—but, aside from that, nothing was changed.

He went to the factory—and I went back to Vodopyanov —and they took me back as if nothing was amiss.

I wanted to fly.

Up there, it was better up there than down here. Flying made it all small somehow—and after you were up there for a while, it almost made it all go away.

And then things seemed to settle a bit—bad, yes, but no worse—and for months it stayed as it was, unchanged from the conditions I had returned to—and as the months moved stubbornly into spring and then summer, all that alarm seemed to go with it too.

Had anything happened? Nothing.

And even the crazy escape schemes I had contrived back in December, lying sleepless and spinning with some fabulous scheme, even these began to leave me. Yet I lay there so many nights in January and February, sleep nowhere near my bed, my brain seized by some new marvel of escape. Was I not a pilot, as skilled as any who flew? Did I not have access to an airplane, to fuel? Would it be all that preposterous to make it off the ground with Miriam with me?

Look, Comrades, the kid has been driving me crazy. If I don't take her up, she will drive me out of my mind.

And go where with her when I got her up there? What range did anything at Vodopyanov have? And if I could get a plane with any real range and get Miriam in it, even then there would be no place safe to go. There was no flying far enough to fly out of the Soviet Union.

So do what? Fly over the consulate and scream? Get up there with a chute and get the plane to Moscow and grab Miriam to me and jump? Could it be done? Jump out of some plane with a kid on your chest? Do it, actually *do* it, and land yourself on the consulate roof?

There was nothing I wouldn't think of, no notion I wouldn't consider—night after night through January and then February— until I came always to the end of the thought: *And leave what behind?*

The bodies of your father and your brother, your father and brother dead because you ran—and got nowhere nohow in the end.

And when March gave way to April, my nights gave way to sleep, and the alarm seemed all for nothing now—there had simply been no change. Our neighbors by the score were missing, but those that remained, remained.

It was quiet in the Village all through April and May, and I saw Leo and Lucille hardly at all. They had since moved into Sotsgorod, and I was not going to the factory—if Sam and Leo talked, that was where they did it.

There was sun now to raise you up, and with the melting of the snows, the earth revealed itself, still there beneath its once awesome but now forgotten burden—and you could not resist the biology in you that moved in measure to the seasonal tide. The earth lightened, and you lightened with it—and there was no reason not to.

May became June and it was a wonderful June, and all the panic of winter vanished no more noticeably than had the last resistant patches of snow. They were blots on the green landscape here and there, remarkable not for what they were the last of, but only for their persistence, and then, in the morning, some morning, they were gone—and who remembered the fearsome torrent they had belonged to?

You think: *It will never snow again.*

Sports were all anybody wanted to talk about now, and I right along with them, and I wasn't the least surprised to be invited back to *Spartak*—why should they not want me?

I was good, one of the best—a star athlete for Gorky.

I was happy to go—happy to run. And in no time I was training at the fields every day, getting set for the *Spartakiad,* which is a sort of nationwide junior Olympics.

It was great, being back at a favorite thing again. Right away, they wanted me to know it was all right if I wanted to move into the dormitory at the Gorky stadium, and I said that was perfectly fine with me. I just wanted to use myself around the clock, to go around and around that track, just run all that winter and cold and worry right out of me, and so I moved there, had a place there, and didn't go home—and there was nothing any longer to worry about, nothing to make me say no.

June was July now, and I was running, doing all the rest of it, feeling the world fall away from me as I ran, the time of the meet in late August the only reference I had outside of the region of mind I had drawn for myself. I ran the same course every day, and in my head there was nothing but my feet touching turf, the speed I made a motion in my mind.

And then the heat of July came, and the days sped by with the action of my feet.

I ran. It is all I can remember of this time.

One of the coaches called me over after the session on July 20th. It was not about anything I'd been doing out there on that track.

He had a message for me, this coach. The head man at the Gorky *Spartak* wanted me to stop by his office.

Why?

To chat.

Chat?

That's right.

When?

Now.

His name?

Chernov. Comrade Chernov. Right now.

I had to go across Gorky to get there. I went—I went by streetcar—and I remember how jammed with passengers it was and how I was proud of my clothes, how they suggested to all those passengers around me my status as an athlete. There was no special treatment, no medals on a uniform to get me a trip without fare or a better place to stand—but some people looked at me, the purple T-shirt I wore. I was an athlete and they knew it, and there was some color in me now, running in the sun, day in and day out.

It was a good day—and I felt good.

That is one of the things I remember—how good I felt.

This Chernov—surely what he really wanted was to make the acquaintance of a fine athlete—the man who would pace the Gorky team, the man who would bring honor and credit to himself and to all concerned.

Perhaps this Chernov wanted an autograph—*With best wishes from your friend Victor Herman, the Lindbergh of Russia. 20 July 1938.*

There were two men there with Chernov—and I knew one of them.

He was a gymnast, a man named Isaev.

The other man was in uniform—an Army lieutenant.

Chernov stood behind his desk, his arms folded pleasantly in front of him.

I said, "Good afternoon, Mr. Chernov. You called for me. I am Victor Herman."

The man Isaev said, "That's right. I attest to it. This man is Victor Herman."

The lieutenant came toward me, one hand on his holster, his other hand holding something in my direction.

"This is a paper for your arrest," he said.

I reached to take the paper, but the man withdrew it.

Perhaps it was for Chernov's benefit—to display what a sportsman I was. But I remember smiling in his direction. And then I said, "All right, I'm arrested."

"The man is Victor Herman," Isaev said. "Thank you, Comrade Chernov," he said, and signaled the man in uniform, who promptly took me by the elbow.

"All right," I repeated, "I'm arrested. I'll get my things. I'll go with you. We'll get this over with. I'll get my things and we'll get this over with."

Perhaps I was relieved. Perhaps it was still not real to me. There was nothing all that clear in my mind—except the motion of my legs along the oval course I had been covering—with my body and whatever else in me—since that first good day in June.

"We will take care of your things," the man Isaev said.

It's extraordinary what a person will say in such circumstances—what will capture his attention and what might come from his mouth. I suppose they would say that it is shock which accounts for these curious oddities of behavior. Or perhaps that it is some sort of momentum of language, the mere ceremony of words carrying us along.

I said, "Thank you."

TWENTY-THREE _____

I sat between Isaev and the lieutenant, the three of us in the back of the touring car that was waiting outside.

This Isaev, he was not a man I disliked. On the contrary, I admired him—he was a first-class gymnast, and, as Russians go, a friendly fellow, always full of high spirits and truly dedicated to sports. Like me, he was a devoted competitor—and we had often talked about things, about famous athletes and world's records and sometimes even about his job with the NKVD.

So what if he was a member of the NKVD? There were many who were. You got used to it—after a while you did not give such connections a second thought, what a man did when he was not

doing his sports. You just understood he was a man like you—
a man for whom sports came first and for whom everything else
was incidental, of no great importance at all.

I said nothing as we drove—and they did not speak, the man
Isaev and the lieutenant on my other side. The day was as beautiful
as any I'd ever seen, and it was a pleasure to be driving in that
excellent automobile, and whatever it was that lay before me, I
would see it through and get it all over with in no time at all.

We had stopped to let a crowd of schoolchildren cross in front
of us, and it occurred to me to be concerned about the *Spartakiad,*
and would I be back from wherever I was going in ample time to
make the meet. I put the question to Isaev—my manner offhand, in
just the mood that the thought had come to me.

Isaev did not look at me when he replied. He kept his attention straight ahead.

"Not this year, Victor," he said.

The driver started up again, and I remember thinking Isaev
was probably overstating the matter—that I would of course be
through with my business in time to make the meet, that if he had
said not this year, it was only to spare me from thinking about it,
only to help me to keep my attention focused on what was immediately ahead.

I took it as a kindly gesture—and I felt a little sorry for him,
for Isaev, that his position with the NKVD had obliged him to take
part in something he had no heart for.

But when Isaev spoke in reply to me, the lieutenant said,
"There will be no talking," and at this Isaev reached for my hand
with his hand, and he took my hand in his and squeezed.

I was undone by what Isaev did. His taking my hand like
that, it was like a hammer had hit me.

Wake up! This is real!

What kind of nonsense had I been speaking? This is happening!
Something is suddenly very wrong! This is real!

"Isaev," I began. "My friend, listen—" But the lieutenant cut
me short.

"No talking," he said, smacking his fist on my knee.

I said, "What have I done? I am innocent. I have done nothing, I swear. I am an American, and I tell you I am no enemy—I
am innocent!"

Again the lieutenant pounded his fist against my knee.

*   *   I said, hunching forward and trying to look into Isaev's eyes. "This is crazy! I am an American citizen. I don't have anything to do with you people! You people can't do this!"

And then I threw myself back against the seat and kept shaking my head and sort of chuckling—this was all unfathomably absurd, I would show them by chuckling, they would be made to appreciate that I at least knew it if they did not.

My mind began fixing on all sorts of elements that I took to be the critical components of the scene—not on Isaev and the lieutenant and the driver, but on the quality of the ride, the pitch of the sun in the sky, the color of the street as the sun glanced off it. I was going to commit to memory the precise distinction of each of these things—to know that we drove in a Ford Model A, that one of the shoelaces of Isaev's sneakers was untied, that I wasn't wearing socks, that the date was the 20th of July. . . .

The 20th of July! Nearly four years since I had jumped out of that plane, since I had pushed myself up and then out and then gone for 142 seconds in a deafening deadfall, my consciousness peering mindlessly somewhere to the side of me as I plummeted like granite to the ground.

What a day it was, the sun pouring out of the heavens in reddish hues as it lowered itself in the sky. We turned and took the bridge across the Volga, and the light from the water flashed over the car. Amazing. Only four days ago I had been swimming here even though I always preferred the Oka to the Volga.

What was I panicking for? Was I not innocent? What in the world could I be guilty of? Besides, I was an American—so whatever I might have done, it was none of their business! By nightfall it would be all over, everything cleared up, the error admitted, apologies conveyed.

"Where are we going?" I said. "I demand to be told! I am an American! You will pay for this! This is kidnapping! You cannot do this to an American! I promise you both, you will pay!"

I kept screaming at them, waiting for the lieutenant to slam his fist into my knee or my face. But he did nothing. He only looked at me, amused—and then he said, nodding toward some pedestrians who were staring, "Look, Lindbergh of Russia, the people are applauding."

It was a forty-minute drive, and it ended in front of a four-story building on Vorobevka Street, a white building, a building constructed of limestone. It was a building I knew very well—because it was central to things in Gorky, and not very far from it was the *Dynamo* gymnasium where in winter I had sometimes trained in basketball and done some boxing too.

It was the headquarters of the Secret Service, this four-story limestone building on Vorobevka Street. You didn't live long around Gorky without knowing that.

I had passed this building many times, diverting my eyes from it as the law required. Everybody in Gorky did that, looked away from the building when he passed. It was a law there—and one of the first ones you found out.

The gates were opened and the car entered and then swung around to the back, the lieutenant leaping to the pavement even before we'd entirely stopped. He jerked his gun from his holster and held it lowered at his side.

"Out!" he said, and I stepped from the car with Isaev coming behind me, prodding me gently.

It was a Nagan, the lieutenant's pistol, I couldn't help noticing—and again I was consumed with the mad notion that it was through my observation of minutiae that I would achieve some power over these people, some control.

He motioned me forward with his gun—and Isaev jogged ahead, opening the door to let us through.

I entered with a strong athletic stride. I entered that way—with a swagger, I suppose.

TWENTY-FOUR ————————————————

I stood before a squat desk, a man seated behind it, two men to either side.

"This man is Victor Herman," the lieutenant said, and placed the paper he had shown me on the desk.

"I confirm that," Isaev said. "He is Victor Herman."

The man behind the desk picked up the paper and handled it as if it might carry some contagion.

He did not look at me.

"You are Victor Herman?" he said.

"Yes," I said.

"Speak up!" he said.

"Yes," I said.

At this, one of the men standing to the side of the fellow behind the desk came forward and with the toe of his boot he kicked me in the testicles. I dropped to the floor, blind with agony. I clamped my mouth shut and tried to draw breath through my nostrils. I could not breathe. I thought: *I am going to suffocate.* In my writhing, I tried to crawl across the floor, as if breath were over *there.*

They grappled with me to get me off the floor, and when they had me standing, they dragged me back out through the door and into the rear courtyard. The touring car was gone, and in its place there was a van, dark green, the same sort of van you'd see used all over for bread deliveries, and I'd seen plenty of them from the ground up, because we had assembled them all at the plant. Only in the back, this one had been redone and, instead of a plain flat bed for stacking bread, there was a narrow aisle, and on either side there was a rack of lockers, the sort of thing you'd see in schools for keeping books and other belongings, eight of them, eight of these lockers on each side, metal, with slanted slits, a little grillwork on them, in the front.

They pushed me up and then turned me right toward the first locker on the right, and then they yanked open the little door.

"Get in!"

"Can't," I managed to say. "Too small."

"In!" I heard, and I don't know how many of them were doing this, but they pushed me in there and slammed the little door closed and then snapped a padlock home. I could move my head and just one of my hands and that was all. I tried to push up on one foot, but then I let myself go into a slump that jammed me into a sort of propped-up position. It was as good as I was going to get.

I waited.

I don't know how long it was. But I know three others were loaded. They brought them in one at a time, and it was easy to count. It gave you something to do.

It was hot in there—and my clothing made it hotter, dark colors that took up the heat—the purple *Spartak* T-shirt I wore and dark blue regulation trousers. I remember thinking how fortunate that I had no socks on—and that my tennis shoes were white. I remember thinking all sorts of nonsense. I even remember thinking that what was really happening was that I was being punished—because I had been boxing and because my mother had told me again and again not to do it—not to risk another injury to my liver. I had defied my mother's warning, and this was what I was getting for it!

I remember thinking even that.

And then that, like my father before me, I was on my way to be hanged.

We were moving now, had been moving some while, and I could tell we were traveling toward Miza, because that's where the airdrome was, and I could hear them, hear engines, and we'd been going uphill, very sharply uphill—and so that *had* to be it, toward Miza.

The van leveled out and continued on for a time, and then it made several turns and slowed and stopped. I tried to see my watch. Why did I want to see my watch? Anyhow, I tried. But I could not do it. Was there any value in knowing the time? Yet you do these things, try to carry out the checkpoints that are routine for you—it is perhaps a way of containing yourself within something familiar while an alien circumstance forms all around you.

I could hear the van doors open and see the light flash in. Then I heard a locker open and a man being pulled out. I waited for them to take me, but the doors closed again and the van moved on and then stopped and the same thing was repeated. Again the van moved on, made a turn, went forward and stopped.

The van doors opened a third time, and then the locker door was opened, mine, and two uniformed men took me by the arms and pulled me out. They got me out and onto the ground and then closed the van doors behind them.

There was another four-story building in front of me, this one red brick, no windows—and from where I was standing I could see seven other buildings roughly like this one, except they had windows—barred, but windows.

"Where am I?" I said.

The two men that stood to either side of me said nothing.

They had their revolvers out, the guns held slackly at their sides. They moved me forward, shifting to positions to the front and rear of me, and we walked about thirty yards and entered through a low iron door. I came out into a small room, what I supposed was a sort of guard's room. The men with me and the men in the room muttered several exchanges between themselves. I paid no attention.

"All right," one of the men said. "You, prisoner, you will undress!"

I wore no undershorts, and when I had pulled off my purple T-shirt and blue trousers, I stood there naked in my tennis shoes, the six or seven of them that were in that little room all scrutinizing me as if they had never seen anything so ludicrous and disgusting.

"The Lindbergh of Russia?" one of them said, and the others started laughing.

The one who had told me to undress, he came up to me and yanked down my jaw and looked at my teeth. He raised each of my arms and looked under them. He told me to bend over and pull my buttocks apart, and when he looked at me there, he whistled and then said in mock admiration, "The Lindbergh of Russia! How splendid, how splendid!"

They all started laughing again, and then they stopped at a command from the one who had examined me. They went to my clothing, the two items I had dropped next to me on the floor, and put these things on a table and searched them.

There was nothing there—a few coins, my wallet. These they gave to the man in charge.

I said, "You will find my temporary living permit in there. I am an American. It's pink. You can't miss it."

"No noise!" the man bellowed back at me. "Hands behind your back, head down, no noise!"

I did as he said.

I stood there. It was all real to me now. It had taken time, but now it was all real, very real. I began casting through everything that might present itself as a potential resource—what was there I had that might possibly help? My mind began working the way my body would work—in the ring or there, the other runners all against me, on the track.

It was then that I first thought—for the first time in my life—what it might mean, one way or the other, that I had not been circumcised. To my father, the Hebrew custom was a thing to be shed, and all other religious practices with it. He would not let them circumcise me, not matter how Rose protested—and when I was six, seven, in there, she told me. Had my father's willfulness brought about something that would make a crucial difference?

A Jew, his circumcision brands him. It confers on everyone everywhere the knowledge of what the man is. To be sure, there are men who are not Jews and yet whose custom is the same. Yet to find a man circumcised is to begin to suspect: *Is this a Jew?* But I was not marked in a way that would reveal me, not set off in a way that would single me out.

Would it be this that would save me?

Or would it happen that my own body would contradict the one appeal that might work? For if I were seen as a Jew, would not another Jew help me?

But to be seen as a Jew might add just the stroke more convincing someone needed to conclude the deliberation of my fate.

My father had gotten me here. It had been his large belief that had done it. But it was also my father's strong belief that left me untouched by the common practice of our race. His conviction was like a great rock that he pushed before him and onto which he hoisted his wife and children to take a lifelong ride. He would push it and push it for all of us to ride, never thinking that as it turned the less nimble might fall off, be caught and ground underneath.

Then where had I fallen?

Again I asked them—and this time I was given an answer— *Spets Korpus*—Special Building—a building for political prisoners.

Spets Korpus.

So be it. I knew where I was.

TWENTY-FIVE _____

I was told to take off my tennis shoes. I did, and they were searched, each one inspected by a different man.

The laces were removed and the tennis shoes were handed back to me, and then they gave me back my T-shirt and trousers, but they had taken the belt from my trousers and had cut away the buttons from the back pockets, from the fly, and from the waist-band.

I got back into my clothes and stood there.

"Hands behind back, head down, no noise!" the same man said, the one who had been giving the orders. I did as I was told, and with my hands behind me I stuck my thumbs through two belt loops and kept my trousers from falling.

I was moved through another low iron door and then a second one, and then we came out into a large area, four levels of cells, three tiers of cells rising on two sides.

One of the two guards with me called out, "Two!" and from above another guard called back, "Two! Two is ready!" Then the first guard called out, "Thirty-nine!" And from above the reply came, "Thirty-nine! Thirty-nine is ready!" The guards with me had stationed me at the foot of a stairway, iron steps rising to the second level. "Up," one of them said.

I climbed the stairs to the second level, and I was yanked up the last step by the two guards who waited for me on the second landing. They took me by the arms and moved me along a thickly padded walkway. We passed one steel door, then another and another.

"Hands behind back, head down, no noise," one of the men with me said.

I started to say, "I know," but caught myself in time.

We kept on going, all the way along that walkway, and then they stopped me about five yards from the end. It was then, when they stopped me there, that it first came to me, the silence! Our footsteps on the padded walkway gave scarcely any sound at all, and when that stopped, the little sound we made, the silence was im-mense, people just breathing somewhere, a kind of hiss almost, like a hiss of open mouths, just breath, maybe lungs whistling there in the dark, hot air, and the heat was like wet wool pasted all over you.

The guard in front of me produced his key. It was amazing. It was downright comical, this gigantic key he was fitting into the lock in a door, and I kept thinking how comical it all was—could they not see it? A key like that, it was impossible that they did not see the humor of it.

He got the key in there and actually used two hands to turn it. Then the two guards together, in a hard sudden motion, as if they would shout out "Surprise!" as they did it, hauled back powerfully on the door.

The appalling distortions of men in there and the gas that rushed out from their midst, it was the first time in my life that I tipped forward toward the precipice of a faint. For an instant I did not think my legs would hold me—and though I kept myself standing, another man inside me staggered, reeled crazily, fell spiraling into a massive swoon.

"In!" the one guard said.

He did not push me. Neither guard did. They stood there with me, watching. I breathed through my mouth and held it. I bit down on my molars.

And I walked in.

I made sixteen—sixteen men in that space, a space ten feet by five and a half feet, and to the ceiling eight feet or an inch or so higher.

I will tell you what Cell 39 was like—and this is what it was exactly—the space ten by five and a half, and to the ceiling eight feet, maybe somewhat higher. There was a window opposite the door, although from outside I had seen no windows. Over this window there were boards and no light came through, and you only knew there was a window there because later on they told you. On either side of the space there were three benches, and on these the men sat—and they sat in the position. The floor was concrete, dark gray—the walls were concrete, also dark gray—the ceiling the same. Over the door, very high up, just under the ceiling, a bulb, maybe twenty-five watts. It never went off. It always burned, the little light that came from it constant. The door was iron, and in it there was a peephole and, lower down, a slot, the feeder. In front of the door there was the big pot, the cauldron, an oil drum cut approximately in half. It was the *Parasha,* the pot where the steaming mess from us was collected. It had a lid, the *Parasha,* a disk of wood that went over it, and as spectacular as the smell from it always was, the gas that boiled up from the *Parasha,* it was a thousand hells worse with the lid off.

You sat—in the position—behind the muzzle. The muzzle— the *Namordnik*—the boarding that covers the window. No looking out, no looking in—and no light except from the bulb over the door that always burned.

The metal door behind me slammed closed. I stood there, trying to get my eyes used to the light, and then I moved before I was ready and banged my knees into steel. It was the pot—and I almost went down across it, but pushed myself back up, my hand on the lid. It seemed fuzzy, a thing with growth. I snatched my hand behind me as if to shake something off.

The men on one side reached out their hands and led me along, passing me along to a place on their shelf. I was lucky. It was the place at the end of their bench, a place as far from the *Parasha* as you could get.

I sat there where they placed me, where they gave me a place, these figures of men that lined three sides, all seated now as they had been when that door was hauled abruptly open, their hands on their knees, their backs rigid, their faces all turned toward me as I stood there with the guards in the doorway, my brain struggling to check itself from the well of falling that opened before it, all those terrible faces staring, all turned in the same direction, the eyes in them wide, staring, every man's hands on his knees, his back like wood, mouth open, breathing.

It was the position that they sat in—and that's how they were sitting now, the steel door closed, no one there to look at now, yet their faces all still turned there, their eyes all fixed on that one spot, and staring—all save the one man who lay on the floor under the bench on the other side.

There were fifteen of us seated, and the sixteenth man was under there, on the other side, curled into himself and, like the rest of them, he was facing the door, his eyes fastened, as theirs were, on that peephole high in the door.

We sat on removable boards placed on benches on each side. That's how you sat, and this put your knees less than an inch from those of the man that sat across from you.

I sat as I sat, leaning back against the wall—I had to push myself back to reach it. It was incredible that the rest of them sat that other way, at the very edge on the bench so far forward on the boards, their backs rigid and inches from the wall. I just sat as I sat and studied the man that was all curled into himself under the bench on the other side.

"What's wrong with him?" I said, and no one answered—no one even turned.

"Is he sick?" I said.

Just that staring—and no reply.

"He looks sick to me," I said. "Mister, are you sick?" I said.

There was nothing, no answer, no motion from any of them—except on the other side, on the end, the end near the door, a man darted his finger to his lips. He did not turn to me when he did this. But the movement he made was so startling—since nothing else in there moved—my attention leaped to his signaling finger and I heard it like a shout. It was a motion I will never forget, so jarring was that little movement, his finger pressing at his lips and then his finger pointing. To the peephole.

It was none of it difficult to understand. It was simply a question of whether you wanted to. I looked around at them all, and I considered what could have gotten men to do it, what force it was that held them that way, like wooden cutouts, like dolls propped up and then nailed to where they were.

You did not get men to sit like that without good reason.

I needed no convincing. It was all the instruction I would need.

I assumed the position—and, like them, I directed my attention to the peephole and kept it there. It was how the day was passed.

It was how the days were passed for one year.

I began that one year by testing myself, doing this as I had done everything before it—the sports, the flying, the jumping, all of it—as if I were launched upon some competition. I would try to do it, sit that way, stare like that, more utterly than did anyone else. There, across from me, under the shelf—*there* was one that could *not* do it, a fellow who had succumbed to the press of competition.

He could not sit. He fell.

I sat. I sat as if the sitting would make all the difference, as if no one had ever done it better, that no one ever would. I sat in the position, staring, thinking insanely that at the end of this the award would be given, the winner named.

But there was no end to it—and no winner named. There was just this—the sitting, the staring—and all it got you was one reward, the absence of something—and that absence was no beating.

The key—that comic key the guard had used? It had a further use, as I would find. It could do more than open a door. His fist through the leather loop that held the key, the guard could make it do more than just open the door.

I started the first year like that, drawing myself into the position as if someone had called, "Ready? Set? Go!" and a gun had gone off, and every muscle in me tensed and then exploded, and like that, sitting behind the muzzle in the position, I ran.

That is how I started. It made a beginning. It got me through, the idea I had—the idea to do it very, very well.

They were all shorn, these other men, the hair on them clipped ragged against their fleshless skulls and faces—and elsewhere where you could see a patch of nakedness on their bodies, the hair was cut, the job haphazard, away from the skin.

They were old men, all of them old by my youthful standard, save one that was about thirty. At twenty-two, I was the youngest by far. Then why had they favored me with one of the two desirable places, the two places farthest from the pot? But it may have been the self-sacrifice that sometimes expresses itself among veterans, the old hands making it easier for the newcomer until he sees what he really faces. Perhaps in time I would be made to give my place up.

The old man on the floor was sick, all right, too sick to use the pot without help. Two men would drag him to it and hold him there if he had to pass water, or on their arms raise him in a sort of seated affair above the *Parasha* if it was his bowels that had to go. *Heart,* one of the men who held him once signaled to me, a look in my direction and a brief tap on the sick man's chest. Or maybe *lungs*—who knew? Sick was all that mattered—and why weren't they all? The heat was enormous—and the heat was the least of it. The smell, the boards, the position, the light, the air a seventeenth organ that pumped a fetid scoop of life back into your chest so many times—you began to count them—a minute.

You heard the steel door bang shut and the little click the huge key reversing the tumblers made. You heard that and you heard a judgment, as absolute as a blade parting your body from your head. The scream began with that, with the little click that you just heard, that little click and the thing that followed it—the mind's one speech to the heart: *I am here.*

It was a sentence that drove the gorge in you flashing up to your brain—*I am here.*

Nasterov—that was the name of the man on the floor. I found out when he died. That was generally how you found out—how you got to know the name of a person. Somehow you only found out a name when the person that had it died. Someone told you.

It was the only headstone anyone got—your name moved from a man who knew it to a man who did not.

Twice I thought to look at my watch—to see how long I'd been sitting in this remarkable posture, back straight, hands on knees, head turned, feet off the floor, eyes where they were—once to see how long I'd been doing it and a second time to see how close to the dinner hour it was. But I did not look. I kept my eyes fixed on the peephole. If they could do it, I could. And besides, there was no watch on my wrist anymore. How was it I did not know that? And how was it that between the first time and the second, between the two times that I had that thought, the thought to check my watch, that I had completely forgotten there was nothing on my wrist anymore, not anything there at all?

Yes, of course, the first day is the hardest. Every blessed one of us, every mother's son, knows a simple thing like that.

I kept repeating this sentence over and over in my head—*The first day is the hardest*—as if it were the most dumbfounding wisdom, the wisdom of the ages—*The first day is the hardest*—as if all human intelligence, the very key to the universe, rolled in resplendent evidence across the highway of those six words.

I heard something! Outside. Not the organic meaty mutterings of men just breathing and snuffling and stifling coughs and squeezing farts back in or out, but something else—metal moving? And there was a collective stirring as it came. I wanted to look at the others, raise my eyebrows to suggest a question. Someone could motion back to me, some gesture, some signal—the metal and the stirring, it's . . .

But I would not do it. I would not look away from the peephole.

Was I winning this fantastic competition? Was anyone noticing? Was anyone keeping score?

The metal and the stirring got closer, and that was it, it *was* metal being dragged—but on something soft.

The padded walkway!

There had been padding out there on that walkway! Or had there been? Perhaps I had only imagined it. Padding in a jail?

But who could remember anything from so long ago.

How long?

How long had I been here like this?

Was anyone keeping score?

And now there was a real noise—and it was the slot—the feeder—moving—and something getting shoved inside.

I looked and when I looked I saw that everyone was looking. Had they looked first? Was I the last one to give in?

I saw the man at the end on my side, the man next to the door, put out his hand to the feeder and pull back a wooden bowl. He passed it down and pulled back another, and then another, passing to this side and then to that side, and the first one came to me!

Of course! Of course!

This was proof of my winning. This wooden bowl I had, and the first to get one, this was my reward!

The first day is the hardest.

Now wooden spoons were put through the feeder one at a time, and each of these was passed around among us in the same sequence as the bowls.

And then the feeder slammed shut—and I saw the others, bowls in their laps, spoons inside them, resume the position, exactly as before. And even the man under the bench opposite, the man on the floor, he too had his head craned at this crazy angle, his eyes on the peephole, his body all curled into itself, exactly as before.

All right, then—if this was their game! The test was not over? Very well, then! I would show them again—once more I would prove just who it was in here that could last the longest, just who was the *   *   to outlast them all!

I too resumed the position.

And waited.

We had bowls and spoons. Surely that meant food. But what? And when?

And then there was that dragging again—and the stirring that always came with it—a soft sound but loud enough, and clearly it was metal on carpet. Surely I had not imagined it. Wasn't there— there *must* have been—carpet out there?

I do not know how long it was.

The first day is the hardest.

But then the feeder opened and when it did your bowl was

passed to the man beside you, the man closer to the door. It went down your side and in a while it came back to you, and in it there was a dry sphere of porridge.

How big? Smaller than a baseball. About the size of a golf ball.

You ate it and waited for more. For at least bread? For water? But that was all.

And the size of the sphere you got never varied. Unless you did not get any at all.

And the spoons and bowls went back again and then out the feeder in the door.

And the men took up the position again—and I with them.

The first day is the hardest.

No! It is the first night that is the hardest!

It was extraordinary, what I saw that first meal in 39—a thing that became so customary for me that in this telling I almost forgot it.

When the bowls came back with something in them, no man ate until every man had his bowl—and you could see how some of them were trembling, so great was their passion for the awful ball of paste that squatted in their bowls. It was staggering, this monstrous *politesse*—and it was the same every time, at each of the three feedings—for all the days of all the months of the year I sat there with them, that I sat with them behind the muzzle and in the position as these men died.

I had already swallowed my little ball of cereal. I looked up from my bowl to see that—to see the others all still waiting for the last man's bowl to come.

I did not do it again.

But the fraternity in 39, it was not the rule in prison—nor would it be the rule in what was to come—in the vastly harder conditions of the camps. It was exceptional, I later discovered, these human gestures that were the practice in Cell 39. Because here men shoved their backs against their hunger and waited, but there, in the camps, men would tear at your lips with their teeth if so much as a smear of some food were still on them.

It is the thing never to exhaust your wondering—the behavior of men, some like this, some like that.

But it is the first night that is the hardest.

When night came, I found out who the Elder was.

It was the rule in 39—that there be an Elder—and it was he that made all the others—what few rules that would keep us secure from the disorder that always pounded to get in.

A man was appointed Elder by silent consent. It was, in a word, understood—a natural recognition among men. He was the man in 39 the longest—or he was the man whose presence seemed to vest in him some sort of unquestioned moral authority.

He was, the day that I entered here, a man who elected to sit next to the door—and therefore closest to the pot, and thus in one of the two least favorable places.

So much for this man's moral authority. He possessed it—in the extreme.

The Elder was Sergeyvsky—a tall man, dark hair, dark features, the son of a priest, a man high up, a cardinal, a bishop, I don't know. And when he died, there was another, another Elder. But first there was Sergeyvsky, and he was the only man I heard talk until that first time in the bathhouse when we were taken to get our hair clipped, our clothing scorched, and our bodies showered.

It happened that first night—night? It was after the time of the meal, the ball of porridge, is all I know. The tall man next to the door stood and moved to the pot. Such a movement made you jump. Nobody moved for hours and hours, and when a man moved, it made you jump.

The tall man stood and stepped to the pot. I kept my eyes on the peephole. I did not want to see him do it. If I did not watch him do it, would it not follow that he would not watch me? It was awful, holding your bladder and your bowels because it seemed easier to hold back what was pushing in you than to go near that thing and drop your pants. Would you have to look inside? Would it be possible to do it without seeing inside? And the smell that would touch you if you were that close to its source! It would coat you, that smell, and never come off. The fuzzy texture of the lid, I could still feel it, a *growth*—I could imagine something brown and mossy taking root on the palm of my right hand. I rubbed it against the knee of my trousers while the tall man stood there, so tall you saw his head and not the peephole. He raised the lid and held it to the side and dropped his pants to the floor, his feet planted on our side of the pot, knees bent slightly, in something of a squat. I did not want to see—not his eyes certainly, but they were in my line of vision to the peephole.

He raised his finger to his lips and he looked at me—and then he spoke, a whisper only, but in that silence the volume of it seemed very great. He made groaning sounds as he whispered, as if he were straining to pass his stool—but I could see it was not that, that he groaned to hide his whispering—and this is what he said.

"You can see the rules. You will see more. Break a rule and no man in here eats. For three days, no food for us—you, the rest, all of us. You they beat with the key. The rest of us, no food, three days—and three days the same for you. You understand?"

I nodded my head.

"Do you have news? From outside? Anything?"

I shook my head.

He pulled his trousers up and knotted them at the waist. He returned the lid to the pot.

Nothing had come out of him. I did not look but I knew it hadn't. Would you not hear a splash? Some wet or smacking sound?

Not one other man in all that time that first day and first night rose from his place to use the pot. It was impossible! But that is how it was—and in less than a week I knew why.

You held it in you, whatever there was. Not from shame or anything like that. You held it in you because that is all there was, and it helped you feel filled up.

Shame? In a place like 39? No, there was no prospect of shame left in you after one day and one night. After one day and one night, you were the only man in that place, no matter how many there were. The rest were like your fingers and toes, parts of a gross organism that occupied a certain cube of space. There was no one there but you.

Oh, but the pot was used—enough that your skin will never lose the smell of it. It is in you forever, the stink you breathed and stared into for one whole year.

TWENTY-SIX _____

I never knew the second Elder's name. It was an exception. He did not die in time.

Sergeyvsky did—dying in time to have his name passed from man to man until it came to me and then was passed to this page.

It is the only headstone that he has.

The second Elder lasted until my leaving—and if his name is known, it will be another that must set it into the record.

Not even when they called you out from 39 did you hear the man's name they called. Instead they called a letter—and you knew yours. You learned it and never forgot it.

The feeder would open and a voice would call in, "Get ready!" Then the letter: "G, get ready!"

And if you were "G" and you did not get ready, they came in to you and they had the key. Only one guard could fit between the benches, but it did not take two of them to do it. One could do it—use the key on you, his fist around the leather thong and the key coming down on you from whatever distance he could get in that space.

It was like a war hammer, that key. You did not want to get it.

So you didn't forget your letter once they gave you reason to know what it was. It did not matter whether the letter they gave you had anything to do with your name. Nothing like that mattered anymore after a time—a thing like a letter matching up with your name—even a thing like a name, not even that mattered after a time. But I was "G." And in my case, the letter matched—"G" for the first letter of my name in Russian. But who knows if that is why they chose it? It was "G," and when they called it and said, "Get ready!" I did.

How long had it been since the ball of porridge? How long since the feeding? What time had that been? And was it possible? That the light never went off and that we sat like this—from morning to night and then on through the night back to morning?

The first night is always the hardest.

I wanted to use the pot. But I would not do it. I would not go near that thing—not yet. Perhaps by morning. . . . But was it morning already? Had night come and gone, and was this the start of the second day?

I sat in the position and waited.

It was as if a thousand windows were shattering—thick sheets of brilliant glass splintering! It was a bell—and the crack it sent through my brain brought me in a leap off the benches.

I fell onto the man across from me, and he pushed me back, but on a signal from the Elder the others were all rising, and it was a thing to see, these fifteen men rising after how many hours as they'd been. They did it by stages, slowly coming up—and I rose too, or tried to. But my legs would not carry me up. I think I laughed a little, and then I quickly shut my mouth.

Break a rule and no man in here eats. For three days, no food for us—you, the rest, all of us. You they beat with the key.

My legs would not work. How long had I been sitting like this? Two days? Three?

And then I got myself standing—and I just stood there like the rest. There was no room to move, with all the men standing—and what about the man on the floor? But it was only seconds that we were standing—because in seconds all those men were lying on the floor, one man up against another, on their sides and still facing the door, their heads all one way, their feet the same, and each man's hands held to his mouth as if in prayer.

You can see the rules. You will see more. Break a rule and no man in here eats.

Even the sick man, he too was stretched across the floor with the rest of them, his body forced out from the curve it wanted to go in, his hands up there by his mouth.

Did all these men pray? Is this why they were in prison? Practitioners of religion in a Communist state?

I got down as they were—my head where theirs were, my weight resting on the same side, my face toward the door, my hands to my mouth. I squeezed between the last man and the wall, and I got down there on the concrete floor—but I did not pray.

Could I sleep like this?

If I had sat like that—then could I not also sleep like this? If they could—could I not do it also?

They slept. It was something you knew without seeing—the change in the breathing that jammed the air.

I lay there.

I am here, I told myself—still disbelieving.

I am in this place, locked in here, and I am lying like this, squeezed between a man and a wall, and against him there is squeezed another, and another after him—and they are all sleeping —and I will sleep too.

But I could not. There came the rain of all that had been building since the little click in the door. It was a deluge, the torrent of questions that fell on me—and the guessed-at answers I gave each of them and then retracted and then replaced with others, one no surer than the first, a downpour that held me on the point of consciousness all that long first night.

I did not sleep.

Sleep?

Surely they would any minute discover their mistake and call me out of here. Say, "Our profoundest apologies, Citizen Herman, we only moments ago were informed that you are none other than the Lindbergh of Russia!"

Call me out and say, "A thousand pardons, Mr. Herman, no one told us you were an American and the President of the United States just called us to so advise us—and we can't explain it, but really, old fellow, this has been the most wretched mistake. Surely you and your President will find it in your hearts to forgive us."

Call me out and say, "Dearest fellow, my good young man, you must please, we beg you, excuse us. You are the very likeness of yet another Victor Herman, a traitor, a spy, a looter, a rapist, and a thief of the vilest condition. But, alas, and so luckily for us all, the filth was only moments ago apprehended and confessed himself there on the spot, completely freeing you from any suspicion of crime. Here, dear fellow, have a bit of tea and some cake, and let us all please make an immediate effort to put this grievous matter to rest. May we call a car? Our driver is waiting."

Say to me, "Ah, Vickie, beloved, good son—your father only wanted to teach you a little lesson. You must never, never again touch a gun. Fly a plane. Eat an apple when you are falling from the sky. Not write your sister Becky. Not do as your mother asks. Outrun your brother Leo. Forget to bring a little something special for Miriam. Not chew your food or eat it so fast or speak when you are not spoken to or do anything ever and forever again when your papa and your mama tell you no. Promise? Swear it! Say, 'I swear.' I want you to be a man, so swear!"

And that is how my head worked until it worked itself into worse—sleep heaving against me from one side, the hard slab of reality, a wall, slammed against the other.

How long will I be here?

These other men, what crimes have they committed?

They are guilty, and will they therefore not try to make me guilty too?

How long have they been here?

How long will I be here?

Dare I get up now and go to the pot?

My hands. Should I pray?

When they call me to question me, what will the questions be?

When will they call me to question me?

If I tell them I am innocent, will they answer that I am guilty?

What could I be guilty of?

Will they not question me?

Should I pray?

How long will I be here?

In the morning, what will the food be?

Eggs? Will they be scrambled? Fried?

My hand! The one that touched the lid! Dare I have it near my mouth?

Which hand touched it?

Touched what?

Should I pray?

I am here!

How long will I be here?

Should I pray?

Pray to what?

But if prayer cannot help me, what can?

Should I pray?

The first night is the hardest—and each one, each night thereafter, is your first.

In the course of the night the Elder would wake all the men, to turn them—and each one would get up and reverse himself, all heads now at this end, all feet where the heads had been, from one side to the other, faces toward the door, your hands both in view. Four times that first night he waked them and turned them—but it was never necessary, not once, to wake me.

How had I come from Ironwood Street to this? How from there to my place on this floor? How in a life does one go from 6094 Ironwood Street to *Spets Korpus,* Cell 39?

The answer was easy.

Here is how you do it—just stand where your father stands you—and when he moves, you follow.

But I loved my father then, and I love him still—with all that there is in me to love. I lay on that floor that first night, turning when the Elder turned the others, sleep an art I had somehow forgotten, and in my heart I loved my father.

He went and, like a loving son, I followed.

I would do it even now. It is what a son is—and one must be a father to know it.

Svetlana and Janna sleep here now—in beds given them by friends here in Detroit. My daughters sleep in the room next to mine—and no one turns them in the night. And if I should go from here, they would follow—and Galina, my wife, she will follow too.

It is what loving is—and one must love to know it.

PART 2

FROM CELL 39 TO THE CELL THAT HAD NO NUMBER

TWENTY-SEVEN

You did not know it was morning until they rang the bell. Only by the bell could you mark the intervals of time—for the light never changed—and how long does it take for the body to forget the pulses that are natural to it? Not very long—and in Cell 39 less time than that.

All that night the Elder turned the men—and I turned with them, sleepless until the morning bell. He turned them four times that night, and not long after the fourth time a guard came in and used his key, whipping the thing with remarkable force. I saw it all —and heard it—saw the door open, the guard enter, stepping on the men until he found the one he wanted, a man four down from me— and then I heard the guard announce the infraction: "*Both* hands in view!" and heard the first blow hit.

Iron on flesh makes a terrible sound.

I shut my eyes and then I opened them. I saw it all. It was like looking into that mirror during the surgery on my liver—it was something I had to see—to know what it *was,* this thing that sometimes happens between men, what one man will do to another.

Yet all the men were fed that morning—despite the rule the Elder said was so. The bell rang and everyone took his place again, even the old man on the floor, going back to his curl under the shelf opposite, and everyone took up the position again, and I followed suit just like them all.

What would it be? Eggs? Scrambled? Fried? My stomach howled for anything save that porridge—and the long night had made me ravenous, hungry in a way I'd never quite been before.

I sat in the position—and, like the rest, I waited. But after a while I wondered if I was the only one waiting. Could it be that no food would come?

Several times I had to check myself from leaning forward and making some sort of motion to the Elder—I could raise my eyebrows and make feeding motions to my mouth. Or I could just rub my belly and smile. Or maybe raise my eyebrows and rub my belly, perhaps that would be better. Or better still, I could make chewing motions—wouldn't that be the least infraction of the rule? What if I went to the pot? That was allowed. I could go to the pot and make chewing motions. But I would not go to that pot. No, that would take a time yet, to get me near that thing.

Was it possible to use it without looking inside? I thought about how I would go about using the pot when I could resist it no longer. I kept trying to figure out some sort of eye and hand movement that would keep me from the worst of it. It was a good thing to think about, this problem—something worth giving some study to. That's what I needed—something to think about—other than food and when they would call me to tell me what the charges were or that the charges had been dismissed or that a mistake had been made or to ask me questions that I wouldn't know the answers to or to tell me that I was going to be shot or to hear me tell them that I was an American citizen and that I wanted to be released this instant or to ask me why I had eaten an apple while falling from the sky—*and what would I say to that?*

I need something to *think* about—so I wouldn't think about the kinds of things that I *was* thinking about—and above all I needed *not* to think about food.

But how exactly does one do that when it is hunger and hunger and hunger that is all that his body feels?

I waited.

I sat in the position.

I studied the problem of how I would do it when I had to do it, had to go to that pot and lift the lid that had a kind of furriness on it. And if that's what the top had on it, what was on the other side?

I heard it. Again. That same soft noise, the dragging, metal on padding? And there it was, the general stirring out there that seemed to accompany the dragging. It was what had preceded the last feeding. How long ago had that been exactly? The last feeding—had I missed a day?

I had to get possession of myself. It made me panic to think that I could have perhaps missed a day and not known it. I got dizzy just thinking that—and I had to get better control of myself. This would never do. I had to get something inside my belly, something like scrambled eggs maybe and some bread and butter and a good glass of milk—because if I kept on this way, I'd never make it.

I sat there.

I tried not to think.

I could sense something restive in the other men—but I dared not look to make sure. Surely they were not moving, but I could sense some sort of unexpressed motion in them, a kind of general urging forward.

The noise outside! That was it! They knew better than I, of course, and they knew it was coming—food!

How long would it be in coming—and when it came, what would it be? But first of course there would be the bowls sent in—or dishes this time—of course, *dishes* for eggs—and then we'd have to get utensils—so it would all take time. I must be patient. It will take time for the thing to get set up—time to dish out the eggs and the rest—time to handle each man's serving and how he'd like his coffee or tea fixed or whether he'd like milk instead.

The dragging was at the door now—that much I could tell. I was learning fast—and perhaps in time you found yourself hardly remembering when you needed to talk to get things understood or needed to stand up or walk around to feel good. A man could get used to anything in time. Hadn't I gotten used to Sam coming home bloody and torn? And what about boxing? Hadn't I gotten used to getting hit—and hitting? Of course I had—and that hadn't been so easy at first. And think of all the other things I'd gotten used to—and that really required some doing. Flying an airplane, for instance —and jumping out of one. Hadn't that taken a tremendous amount of getting used to? Just imagine! And going on a ship for the first time and not getting seasick. Hadn't I done that? If I had done all that, what couldn't I do? I could learn to keep my mouth shut and to listen and never miss a trick! Why, I'd probably hear a thousand times more than I'd ever even known existed! And hadn't I been sitting in the position all morning and not even noticed it once? I didn't even feel like leaning my back against the wall, it was that easy to do, and who even thought of it?

The feeder moved! And they were pushing something through! If the sequence was the same as it had been at the last feeding, then I'd get the first dish!

I was ready.

I looked and saw the Elder pulling through a bowl.

All right. I was ready.

It was passed down to me—and it wasn't empty.

It had water in it. Hot water.

Of course!

For bathing. For washing your hands. Washing your face?

I watched the others. I knew the rules. No man does anything until every man is ready, and then everyone does it together.

I watched to see what they would do.

But when every man had his water, they began drinking it—drinking the hot salty water—and when I saw them do it, I did it too.

That was breakfast—the second day—and breakfast for a year of days thereafter.

And lunch was another bowl—only with this wooden bowl you also got a wooden spoon. And this time the bowl held more hot water—only flavored in some way, a fishy smell or a grassy smell—and there were always a few bits of leaves in it—and you were glad there were.

Supper the same—the ball of dry porridge.

And those were your meals—all three—and you never got any other food.

One year!

In the morning, the feeding was "tea"—the bowl of hot salty water.

The second feeding was "soup"—the hot water flavored this time, and always a few bits of leaves on the top, and these you were glad to chew.

The third feeding, the cereal—never more than that little ball.

And there would be a fourth item, but you never knew when it would come—a bit of soggy black bread, very sour—and when you got it, it was very good.

It got so I loved that bread. I can taste it even now—and, even in memory, I want it and I love it.

Will a man get used to anything? Some will.

Many won't—and many die. When it gets bad enough, most die.

It is what I saw.

But the bread was good—very heavy and sour—and you'd always find something in it—a bit of twig or some bark. I don't know how they made that bread—but those things were always in it, something like that, something that came out of a forest.

And this is what a day was—the position, the three feedings, and then the position on the floor. A day was this—and nothing more.

And the light was always the same.

But there were four exceptions in the days that you lived—and these are what they were.

Every ten days there was the bathhouse.

Every ten days two men could leave the cell if they were willing to empty and scrub the *Parasha.*

You could get up and use the pot when you wanted.

The fourth exception was the beatings.

And these had two names—"punishment" and "interrogation."

It was the third day—night.

The door was opened sometimes during the middle of the night.

Who will be beaten? Whose hands are not both in view?

But on a word from the guard and a signal from the Elder, the sixteen of us were made to rise—and the old sick man did it too. They marched us out of there and in single file we went down the padded walkway—but Nesterov fell before we got to the stairs, and two of us had to drag him. He was happy to be dragged. You could tell. Wherever we were going, he wanted to go. So we dragged him. It never occurred to me to think he had a choice, anyway. By now I had learned that much. There were no choices.

We were marched down the stairs and through several doors and came out into the prison yard—and they walked us to a corner in that open area—and you could see when you came out into that area that there were lights on in the tiers of barred windows all around you and lots of noise coming from those windows and even men hanging their arms out and calling through the bars. It was a hot night. It was July—and it was a shock—all that noise and humanity in motion and the sense you had of a kind of ribaldry in the air.

It was monstrous, the contrast between what I had just come

from and the carnival atmosphere out there in the prison yard. I knew from the stillness behind me, from the gross quiet of the place and the two times I'd been along the walkway, that back there hundreds of men, and possibly women too, sat as we sat, in *Spets Korpus,* in the position, in silence, behind the muzzle. Whereas it was clear from what I was hearing and seeing out there in the prison yard that life was immeasurably different for the rest of the prisoners, for the thousands of men and women the other six buildings must have, in the aggregate, housed.

We stood outside a wooden structure squeezed into a corner of the yard, a ramshackle affair dwarfed by the massive red brick buildings rising all around it. We stood in a group, the men of Cell 39, two guards off to the side eyeing us. I tried to calculate the time —but there was no telling. I figured it was about three in the morning. Why were we waiting there? And what were we waiting for? I still had no way of knowing what this was all about—and it even passed through my mind that we might be going to some sort of group interrogation. But how could that be? How could you question a group of men all at once? Did that make any sense? But why try to make any of this make sense? Is craziness a logic too?

The door to the wooden structure opened, and in single file we followed the Elder inside. I had to shut my eyes, the light was so powerful—or at least it seemed to me powerful after the bleak constant light of 39. The floor of the room we were in was alive with human hair from wall to wall. It made you want to vomit, the thickness of it and the filth.

I watched the Elder for instructions, but it was the guard that came in with us who gave us the command to strip everything off. When the Elder got his clothes off, he hung them on a rack that was at the other end of the room, and I saw all the rest of the men do the same. I got out of my purple T-shirt and unknotted my trousers and, like the rest of them, I took off my tennis shoes, and all these things I put where the others had placed their clothing. When everyone had his things on that rack, a man came through the door on the other side and pulled the rack back out that door with him.

If this meant we were going to get prison clothing, that was all right with me. It would be good to get into something clean—and certainly it would be good to have the rest of the men in 39 in clean clothes too. The rags they wore were wretched—and if the *Parasha* had not been there to overwhelm it, the smell from the other men would probably have been almost as bad.

"Line up!" the guard with us called, and when we had gotten ourselves in order, a man came in through the door the rack had gone out of. He carried a large pair of clippers, and he went to the end of the line and he began.

His method was designed to give him maximum speed. Beginning with one side of the head of the first man, he cut the hair there, and then, his clipper going without being raised from the man's body, he went down one side, cutting the hair from one side of the man's face, under his arm on that side, then down over his chest on that side, across his groin, down over one leg and then up the other leg, to the chest, under the other arm, to the face, then back up to the other side of the man's head and then onto the next man, repeating the same procedure, and in this manner all sixteen of us added the hair from our bodies to the sea of hair that matted the floor, a mess of human growth of every texture and shade pressed by the men who walked there into something like a nightmare's idea of a carpet. And if you looked, you could see things crawling in it, their nesting places disturbed.

We still stood in line, all of us smaller-looking now, all of us revealed to an extreme beyond nakedness, the terrific light overhead a white-hot poker that probed you and poked you all over. You had stinging places all over you too—from where the clipper had cut you or from where the barber had lost patience with the dull work and had yanked the hair out.

Two of us had to hold Nesterov up the whole time, and even in the July heat and that light overhead, the old man was shivering. On the order to march forward, we dragged him with us into the bathhouse. You got to it through the other door, and I could see another group leaving just as we entered the place—and in time I found out that's how it worked, all the political prisoners in *Spets Korpus* run through the hair-cutting and the showering at night, each cell every ten days.

In the bathhouse Nesterov just got down on the floor. He found a place under one of the spouts and just lay down there in his characteristic curl, his legs drawn up and his elbows wedged in against his stomach.

There were spouts set into the ceiling, and you stood under one of them waiting for the water to come. The guard left you and closed the door behind him, and you stood there waiting, and when the streams of water came they were either one way or the other, a bolt of ice or a scalding flame.

There were about twenty spouts sticking out from the ceiling, and under them the men were leaden in their movements, no matter what the water was like or how it suddenly changed from one impossible temperature to another. They stood under the slamming water and rubbed themselves, and even Nesterov was making little rubbing movements, one leg against the other and the same way with his arms—like an insect.

"No," the Elder said when he saw me opening my mouth to catch the water from the spout I was under. "Don't," he said, and it was startling to hear someone's voice, a man other than a guard. But I had heard Sergeyvsky before—when he had stood at the pot and whispered the rules.

Did the rules not hold anymore? Could you speak here, here in the bathhouse?

"The water is not safe," he said, and I said, "All right," and I nearly jumped at the sound of my own voice. How long had it been since I had heard myself speak?

"We can talk here?" I said.

The Elder nodded—but held his finger to his lips.

"Then why aren't the rest of them talking?" I said.

"What is there to talk about?" the Elder said.

I looked at the man. Was he serious?

"You are the flyer," he said. "You are Victor Herman."

I nodded my head yes. "I am an American," I said. "I don't belong in here. They made a mistake. What are you doing in here—and the rest?"

"My father is in the church," the Elder said, "so I am a spy. Those two there, they are wreckers—they blew up the Gorky bridge. Twenty-five years for that, for each of them—and that one over there, also twenty-five years—another spy. You, Victor Herman," the Elder said, winking at me, "you are a spy?"

"Are you crazy?" I said. "I am an American. And those men didn't blow up the Gorky bridge—because I drove across it just a little while ago—and those two were here when I got here!"

The Elder raised his finger to his lips again. "Softly, please," he said. "You are a spy, Victor Herman—and those men, they are engineers and they built that bridge and they blew it up a year ago. They are wreckers and their sentence is twenty-five years. The others I don't know about—but I know about you, Victor Herman."

"How?" I said. "How do you know anything about me?"

"I know your name, yes? But of course everybody in Gorky knows your name and what you look like. You are the Lindbergh of Russia, Victor Herman—a famous man and a spy."

But then Sergeyvsky laughed, very softly, and I tried to laugh too—but I couldn't.

"How old are you, Victor Herman?" he said, now rubbing himself again, the water steaming off him.

"Twenty-three," I said.

The Elder said nothing in reply—and his question and then his silence left me feeling a kind of sentence had been pronounced. It was ominous, what he had asked and his silence when I had answered.

"Is there soap?" I asked, to throw off the feeling that had settled on me. But I knew there wasn't any soap, and the Elder did not bother to reply.

Soap? What a question!

The water was shut off, and the guard came back in, and this time he was accompanied by the other guard who'd been with us when they'd marched us out and then down the stairs and across the yard. We went into another shed, going out a door across from the one we'd entered by, and as we stood inside that place the rack was wheeled back in and our clothing was on it. But none of the men was going for his clothing. They stood there, waiting—and I did not know why until one of the guards shouted, "Dress!" and all the men went to do it, and I did too.

If the water was hot, it was nothing compared to the scorch you got when you got back into your things. But you did it, no matter how hot they were, and though the rubber on your tennis shoes had been baked sticky and was flame to the touch, you got into them, you got into everything that was yours, Nesterov too, and we had to help him to do it, and he screamed as the clothes went on him.

This was the work of *Zharo Kamera,* the toaster—meant to kill the lice and the crabs and the vermin that flourished on our bodies and in the things that had been on them, and I eventually learned that our cell got the same kind of treatment in our absence, the walls and floor and boards dowsed with carbolic acid from top to bottom. Not that this ever got the smell of vomit off the boards or ridded them of the stains of blood that gave them all the pattern of maps.

As for the tiny parasites that fed on the sixteen men that were the human population of 39, by morning they were among us again and thriving. The hardiness of these creatures is nothing less than wondrous, and it is no less remarkable the great number and variety of verminous life that will all find a little something to satisfy them somewhere on the flesh of one man. You would sometimes wonder where all these things came from—and it sometimes seemed that they came from nowhere else but inside you, that it was you who had given birth to the tiny cannibal horde that fed on you openly as you sat helplessly in the position.

We were marched back in the same fashion we had come, another group waiting at the door to the barber's shed as we started back through the yard, and probably a third group inside that shed and a fourth under the spouts now.

Even before the door was locked on us again, most of the others seemed already asleep in their positions on the floor. I could hear Nesterov groaning a little from his position next to Sergeyvsky, but then he was quiet and only snored, the distinctive wheezing sound that told you it was him.

It was my third night in 39. The other two, I'd lain sleepless until the morning bell, still tormented, when it rang, by all the questions that had come welling up in me during the long, terrifying nights. Nothing I wanted to know had been answered, and it was gradually being disclosed to me that maybe nothing ever would.

I slept that third night. I slept the little time remaining between our return from the bathhouse and the crack of the morning bell. I know I slept—because the man next to me had to wake me to turn me the one time left—and then I was waked a second time, and it was the first time I waked to the bell, a sustained shrilling, a sound gone mad.

The bell was just a short burst. But for minutes and minutes it renewed itself inside your head. It was like a nail introduced into your ear in three distinct stages, each accomplished by a smart blow with a hammer—one, two, three—until a shaft had been opened all the way through to your brain—and then the hammer was turned and the claw was used to grip the nail and draw it out.

TWENTY-EIGHT ————————————————————————

I had been right about what you learn to hear. It proved true—
that in the long silence the ear becomes a thousand of its kind, so
that you could hear the dragging a long way off now and knew it
was the kettle coming with your water or your soup or your cereal.
And you could hear the stirring of men, men far away, moving,
urged forward by expectation—and you could hear the beatings far
away too—and knew how long they lasted and to what extent they
were cruel.

And then you heard the tapping—from what sometimes
seemed close by or sometimes seemed a long way off, a kind of
cadence always, and so you reasoned that it was not some random
thing moving through the walls but that it had a purpose, that it
was in fact a code.

But I did not get a chance to ask about it until the second time
in the bathhouse, and when I did, that is what the Elder said, that
it was a code.

"Do you know it?" I said. "Do you know how it works?"

"No," Sergeyvsky said. "I only know it is called the tap language. But it is useless to us—we have nothing to tap with. Every
spoon is counted. What else is there? In any case, we do not know
what it means."

"We could tap with this." I said, showing him a piece of soap
about as big as my thumb.

"How did you get that?" the Elder said.

"There," I said. "From over there in the corner."

"How tap with soap?" he said. "Soap is too soft."

"This piece?" I said. "Not this piece. This piece is too hard to
melt anymore. It's like stone. That's why it was over there."

"It is no use," the Elder said. "You do not know the code—
and if they caught you with the soap or heard you tapping, it would
be no food for any of us and maybe shooting for you. Besides, there
is nothing to say," he said.

"There is always something to say," I said. "That's what a man
does—he talks—he finds something to say, no matter what."

The Elder turned away from me as he had done that time before—when I had answered "twenty-three" and he had just smiled very slightly and gone back to rubbing listlessly at himself in the hot water, and then the water had gone abruptly cold, but he had not reacted at all.

I put the soap between my buttocks, and it was in this fashion that I got it back to the cell. I kept the soap there all that night, and in the morning I took it out and put it under my arm. I kept the soap in just this manner throughout the year I spent in 39, holding it between my buttocks when, every ten days, the night came that we were taken to the bathhouse. It was only when I went to interrogation that I had to pass off the piece of soap to someone else. But only Sergeyvsky would take it from me, only he had the courage to do it—and when he died, the Elder who replaced him, he too would hold the soap when I could not.

But what good was the soap until you knew the code, until you could understand the tap language and use it to speak back?

It was in the fifth week that I began to figure it out.

By the fourth day I was resigned—at least insofar as I gave up thinking about some sort of immediate release. I believed release would presently come, but I gave up expecting it to happen the very next hour, or the one after that. The hours became days and the days became nights, and you went from the sitting position to the reclining position, and the days and nights were in due course weeks—and you knew what your life was, the feedings and the two positions and, for some of the time, blessed sleep.

No man left 39—none was called out for questioning or for trial—and when I left—I left with the rest of them, for the trip to the barber and the bathhouse and then back again, and the weeks became months, the incessant light sometimes making you crazily think you had been imagining it all and that all this time was one long, long day. You moved not at all, except when you changed from the position on the bench to the position on the floor, and, every ten days, when you went to the bathhouse. No, there was one other time you got to move.

The pot.

You had to be blind with pain to do it the first time, to get up with the thundering in your bladder and your bowels suddenly uncontainable, to get yourself over there bent in the crouch the pressure forced you into, and to reach out your hand and take off that lid. But I did it that first time and held that lid away from me toward the door, and with my right hand I unknotted my trousers and let them fall, and when they wouldn't go far enough, I pushed them down. You had to use a sort of half-squat to get over the pot because you could not touch the rim. You did not want to let it touch you, but you would not anyway—because it was sharp and the metal was ragged and could rip snags in your skin.

It wasn't so bad, having to do that in front of the other men. It was the same for them, and it wasn't so bad—and no one really saw you—for their eyes stayed fastened on the peephole, staring there, unseeing, really. Like you when you were sitting in the position, the others were asleep behind their eyes. And if you kept your wits about you and had very good control, you remembered not to look down—because you did not want to see into the pot.

And after the first time, it was easier—like all the enormities that made up your life in 39—after the first time they were all easier. It happened. The feeling began to drain out of you.

Like them, you lived as if dead. Until if it had not been for the tap language to snatch you back to the sphere of thought, you would have, like them, let go of your mind and let it drift to a region somewhere to the side of you.

Every day, through all the hours of sitting, I strained to hear the tap language, the bits of it that I could. It was mainly near feeding times that you heard it—at first when the feeders themselves were being opened and then during the slight bustle of meals.

I listened to catch a length of it—and this I would memorize to hold for later study. It was easy to do—there was nothing else to crowd the cadence of the tapping out of your mind. You heard a phrase or two, and it was easy to hold it in your head—and go over it and over it in search of the key. How difficult could it be? It had to be something relatively easy—and I knew it wasn't Morse code —because that was something I had learned back in Detroit from listening to an adventure program on the radio, and I knew it wasn't that.

I had nothing but time to figure it out, and in time I did.

How ironic that what I decoded that very first time turned out to be a message about the tap language itself. It was the same message repeated all day—and it said: *101 tapping. Punishment tapping ten days isolator.*

But what was an "isolator"?

I didn't know. Whatever it was, it would be bad. But exactly what it was I did not know.

But now I knew the tap language!

And I tapped back *Understand*. And it was wonderful to do it —to know that in this way you could talk—that you could hear someone say something and say something back in return. It was, I think, what saved me from insanity that year in Cell 39—decoding and encoding tap messages—so that I had something else inside my mind except the two positions and the three feedings and the awful thoughts that came in the night. It was a way to escape myself and to extend myself beyond the dread volume of space I inhabited. It was how I moved myself out into the world and brought the world to me—and in the doing of this I kept a part of myself alive, the part that is mind, the part that is voice, the part of you that you think is irreducible but which can be made to disappear.

As for the tap language, it worked in accord with the alphabet —the Russian alphabet containing thirty-six letters, but the six least used ones are discarded, leaving thirty. Of these thirty letters, you form six groups of five letters each. The first tap gives the group. A pause. The second tap gives the letter's place in that group. Hence, tap, tap—pause—means second group of letters—followed by tap, tap, tap—pause—the third letter in that group. Tap, tap, tap, tap—pause—*fourth* group of letters. Tap—pause—*first* letter in that group.

But it was nowhere so cumbersome as it sounds set out here. On the contrary, after a time you executed a message with considerable speed, just as you decoded those whose tapping you listened for. It was a good system—you could cover a lot of ground with it and at a pretty good clip—and when you had nothing else to do all day, it was easy to pick up skill, to get very fast with it, both the encoding and the decoding.

And that was the first message I decoded—*101 tapping. Punishment tapping ten days isolator.*

And I had answered *Understand*—and then, when the message came the next time, I knew better, and answered *39. Understand.*

But about a month later the tap language was improved— and it took a long time before everyone understood. It was this, the improvement—the message would come, and at the end of it the tapper would add a fast burst of taps, exactly five of them— and that meant *Did you understand?*—and if you did, you would do the same thing back, a burst of five fast taps. But if you didn't, you would rub whatever you were using to tap with, you'd rub it back and forth across the wall, also five times, and then he'd repeat the message if he could.

Punishment tapping ten days isolator.

I was never caught tapping. But I found out what the isolator was.

I had to go there to find out.

It would have been worse had I been caught tapping—because then the others would have suffered too. I knew that they mostly did not want me to tap. It wasn't for them that I was doing it. It was as the Elder had said. So far as they were concerned, what was there to say? They had no interest in it one way or the other—and if it happened that I was caught, then they too would pay—and they knew it.

Among the fifteen men who shared 39 with me, it was only the first Elder and then the second who had any interest in what the messages that came to me were—and in the bathhouse, if they asked me, I would tell them. But it was not a great interest of theirs —and the messages were chiefly not worth passing along.

20. Man called out.
85. Man yesterday shot.
21. Man beaten.
21. Man sick.
74. Interrogator named Resnick.
99. Is Resnick bad?
74. Yes.
58. Light went out.
108. Elder says stop.
28. Man called out.
39. Man died. Nesterov.
38. Understood.
38. Man died. Nesterov.
37. Understood.
37. Man died. Nesterov.
30. Understood.

And it was thus that a message of no great importance was passed from cell to cell. A man was dead. His name? What did it matter? But it went, that name, melodically, from cell to cell, as if in it there reposed a most excellent music, *Nesterov,* until all the tappers in *Spets Korpus,* and anyone they chose to tell, knew.

You got better and better at the tap language, until you hardly felt handicapped at all—and after a month or so at it, every time you tapped you thought you heard your voice doing it and not the piece of soap you used against the wall. It was the same way with what you heard—they were not taps any longer, they were the voices of men speaking—and you could hear every nuance in their speech, every hint of character that distinguished one speaker from another. And it got so that you did not need to hear a message completed, because you knew what the tapper in 38 was going to say before he finished, and he knew the same thing about you. And you tried very hard never to scrape a *no* in reply to the burst of five that came at the end—because that would threaten to wear out your soap. You tried very hard to understand—and in time it wasn't at all difficult to do, sitting in the position, risking one hand behind you, reaching back there to the wall. *Ten days in the isolator.* And what was the isolator? But I sat at the end of my bench, my right arm toward the far wall, toward the wall away from the peephole. So the danger was less that way—and I was never caught.

But in time I went to the isolator, anyway.

But before that I went to interrogation.

And before that, Nesterov died, and for the little it was worth, everyone in *Spets Korpus* knew.

The trips to the bathhouse were how you learned certain things—how I learned, for example, that the toilet for our floor was in the corner at the end of the walkway on our side, that the toilet came right after 39.

It was a good place to be, Cell 39—because you could pick up a lot of messages from men that did their tapping in the toilet. It was the safest place to do it—to tap. It always took two men to drag a cell's *Parasha* to the toilet and two men to dump it out, but while one man was washing the pot, the other man could tap, the tapping not so noticeable because of the washing and the water. So I learned that Cell 39 was a good place to get messages—and that we were probably getting the bulk of them on our floor.

You always found out a little something new every time you went to get your hair cut off and your body dowsed and the vermin

baked out of your clothing. But it was always bad coming back—
bad that you had to come back at all—and worse because the
stench of the *Parasha* had to be gotten used to all over again and
because you had to watch out until the puddles of carbolic acid
dried up.

And it was also bad going out into the open air—after ten
days and ten nights in the air you inhabited, the little air that could
fit between the bodies of all those men in a space ten by five and a
half by eight. The air we lived with went from one man's lungs to
another's, and it always had *him* in it, and the gas from his bowels,
and the sweat from his skin, and what he belched went into it, and
what the *Parasha* gave it, that was in it too, and from under his
arms and from his stinking crotch, and from the carbolic acid, all
of this made its contribution, and also the vomit and the blood and
the filthy things that crawled everywhere, and this was the air you
breathed—and if you didn't, you died. So that when they called you
in the middle of the night, and you went out there—it was at first
not so bad so long as you were on the walkway and still inside.
But when you got outside and into the night air, it was as if whiskey
or dope was doing its work on you, and you got dizzy and nearly
passed out. And like whiskey or dope, it made you actually sick,
that night air—actually sick to your stomach—and it was madness
—because you started gasping for the foul gas you'd been living in.
You were like a thing from underground that had to breathe grit.

That's what Cell 39 could do to you—it could make you so
used to what it was that life outside it seemed electrified and fatal.

In summer there was always a mist on the walls of 39. It is
something I just remembered, that mist. A curious thing, even
though it was caused naturally enough—by the moisture our bodies
gave off and the heat that came from the radiator under one of the
benches.

It is what you would expect, that radiator—heat in the
summer and none when the months went from autumn to winter.
But the mist was with us until September, late in September, and it
was back again in late April. I know it gave me a very strange feeling to see it, that wet haze that lay all along the dark gray walls.
I suppose it's the same feeling you get in a steambath or in a
steamy bathroom when the hot vapor condenses on the cool tiles
and the mirror. Everyone's seen that—and I think most of us have
felt what I am talking about.

It's just a strange feeling. I cannot describe it. It is almost as if you are floating, as if your body has become vaporous too.

I had that feeling in Cell 39. Until the autumn came and the radiator shut off, and it got very, very cold.

TWENTY-NINE _____

Nesterov died after the bathhouse. A month later Sergeyvsky died too—in the first case, death came from some kind of choking, and in the second the man just fell over and there was blood running out of his ears.

It was onto the lid of the pot that the Elder fell forward from the position and the blood from his ears streamed along the disc of wood and then spilled into the *Parasha* below.

I tapped it out. And perhaps the message went from cell to cell.

Maybe it was what my mother had—a stroke, a bleeding in the brain.

But between the time that Nesterov died and the time that Sergeyvsky followed him to the grave, I was called.

They called me out—for interrogation.

"G!" came the shout from the guard through the feeder. "Get ready!"

It must have been about midnight—about two hours after the second bell.

I got up and went to the door. I got up and stepped between the men lying there and positioned myself at the door. And it is extraordinary what happened to me, how I quite suddenly changed inside. I could feel myself trembling all over—but it was not from fear. It was rage—it was anger that was going through me, and eagerness—and as I stood there waiting for the door to jerk open, I began to feel incredibly renewed—an energy waiting to get loose. I could scarcely contain myself—and I began to rehearse all the things I would say, the wrath I would explode with when I finally confronted my captors. My arms and legs were actually buzzing with the fever that was building in me. The shout through the feeder was "Get ready!" and that's what I was, the heat in me terrific. I could feel it in my face, the skin on my face and my neck warm with it, actually itching. There's no other way to say it—I was *seething*. I stood there burning up with rage. And *still* I waited and the door didn't open—and I thought that maybe I should call out, "Herman is ready! I'm ready!" But I didn't do it.

I just stood there—and when the door was finally opened, thrown back with that powerful abrupt movement that seemed routine to me now, I took a hard look at the guard and stepped forward and then all the way out of Cell 39, feeling myself utterly restored to the man I had been the day I had entered that small hell behind me.

I stood on the padding in the walkway and waited with rising indignation while the guard heaved the door closed and worked his gargantuan key in it.

"What time is it?" I asked.

"No noise!" he wheeled on me and shrieked it and then flipped the key back and forth in my face. "Head down, prisoner—hands behind back, no noise!"

I did as I was told and when my head was down, he pushed me along the walkway, and I moved ahead with him following.

"Down," he said, and I took the stairs fast, my legs pumping even though my arms were behind me. I felt great—angry and great! I thought about crazy things—about taking on the Goldmann boys and their cousins, about taking on all four of them at once—and I thought about that first time shooting, there in the small stadium behind the American Village. My * , how long ago that seemed to me now! But I kept thinking about it—how all those men and boys stared, how I put five in a row dead center, how amazed I was to have done a thing like that, and then the commander or whatever that Army man was, his getting up out of his squat and coming over—and that night, in the eating hall, and the little dark green box.

And then I thought of my father, his wooden spoon gripped in his hand, standing there by his place and looking up at the other man, and looking small and inconsiderable to me—and I thought about how I'd felt shame then—such a queer confusion of pride and shame—and how I'd even thought for an instant that maybe I shouldn't take the medal, that if I did not take the medal, it might in some way enlarge my father, make it okay that he was standing there with a wooden spoon in one hand and his other hand sort of reaching for the table, not really knowing what to do with either hand, and half-turned to the man in uniform and half-turned to me.

Why was that in my head now? And I couldn't get rid of it, couldn't get that picture of my dad and the other man, the way they looked standing there, I couldn't get it out of my head. There were other things to think about—what I was walking toward, what I'd see when I got there, what I was going to say. What *was* I going to say? And maybe I wasn't going to be seeing anybody to say something to. Maybe they were just taking me outside for something. Maybe they were . . . and the thought went through me like a pile driver: *They are going to shoot me!*

"Where are we going?" I said, and I turned when I said it to make sure he heard me—and he just smiled in reply, and I could see how he had dog teeth and one of them was rotted.

We were on the first floor now, and since he gave me no directions, I kept to the same route that I was used to, the one that led out into the yard and the bathhouse. He let me go. He didn't stop me—and then I realized what a mistake I'd made—*don't go outside* —whatever it is, it would be better to stay inside!

But we were in the yard now, and there was a van there, just like the one that had brought me here, and I started heading toward it, and still the guard let me go.

"Up!" he said when I was within ten feet of the van.

I got in—and when I was struggling to make it up with my hands still behind me, the guard shoved me from behind.

He pulled up after me—and I could hear him breathing hard. There was another guard in there, but he seemed to be paying no attention to us. The first guard turned me, he turned me to the only locker door that was open. Were all the others occupied? Were people already in there? "In!" he said, and when he said it, the other guard was right behind him and together they pushed me down and in.

They pushed me so that my face was rammed against the metal in front of me and away from the vents in the locker door. I was stuck like that. I couldn't move—and one of my arms was taking too much of my weight. But then the van bounced—I guessed it was the first guard jumping off—and the rear doors banged closed —and immediately the van pulled ahead—and the motion tilted me in a way that I could move a little better and at least relieve the strain on my arm. But there was no reversing my position in the locker, and even though I knew I had air enough, it made me uneasy to be turned away from the vents.

I tried to concentrate on interpreting the features of the drive —listening and feeling for hints—and it wasn't hard to do—because everything matched another set of things remembered, only this time it was all going backwards, and we were going down the steep hill instead of up it—and I knew that when we stopped and the door opened and they got me out, it would be in the courtyard behind the building on Vorobevka Street.

I was going there! Was it to receive an apology? Was that it— they would make their excuses and release me directly from there, from NKVD headquarters in Gorky? Was that their jurisdiction, this business, this mess that had been made? But why at this hour of the night? Why, if you wanted to make amends, would you take a man out in the middle of the night and stuff him into a locker to get him where he would receive your apology?

We stopped. But my door did not open. I heard another locker rattling and a man getting out. I could hear him fall down as he walked through the aisle toward the rear of the van. And the van doors opened and then they closed. In a little while, another locker opened—and it was the same thing, the van doors opening and then closing again. There was an interval of about five minutes between each of these exits—and I quickly multiplied five times thirteen— to get an idea of how long I was going to have to wait. If I was the last man in, then I would be the last man out—and if all sixteen lockers had been filled, then it followed that I'd have to wait over an hour to get out.

I settled back into a slump to wait. My arm hurt again and my nose and lips were flush against the back wall of the locker. It was very cold.

But there was motion right behind me and then I heard the door move and felt myself being pulled back by the shoulders. I backed out and stood in the aisle, and, with my arms behind my back, I tried to rotate my shoulders to loosen the stiffness in my neck.

"Head down, hands behind back, no talking." It was a new guard. I followed him to the rear of the van, and when the doors flew open, I jumped down. I was pleased with the way I did that, pleased that my legs held and that I didn't go over onto the pavement. I could see the cobblestones, but not the building, not where we were going. I could see a guard's boots ahead of me and I could see the cobblestones, and I followed the backs of his boots. But I didn't have to see the white building to know. These were the same cobblestones.

I could see we were getting to a doorway. The guard in front of me said, "Stop!" Another guard's boots came into my field of vision—and I heard "178," and then my elbow was taken by the new guard—and I followed him inside. We went all the way to the end of a corridor on the first floor and then we climbed a flight of wooden stairs and came out into a hallway, and I followed him all the way to the end of that hallway on the second floor to another flight of stairs. We climbed these to the third floor and again came out into a hallway and started along it toward the other end, but this time the guard in front of me paused at each doorway on the right side, a pause of several seconds for each doorway. At last we were at the end of the hallway on the third floor, and again we climbed a flight of wooden stairs, and it was the same on this floor, always that pause at each door on the right side, until we came to one and stayed there.

I stood waiting. I raised my head a little. There was a whitewashed stencil on the door—it gave the numerals *178*.

I waited.

I heard an unbelievable scream. It was the first time I had heard anything like it. It was the kind of scream you imagine a woman makes in childbirth. It was a scream like that, not hysterical, but more a stupendous howl of exquisite agony with relief mixed into it.

I looked up. The guard said, "Head down."

I waited. I tried to decide where that scream had come from. What had made it—a man or a woman? It was that kind of scream —beyond gender—but a perfectly human sound. In fact, I remember thinking that it was the most human sound I had ever heard— what I mean is that it seemed to suggest a declaration of something at the very bottom of what it feels like to be human. That's all I can say about it—that sound.

It was remarkable. It was truly unbelievable, and I have never heard anything like it since. Even though I came to see men and women in states of appalling torment, I was never again to hear anything like this—that one transfigured scream—and on either side of it silence, a perfect silence.

No, I must correct that. There was a time when I heard something even worse. But it did not come out of a man or a woman. It came out of a girl—and it was not a solitary perfection of the sort I am trying to tell you about. It was worse and it was different—and there were many of them, those sounds that girl made. They went on for a long time.

The door in front of me opened, and I heard the guard say, "Prisoner Herman." And then: "Do you need me?"

The voice that answered was not like the other voices I had been hearing. It wasn't loud and it had nothing brusque in it. It was a high voice, very pinched, very like the voice of an adolescent boy —or the kind of voice a woman will sometimes have if she has a great deal of man in her—it was a voice like that, hoarse, damp, as if the throat needed clearing, a breathy, wet contralto.

The voice said, "No," and the guard pushed me forward— and I entered that room and when I made those three or four steps forward it was like stepping onto a wing and taking a mouthful of the rushing air, getting a good mouthful inside me, and then pushing, pushing myself out from what held me up, and jumping, going out there into whatever would catch me, and it's the air itself that does it, it's the air itself that embraces you, and you let go and go limp and career through it all the way down, deadfall.

I looked up when the door closed behind me. I had already seen the highly polished boots—and I could tell from the size of them and the legs that went into them that he was big. But I was not ready for how big he was. He was about the height of Sergeyvsky, but broad—heavy thighs, and a very wide waist, and very meaty in the chest and shoulders.

He wore the brown woolen trousers of his uniform, and they were tucked into the tops of his boots and the material was pulled very tight. His jacket was off, and even though it was cold in the room, his sleeves were rolled up past his elbows. His arms were hairless, and the skin was white, the meat in them dense. That's what they looked like, his arms, as if they had a kind of ponderous weight.

He turned away from me before I could see his face. He was striding now, walking to the desk that stood in front of the wall opposite. There was a window behind the desk, and a chair. And there were chairs on either side of the desk, like the chairs I'd seen in schools back in Detroit. In fact the chairs on either side of his desk were exactly the same kind of chairs I'd seen in the principal's office at Cass Technical High—and certain teachers had them too, the very same kind of chair.

He went to the window and looked out. It was dark out there. What was he looking at?

Then he turned and took up a position behind his chair, his arms supporting his weight as he hunched forward on it. It was no problem seeing his face from where I stood just inside the door. The light was strong in the room—and from where I was I could see his lips weren't right. When you got a better look, you could see that it was really the lower one that was off, the skin sort of scrambled and puffed out and lopsided, as if a razor had sliced straight down and the ends of the separated flesh had been yanked together, one over the other, and then sewn up. In the light from the little lamp that sat on his desk, his whole face looked disorganized because of that lower lip. But when he pushed himself erect and stepped around and into the light that came from overhead, I could see that his face was otherwise very ordinary. It was just the lip that wasn't at all right, and the place where it was pleated was very red. It looked raw—and it glistened in the light.

He still had not spoken. He just studied me, his face without expression. He had his arms folded, and he just stood there looking me up and down. He seemed two, three times my size, his total bulk. I stand about five-eight. This man was more like six-three— and I guessed his weight was well over 200, solid. I tried to recollect my weight when I'd last gotten on the scales at *Spartak*. I used to weigh myself there every morning I trained—and sometimes when I got finished in the afternoon I'd do it again. But I was always the same—a little over or a little under 135.

What did I weigh after the meager diet of Cell 39? I had no way of knowing. I could only tell how much I'd lost by the longer and longer tails to the two ends of my waistband that I knotted to keep my trousers up. I was suddenly aware of my clothes. It was as if I had actually forgotten what I'd had on all these weeks since July 20th. Somewhere back there in those weeks I'd begun to lose sight of a kind of catalog I suppose we all keep on ourselves, a kind of everyday accounting—what you wear, what you eat, how you feel, a list of how and what, a whole array of routine things that you're more or less not mindful of during the course of a day and yet they constitute the index to that day.

I wore what I'd been arrested in—except I had no belt in the loopholes of my trousers and no laces in my tennis shoes. And my fly was open—the buttons there had been cut off—and I could only hide myself by overlapping the ends of my pants when I tied the knot to keep them up.

Still he did not speak. And I began to think, well, it is a contest again—who can keep silent longer? And then I thought, * , now is the time to speak up! Now is my chance to set things straight! I began to think what my first statement should be —and although I was not entirely satisfied with it, I thought I had a clever one. It would leap us ahead in whatever exchange was coming up. I was going to say, "I demand to know who's told lies about me!" I was going to say that—and I was holding it in me a while longer to give it further consideration for just an instant more, to make sure it wasn't something that would trip me up, to make sure it was precisely the best statement to open with. But before I could get it out, the man spoke. It was that same curious voice—a notably unpleasant voice. Not the attitude that underlay it —that was not what was so unpleasant. It was instead that the voice did not go with the man that had it. And when you heard it, you wanted to clear your throat—or say something to the man about it, perhaps suggest to him that he cough out the phlegm that was making him sound like that.

He said, "I am Belov." Just that one statement, and then he made a half smile, and it resulted in something hideous, because you could see his lower lip wouldn't stretch enough, and his effort to smile aggravated the distortion you saw in his face.

It is astonishing what one will say in certain situations. Later on, you're amazed at what comes out of you. You say something that has nothing to do with the things you've been getting ready to say. It is not that you don't say the *right* things—because that's the point. In a kind of way, what you say is *exactly* right—too right— as though one were reading from a chart where it had all been worked out in advance.

I said, "Good evening, Comrade Belov."

And I stood there waiting. When he said nothing more, I turned slightly, one way and then the other, and gazed at the room. It was just a whitewashed room, nothing at all on the walls—across from me the desk and the three chairs, perfectly balanced, and be-hind, the one window. Did it give out onto Vorobevka Street? Onto the courtyard in the rear? Or was it a side window?

I thought to go to it—to do something to break the crazy silence and waiting. If the window showed Vorobevka Street below, then I might see people out there, even at this hour, and that would be pleasant, it would be wonderful. Would I recognize some-one? It is true, I was four stories up, but even so I might see some-one familiar to me. After all, this was Gorky—I'd lived in this region for over seven years—and wasn't there a *Dynamo* gymnasium nearby? I might see someone I knew even at this hour. Were there streetlights out there?

I started to make a move toward the window and then I stopped myself and acted as if I had just been shifting my weight—and, when I did that, the corner to my left and behind me came into view.

It was not whitewashed, like the rest of the walls. The rest of the walls glowed white, empty of everything and white. But the corner to the rear and to my left, it was painted dark blue—an area about four feet out into either wall and about seven feet high was painted a very dark shiny blue, and I could see from the flash where I was that it was an enamel. It was so shiny that it looked like an enormous right-angled tile had been pushed across the floor and leaned into the corner.

I looked away from this as if I had seen nothing of note. I studied the window again. It was barred. What harm, then, if I walked over to it and had a look outside?

But I stayed where I was.

I just kept looking at the window across the way and waiting for the man to say something else. It was the usual kind of window you saw in big Russian buildings in those days, doubled, to protect against the cold, the exterior glass opening out and the interior glass opening in—and between them there were bars.

Was he never going to talk again? Was this perhaps how it worked? An interrogation? Or whatever this was? You just stood a while together, not speaking, and then it was over with? Could it be that he was judging me in some kind of subtle way? Could that be it? That this is how they made up their minds about you—they put you into a room with a man and he looked you over closely and then he went out and told them what he thought?

And then my mind started turning against me—and I could feel myself losing control. I began to think that perhaps he had already spoken a great number of sentences—and that I simply had not been paying close enough attention. It startled me, this thought. Was it possible? Had the man—what was his name?—had he already asked me dozens of questions, already given me every opportunity to clear myself, to get myself out of this, and I had not heard, had instead been looking out the window or at some blue design in the corner?

Had I already missed it all? And failed some kind of test? Could this have happened to me—had my mind done this to me? Had those weeks and months in 39 driven me insane? Made me deaf? Delivered me into some kind of waking trance?

What had he said? He'd given his name!

It was . . . Belov!

I swallowed with relief.

Belov! He said—*I am Belov.*

Who talks like that?

What a queer way to talk.

And, that's right, I had *answered*—I had said. I had said . . .

I had said something stupid, something dull.

I had said—it was amazing—how long ago?

I had said: *Good evening, Comrade Belov.*

I waited.

I tried not to look at his face, at his lip.

Was that it? They stood you here and the test was to see if you could *look* at his lip? Or *not* look at it?

I couldn't decide. It seemed to me that perhaps this made sense—it had to be one or the other. But I could not decide which you were expected to prove.

I tried to look at his desk—to see if there was anything on it. I couldn't tell.

And then I looked at his face. If that's what they wanted, I would do it—and it was then that I noticed something else. The man was slightly drunk. I could see it there in his face and the way he was looking at me. It's something that if you're not a drinker you get used to spotting in people—and I could spot it in this Belov. The man was slightly, or maybe more than slightly, drunk.

Perhaps this accounted for the man's silence. Perhaps he was drunker than I surmised. Perhaps he was asleep on his feet.

And then he spoke again.

"I am your interrogator."

And that was all he said. I waited for more—but nothing came. I repeated the phrase in my head, tried to say it the same way he'd said it, figuring I could make up my mind about how drunk he was.

It was the ensuing silence and my distraction perhaps that led me into saying the second crazy thing I said. But what was I to say?

I said, "Thank you for telling me that."

I had to say something—and what should I have said? I am Victor Herman? I am an American? Did he not know these things? Was it not better to be extremely formal, extremely civil? To let the statements follow some sort of ceremonial pattern that only this man could guide us through?

He dropped his arms from where they were folded in front of him and took a step closer to me, moving his hands behind his back as he came. He stood about three or four feet from me now— and the deformation of his lower lip seemed to glare in the light, it was that inflamed even though you could see it was something that had happened to him long ago.

I couldn't take my eyes off it now. He blocked my view to the window across the way and there was nowhere else to fix my eyes. I could have looked down to his chest—but wouldn't that have appeared guilty or servile? Wasn't this the test to establish my innocence? Wasn't the imperative thing that my bearing, my least gesture, my every move all convey the testimony of a man who is without the slightest guilt? I should look this Belov right in the eye! But when I tried to do it, that twist of flesh drew my attention as if it were a wound I myself had inflicted—and it was impossible! It would be a wretched mistake to gape at that tortured lip—yet I could not take my eyes from it. So I stared—knowing as I did it that this was a critical misstep, that clearly the man must be sensitive about such a thing, such an ugliness to have on a face. Who could not be uneasy over such a thing, even if he were born with it? No man could ever get himself indifferent to a malformation like that!

The lip moved! He was saying something.

In that womanish voice, very breathy and very hoarse, this Belov said, "You will tell me about your counterrevolutionary activities. I will hear every one."

What?

Could this be what the man had said?

Could I trust my hearing anymore?

But that is what he said, and I for the third time said the wrong thing. To begin with, I hesitated. It was in my mind to show the man that I was giving his question serious study, that I was a prudent fellow, that he could rely on me, that I would of course weigh my words for gravity and precision before speaking—when I simply should have laughed in the man's face.

At last, and with great composure, I think, I said, "No, I have done nothing counterrevolutionary. I am, of course, an American —and this is not my revolution. I have nothing to do with it, one way or the other. But you have my word on it, in any case. Really, I have done nothing counterrevolutionary. I don't think in such terms, really. I am not a political person, you see. Perhaps you don't know, but I'm a sportsman. I'm not at all interested in politics, one way or the other, I promise you."

All through this speech, I kept trying to stop myself. The first sentence would have been enough. Certainly by the finish of the second sentence, I'd said all that needed saying. But the words simply carried me forward—into what seemed to me further qualifications that were necessary. And then I could see that he wasn't listening to anything I was saying, and that made it all worse, just added to my uneasiness with what I'd already said and urged me on into the next sentence and the next, trying to work myself up into a sentence that would compel his attention to what I was saying, and anyway, it was so good to be saying *anything,* to be talking at all.

But it would have all come out the same, in any event—no purity of language or impression of candor would have improved my claim in the slightest. Nor would indignation have helped me, the anger I had so pleasurably held in store.

In time I was to learn that only guilt would help me—and it's no good learning that when you're innocent.

"Turn around," Belov said.

I did it immediately.

"Walk into that corner there, the blue one."

I took a few steps forward and stopped.

"Keep going!"

I started up again, slowly now.

"Stand two feet from the corner!"

I reached what I took to be two feet from the corner and stopped.

"Face the corner."

I stood there. It crossed my mind that something like this must have happened to me in grade school. It had happened to all the boys at one time or another, so it must have happened to me at least once—but I could not remember. Didn't they put a dunce's cap on your head—or something like that?

I stood there. I could tell he had not moved.

All right, then I will stand here.

Should I turn around and say, "See here, Mr. Belov, I demand to be put in touch with the American consulate! With a lawyer! With a judge! With your Mr. Stalin! With the President of the United States! With my father, Mr. Samuel Herman, a tireless and dedicated Communist like yourself! With my mother! That's right, my mother! I promise you, *she* will explain how all this happened! Call my mother,   *   it!"

I stood there. I faced into the corner. There was nothing to see but that dark blue enamel. It was painted right out from the corner onto the floor beneath my feet.

My trousers had loosened and I reached to knot them tighter. But I never got my hands there.

He came fast when he came. For a big man and a man I judged at least moderately drunk, he moved with surprising speed. I could hear every brisk step he took, those boot heels reporting his heavy rapid march across the wooden floor.

He never hit me anywhere but in the kidneys. He would hit three times on the right side and then pause. And then he would hit three times on the left side and pause. He always took his time. No matter what happened, he was never hurried and he always paced himself, three times here, but slowly, one . . . two . . . three. Then a longer pause—and now three times over *here,* one . . . two . . . three. And after a series of three, he would return to one of the chairs and sit a while. Sometimes he would sit for as long as half an hour —drinking a bit from a bottle he had, beer sometimes, whiskey sometimes—and then he would rise—I could hear the weariness in it, in his motions—but as soon as he was standing, he came across that floor very fast—and then it would be another series of three, on the right, then on the left, always in the kidneys.

It would start always after twelve, sometime after twelve

o'clock, and it would not finish until dawn. I would go in the van, in the locker, and we would climb the four flights of stairs, always pausing on the last two floors at each of the doors on the right side of the corridor, and then we would stand before the door marked 178 and wait. We would wait sometimes ten minutes, sometimes more, and then I would go in.

Belov would say, "You will tell me about your counterrevolutionary activities. I will hear every one."

And I would answer.

And he would say, "Go to the corner."

And I would go there. And after the first time, he used manacles or cord. After the first time, I could not raise my arms. I could not put my hands up to ease myself into the walls. After the first time, I just went into the walls.

After the eighth time, he tied my fingers together—one finger from each hand. Maybe this gave him more room to move in, a better target, with my hands fastened together in front of me.

The first night I did not fall.

But I fell the second night—and after that I fell every night. But falling did not matter.

There was just the one question—every night I walked into that room, the same question—and then I would go to the corner and stand.

But Belov never tied me or manacled me. A guard did that—and then the guard would leave the room.

He never took my shirt off, either.

When I think back on it, I think this Belov did not like to touch me. It is the impression that I have—that the man could not bear to touch me.

But the eleventh night he did.

With the tips of his fingers he felt along my back. He inched along from side to side and from top to bottom, pressing as a doctor does—and asking, "Hurt? Hurt here?"

But I never said yes.

Still, he found the place where I winced—and then that's where he hit.

Do I owe God that this Belov did not like to touch me? Do I owe God that my shirt was never taken off me? Is it God I owe that the scar where they healed my liver stayed hidden from Belov? Or is it God I owe that Belov lived to hurt me?

He hurt me for fifty-five nights.

From sometime after twelve until dawn, that man hurt me—and then he would call the guard to take me down and pass me along to another guard to walk me to the van, and in the van there was a third guard to put me in the locker—and I would walk out of Room 178 and down those four flights of stairs—_head down, hands behind back, no noise_—and ride the van back to _Spets Korpus_, Cell 39, and I was always there in time for the morning bell.

Those fifty-five mornings I gulped my hot water down. It did not matter how hot it was—I gulped it—and I was grateful to be on time. I never missed that first feeding. I always made it back before the first bell—and fifty-five times I made it back.

After fifteen mornings, they shared. It is one of the memories that makes me cry. Of all the things I will remember, of all the things that are printed onto my thoughts until I will think no longer, only three or four make me cry.

This is one of them—that they _shared_ with me, all those mornings from fifteen to fifty-five, each giving a little, until I had a second cup.

Yes, I owe God for that—and admit it. Or I owe _man_—both my gratitude and my hate.

What is it I should remember? Those fifty-five nights? Or the mornings when they shared?

THIRTY _____

I hurt inside, and I passed blood the second morning. The Elder saw it and shook his head, and then he looked back at the peep-hole and stared.

My water was blood.

I put the lid back and went to the end of my bench and took my place.

I sat in the position—and, like them, I stared.

I'd had two nights of the fifty-five that were going to be mine—and I was struck dumb with surprise.

Why was this happening?

It *was* happening, wasn't it?

I searched for what was wrong. I sat in the position, my eyes locked on that peephole, my mind traveling all the way back—back through all the years in Russia and back through the years before that. Was there something there? Perhaps there was. If I could only think hard enough, the thing I'd done would spring out of hiding and the basis of my guilt would be clear.

*Counter*revolutionary?

Surely I would find something to fit that.

But how far back should I go? Could I stop at Ironwood Street—or should I go all the way back to Henry? Maybe back to Ferry would be good enough. How old was I when we moved to Ferry?

I hurt inside. And I was passing blood.

The third night I could not hold myself up in the locker. It was a longer wait going and a longer wait coming back, and both ways I could not hold myself up in the locker.

Some nights they would not pause. Some nights they would run me up the four flights of stairs, trotting me along the hallways to the next flight. But then at 178 I always waited, even the nights they ran me. Never much more than ten minutes—but always a wait about that long.

But then we would go back to pausing at doors again—on the third floor and on the last.

By the fourth night, I depended on his voice to get me through. It was something I could loathe. I could despise his voice, seize it as the thing to turn all my hate on. If I hated it enough, it would get me through. I would make up things to think about it, perhaps even to say about it—how I could humiliate him with ridicule, such a preposterous voice on a grown man, a brute of a fellow like you!

Belov! Swine! Pay attention! You have the voice of a freak! Listen, Belov, I am laughing! Your voice makes me laugh, Belov! Such an embarrassment, a puny thing like that on a big dumb cluck like you! Do you hear me, pig? Victor Herman is laughing. Please believe me, I can't help it—it is the voice of a toad. Belov! Dumb cluck! If a tumor could talk, it would sound like you!

In the barber's shed and in the bathhouse, they saw me. They saw my back—and they stared at it no differently from how they stared at the peephole. And the second time in there, the Elder pulled down the skin under one of my eyes and looked.

"What?" I said, half-angry, half-surprised.

"Blood," he said.

"So, blood," I said. "I am a man—so I bleed."

I did not want his sympathy. It would make me cry to have it. I only wanted my rage now—and something even stronger than that. It was resolve I wanted.

"The * with it!" I said to the Elder—and went back to rubbing myself in the water.

"Talk," he said.

"What about?" I said.

"Tell them something. Make something up."

"The * with it!" I said—and walked away to another spout. He followed me. "Think," he said. "Make something up."

"Did you?" I said.

He looked around. He said, "We all did."

"And where are you now?" I said. "What good did it do?"

Again he looked around at the other men standing under the water. "Flyer," he said, "we are alive. For none of us is there torture anymore. Think, flyer—you are a spy."

"I am an American," I said. "How could I be a spy? For what?"

"Save your life, American," the Elder said. "Think, idiot—your life!"

On the fifth night blood came from my penis when he hit. He only had to hit a little bit, and some blood would seep out or spurt out—and from my rectum too.

On the seventh night, from my nose, the same—a little bit, seeping—and more from my penis and rectum, from there it came in small splashes.

On the eighth night he said something else before he said, "You will tell me about your counterrevolutionary activities. I will hear every one."

Before he said that, he said. "Your trousers are ruined. Get another pair of trousers. These trousers are full of blood."

Then he asked me the question, and when I answered, he said, "Go to the corner and stand there."

On the ninth night, he said, "No new trousers, prisoner? You must get new trousers. These are ruined. These are no good. Throw them away."

And then he asked me the question.

On the tenth night I fainted for the first time. But I got up and then he knocked me out again. This time I stayed down and he let me stay there. I came around and stayed down, and he gave me some time. But then he got me up again.

He said, "Turn around."

I stood there. I could feel the tickling as the blood went over the clipped hairs on the backs of my thighs.

I saw him walk to his desk and lift something. He held it up. But the overhead light cast shadows where he was and I couldn't see what he had.

"See this, prisoner? A file on you. It tells us everything. We know everything. So why are you stubborn, prisoner? You will tell me about your counterrevolutionary activities. I will hear every one."

I said, "If you know everything, then why do I have to tell?"

He smacked whatever he had in his hand. First he smacked it with his hand, and then he smacked it down on his desk.

"If you tell, then you go free! We give you a sentence, and then you go free! Now, prisoner, begin!"

Would he kill me? Was the Elder right? What if they didn't want to, but they killed you anyway? What if the next punch did it? Was this bleeding from my liver? Does the liver make you bleed like that? How much could you bleed and still be all right?

"All right," I said. "But give me a lead—tell me where to begin."

Was my voice pleading? Or did I mock him? Had I been mocking his voice? When I talked, did it come out as mimicking him?

"No, no, no," he said, his meager wet voice barely audible from across the room. "I must see if what you say coincides with what is written here. All right, begin!"

I wanted to faint again. I wanted to sit down. I longed for the position. To be back there in the position, that would be paradise.

"I'm sorry," I said. "I can't think of anything."

"Turn around!" he screamed in that pathetic voice. "Face the corner!" he screamed, and he came at me across the floor in a fast march, and I went down when he hit.

That night I kept falling. That was the tenth night. I fell and I stopped getting up. So he kicked me instead. He let me lie there all that night and didn't get me up to punch me. For the rest of that night, he kicked me instead—and at dawn they took me out.

The eleventh night I went down with the first blow. He tried to get me up, but he could not get me to stand. He tried, but it would not work—and I could not help.

I heard him go to the door and call to someone in the hall, and then that man came and together they got me up. And then Belov told this other one, a guard—I could see it was a guard now—to go get Tolya, and the guard left—and Belov held me pressed against the wall, his hand gripping me at the throat, his shoulder pushing up against me.

The guard returned. He said, "Tolya cannot come."

Belov dropped me. He cursed. His curses seemed comic, that ridiculous voice straining for force, for an expression of outrage.

After a while—how long? It could have been days but it wasn't —after a while Belov was back. Was this other one the man Tolya?

They had a bag of dried peas. Small dark peas. They spilled them out on the floor where the blue was, and then they hoisted me and kneeled me on the peas. They got on each side of me, Belov and the man Tolya, and each put his weight on a shoulder and moved me around in the peas. Then they'd lift me and then they would drop me, each working a shoulder, and in this fashion they moved me all around on my knees on the peas, all around the blue triangle painted on the floor.

There was nothing more that night. There was no more hitting that night.

But the next night was like the first.

And then the thirteenth came, and that was different too.

He asked the question. I don't know how I answered. I don't know what I said. Yet it was the same—it came to the same thing— but Belov did not send me to the corner when he heard whatever it was I had said. He took me by the shirt and pulled me to a chair, one of those school chairs to the side of his desk.

He picked up a pencil, the kind that is faceted, five sides.

He said, "Put out your hand."

He took the pencil and placed it perpendicular to the crease between my little finger and my ring finger. He started with the right hand. He did all the creases on that hand, and then he began on the left hand, and did all the creases there too. He went from one crease to another, from one hand to another, the pencil between the fingers and Belov squeezing them together and then holding them that way for minutes at a time. Then on to the next crease.

He called for Tolya around three in the morning, and Tolya worked the pencil and Belov worked the pliers. Tolya moved the pencil from crease to crease and then he squeezed two fingers together, and when he had them good and tight, Belov gripped the pencil in the jaws of the pliers and turned.

Belov did the turning until dawn that night. Tolya worked the pencil.

All the skin was off by dawn. Each time enough came off, Belov picked it up from the desk top with a slip of paper. He used the slip of paper like a shovel and picked up whatever was big enough and slid it back off into the ashtray.

They had it all off by dawn.

And when I stood to go, Belov said, "Look, prisoner." He pointed to the top of his desk. "You see?" he said. "Clean." And then he tapped each of my hands with the pencil. "You see?" he said. "Clean too."

For weeks after that thirteenth night, I had to be very careful in either of the positions, sitting or reclining. I could not let my fingers go together—because when they did, they stuck—and it was worse if you had to get them apart.

It took a long time. But they healed.

If you live, it heals, whatever it is. Even the wounds they didn't know they were making, those healed too. If you live long enough, it all heals—and the scars inside and out, they are just a toughness.

They are, for all of us, what toughness is.

The fourteenth night it was just Belov again—and punching in the kidneys, first the right, then the left—three on each side, altogether a series of three—and then he would rest.

But on the fifteenth night, it was Tolya and Belov, the both.

They sat me in a chair. They each came with the other chairs and sat themselves before me. And each man had a pencil. Tolya took the place above my left eye—and Belov took the place above the right.

It wasn't bad at first. But it got bad. It just took time to get bad —and then it quickly got much worse. They never changed the force of it. It's hard to remember, but I think the force was always the same. It just took time to get very bad—and then, once it got that way, I thought nothing could ever be worse.

It was just a simple thing, what they did with their pencils. It's something you've seen kids do—and teachers have probably seen it many times—and maybe even some teachers have done it to kids. A simple snap—holding the pencil at one end, a fingertip at the other, pushing at the bottom, pulling back at the top, get a tension in the wood, then let go.

They did it like that from after midnight until dawn. It was the fifteenth night. Each did one side—just an inch or so above the eye. Tolya on the left side, Belov on the right, maybe a minute between each snap.

It wasn't hard at first. It didn't seem bad for a long time. And then, very quickly, it got worse.

It's hard for me to look at a pencil now. I don't want to be angry anymore. But who can live a life and not see pencils wherever he turns?

It hurt to chew the bread ration after that. It was a dense bread —very heavy. You had to chew it hard to get it down. But mostly it did not come.

I think it is not wrong to say that Belov made my days easier. The nights he used me, the days after were easier—easier because there was something in me, a hating, and not the spacious vacancy of routine days.

Belov gave me my loathing to think about—and where I hurt and would I live to be hurt again another night.

He was hurting me. Was this worse than my never being called out? I heard "G! Get ready!" and I knew I was not forgotten, not like the others who sat this day and that day and the one after that, for how many days to come?

For fifty-five nights I was not forgotten, and I have Belov to thank for that—those fifty-five nights. But there were timeouts— and these fell on the sixth, the twelfth, the eighteenth, the twenty-fourth, and the thirtieth days of the month—in my case the *nights* of those days for these were the "free" days in the Stalin month, a month based on the six-day Stalin week. Instead of the seven-day week, in those days Russia observed a six-day week, to eliminate the traditionally religious character of Sunday. The sixth day was free day, and the nights of those days Belov enjoyed a holiday from the labors he performed in Room 178.

Stalin also ridded the days of the week of their names, and they were instead cited as first day, second day, third day, and so on— until you came to free day, and on free day Belov rested.

Me, I wish he had been more industrious, more conscientious, more dedicated to the great Russian push forward—because it was always harder to go back after a free day, always harder to pick up again where we had left off, always harder, after that little interval, to wait my turn at Room 178. Many Russians did, many worked on free day, just as they did on the other five days of the week. But Belov rested.

And I sat in 39 in the position wondering how—how conceivably the man could find something more entertaining than the chores he carried out in Room 178. Sometimes I would interrupt the diagrams I drew on the peephole with my eyes or the little games and tricks I would play on that small ring of glass, sometimes I would interrupt these exercises to think about Belov and to try to guess what he did when he did not do something to me.

Torture? It is terrible, of course—and for each man it is terrible in a different way. But the position, sixteen men like sixteen stones, all staring in that silence until a bell goes off to shift them from one condition of petrifaction to another, the position was worse —and it is terrifying—terrifying even to *see,* and infinitely more terrifying when you know what you see is for you as it is for them, and you know that you are a petrifaction too, that you are like them, like *that.*

I drew diagrams on the peephole and played all sorts of games. I made my eyes draw blueprints or I'd draw numbers backwards and upside down—and sometimes I would use my eyes to contrive a very elaborate design, and then I would turn it around to see what it looked like on the other side, or I would make the drawing and then tilt it, tilt that coin of air into different angles to see the way the altering perspective would change what I saw. Or sometimes I would whirl that coin of printed air to see what it would do.

I kept on doing these things all day long—while I waited for the night and for when Belov would have me called out.

He called me out fifty-five times—but after the eighteenth time, they were all the same, except for the time they burned me and for the night before that, the fifty-third time.

It all went the same that fifty-third night—the van, the locker, the stairs, the pausing—the same. And I waited at the door of 178 just as all those other times I had. Then Belov called me in.

He stood in the middle of the floor, directly under the overhead light. It made his face dark, that the source of light was directly above his head, and you could only notice the ruined lip as a some-what darker place.

"Welcome, prisoner," Belov said, his manner detectably jovial. "Come stand here, prisoner," he ordered, and he motioned to the floor at his feet. "Now then," he said when I was where he wanted me, "did you miss me last night?"

"Yes," I said, both meaning it and meaning also the sarcasm he obviously wanted.

"Very good," said Belov. "Now, stand up straight, please. Why do you not stand straight and tall like me?"

I made an effort to straighten my spine, but the pain stopped me, and even without the pain I couldn't have done it.

"Very good," Belov said and smiled, his upper lip stretching while the lower one struggled to follow. "But you still have the same filthy trousers. They are disgusting. I tell you, you must throw them away and get new ones."

"I intend to," I said.

"Excellent," Belov said. "Now follow me."

He walked to his desk and sat down behind it and he gestured with his head for me to take one of the other chairs. I could see a large sheet of paper on the desktop, two columns of typing on it from top to bottom. He saw me looking, and he looked too.

"Does that interest you?" he said.

I said no, that it did not interest me.

"It concerns you," he said.

"I see," I said. "And how does it concern me?"

Belov stood up and turned his attention to the window behind him. He seemed to be studying something out in the street. Or did the window give onto the courtyard in the rear or simply onto one of the buildings on either side? I still did not know.

"Tell me, prisoner," he said, still gazing out the window, "what is it you think of when I say *blue?*"

"Nothing in particular," I said.

"Oh?" he said. "Then what is it you think of when I say *corner?*"

"The same," I said, without hesitating. "Nothing special."

Belov turned away from the window and stood behind his chair, and then he pulled it back roughly and sat down.

"Prisoner," he said, "we do not need you any longer. We are going to set you free. We have been testing you and you have been tested enough. We know what you are made of now. We know you are made of good stuff. So, let us be friends now that it is all over."

I said, "All right."

"Very good," Belov said, and he reached forward and picked up the sheet of paper, and with it a second sheet of paper that was underneath. He took a fountain pen from the pocket of his brown shirt and uncapped it and handed it to me. He said, "A list of names. You will sign at the bottom before you go free."

"Whose names?" I said.

"It does not matter," he said. "Just names." And with this he put the paper back on the desk in front of me and put the second sheet of paper on top of it—so that only a blank area on the bottom of the sheet underneath was visible.

"It does," I said.

"Does what?" Belov said.

"It does matter," I said. "To me it matters."

"To a man that is going to be free, what can matter?" Belov said, and again he worked his lips into that hideous smile.

"How do I know that my father's name is not one of those names? Or my brother's?" I put the fountain pen down on the edge of the desk.

"Prisoner," he said, "you vex me. You trouble and you vex me. *Sign!*" he shrieked and lifted the pen and held it toward me.

"Nothing doing," I said and stood up.

"Very good," Belov said and also stood. He stepped around the desk and strode to the door, opened it, and called out into the hall.

They took me down those four flights of stairs and then down another flight after that. They took me to a room down there, down there in the basement. It was a small room and it was dark.

There were men in that room. I don't know how many. But as soon as I was in there, I could hear them moving around. They had a light. They turned it on and it was very bright—it was like the light that auto mechanics carry around to work with under a car, only it beamed in just one direction. The direction was my eyes. Wherever I moved in that room, the light they had kept shining in my eyes. And then it would suddenly go out.

I didn't know what to do. First I stayed where I was. For maybe three minutes I didn't move and then I moved around a little—but no matter how I moved, I didn't bump into anyone—just into walls.

It was a small room. I could hear them move when I moved, but when I kept still I couldn't hear them. They kept still when I did, and then the light would come on again, the beam aimed perfectly, always in my eyes. I stood there, and then I moved—and the beam followed me wherever I moved—and after a time it went off again, and it all continued as before. Sometimes I could hear them whispering—but then they would quickly stop—as if they could tell that I was hearing them—and then the light came on again, and then, this time quickly, it went off. And it was like this for about two hours— and then they started hitting me.

I didn't know how many of them there were. I could only tell the things they hit me with. They hit me with belts and with wooden clubs and a metal rod and with different things with different weights and different shapes—and the things they hit me with kept changing all the time—and then, abruptly, the hitting would stop and the room would be quiet again and then the beam of light would come on, come on and then go off, and I could hear them whispering and then hear them stop—and they would move whenever I moved, and it was all like a children's game, and you began to think of it that way until they hit you the first time again and waited, as if that first blow was an introductory note in some musical composition that demanded there then be a pause before the entire orchestra came crashing down around your ears.

And then the hitting commenced again, without interruption, different things with different shapes and different weights, but never once that I know of did they hit me in the face or head or neck. But perhaps they did. It was hard to know.

That was the fifty-third night—all that I can remember of it.

I do not remember going back to 39. I was there in the morning by the first bell—but I do not remember getting there.

I remember only my waking up to the bell. I was lying by the pot. But the bell must have already gone off because the others were already in the position. And when I opened my eyes, I saw the man that sat facing me open his eyes wide to the man that sat behind me, and then I felt a heavy blow in the middle of my back.

I coughed. I coughed, thank God. I coughed up clots of blood. I nodded and got to my knees, and on my knees I made it to my place and pulled myself up—and, like them, I was sitting—and, like them, my eyes were in position on the peephole. But that day I could not draw diagrams and blueprints and pictures and designs with my eyes. All that day after the fifty-third night I cried, but no tears came out.

All that day I waited for the night. But they did not call me out. It was a free day.

Belov was resting.

All that day I cried—but no sound and no tears came out.

The Elder must have turned us that night. He always turned us at least twice. But I do not remember his turning me that night. I do not remember how cold it was that night. I only remember a feeling I had—a feeling that inside me something vital, something alive and pulsing, had stopped. Everything soft and moist had been wrung out of it, and it was dry now and hard as horn, a small thing centered in my belly.

It has been in me ever since, this small hard thing.

In the morning there was a coat over me—a long black coat made of fur. It was the coat of a man who had come in with it, a man who had joined us a week before. He had come as he had been arrested, in his long black coat—just as I had, in T-shirt and cotton trousers and tennis shoes, long, long ago.

It was winter now, and the man who was new to us put his coat over me.

But that morning when I waked with the coat over me, I was not the man who had fallen into the black sobbing slumber of the night before. I was not that man nor the man I am in Detroit today. I was instead that other Victor Herman, the one who endured an ordeal of eighteen years. It is *that* Victor Herman who did it, and that man is alien to me now. He is a creature they made one night in a basement. All it took was a very bright light that followed your eyes as they moved. It took a very dark room and that light, and men who moved when you moved and who whispered in the dark. It took never bumping into them and a light that went on and off and whispering that would stop when you heard it and the surprise of clubs that touched you in the dark.

THIRTY-ONE _____

They called me out the next night. But it was too late for that now. They put me in the van and they put me in the locker and then they took me out in the courtyard behind Vorobevka Street. But it was too late now.

They took me right to the basement and they put me in a dark room.

Was it the same room?

The light came on. Then the whispering. And when I moved around, they moved too.

I stood still. The light went out.

It came on again—and it was very silent in there.

I stood there, motionless. The light went off. They whispered. The light came on. And then it was silent again.

"Prisoner!" a voice said.

"Prisoner!" another voice said.

There was a long silence—and then the light went out.

I heard them whispering—and then silence.

I waited for the first blow—it would come as an announcement. Then the rest would come.

I heard them whispering again.

Was this the same room? Were these the same men?

"Victor Herman!" a voice said.

The light came on.

"Victor Herman!" another voice said, and then a third voice said, "Tell us what we want to know or die tonight."

The light went out.

I stayed where I was. I heard them whisper and then move around and then it was silent again.

I screamed into the silence. I screamed with all it was in me to scream.

I screamed, *"Nyet!"*

And then in English, softly, to myself, I said, "No."

They hit me with boards and then with something small and heavy. It was iron.

I pushed up, stepped out, took a mouthful of rushing air, and jumped. I fell deadfall, careening. But I could not fall into the next morning. I tried. But I could not do it.

I kept waking up. A burning in my leg kept waking me up— and I would wake up and feel it and smell something awful in that room and then I would fall again, go spilling over backwards into the tumbling dark. But no matter how hard I tried to catch the sailing air and keep careening, I could not fall far enough.

I kept waking up. It was a sensation of burning that kept waking me up—and always to a smell I had never come across before. Such a terrible smell, I would say to myself—what is it? But before I could think very clearly, I was lost in a long somersault, the dark going one way, my body going another, an impossible vaulting that divided me from space itself.

This time I made the jump last until morning, and it was the bell in *Spets Korpus* that woke me.

They burned me. They had burned me that night, a round shape inside my left ankle.

I do not know what they did it with. But by the time they did it, it was too late—and too late for the fifty-fifth night too.

Still, even after this, they still called me out.

"G! Get ready!"

I stepped between the men and stood between the *Parasha* and the door, and when the door was pulled open, I stepped out. I moved along the padded walkway with my head down and my hands behind my back. I went down the iron stairs and through the small doors and across the prison yard and into the van, and in my locker I made the ride to Vorobevka Street.

Had they killed me the night before?

They had not.

Would they kill me tonight?

We did not go to the basement. We went along the usual route, and we did it in the same fashion, from one end of a corridor to another and another, pausing by the right-hand doors on the last two floors.

I stood before 178 for the fifty-fifth time. I waited, and after the usual interval of waiting, Belov opened the door. The guard took me in, tied my fingers with the cord that Belov gave him, stood waiting for instructions, was dismissed, and left the room.

Belov? The same—no matter how cold it was—his jacket off, his brown shirtsleeves rolled well beyond the elbow.

There was only one difference this time.

He did not ask me the question.

He said nothing, in fact. He did not even tell me to go stand in the corner.

He just pointed there and smiled.

I decided, do it now—because you might not get another chance.

I made as if I were going to turn toward the corner, but instead I took two fast steps forward and with whatever I could scrape from my lungs I spit in his face. I waited until I could get a good look at it—I wanted that picture for the peephole. I wanted it to die with if that's what was going to happen in the hours ahead. I took a good look at the gray muck I had gotten on him, and then I wheeled around and walked into the blue corner and waited.

I could hear him making little squealing sounds of terror, the sounds a man might make were he to discover a fat furry spider clinging to the tip of his tongue.

I waited. I could hear him squealing and yanking open drawers in the desk.

It was the best I could have done. The spit, the thick spit of a man you were too dainty to touch, his spit, his mucus running on your face—let it drive the bastard mad!

I waited. And Belov was more or less quiet now. I could hear him snuffling, a man straining to organize himself. And then he came. He came in that brusque march that I'd come to know as the processional of his assault. I waited for him.

He could kill me. But that's all he could do.

He counted. *One! Two! Three!* On the right side, in the kidney, and then on the left. *One! Two! Three!*

I counted with him. But I never made it to one again.

I came up out of sleep all at once. I must have given a shout. I had that sort of feeling in my ears—as if just moments before I had used my voice to shout. I sat up all at once—*I was in a bed!*

How long had it been since I had been in or even seen a bed?

I was in a kind of hospital ward—iron beds, sheets, blankets—but it was cold.

They kept me there more than a month—there in the Gorky prison infirmary.

I was bleeding inside. Most of the others were too—but they wouldn't talk. No one would talk—not even Romanoff, the one man I recognized from the American Village. He knew me and I knew him, but he wouldn't talk—except once—once, when we were alone in there, he whispered to me for a little while. But the next day he died. Most of them in there died, but I didn't know who they were. I knew Romanoff, though—I knew him from the Village and from back in Detroit. Everybody who was close to the Socialists knew him back in Detroit—and this was because of the time Romanoff had knocked over the mounted policeman during a workers' demonstration downtown. It was the 6th of March, 1930, and thousands and thousands were there, and so was the National Guard and the city police and the state police, and police mounted on horses—and Romanoff had knocked one of them over. It was a thing to impress a fifteen-year-old boy, seeing that big man do that, put his shoulder to that horse and shove. The man's back was to a plate-glass window when he did it—and the horses were driving the people against the glass—and then I saw Romanoff, a truly huge man, do what he did, put his shoulder to the front of that horse in something like a tackling motion—and shove. The horse went over and so did the policeman. It was a thing to see, and many of us saw it—and talked about it afterwards, and about what a brave man Romanoff was. The cops beat the ∗ out of him after that—five, six of them clubbing him—and we talked about that too, all the kids I knew.

And here he was now, the same man—and whenever I tried to get him to talk he'd just put his finger to his lips and look at me. But he whispered to me the day before he died. He whispered that it was all okay now—that as soon as the bleeding stopped, he was going to go free—he was going to get himself on the first boat and go home. He was going to get himself as far away from this as a man could get.

I said, "Why are they setting you free? Tell me, so I can help myself."

He whispered. He whispered, "I signed a paper."

"A paper?" I said. "What was on it?"

"It said McCarthy, the engineer in the Village—it said he was a spy."

They took Romanoff out of there the next day. It was early in the morning when they did it. Three went out that day, the same. In the month or more I was in that infirmary, many went out, never a day when one didn't go.

Bleeding inside, I believe it mainly was—all this bleeding inside. But some bleed the way my mother bled—their own doing, the body purging itself of something. It's meant, I suppose, to clean you out when life's deposited too much inside you—and it does its job at any cost.

I was lucky in that infirmary. It was my first luck, the first time being a Jew saved me instead of hurt me. There was a doctor there— a trusty, and therefore a criminal and not a political—and I recognized him for a Jew, and I told him I was too—and to convince him, I would talk to him in Yiddish. It made a difference, that he was a Jew—or maybe it wasn't that, maybe it was just because I was young. I don't know. But I think it was the first thing—and he got food for me—an egg now and then, and now and then a glass of milk, and sometimes vegetable soup and potatoes, and at night, even when the Jewish doctor didn't get it for me, I got real tea with sugar and a roll.

It was good, that milk now and then—and the egg.

It would be a long time before I would have either again. But it would not be a long time before I would eat tree slugs and rats— and worse.

I built myself up. I was strong from that month or more. I stopped hurting inside after three weeks, and by four weeks I was strong again.

I was strong when they sent me back to the second floor of *Spets Korpus*. They took me down the padded walkway to the cell in the corner. But the men in 39 were all different—except for one. Only one was the same, and he took a place next to me after the night bell. He lay down behind me, his back against the wall, and I heard him whisper from behind me:

"Flyer, the others—all dead."

And then I felt him poking something under me, trying to poke something under my side. I took a chance and felt there.

It was the soap!

I got it between my buttocks but had to get it out again around twelve. I had to pass it off to the man behind me.

They were calling me out.

"G! Get ready!"

I'm ready, I thought.

I went into the van and into the locker, but there was no trotting up the flights of stairs or pausing at the right-hand doors, nor was I made to wait in front of Room 178.

Belov!

He was sitting behind his desk. I could see that something was tremendously different—but what? And then I saw it—that he had the jacket of his uniform on and there were medals all over it.

He said, "Comrade Herman, good evening. Please sit."

I walked across that wooden floor and took a chair.

"You have been in hospital," he said. "I am sorry. You are better?"

I nodded my head.

"Very good," he said, and I was thankful he did not follow it with a smile. "Now," he said, "it is time you know the truth. There are two ways out of this, two ways only. You either die or you go to court. Do you want to die?"

I said nothing. I just shook my head.

"Very good," he said. "Then for you, my friend, it is court. But," and now he smiled, "to go to court, first I must have material. Do you understand?"

I nodded my head.

"Very good. Now, in this connection, I ask you—the engineer, McCarthy, do you know him?"

I nodded my head.

"Very good. This is, you see, material. I tell you McCarthy is a spy. We have proof and we know it. He has agents here, other Americans. Together they pass information to the American consulate in Moscow. It is forbidden. You say you know him?"

I nodded.

"Very good," Belov said and produced a paper from the center drawer. "This covers the matter. It tells about McCarthy. It says on a certain day you told him how many trucks and cars were produced on a certain day."

"Which days?" I said. "Which day did I tell him and which day of production?"

"Comrade Herman," Belov said, again smiling, "these things are of no consequence. Just sign."

I said, "But it would make no sense. To begin with, I had hardly anything to do with the plant. And even if I did, why would a worker be telling the chief engineer what his day's production was? And besides, the newspaper always reported the daily production, anyway."

"But that is just the *point,* Comrade!" Belov said, that impossible voice pinching itself farther up the scale to express his satisfaction. "It is foolish, yes? Very good. You see, you will sign this paper. I will then send it to the court, and you will then go to the court— and you will tell them, look, see, this thing is foolish and I deny it all, and the court will let you go—because of course you will be right. The court will say, why did you sign? And you will say it was the beatings. Is this fair?"

I wanted to nod my head, but I didn't. It made no sense. But wasn't I crazy to question it? If I said no, what would happen? And wasn't it craziness to expect anything but craziness from them?

"It makes no sense," I said. "You realize that."

"Of course," Belov said. "That is why it works. There is no other way. Except we send you back—and in time, I don't know how long, you die. Here—sign."

I signed.

Belov called for the guard—and I was taken back. It was strange, returning from Room 178 before dawn. It was strange going back there in the night. And it was awful living with the *Parasha* when I knew I was getting out.

I *was* getting out, wasn't I?

Another month passed. Belov called me out. It was the same as before, very formal—dressed up in his medals, his manner amiable.

"Comrade Herman, good evening. Please sit."

I sat.

"It distresses me to tell you, but the paper was sent back. The court says insufficient material. I am sorry."

"I am sorry too," I said. "What do I do now? Could we add that I told him the daily production for a week?"

"No, no, no," Belov said, "that would never do. Tell me, you were the captain of the American Village basketball team, no?"

I nodded my head.

"Very good. Then I will write here that your team played the Pavlova team, and that you told Engineer McCarthy the score."

Again I said, "That makes no sense. We never played Pavlova. There was no score."

"Exactly," Belov said. "Is this not what we want? Something foolish? Something you can dismiss with a wave of your hand? Here, I will write it and you will sign."

I signed.

"Very good," Belov said, and he took the paper and returned it to the middle drawer.

He stood up and I stood up too. He walked to the door and I followed him, my eyes drawn to the blue corner as I moved across the floor.

"Very good," he said again at the door. "You have enough money? To return home when we release you—you have enough? For the streetcar, perhaps?" He put his hand into his pocket.

It was incredible. That hand—those hands—what they had done to me.

"Not necessary," I said. "I'll get home."

"Very good," he said, drawing out his hand. "So, Comrade Herman, I will see you perform at *Spartak,* yes?"

I nodded my head, and with that Belov opened the door, and the guard took over—head down, hands behind back, no noise. But the locker didn't seem so bad anymore—and when I walked into Cell 39, that didn't seem so bad, either. And after the morning bell, they moved me out of there. It happened so fast, the soap was still under my arm.

They walked me down to the first floor and put me in Cell 18.

It was really happening.

I was alive—and I was getting out!

For the first time in a long while, I thought of my father. I thought of Leo and Miriam and Sam.

I thought of my mother that day too. I wanted to tell someone what was happening—and she, most of all, was the one I would have liked to tell.

And for my father, I thought—let him see that I have been tested—and that I proved myself a man.

THIRTY-TWO —————————————————————————

I was in Cell 39 somewhat less than a year, sixteen men and the *Parasha*—a block of air and sixteen frozen men, silent behind the muzzle, in this position or that one.

In Cell 18, 137 men—and I made one more. There were make-shift cots there, three, four, and men all over, on the cots, under the cots, all over the floor, on wooden tiers that went up to the ceiling.

But there was no position here, neither one—and it was worked out that you slept in shifts—and so long as it was your shift, you could sleep, and it didn't matter where you faced or where your hands were, and you could sit any way you wanted to—or could manage.

There was only one place free and it was a place under a sick man. He was on the tier right above me and he was very sick, and his bowels never stopped running, it seemed, and when they did stop, then gas came out instead of the little belches of watery stool. But I couldn't get another place. I could see Janssen, one of the Americans from the Village, but I couldn't get to him right away. I had to keep my place on the floor under the tier with the sick fellow over me. I had to keep that or I'd have no place to lie down at all. But then I saw Janssen better, and I didn't want to go over to him. He had little bubbles of blood coming out of his mouth. His lips were pressed together and every so often some bubbles would appear. He fell over late that first day, and I asked about him when he did. Nobody knew why or nobody would say why—but that night somebody said the American had broken ribs and maybe one of them had punctured a lung. But by that time they'd taken Janssen out—and you could see he was dead when they did it. I got his place when they took him—and that put me up front near the door. It was better, even though it was near the pot.

It was a big one, the *Parasha* in Cell 18—and it was bad being near it. But it was worse being under the sick man. It was all human waste, one way or the other. But his you could smell the sickness in, and a foul gas that proclaimed the headway death's work made.

The food? The same—but a man could talk, and if he wanted

he could move around, although you might lose your place. But you could stay in it and shift yourself around, or lean against the next man or against a wall if you could get to one, and some men some-times had the cots.

There was the same light here, always going, a bulb over the door—and there was a muzzle also, but in 18 it was shorter and some light got through the top.

It was all different, anyway—and the difference made it better —and it was easier to tap. Sometimes I did it, and I always listened. But there wasn't much to say—and less reason to, now that you could actually talk.

Just short of a month they called me out.

I went the way I always went—in the locker in the van.

It was Room 178 again. But there was a difference—and it filled me with excitement.

This interview was going to take place in daylight! Clearly this must mean something in my favor. Wasn't there some likelihood that I might be released this very day—indeed, from this very room?

The guard knocked and Belov opened the door.

"What's this?" Belov said.

"The prisoner," the guard said.

"I did not call for him," Belov said. "He does not come here. He goes to court. Take the prisoner to court."

To court! Everything in me soared. Was this true? To court? I wanted to run—I wanted to run all the way back to the van. Would I be late? My * , would this error mean that I would miss my moment? That my case would have to be rescheduled? That my plea would not be heard for still another month?

"Good day, Comrade," Belov said to me. "It is very good to see you. You are feeling well, I hope?"

"Just fine," I said. "Thank you," I said. "Good to see you too."

Come *on,* I felt like screaming into the guard's face—let's *move* it.

"To *court?*" the guard said. "The prisoner goes to court? Right now?"

"But of course," Belov said, and smiled. "They are expecting Citizen Herman in court."

"Then I will see that he is taken there, Comrade," the guard said. "Right now."

"Yes, *do,*" Belov said, still laboring with what I imagined he hoped would be something like a human smile.

"Head down, hands behind back, no noise," the guard said to me as he marched me back down the hallway, his revolver out and held down at his side, no different from how things were whenever they moved me from place to place.

They put me back in the locker and the van pulled away from the white building on Vorobevka Street, and when they let me out we were back at the prison again—but when they took me out and marched me across the yard, we entered a different building. I could tell we were in one of the jails for criminals now—it was chiefly the noise that signaled the difference.

They walked me up to the second floor and stopped me in front of Cell 21. The noise in the place was terrific—and the *light*—and then I realized that the place was airy and that windows must be open somewhere. It was summer again, and the jail was cool and not unpleasant inside.

A new guard was unlocking the door of Cell 21 when what was going on first began to register with me. I must have been dreaming —I must have been overcome by the flush of happiness and by all that noise and air and light.

"Wait a minute," I said. "This isn't the court. Belov said take me to the court!"

"Shut up!" the guard said, still working the key in the lock.

"Hold it!" I shouted. "I'm supposed to go to court! Something is wrong here!" I shouted. "What's wrong here?"

"Shut up! I tell you to shut up!" the guard said.

He pulled open the door.

"Inside!" he said.

It was large, this cell—larger than Cell 18 in *Spets Korpus.* There were berths around the walls, upper and lower decks—and there was a small table in the middle of the floor. Some of the berths even had bedding—and many of the berths were free. But it was crazy, because I could see men lying on the floor, *under* the berths— even though some of the berths on the first deck and many of them on the upper deck were unoccupied. Why were there men lying on the floor, then?

In this whole cell, bigger than 18, there were only nineteen men. It was unbelievable.

After 39 and 18, it was unbelievable, all this space—and the

My father had himself photographed in 1905.

That's Sam on the right in 1902, at a political meeting in Russia, and here he is again, second from the left, four years later, at another meeting.

My family before we left Detroit—Leo, me, Rose, Sam, Rebecca. Miriam was not yet born.

This group picture was taken aboard the *Leviathan*. I'm third from the left in the back row.

I'm in my cadet's uniform even though this was taken just after a meeting of the auto workers at the plant.

It was 1936, and I was teaching parachute-jumping. I can't remember the woman's name.

above: Here's how I looked a month or so before I was arrested.

above right: Picture taken of me two weeks after I was finally released from the camps.

left: My younger sister Miriam, who became a doctor in the U.S.S.R.

It was 1949, the year I "married" Galina.

Galina when she was twenty-three.

This certificate was given to me to signify that I was an exile. It was valid only in the district of Krasnoyarsk.

Galina and me in Krasnoyarsk. It was 1949.

My firstborn and me in 1952.

Svetlana not long after the three of us got out of the chop-out.

Svetlana in Siberia. The year was 1956. She was four years old, and very hungry.

This picture of Galina was taken by her parents in 1956. She was visiting at their farm in Zikova Village.

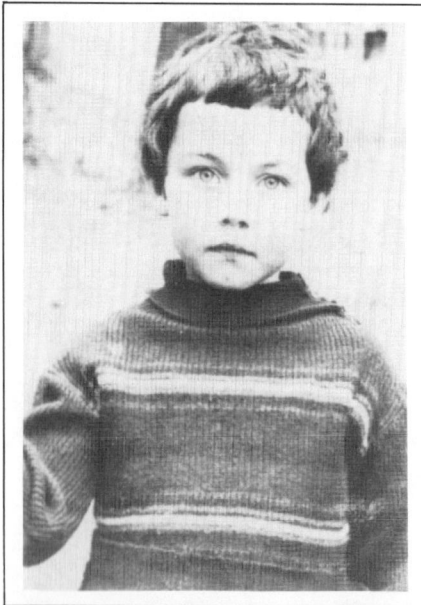

The boxing team I coached in Eneseysk, Siberia. The first man holds the trophy we won in 1954.

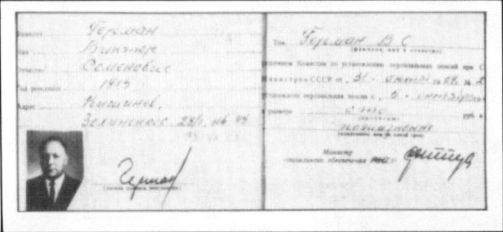

My cousin David Herman, the man who engineered my escape.

The certificate warranting that I was to be awarded a lifetime pension of one hundred rubles monthly.

During the time when the Soviets were trying every blandishment to secure my silence, I received the Jubali Medal, "for heroic labor." The award was made by The Supreme Soviet of the U.S.S.R. in connection with the 100th birthday of Lenin.

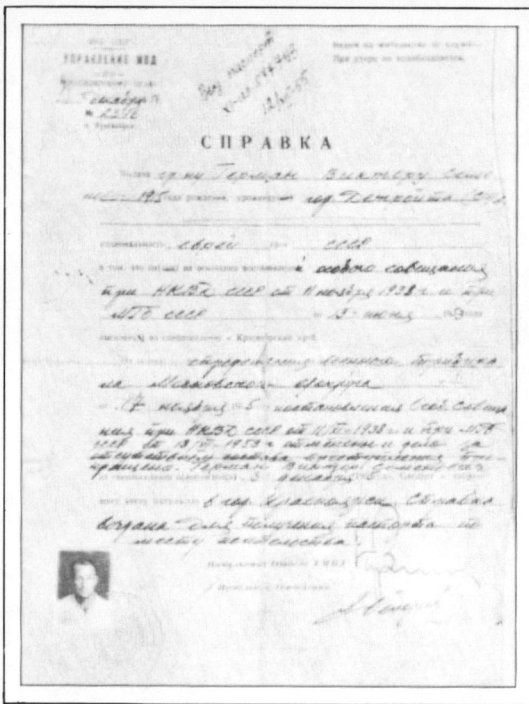

СПРАВКА

This document freed me of all charges. It cites my nationality as U.S.A. and says that I am a Jewish citizen of the U.S.S.R. Its text amounts to the following statement: that in accord with a special meeting of the NKVD in 1938 and another special meeting of the KGB in 1953, I am exiled to live in the Krasnoyarsk region. Further, that on the strength of decisions made by the above organizations and thereafter by the Military Tribunal of Moscow, this in 1955, all charges against me are abolished and the case is dropped for absence of "corpus delicti."

The girls and me before a little party I gave for them after they were released from the U.S.S.R.

light and the air in the place. And all these men were young—any-where from seventeen, say, to thirty-five—and there was something else you could right away see that was different about these men—and that was the expressions on their faces—and the tattoos on their chests and arms.

"Inside!" the guard shouted.

I started to go in—and immediately I saw it—white—on the floor—*a white towel!* Laid out there on the floor just inside the door, right where the *Parasha* would normally go, there was a perfectly clean white towel. I looked at it and then I looked up at the men in front of me—and they were very quiet suddenly and they all stared back at me, watching.

Again I looked at the towel and back at them and then at the guard, but the guard was closing the door behind me.

What was this, some kind of joke?

I stepped carefully around the towel and continued on into the cell, trying to decide where, among all these free berths, I was going to take a place. But as I turned to sweep the berths a second time, still unable to make up my mind among so many choices—how long had it been since I'd had a *choice,* a choice of anything?—two of the younger men, boys really, about seventeen or eighteen, pulled themselves out from underneath the lower deck and came up in front of me, and then walked all around me, and I turned with them as they circled me, and I could see they were leering at me, looking me over as if I were some contemptible class of man scarcely ever seen in a public place.

Was it my clothing? The purple T-shirt and the dark blue cotton trousers and the white tennis shoes? Was it the *Spartak* train-ing clothes I still wore? Or had my months in prison, in the position behind the muzzle, so changed my appearance that I was as dis-tasteful to look upon as Belov's twisted lip? Perhaps I *did* look strange. Who knew? I had no way of knowing—there had been no mirror for me to stand before to see what sort of transformation must have come over me.

The boys kept circling around me, and I got tired of rotating with them. I stood still and let them circle, and I let my attention go back to the open berths, looking them over to see which one I would take.

One of the boys said, *"Zdryuch!"*

It was a word I'd not heard before.

At first I ignored it, but the boy repeated, *"Zdryuch!"*

I answered. I said, "I don't understand you."

"Undress!" the boy said.

* *   I said.

And like that, they walked away from me, and then pulled themselves back under the lower deck on my left side. But just as they went under, two others came off the berth right over the boys —older fellows, about thirty, each one about that age, and bigger.

They came at me slowly.

It was not hard to tell why. It's something you learn—that look in a man's eyes—there is just no mistaking it. It means what it means, and there is no other look like it.

They fanned out slightly as they came, and when I could see they were going to fan out even more, I moved. I didn't wait—I went to them. I took the man on the left first—punching in the poised style I always practiced in the ring, nothing hurried, almost a kind of slow motion, and I imagine it is the unhurried pace of it and the almost stylish look it has that disarms a man—he can't believe it's ever going to reach him, so slowly your fist seems to move, and perhaps he thinks that when it does reach him, what force could there be behind it, a punch that is not thrown in rage?

They both went down. It was an easy performance. These men were not boxers—they were fighters. There is no match between the two. I hit them easily—and hard—first a combination, the man on the left, and then I pivoted and took down the second man with a left cross to the face, and when he doubled, I hit him with another left under the heart.

And then I lost the control I had. The boxer went out of me, and it was all fighter now—the rage that had simmered in me all those months and months boiling now into a fury that went off in wide shaking waves along my arms and legs. I grabbed the second man's head by the hair and yanked him a ways up from the floor, and in one motion I was straddling him and in a crouch over him, and I was methodically ruining his face with short rights—in the nose and under and over the eyes, and then three hard tight ones into his neck.

And I thought, I will *kill* him—and I stopped.

I jumped away from him as if I had touched flame.

I will kill, I thought. And I thought of Belov.

Let them push me, and I will kill.

I stepped backward, one step at a time—watching both sides of the cell. I want one more to come at me, I thought. The next one *I will kill.*

I stood on the white towel, my back to the door.

I could see them murmuring to each other. I stood my ground and waited, my fists still balled. I wanted to dance around a little bit, maybe even do some shadowboxing, keep myself limber, show them I had done plenty of boxing and plenty of fighting, that I was no one to start up with—and then I thought, no, *don't* show them, let them come—because I will kill the one that comes—and maybe that's what I need, *to kill someone.* Belov!

Let them come! Now!

I glared around the cell. I looked at each one of them, inviting each one of them to come. I slowly moved my attention from man to man, my brain calling *Come! You! Come!*

It was then that I noticed the man on the upper deck, in the corner by the barred open window. How could I not have noticed him sooner?—up there and smiling at me, pillows propped all around him to support his back and arms as he leaned against the wall, smiling at me and murmuring with the five men who had gathered on the floor below him.

I did not smile back—I just kept moving my gaze around the room, going from man to man. I could see where some men had lots of bedding, sometimes two or three mattresses and a couple of blankets and other men had none. I kept looking each man over, first looking now to see how much bedding he had, if any—but then I jerked my head back to the far corner where a sudden movement had flared on the outer edge of my vision.

And here was the one—here was the one I wanted, and he was coming—and let him come. *You! Come!* my brain crooned to him —*you are the one I will kill.*

He had been murmuring with the one in the corner, this one, a man actually wearing a suit, a nice blue suit, and he held his left arm behind his back and his right arm in front of him, the elbow centered near his belly and the arm out in front, and there was a handkerchief draped over his hand, a nice clean cotton handkerchief with a very colorful design, and he was coming at me, his arm out in front of him, his body behind that handkerchief.

Perhaps he expected me to stay where I was—and wait for him. It must have been that—because he wasn't ready when I came

—I could see the amazement in his eyes as I started to run at him. He didn't backtrack, but he stopped and just stood there, clearly stunned to see me run at him, his arm still out in front of him, that handkerchief over his hand.

I took the wrist behind that handkerchief hard in my right hand and with my left I pounded against the point of his elbow, and then I shifted to my left and turned hard and this time with the heel of my left hand I slammed that elbow a second time, and this time when I did it the arm was straightened out and when I hit I pulled back on his wrist with my right hand—and I heard the arm snap.

He didn't fall. He eased back toward a lower berth and halfway sat, his face bleached of all color, the arm hanging like a dead snake whose teeth still gripped the shoulder they had pierced. The man did not scream. Maybe it hurt too much to scream—or maybe he was in shock. I don't know—I only know he'd hardly made a sound— and he still didn't. He just slumped in that half-sit against the lower deck and looked at me—speechless, his face emptied of color, his expression blank.

Now, I thought. *Now I will kill him.*

The knife was still at my feet.

Not a knife. I would not use a knife.

My fist—Belov—the Goldmann boys—the trucks fanning out into Camp Farmington—my father standing with a wooden spoon in his hand—my mother's things fingered in the dirty light—Frank, Frank the good old boy who teased me in the yard—the basement— the whispering—the light that went on and off! This, this!

My life!

My fists! I dove at him. I caught him by the hair with both hands and dragged him away from where he sat. He sprawled out in front of me, whimpering now as I dragged him back out of there by the hair. I wanted it in the center of the floor, where they could all see it—I wanted it out there where I could *move.* He was crying now and snatching at my shirt and at my face with his left hand— but I got him out into the center of the floor, and I knocked aside the little table as I backed up with him and then I ducked under him, and his chin came down on the back of my neck. He would not stand but he was standing enough, and I had my target, his belly and his heart—and I went at it and held him up, and it was like working the heavy bag, no resistance in it, just the dead weight, only this time I was going to open it up, and I felt everything sag inside him, go soft, and the only thing in my head was the rhythm and how long it was going to take before his whimpering quit, and then there wasn't any blue in front of my fists, two lefts, two rights, but it was *brown*—and I jumped with fear from seeing that, and I stopped.

He came down on top of me like a sack, and when I pulled back from him he went to the floor in a crazy melting motion, a sack of grain with its bottom split open and the stuff running out.

What next?

Who next?

I turned around and walked back to the door—and waited. But the door opened behind me—and I stepped away to the side.

There were two guards there. They came in and saw the man.

One of them stayed by the door, near me, while the other one, the one who had taken me when I reached the second-floor landing, he went to the man in the blue suit and bent over him.

"What is wrong with him?" the guard said. *"Korzuby!"* he shouted down to the man on the floor. "Korzuby, what is the matter with you?"

Korzuby, Crooked Teeth—it was my first experience with the nicknames that all the criminals were known by. For years and years after this, when I was with criminals and no longer with the politicals, it was how a man was known—by a name he had picked up during the course of his life in and out of one sort of incarceration or another.

"Korzuby fell out of his bed," the man in the far corner called. "It was a bad fall. Very bad."

"Come on, Korzuby," the guard shouted down at the man. "Get up, get up! It's the doctor for you."

But the man in the blue suit wasn't moving. The first guard called the second one for help, and together they took the collar of his jacket and pulled the man in the blue suit across the floor and then out the door. But before the door closed, one of the guards stepped back into the cell and called up to the man in the corner.

"Enough! No more today!"

And I saw the man in the corner make a two-finger salute in return.

The door closed—and I heard the lock turn.

The ✻ with it! I took a berth and went to sleep. It wasn't easy—I was all jumbled up inside—worried about myself—worried

about what I'd done and what I had almost done—and I suppose I was trembling—and spent—and sad. But the   with it, and the
* with them! I would sleep.

And I did.

It was night when I waked up—but it was not a night anything like night in 39. Some men slept, some walked around or sat in groups talking and laughing, and one group was playing cards, another feature I was to find typical of life among criminal prisoners. Cards were also central to their social order, such as it was—not only was it their favorite pastime—a pastime I would later see pursued for human stakes—a nose, ears, an arm, a life—but it was also the basis of the ranking among them. Based on the Russian deck of thirty-six cards, the sixes, the *Shesterki,* were the lowest, the servants, and these graded up to the sevens and the eights, for example, they being the *Voysmerki,* until you went all the way up to the kings and the ace—but only one ace, and he was the *Atoman*—and this of course was the fellow on the upper deck in the corner, the smiling man with the extra pillows and the extra mattresses, more than had any other inmate in Cell 21.

And some had none—no bedding at all—and still others, sixes, the lowest in this order, they were made to sleep on the floor—despite the berths that might have held them.

It was around a deck of cards that the ranking of the criminals was organized, and I would come to find that they played cards with a great passion, and often. Indeed, everything about the life among them was new to me—and especially this was so of their jargon—a brand of Russian slang I had not encountered before. Hence, that command *Zdryuch!* which I had not understood.

I sat up on my berth and then I stood up. I looked around for the one I would try—and I spotted him—a man standing by his berth and watching the card game in progress around the little table. My man was against the wall opposite.

I strode across the room. I pushed him aside. I reached down and scooped up his pillow and his mattress, and carried them back to my berth. I made a great show of carefully installing these things in my berth—and I listened for a sudden motion from behind me.

There was nothing.

I lay down and turned to the wall.

"Hey!" I heard. "Hey, fighter!"

I didn't turn around at first.

"Hey, fighter! I want to talk with you. It is the *Atoman* who wants you, fighter! Come here!"

I turned around very slowly.

"You calling *me?*" I said.

"Yes. Please," the man in the corner answered, smiling. "You, fighter. Please!"

I walked over to him—and as I went I could tell the others had stopped what they were doing and were watching me as I went.

I stood under his berth, and he leaned himself around to address me confidentially.

"Who are you?" he said. "Are you a person? Are you an *Urka?*"

"I don't understand," I said.

"An *Urka,* a person. Please, fighter, are you a wolfblood? Are you one of us?"

"What *are* you?" I said, standing under him, but my attention more or less elsewhere, my gaze straying among the others.

"I am the *Atoman,*" he said, "the chief here—and you, fighter, what are you? A wolfblood, yes? One of us, yes?"

I guessed what he was getting at—but I let him think otherwise. To him, there were *Urkas,* wolfbloods, real persons—and then there was everybody else—the world divided between those who committed the crimes of theft and murder and those others who didn't and therefore didn't matter at all.

"No," he said, "you are no *Urka*—but you are. A wolfblood, he shows it with the towel—but you did not. You stepped around it, fighter. I know. You are no *Urka,* but I say you *are* one. Hey, fighter—hey, *Urka!* Next time you wipe your feet on the towel, yes?"

"Sure," I said. "Why not?"

"*Urka,* fighter—don't worry, the *Atoman* will teach you. Here, you tell me—who are you?"

"It doesn't matter," I said.

"So be it," he said. "But come, the *Atoman* will teach you. Here, you come up here, all right, fighter?"

And he put a hand down to pull me up. I let him. I pulled up into the berth next to him.

He taught me things, that man—and if he hadn't, then I might not have made it through. It was from him, from the *Atoman* in Cell 21, that I began to pick up the criminal lingo that would allow me to pass as one of them when it was most crucial that I be able to. And it was from him that I found out why they'd sent me to 21, why I was no longer with the politicals.

"They put one in here—and we do the rest, you know?"

"No," I said, "I don't know. What do you do?"

"We work on him—it is a service we perform—for favors. And what the * do we care? We hate them, yes? Spies, traitors, counterrevolutionaries, Jews, professors—they are all alike. We give them * , believe me. They talk—they go out of here and they talk, believe me. But you, fighter, you are okay—an *Urka*— you are like us even so, yes?"

"Sure," I said. "You can count on me," I said, and I ate the food he had and I protected him from newcomers to 21 who thought they might like to be *Atoman* instead, and it was good for me that I did all that, that I had bedding and extra food and learned the things I had to learn to survive. And I fell into the life of an *Urka,* a wolf-blood, a real person.

I learned there, in Cell 21—and again, I built myself up—air, light, and the things I needed when I needed them.

I was the one king to his ace—and thus I began the long game among killers, among fellow captives no less murderous than my captors were, among the strategies of ragtag cards colliding on a playing board that in time would become the frost and the woods, where winning was just staying alive to play another day, and where you did it with cunning, with a heart hardened to the misery of those less able to play, and with the luck that makes the decisive difference in a pitiless game of chance.

It is what living as a prisoner is—a game of chance even deadlier than the one all men must everywhere play—because here death was not one specter but many—and the rule is you cannot run. Run where? Into what? A wall? Bullets? The frost?

I played to play another day. I was like them, in the end—in the end, I was an *Urka* too—and I was there with them the next time the sixes snatched the towel up in reply to the noise at the door. I watched the sixes spread it there, laying it out there in the path of whoever was to enter and be tested. I sat on my berth next to the *Atoman,* and perhaps I was even interested. Would the poor devil prove to be the *Urka* I was? Let me see—and, like this, I became as much a part of them as I had ever been of anything else. And, like this, as one of them, the hours for me passed, and all the life that preceded thinned and then vanished.

Miriam? Leo? My father?

Did I think of them as I stood my ground in Cell 21? No, I did not let myself think of any of what lay behind me—or of what might have been the lot of those that were all in the world that I loved.

How could I?

I stood my ground and looked around for more ground. It is what a wolfblood does.

THIRTY-THREE ——————————————————

In twenty days they moved me from 21. They did not move me to court. They did not put me in a locker and take me somewhere in the van. They did not release me from the white building on Vorobevka Street or from anywhere else.

No, they moved me back to *Spets Korpus*.

But not to 39.

They moved me to the basement.

To a holding chamber—to the place they put you in before they took you out for good.

I went from 21 to the death chamber in *Spets Korpus*. But I was an *Urka* when they took me.

In the basement all the death chambers were on one side, and there were three of them. Across the way there were the isolators. But I don't know how many—I could never see to tell.

It was the same as 39—no light, just the bulb always burning, and the size was just the same. But there there were four bunks—and seven men. No blankets, but straw mattresses and straw pillows, no different from 21, and it was, in this respect, not so bad, and the food was all right, three feedings a day, and not bad.

Sumbatov, he was one of the others that I remember, a young Georgian, a man who had been in charge of an underground air-drome in Sukhomi, a city to the south—and as for him, he'd been accused of treachery, of letting Turkish planes fly over the Black Sea into the territory of the U.S.S.R. And another I remember, but not his name—he was a ship's captain from Novorosseisk, and the accusation against him was that he burned down his ship while it was docked in a foreign port. And the two engineers from 39, they were also there—and not, therefore, dead, as I had been told. Not yet.

The ship's captain, they took him out my first night there.

Sumbatov and I talked that night. The others had not seen them come, not seen the four of them there at the door, the three in black leather with two tight belts crisscrossed over their chests, and the fourth man, the one who held the large revolver and who did the work that was to be done. But Sumbatov and I, we had seen them when the ship's captain went out the door—and we talked, he and I, the rest of that night.

The seven of us slept in shifts, anyway—and Sumbatov and I, we were day sleepers, four bunks for three in the day and four at night—but now there would be an open bunk for a day sleeper who wanted to move to the night. It was better to be a day sleeper, I think—because they only took you out at night. But for some men I suppose it is better to be sleeping when they come.

I had a lot to eat. Nobody ate much—and there was a lot left over for me. I ate—but the other politicals, they didn't eat much at all—nor did they sleep much either. They were waiting to be taken out. But me, I ate and I slept—because it was all too late now, and wasn't I a wolfblood? And to　✱　with this and that! This and that were both just one thing in the end—and that one thing was death, and the　✱　with it.

The *Parasha* was small and it was emptied every day, and you could get water whenever you wanted it, and the guards let you talk or tap—and I had extra food, leftover food because the others would not eat.

And there was no position here—and you could tap and talk all you wanted—because it didn't matter anymore—they were going to take you out—and the job was just to wait for it the best you could. I did it by eating and sleeping—and talking with Sumbatov. Weren't we both flyers?

We passed the time that way, Sumbatov and I—until the night the feeder opened and they called him.

I saw him give a start when the feeder opened—and then when his name was called—not his initial, but his whole name—he jumped up where he stood and looked around, uncertain. He called back, "Do I take my things?"

And the answer came. I heard it.

"No. You will not need them anymore. Get ready!"

And then the feeder slammed shut.

He stood there. He looked at me. I didn't know what to say. I liked this man, this handsome young Georgian—but I did not know what to say to him. He gathered up the few belongings he had and passed something or other out to each of us, and then he stood there waiting for the door to open.

How long did Sumbatov stand by the *Parasha* waiting? An hour? Two hours? And then he sat down by the door. And still he waited, and he would not talk. Toward morning, he was still there waiting when I drifted off into sleep. The last thing I saw was Sumbatov squatting silently by the door.

It was just a joke.

They didn't take Sumbatov out that night—nor any night for a week after that. But in that week his hair fell out, and the little that didn't, a fringe that went from one ear around the back to the other, that turned white.

Sumbatov was an old man when they called me out. My call came thirty-five days after Sumbatov's joke, and by then the young Georgian was old.

Like him, I stood at the door and waited.

There was nothing I had to pass out—nothing that was mine to give to each that was there, and there were fewer there when my turn came.

It was night. But I was a day sleeper, and wide awake.

I got up when they called me—"G! Get ready!"

And I did not have to wait long at all.

In minutes the door opened—and they were there, the three in black leather and the man with the revolver. I walked into the corridor a few steps and stopped.

"Head down, hands behind back, no noise."

"All right," I said.

I stood there. One of the men with rifles came toward me, and the other two followed. The first one pushed at my mouth with something—it was the gag—a rubber ball.

I opened my mouth and let it in.

So be it—and to * with this and that!

I don't know what I thought of. I don't think I thought of anything special. Perhaps I thought about the rubber ball. I don't know. Or about Sumbatov and his hair turning white.

They stood around me, the three with the rifles and the black leather uniforms and the belts that were drawn taut in diagonals across their chests—and the other man, the one with the revolver, he was in a long black leather coat—and he stood off from us, under the little bulb that hung from a cord overhead.

Then he came over closer—and I could see how clean his shave was, and how terribly erect he stood. He spoke to me, rather gently, I thought. He said, "Keep your head down. Make no noise. Do not turn around. When I tell you to walk, go that way, and go straight and don't turn around. All right, now walk."

I started in the direction he had pointed, and when I started the three with rifles grouped themselves around me, two with bayonets touching my sides and the third man leading the way. The fourth man, the man with the revolver out, a revolver that looked much too large, he was somewhere behind me—and in this fashion we paraded to the end of the corridor.

I could hear pounding on the doors of the isolators as we passed them. Were they pounding for me? Or just pounding for themselves?

There was a solid iron door at the end of the corridor, and over it, very high, an arch formed of bricks. We went through it. We continued on through two more doors—doors that were made of bars.

Perhaps that is what I was thinking about—the things I was seeing—feeling—the points of the bayonets, the floor that I walked across, the arch made of bricks, barred doors.

What was there to think about?

We went through the second barred door.

"Turn right!" I heard from behind me, the voice of the man who would do the work.

I turned right—into another long corridor.

"Stop!" I heard from behind me.

I stood there. Stop? Did they not take you outside? To wherever they kept the cars that backfired?

The three with rifles stepped away as the one with the revolver came up. He stood in front of me—and he lifted my chin. With one hand he lifted my chin and with the other he returned the pistol to his holster.

He took the rubber ball out of my mouth.

And then he put his hand on my shoulder and gently shook it.

"Eh," he said, "Herman—we frightened you, yes?"

"No," I said.

I do not think I was lying when I said that.

"Oh, flyer, Lindbergh of Russia—hero, eh? Brave American, yes?"

I said, "You asked me, I told you."

"Very brave, very brave—the wonderful American. Bravo, wonderful American—what a fine hero you are."

He laughed. He was holding me hard by the chin—and then he pinched my cheek and lightly slapped it.

"So brave, so brave," he murmured, and then he shouted out for guards to come, and two of them came, and took me away from there.

But they did not take me back to one of the three death chambers in *Spets Korpus*. They took me instead to Cell 316—up the stairs to the third floor and to the cell marked 316, and here there were over three hundred men, and the place was no bigger than 18.

It was night when I went in there, into 316. But here they slept in shifts too, and there were as many men awake as there were men sleeping, and the Elder was one of the ones who were awake.

I think he was surprised to see someone coming in at this hour, and he wanted to know where I was coming from—so I told him— and he made a man get up from a place and give it to me to sleep or lie down or whatever I wanted. Because there was no place unless someone gave you one.

But I couldn't sleep. I couldn't do much of anything except think about the iron door and the arch of bricks above it—and about the four of them in black leather. I was lying there thinking about the way he'd held my chin and then pinched and slapped my cheek, when I heard tapping going on.

It was from the cell next door.

It said: *Herman dead, shot tonight.*

I think I had already decoded the first two words before I realized what I was hearing.

I looked around for something to tap back with. I was in a frenzy to respond.

I used my knuckles. So what if the sound did not penetrate the thick wall? So what if no one ever heard? It only mattered that I say, over and over, it was not so.

With my knuckles, I tapped:

316: I am Victor Herman.

I kept on doing it, over and over, tapping the very same message.

I am Victor Herman.

I just kept doing it—until the intervals between tapping grew longer and longer, until my knuckles were knocked open, until the skin was all tapped away, until I hurt and I bled and I couldn't do it anymore, and then I fell into a terrible sleep.

Eh, Herman—we frightened you, yes?

I had said no.

It had seemed to me true. It had in truth come to me and hurried from my mouth as it came.

But *yes,* brave man with a revolver! *Yes,* brave Russian in a long black coat who comes in the night to take men out. Yes, you frightened me, fine wonderful Russian hero!

*Bravo, you   *   scum!*

I did it every day for a week—sent that message. What else did I have to do in a day? It was something to do, to say that you lived.

I was in 316 for two weeks—and again they moved me, this time to a place they called The Club, a large tall room that had once been the prison chapel. But since the Revolution did away with what it had been used for, that big room was now a place to keep men. It had been rigged up to provide three levels, three platforms —and the old men were on the first one; above them, on the middle level, the politicals were kept; and on the top, the criminals.

I just went ahead and climbed up to the third tier. Was I not a wolfblood now? Wasn't I entitled? It was better up there, more light, more air, more freedom.

There were somewhat over 1,200 men quartered in The Club, and the fewest number occupied the topmost level. It was, of the three platforms, the best one to be on.

The criminals handled everything—the distribution of the food that was brought in big kettles, who got it and who didn't. It was the same with sleeping places and bedding and everything else—the criminals made the rules and enforced them.

I made sure I got my share and I didn't care who, besides me, did or didn't. There was no will in me to make a revolution, to worry about this man or that man getting his fair share. I made sure I got my share, and that was the end of my caring. I saw the sick and the feeble denied, and I did not care. The strong took and the strong survived—and that was the way it was—because you meanwhile had all you could do to protect yourself from the ones with real power—the ones who put you in here in the first place.

But I was only a month in The Club. Again they moved me—this time to the *Spets Korpus* subbasement, to a cell where there were ten men, counting me. The tiers were both on one side, and I took a place on the top one.

It had no number, this cell—or at least none that I ever saw. There was nothing on the iron door that I could make out when I had stood before it to be let in—and no one in there, none of the other nine men, knew otherwise. It just had no number, so far as we knew. And we let this convince us that it meant something special—that it was the last holding place before they set you free.

We all of us thought that, that freedom was just a matter of time now, and when they called us out—all of us together—that did it! There was a kind of uproar, men hugging each other and kissing each other, men jubilant as I'd never seen them. They called us out and told us to take our things—who among us had things?—and in a group they marched us out into the yard. We stood there in the cold—the ground was mushy from melting snow. It was a very cold day.

The guards called for us to line up, and you could not take your place in line without being seized by the fugitive thought that what they were going to do was shoot us.

But, no, that could not be. Could it? They never did it like this. Ceremony was ceremony—the three in black leather and the officer with a gun—and this business, it had no ceremony that I could see.

I took my place in line.

I was shivering a little, but mainly, I think, from expectation. It was going to happen—it really was—and I felt Miriam leaping into my arms, the exuberant weight of her small body, and I felt my father clasping me to his chest, our hands at each other's back patting and patting to show it was all right, that everything would be all right forever again.

Or were they all dead—my father, my brother, my sister?

An officer strode into the yard, a man who wore the insignia of the NKVD. He walked to the end of the line nearer him, and I could see him handing something to the man that stood there.

I counted.

I was eight from where the officer began.

What was it he was passing out?

And as he drew nearer, I could see what was in the hand that he held at his side—little slips of paper—and each man was getting one of these.

What would it say? It would say . . . *Released. Hereby freed. Innocent. All charges dropped.* It would say, *Go home and be happy and forgive us and live a long life.*

He was one away from me now—and then he was in front of me and I heard him say, "Name?"

"Victor Herman," I said, my teeth chattering.

He spread apart the three little slips of paper he had left, found the one he wanted, and held it out for me to take.

"Here," he said.

I looked down. I saw my name printed there, very carefully printed out. I kept looking at it in bewilderment.

My name?

The officer was standing in front of the man after me. I touched his sleeve and I said, "It just gives my name. What is it? I don't understand."

He glanced at me. He was handing the man next to me the slip of paper for him.

"Turn it over," the officer said.

I did.

There was nothing there but a numeral. It was marked there in red, very large, with a circle around it, the circle also in red.

It was "10."

Ten? But what does ten mean?

The men were all looking at each other and a few were talking and most were silent. They were comparing numerals—*What one did you get? Three? Seven?*

Herman—*ten?*

No one ever told us what those numerals meant. But it was not necessary to tell us. What they meant became clear enough in no time at all.

There was a van parked in the corner of the yard, and when he had given each man a slip, the officer turned to one of the guards, and then the guard stood away from him and called out.

"Heads down, hands behind back, no noise—and in single file you will march to the vehicle there. Now march!" he shouted, pointing to the van in the corner of the prison yard.

We walked across the yard in the direction of the van. We went there in a very orderly fashion. No one cried out. No one tried to run.

Why?

It was not weakness, no. Nor was it fear so much.

I think it was something other than that. I think it was uncertainty—and shock—and not believing, even then, that the numeral you were given meant what reason insisted it must mean.

Your heart looked wildly about for some other reason—something cunningly hidden, something too wonderful to occur to you without a consideration of all the attractive possibilities.

Ten! Did it mean ten thousand rubles in the way of compensation for your hardship? For being wrongly arrested and wrongly tortured and wrongly robbed of more than a year of your life?

It *must* mean something like this. But what? What exactly did *ten* mean, and why was the marvelous news merely implied? Was this some sort of Russian idea of whimsy? *Ten?* Did it mean in ten days I could go home? Did it mean that for ten years the Soviets were going to give me some sort of pension, a kind of evening of a score that had showed a debit on their side of the ledger?

Surely it meant something like this—but what?

Yet why were we being pushed down and into the lockers? And why were the others, the other nine, so silent?

And why was I feeling so queer again, as if again I had taken one step too many and again tripped over a precipice into dream?

The van pulled out. I was thrown against the forward wall as we began the steep grade down toward the city. I rested my weight against the angle of descent—and there, alone in my locker, my body pressed in the direction of the van's motion, I let it into me. It had been seeping in from widening fissures, and now I let it all in, through cracks that opened to flood me with the clangorous knowledge. It was an ocean, that knowledge. *Ten! Ten years!*

I had been given my trial.

Sentence had been passed.

Everything had been reduced to a numeral. See your name on one side and then turn over to the other side. See a numeral and a circle running round it.

I had been tried and sentenced—and the sentence was ten years. I added the years of my sentence to my age. It is an addition every sentenced man does.

I was twenty-four when they let me out of the Gorky prison. When they let me out of wherever I was going, I would be thirty-four.

It was easy—you just added ten to whatever you were.

PART 3_____

**STALKING RAT IN THE JUNGLES
OF THE NORTH**

THIRTY-FOUR

It was 1939, early September—and the air was cold. Troopers ringed the railroad station in Gorky, but I did not see them until I had been unloaded from the van and stood waiting with the others in the mushy snow that lay in patches that gave way to mud.

They marched us to the outskirts of the station. There was a prison wagon there, a Stolypin wagon. Along one side there were windows with steel-mesh netting ballooning out from them, and we could see guards inside walking up and down.

My group was loaded next to last, and it was chaos inside when we got in there, more men than there was space to fit them in, even with squeezing, and there was panic now—because the meaning of the numerals circled in red was understood. There were windows on one side of the Stolypin wagon, so that when you looked in what you saw were guards walking up and down. But on the other side there were no windows, because a row of windowless cells ran from one end to the other, and in each of these there were four bunks, two lowers, two uppers, and in each of these cells fifty men were to be transported, but fifty men in such a space was about double what even extreme crowding would permit. And yet it was done.

There was something approaching pandemonium in the cell that I'd been assigned to. But the lock had been turned and there was no getting out now—and the thing to do was to stay alive until you got where you were going and they let you out. Men were tearing men from the upper bunks and forcing themselves into places up there, where you were safe at least from being trampled and could maybe breathe a little better.

I did it too. I grabbed at the legs of the man nearest me and just dragged him down from where he was perched and scrambled up in his place. And then I pulled my legs up after me and squatted well back against the wall.

We were more than two hours in that station waiting to move. I figured things might get a little better once the motion of the wagon was felt and men were lulled into a kind of quiet. The waiting made everything worse, and some men were dead before we got out of the station.

But then we could feel the jolts and hear the ugly banging as something, an engine or another car, coupled onto us—and then there was the squealing complaint of metal moving as the Stolypin wagon began to roll.

The cells were made of bars, so if you were in the right position you could see out through the steel-mesh windows across the way.

There was only one thing we wanted to see—and that was some landmark that would indicate our direction. Because there was only one question you wanted answered now—and that was _which direction?_

You could live with any answer save one.

But that one was the answer we got.

We were heading _north!_

I could see enough to tell we were heading toward Vyatka, a place called Kirov now. It was north. You would settle for any direction but that one—because it was already cold back in Gorky.

It spread through the cell like poison gas—_north!_ But it was something to quiet the men—and they all knew it now—_north!_ They sat balled into the small forms the crush allowed them, all of them silent now, gray and silent as rocks.

The dark came quickly, and in no time the cell was all in blackness. There was no light in here, and you wanted one. A man might come at you and yank you from your place, and anyway, it was impossible to sleep. I squatted with my legs hugged against my chest and my eyes wide open to watch for attack.

I couldn't sleep. I didn't want to sleep.

I jostled the man squatting next to me.

"Our direction, it's north, isn't it?"

He said yes, he was sure of it.

"Toward Vyatka," I said. "You agree?"

He said he agreed.

"I've been there," I said. "I've flown over it."

"Oh?" he said.

I could not see his face. There was no telling how he meant this.

"Yes," I said. "I am a flyer. I used to be a flyer."

"Can you fly now, friend?" I heard him say. "Because if you can do it, then teach me how."

"No luck," I said. "Can't spread my wings in here."

"Be glad you can still breathe through your beak," he said.

"Yes," I said—and was quiet for a while.

"You know where we're going?" I said.

"North," he said.

"Of course," I said. "But how far north?"

"Pray that it is not too far."

Too far? What would be too far? How far was *too* far?

"Listen, friend," I heard him continue, "I can tell you this much, and that is this. There are two chances before Vyatka—two camps along the line before north beyond Vyatka. There is Sukho Bez Vodny—and there is the next camp about two hundred miles farther up. That one is Burepolom. After Burepolom, well . . ."

Sukho Bez Vodny—Dry Without Water.

Burepolom—Stormbeaten.

And I was to hope for these?

"I will hope, then," I said into the darkness next to me.

We stopped at Sukho Bez Vodny. Men were taken off. Men were put on. I was left to squat where I was, and the Stolypin wagon moved on, rolling north.

After Sukho Bez Vodny we were fed.

Three loaves of bread, about a pound each, were thrown into our compartment. But the sharing was fair enough. I think each man got a little chunk. But it was impossible to tell if each one did. In any event, there was no fighting anymore.

There was no water. No fighting and no water—it is something I remember.

We stopped again, and this time almost everyone was taken off. I could see the station was called Sherstki. But where was Burepolom?

They lined us up under heavy guard—and then we were moved out. We walked for three miles—and after three miles I had what I was looking for—the *Gulag* my hoping had got me. It was Burepolom.

They ran us through the bathhouse first—first the clipping and then under the spouts. It was the same as it was in the Gorky prison —lined up in groups for the clippers while our clothing was moved into *Zharo Kamera,* and then we stood under the water and rubbed ourselves.

But here they fingerprinted us. Right after the showers, finger-prints—and then they assigned us to work teams, and once we had our assignments we were sent to our barracks.

Three thousand or so people were quartered in the central compound at Burepolom, and there were about twenty barracks to hold them, unpainted wooden structures that huddled against the hard ground. So far as I could tell, there were no politicals here, nor were there serious criminals. Mainly these were men whose offenses had been minor—and the place was really more a work colony than it was a prison. The rule was lenient—as things went. But it was nevertheless a prison, with a high fence going around the perimeter and beyond that a few thicknesses of barbed wire—and of course there were the guard towers placed strategically, and each of these manned by machine gunners.

Yet it was a light camp, as I would discover, and most of the prisoners were there to work off light sentences—three years, five years. In all my time at Burepolom, I came across no one who'd been given a sentence equal to mine, and yet this was something else that I would in time discover, that ten years was the minimum for a political, and that shooting was the other alternative. At least that was customary.

But remember that these were exceptional times—and that everything I describe was played out against a backdrop of routine chaos. It was the way things were at the time, and for a long time after that—and it is difficult to comprehend what the effects of such chaos can be—because comprehension asks for a certain sustained set of conditions, whereas the times I am telling you about cast up conditions that were no more consistent than were the crystals of snow that descended upon them. Indeed, if there was consistency, it resided in inconsistency.

Think about me for a moment—among the three thousand in Burepolom, so named for the tangle of trees the wind had contrived the forest all around. I was a twenty-four-year-old American in a T-shirt and sneakers and cotton trousers I had more than a year ago put on to run around a track. I stood in the snow and in the freezing mud in a place called Burepolom, and in my pocket there was a slip of paper with my name on one side and on the other a number. The hair was newly clipped from my body, and the lice were re-situating themselves in safer nests.

What was I? A man falling across the length of an alien land. How does one make sense of such a thing? Someone pushes and you go hurtling sidewise ten thousand miles from the stance that was your life. It was as if my body were glued to some fabulous momentum into whose path I had inadvertently stepped.

Birch, maple, and pine—mainly pine—pine trees like an ocean frozen into stalks of black water. It was wood—and it was what I began with—and what I would end with—a monstrous infinity of wood. Was I made to think that my father had been a carpenter? That his father before him had been the same? Oh, yes, I was made to think about that—and to wonder about that. I would have plenty of reason to do so—and time to do the same. But it wouldn't be so bad at first—at first it would be easy—and even rather pleasant. After Cell 39, trees, timber, wood, the wonderfully clean smell of it all, at first it would be an Eden. But in time it would be a coffin that wanted you.

I could see it out there, spreading away in all directions from the camp—a forest. But I did not go there yet. First I went to the barrack.

It had upper and lower berths arranged on each side like a railroad sleeping car, but with no walls between—two uppers, two lowers—and a step away another set of four. The light was good and there were windows, and the door was not locked and you could go to the outhouse when you wanted—and you could do more than that, you could even walk around the camp when you wanted. And there were mattresses and pillows, straw. No blankets, but mattresses and pillows, one for each man.

It was a good place.

I sat on my berth thinking that, trying to convince myself how good things were—and I waited to be told what to do. I didn't ask the other men there. I decided a wolfblood just waits. But I was hungry now—and it seemed time.

I called across to a man on the other side.

"I'm hungry. How long before we eat?"

He rolled onto his side to face me.

"You want to eat?" he said. "Go eat."

"Oh, yes?" I said. "Show me."

He hopped down from his berth and motioned me over to the door, and when I got there he opened it and pointed.

"See that boardwalk? Follow it along."

I went immediately. Food you could just get to? Yes, this was a good place.

I found the eating shed. On a table near the door there was a pile of dirty wooden bowls. I took one and went to a sort of counter affair along the back wall. They gave me *Balanda,* trash soup. It had a wretched odor, as bad as back at Gorky, but there were fishbones in it and leaves and even a bit of fish meat in it too and some grain. I ate five bowls.

"That's good," I said to the man who ladled it out to me. "What else do we get in this place?"

He didn't answer.

I asked him again.

"*Balanda,*" he said, "all you want. Once a day, cereal. Bread? You get what you earn."

"Is that all?" I said.

Again he did not answer. I took another bowl of the soup, swallowed it down, and started back. It was dusk when I started out of there along the boardwalk. Perhaps what I saw would not have affected me so if it had been revealed to me in strong daylight. But the light was darkening now, true dusk, a special time, and what I saw was scribed against the ghostly light of what briefly appears just before early evening truly establishes itself. It is a vacant time, that time between the end of day and the coming of night. It's just a moment, really—it quickly passes—but in it everything is colored by the failing light, both dimmed and made vivid at the same time. It is a strange time—I think children know best what I mean—a fearful, solitary poignance fleetingly radiating from ordinary things.

I saw the line of men in just that sort of light. It made something in me turn over and move itself upside down.

There must have been about eighty of them. They were walking in single file. Each man had his arm extended so that his hand rested on the shoulder of the man in front of him. They were wearing what looked like nightgowns—but whatever they were, they were white, long white gowns.

These men were moving toward me, and as they came I could see how each held his other arm tight against his body.

Each man rested a hand on the shoulder of the man in front of him—except of course the man who led the way—for he was sighted, whereas the others were blind. It was a vision I would rather not have seen, that string of blind men winding slumbrously through the unearthly light. Or was it I that was slumbering? I had that feeling again, as if I were in a dream.

The blind men were coming to the eating shed with their bread ration tucked under their arms, held there to protect it from the sixes who attacked when the line neared the eating shed. I guessed the bread must be very dry and hard and needed the *Balanda* to wet it down and get it soft enough to chew. In Burepolom you needed strong teeth if you were a blind man who did not wish to risk his bread.

I shooed a couple of the sixes away, and then I thought to   *
with it. This was not a world I had made. It was only a world to keep myself alive in.

I made my way back to my barrack, my belly sloshing with the foul *Balanda*. I lay down on my berth and looked around. It was not so bad, this place. Ten years here? It would not be so bad.

I adjusted the straw pillow and tried to get comfortable. Remarkable, how something soft seemed odd to me now. I rolled onto my side and faced the wall.

"Comrade," I heard someone behind me say.

I turned around.

It was the man who had directed me to the eating shed.

"What?" I said.

"Good, eh? The soup?"

He was seated on the bunk across from me.

"Not bad," I said.

He laughed.

"Where are you from?" he said. "Tell me, what is your name and where are you from and what is your crime?"

"Not important," I said. "The usual story," I said. "But you tell me—those blind men, what are they doing here?"

Again the man laughed.

"You saw the blind ones, eh? Bad fellows, those blind men—every single one a treacherous counterrevolutionary, Comrade."

"Yes?" I said. "In what way?"

"In what *way,* he asks!" the man said, and this too he found amusing and laughed. "Visual agitation, Comrade! That is their counterrevolutionary crime! Begging on the streets and being blind, Comrade! It is an embarrassment to the State, a shame upon us all!"

"I see," I said and turned back to the wall.

"He *sees!*" I heard the man say and then heard the laughter that followed.

Not long after I fell into sleep. If I dreamed, then there must have been somewhere among the flashing images the vision of that winding train of white-gowned figures gliding silently through a celestial light.

The waking was clangorous here at Burepolom, someone slamming two pieces of iron together somewhere near the eating shed, and you went to the feeding in shifts—and which shift you were in depended upon which work team you were in and how far out from camp you had to go to do the work they gave you. The farther you had to go, the earlier you went to eat.

I was in Team 1, the team made to do hard physical labor, and when the banging of the iron waked you, then you went to the eating shed before dawn. But the team leader told me to stay back from work the first day, told me the first day was a free day. So I went back to Barrack 1 and tried to sleep. But they called me out of there about an hour later. All the new prisoners were being assembled for instructions. One of the Commandants would call you out, a sort of police force made up of criminals who were big enough and strong enough and mean enough to enforce the rules and to make sure things got done the way the Chief of the camp wanted.

So I joined the others. They were lined up in front of Barrack 3, stamping around and shivering in the morning cold. When we were all there and waiting, a man sauntered over and seated himself in a chair one of the Commandants came running with. I think this man was the largest man I have ever seen—a great lummox of a fellow.

He sat in front of us, his mass so eclipsing the chair it looked as if he sat in air.

"My name is Bobrov," this ox of a man said. "Make sure you remember it. I am head of the NKVD at Burepolom. Make sure you remember that too. Here are the rules. Work good, fulfill your work plan, and you may write and receive two letters a month. But this does not apply to a political prisoner. Work good, fulfill your plan, you may go to the movies once a week. But this does not apply to a political prisoner. Work good, fulfill your norm, you make three days of your sentence in one. But this does not apply to a political prisoner. I tell you, this is not a prison camp—it is a work colony— but nevertheless we have an isolator here. Break any of the rules the Commandants give you, and you go to the isolator. If you are a political, worse will happen. You have Bobrov's promise on that."

He went on to say some more things, but I did not listen. What was the use of listening? It was all the same to me. Was it my imagining, or did this Bobrov glance at me every time he said "political"?

After a while he stood up, and a Commandant ran to take up the giant's chair and to walk behind him with it as Bobrov strode away. Then another Commandant, the one who had called me out, shouted out that all new members of Team 1 should report to him. I walked over to him, the few yards that were needing.

"You are the only one?" he said.

I said, "I don't know."

He said, "Yes, you are the only one. Come with me."

I followed him to Barrack 6, to a window where they were handing out clothing. He stood next to me as the man at the window handed some items out—heavy quilted pants, a quilted jacket, both black, and a pair of grass boots, something the Russians call *Lapti,* a foot covering woven from the underbark of trees.

"Follow me," the Commandant said, and he led me back to Barrack 1. "Inside," he said, when we got there, and then he told me to put the camp clothing on.

I started to do as he said. How well I can remember now the extraordinary feeling that came over me, what this business of exchanging one set of clothing for another meant to me. Because I wanted to keep the *Spartak* clothing I had, clothing that I had worn now for more than a year, clothing that had taken on a certain meaning having to do with life before what passed for life in the Gorky prison. It was clothing that had witnessed my testing, an ordeal of an order I had never before experienced. They were like battle clothes, those tennis shoes and the purple T-shirt and dark blue cotton trousers, and though I froze in them in the cold months, they were like a lucky piece to me now. Had they not seen me through the worst of my days? Was there not some magic in them now? I was going to keep everything on and simply add the quilted pants and jacket and *Lapti,* and why not? In the cold that was clearly coming, I would need all the covering I could get. But the Commandant wanted what I had.

He said, "Give me those," pointing to the things I had on. "Give me those and I will show you how to wear the *Lapti.*"

I didn't resist the order. Perhaps I would be better off without the stuff, better off without the memories attached to them. But now I know that was a foolish thought. How could the mere shedding of a few articles of clothing shed what the body knows?

But I handed the items over—and I could see why he wanted these things.

He put them on—filth and blood and all—and he got back into his quilted pants and jacket and tucked the tennis shoes under his arm. Then he went rummaging around the barrack and came back to me with some rags and paper and cord.

"Here," he said, holding the stuff he had out to me. "Wrap your feet in this first. Then the *Lapti.* Then bind the uppers to your legs. Here."

I took the stuff and did as he said—but he made an irritated motion with his hand, knelt, knocked away my hands, and showed me how to do it.

"Thanks," I said.

He stood up and put the sneakers back under his arm.

"I know who you are," he said.

"So?" I said. "Who am I?"

He said, "I'll slap your brains out if you get funny with me. Shut your mouth and listen. You are the flyer, Herman. I read your papers. You are a political. Mind you obey me or I will tell the others. You are sentenced to ten years. And all ten years you work only at the very hardest physical labor. Do you understand?"

"I understand," I said.

"All right," he said. "I like you," he said. "I am glad to have these," and he indicated the things he had taken from me. And then he handed me a rope and showed me how to tie it around the quilted jacket to hold everything up and keep it tight.

I stayed in the barrack the rest of that day. Around midday I went to the eating shed to get some more food, but they would not let me have it—no more food until I worked, and they would not let me work that day. But that night the Commandant came to the barrack. I was trying to fall off to sleep—the hunger in me rousing me whenever sleep started taking me under.

I felt someone poke me in the back. When I turned around, it was the Commandant.

"Here," he said.

It was a chunk of pork fat, raw.

He watched me eat it, and then he went away to his bunk, and I slept.

It was my second night.

In the morning I went out with Team 1.

I followed the team to the wood mill—all the way to the outer reaches on the other side of Burepolom. The team leader took us around to the back. The job was to work logs that were no good for anything but firewood. The team leader told me my work plan, my norm. It was to saw up twenty cubic yards of wood—twenty cubic yards a day.

"How about gloves?" I said.

"Only when winter comes," he said. "Now go in there for your tools. Tell the old man you get an ax and a saw." The team leader pointed to a shed nearby.

I reported to the shack and asked for an ax and a saw. The old man there went looking among his things and came back with what I needed.

"Carry the ax in here," he said, stuffing the handle of the ax under the rope that cinched the jacket to my waist. "Break a saw, no food for the day." He winked and turned over the saw.

It was a bow saw, a handle at either end but a one-man saw. At any rate, the blade was thin. As for the ax, it had a handle about two feet long, just a rough piece of birch stuck into an ax head.

The first day I broke three saws. And by nightfall, I'd sawed less than three yards. The next day I broke one saw, and I produced a little over ten yards.

I ate the third day. That day I broke no saws and I made my norm—and thereafter twenty cubic yards was no trouble at all. In fact, it seemed to me light work. I enjoyed it. It was building me up, this work. It was good that I had it. I had food, such as it was, and I had work, and the work was easy and it was good for my body.

It went on like this for a month—sawing the bad wood, stacking it, and waiting for a man to come along and mark it. But Bobrov was always watching. If it rained and I went to the tool shack to get out of it, Bobrov would show up and run me back out. If I went over to the clubhouse and snuck into the movies, Bobrov would show up to chase me out. They showed Westerns, American Westerns, old silent films, and something in me was crazy to see them. But Bobrov would always catch me. Once I persuaded the mechanic to let me turn the projector crank. There was no electricity in the camp, of course, and that's how you made the projector work, and he let me do it once. But Bobrov found out—and whatever he caught me at, it was a day or two in the isolator or a day or two without food. And finally he sent me there for ten days. But in Burepolom the isolator was not so bad. It was child's play in contrast to anything in *Spets Korpus*. And the ten days there, they were worth it—for the few minutes I had of Hoot Gibson and something American to see and to add to the things American I'd begun to index in my heart. Bobrov always kept after me. It seemed this Bobrov had nothing to do but slip his mammoth bulk from place to place to keep an eye on me.

It was during this month that I uncovered a piece of information. It told me something about my destiny in this camp and in all the camps to follow. It is something that makes no sense to me even now. I have no explanation for it, nor can I think of any that might come close. But what I by and by discovered was this—that politicals always had inside work, that so far as I could find out, politicals did their work indoors—and especially this was so if they were Jewish politicals. But in this camp and in the slave camps to follow, I worked outdoors—and almost always it would be in the woods, the work most dreaded of all.

Did their papers not tell them I was Jewish? If they did not, then was this in my favor or not? And why me, why was I singled out among all the politicals? But is this not a question every man asks—*why me?* And for every man the answer is the same—*chance,* that is *why you.* And why not? Isn't blind chance the one reliable foreman of the days we live?

Blind chance? If we live at all, for even an hour, are we not already in debt to fortune? Then what man, what woman, what child has a real grievance with bad luck?

If one lives to add things up, one is already ahead of the game.

Three subcamps were attached to Burepolom—and these were Unzha, Nuksha 1, and Nuksha 2. After a month in the main camp, I was sent to Nuksha 2.

It was different in Nuksha 2. It was not the easy life of the main camp. It was the beginning of an inferno.

Why was I sent to Nuksha 2? And from there into the abyss that followed?

As well ask why a falling leaf spins left or right, or spins not at all.

THIRTY-FIVE ——————————————————

Nuksha 2, it was only one barrack. At a little distance from each corner of that barrack there stood a gun tower, and from each a machine gun stared down at you. Just beyond the gun towers, there were several depths of barbed wire ringing the camp, and everywhere there were guard dogs, every single one of them a German shepherd.

This was Nuksha 2, and it was here that I first went to the woods. Nothing but lumberjacks were domiciled in the one barrack that constituted Nuksha 2, and at dawn we went to the woods. It was birch we worked, and birch is hard wood.

I was the only newcomer at Nuksha 2, and it was immediately clear that a newcomer would be made to prove himself. These were all criminals, these men, and they were as hard as the wood that they worked from dawn to nightfall. They hated each other and they hated me, and I hated right back—but it was common hatred of the birch that bound us one to another and kept the fighting in control.

What had gotten me here? Was it Bobrov? Was it my having tried so often to see those silent Westerns? Was birch the price I would pay for those glimpses of something American? Or was it merely Bobrov's whim? Yet the Commandant had said that for me it would be nothing but the very hardest labor.

Thus Nuksha 2—it was what the sentence said.

In less than a week the work plan worsened from what it was at first. Your time in the woods was lengthened until well after nightfall. Since the bonfires for burning branches and the brush we dug out gave light, it was seen that a man could go right on felling and sawing trees well into the night. And with the heavier norm, the snows started, building up quickly in the forest, and that of course made your norm harder still.

The camp rule was strict here—and the barrack was kept locked. But what did it matter? Working the birch from dawn until late night left you with nothing but the strength it took to go out and come back and to stretch out your body and sleep. And the food was strictly governed here, to a degree that seems mad in the telling.

You ate alone in Nuksha 2, and you were guarded when you ate. In the morning and at night, you were called out one by one from the barrack, and from there you went to the eating shack, and the food was doled out to you in exact accord with the amount of wood you felled and sawed, and you sat there in the eating shack and ate it under guard—and you were permitted to save nothing, neither for yourself later nor for sharing with others. Whatever your norm was, that was how you were paid. Me, I was getting a pound and a half of bread a day—because my norm was large and I fulfilled it. That was at the night feeding, the bread—and in the morning and night I got soup and the soup had meat in it. It was mainly horse, but it was meat. And sometimes there was a cereal of some kind.

My norm was eighteen cubic yards—which, for birch, is a big norm, because the wood is that difficult to work. But here it wasn't just sawing that amount—here it was first cutting down trees and then sawing what you needed to make your plan. I ate all right at eighteen yards—but many men could not come near that plan, and they ate not so well at all. It was when the snow deepened and took you into it like white tar that more and more men fell short of their norms and that more and more men began to starve.

But there was one food everyone got—a kind of drink they made out of pine needles. It was the rule—you had to get it down, a half glass every day—the idea being this would give you the energy to do your work. Also, there was another rule that was peculiar to Nuksha 2, and this was that you had to work on free days, and so you worked without cease, from dawn until a little before midnight, and you did it in the deepening snow.

It got bad—as the winter got bad—and as the work fell off and men began to starve it got worse. In time a gang of them tried to break out. I couldn't figure it. Where did they think they could run to? What was out there? But they tried it, anyway—and when they did, the machine guns went to work, and that was the end of the ones that tried.

No one tried it after that. But it was better they killed you when you tried something—because if they didn't kill you, it was the isolator instead—and here at Nuksha 2 the isolator was an open dugout. In winter, the guards would stand up there and pour water down on you and it froze. In summer, they'd use lime, and a man would cough his lungs out.

But I met my plan and I ate—and that's all I did and all I thought about. It seemed to me it was me or the birch, and if the birch was hard, then I would be hard. I would be a man with bark up one side and down the other, and, like a tree, I would stand where I stood.

My time in Nuksha 2 was three months. I did my work and that was my time, not one day of it in the isolator.

But I think I could have taken the isolator there at Nuksha 2. By then I think I could have taken anything.

Yet there was one thing I saw there that made its way through the bark that covered me. Like the line of white-gowned men, it left me, this thing I saw, with a vision that comes to me even now. It is when I see a woman in a fur coat or a woman late in the term of her pregnancy, that the scene in the Nuksha forest flashes in and out of a landscape that is only some safe place here in Detroit, a shopping center, a sidewalk near my house. And often it happens, this vision, when I am looking at Sveta or Janna—or thinking about Galina, my wife.

We had been working the birches pretty far out, and my brigade was getting closer and closer to a line of railroad track that interrupted the forest. One day, toward evening, when we were not far from those tracks, a short train pulled into view, its pace a leaden crawl. We stood a while to watch it pass, but just as it got by us it creaked to a stop, and we could see that the last car was a boxcar, a cattle car, really, and, once the train was halted, guards came running from the front to slide back the door.

There were women in there—fifty, sixty, seventy of them—you couldn't count, it was so baffling to see women like this, all dressed in summer clothing, light dresses and summery skirts and blouses, and some even had on sandals and that sort of thing, and some high heels and stockings, and a few had on spring coats and fancy hats, and there was one with a kind of short fur jacket, not a thing meant for warmth, really.

It was strange to see women, and it was very strange to see them so attired, the snow all around almost waist deep except where we had cleared it to work the birch. Those women, their faces were awful with fear, and the skin was like chalk. Had they been in prison, the lot of them? What else could have taken the color from their flesh?

The guards ordered them out.

I stood, like the other men, with my ax in my hand, and I stared. There was something about what I was seeing that held me to the spot. What was this? What was it I was going to see? But the women just kept coming out of there, most of them jumping badly from the wagon and falling headlong into the snow, righting themselves, and slipping again. It was like a circus act almost, like some crazy interlude of clowns out in the middle of nowhere. Was it some kind of performance that was under way, a troupe of zany traveling ladies who went all over the winter wilderness entertaining lumberjacks in the snow? Was that what their falling into the snow was all about—you were supposed to laugh at such preposterous falling down and getting up and falling down again? And the costumes, were these not also calculated to inspire mirth in the audience of stunned men that stood there gaping, each with an ax in his hand?

But then the women were all out of there and pushing themselves against each other, drawing themselves into a collective embrace to deal with the cold. But in those flimsy clothes? In this snow —with everything everywhere frozen? How ward off this cold except to insinuate yourself into someone else's body? The men, even in our quilts, we were cold—and these women, some of them were scarcely dressed for a cool spring day. And your eye was drawn to the one in the little fur jacket, a thin thing, that jacket, a rag, really, but it caught your attention, and then you saw why it did. You saw that below the skimpy jacket, below that dark curtain of fur, there was the swollen promise of new life weeks away, maybe even sooner than that. She was somewhat taller than the others, or anyhow seemed taller, given that she was notably slender where she was not notably pregnant. That and her pale hair showing where the scarf did not cover her head, that hair, that slim body, and the patrician expression on her face, it all imparted to her something of an aloof presence among the others, something vaguely aristocratic. You noticed this, and then you noticed that the others stood somewhat away from her—or else it was she that was standing somewhat apart from them.

There was a great silence all around, now that the women had quieted. As for the men, we were speechless in the face of this spectacle. I don't suppose any of us or any of them failed to hear the guard who called out the general announcement:

"You sluts will work here with these prisoners until nightfall. You will clear the snow and you will collect the branches to keep the bonfire going. After sundown, you will spread your legs for the prisoner who wants you. But first my colleagues and I"—he swept his arm in a grand half-circle indicating all eleven guards—"will put our thermometers inside you to make certain your filthy holes are the right temperature for these brave Soviet workers." He laughed heartily. He had a thought, and he could barely stand the hilarity it promised. At last he said, "I imagine there will also be a dog or two that will want to warm his   *   . But which of you harlots is pretty enough to attract one of these splendid animals? Well, we shall see, we shall see," and with that the man exploded into hysterical laughter.

Was the man serious? Who could tell? Already the spectacle was so utterly mad, you were willing to believe anything could happen next.

It did.

There was a terrible wail from the woman that was pregnant, and then I heard her call out, "Please! Please! I will give birth in a month!" and then I heard our team leader, a vicious criminal named Pavlov, shout, "All right, the month is up!" He advanced on the woman and kicked her square in the belly.

What Pavlov had done happened fast; it happened before anyone could stop it. It was the same for what was done to Pavlov. No one could have stopped it. But no one tried. In an instant he was dead, hacked to bits by the axes that hit him, his head taken clear off at the neck, but chopped open before it was cut from his body. The snow where his destroyed body lay looked as if pails of blood had been carried to the spot and poured out.

The guards were visibly frightened. They raised their weapons and called the dogs to attention. The kicked woman lay crabbing along in the snow, her hands grabbing and her feet pushing so that she moved in a little circle near to where the trunk of Pavlov's body lay like a continent from which the rest of him—his head, both arms, both legs—spread like major islands, his blood the ocean that separated them from the gory mainland.

Would they shoot us all? Would they release the dogs and start to shoot? I don't know what the rest of the men were doing, but I stayed where I was, my eyes on the dog nearest me. But then the tension seemed to go out of the air, as if it had reached too great an extension for it to be sustained. There was a sort of breathing out. It might not be an exaggeration to say that everyone had been holding his breath. Who had ever witnessed anything to equal this?

The next moment the guards were ushering the women back into the cattle car, and in no time at all they were loaded, two guards lifting the woman who had been kicked and raising her to the hands of the women who returned her to the floor of the cattle car. A signal was given, the little train screeched once and then lurched, and then began moving slowly up the line, the guards who had jumped off her now trotting alongside and, one by one, hauling themselves up and in.

We worked that night until well after eleven. There was no talking. Not that we ever talked much in the woods. But this night there was no talk in anyone. The lumberjack brigade never moved from the zone where Pavlov lay in six parts. If there was talking, it was what that mess in the snow said to us.

What _was_ that man?

And what were we?

This life—the snow, the birch, all of it—what did it kill in you while the carcass of your soul split apart and gave birth to something very alien? But the new thing you were, did it not come from inside?

All those nights and all those days I worked at sorting out my feelings. I suppose I was trying to rid myself of shame, shame that pressed at me after a certain truth had made its initial assault. It is easy to talk about the first part of that shame—my wanting a woman, any of those women, whatever the circumstance of my having her. It was something I had never had and something I wanted to have, and I can understand my wanting not ending at the boundary where cruelty begins. It's easy to talk about that part—

but not so easy to talk about my feelings from seeing the woman kicked and then seeing the man Pavlov cut apart. There was something in this for me that goes beyond horror—or that perhaps stands darkly alongside it. It's something that's no good explaining now—or trying to explain now. My years get in the way, the things I know about men now that I have been one long enough. And there is no going back to recapture the precise composition of my feelings and thoughts at the time. I just know that they were not entirely consistent with what I expected from myself. I know that somewhere in there something like excitement, a certain zest, the agitation of something animal erupted in me.

I worried about it. I worried, and I wondered what were the thoughts and feelings of the other men who had seen these things.

But weren't they all criminals? What could the things in them have to do with the things in me?

I tried to believe that then. I was young enough to believe that then. And now that I am old enough to believe otherwise, I don't want to think about it.

In early spring I was moved to an outpost on the Unzha River —in the outer zone of Nuksha 2. The work was floating logs, and it was easy work after the birch. We lived in tents, and the prisoners were all politicals, men and women, about seventy of us, a few Americans, but mostly Germans and Chinese. It went that way all that summer, the summer of 1940, floating logs and keeping to myself and letting the sun do its work on me. I kept to my silence and the others kept away from me. Was I impersonating that pregnant woman? Was this how one paid for the evil he guessed was in him—by taking on the face of his victim?

Then say I was like her all that summer—not talking, just doing my work and standing apart and begging the sun never to stop.

They moved us all just after dawn one morning that autumn, rounding us up and distributing to each a hunk of bread. I don't know where they all came from, but a heavy guard appeared, each man with a machine gun and a dog. The gang of us were marched out of there—all the way to the Shertski depot, where a Stolypin wagon was waiting.

They loaded us.

We waited.

In time there was that jolt and the coupling onto an engine—and movement.

Movement! From what to what?

North? South?

Again it was north. The knowledge went through that wagon like a shark through water, a frantic whispering and then the long hush until nightfall—when a soft crying began, a few of the women in the cell that all the women were put in.

North. I was going north again. It was like traveling into your bones.

THIRTY-SIX _____

At Vyatka I was taken off, taken to the city prison there. It was a great fortress of a place, dark red brick, a gloomy business about three hundred years old. But after five days they took me out, put me in a truck, trucked me to the station, loaded me into a Stolypin wagon, and again carried me north—north through Zuevka and Yaya and the Kai district—until after six days of rolling north we stopped at Fosforitnaya, a place named for the phosphorus that was mined there.

It was a name you did not want to hear.

There was no being in a *Gulag* very long without someone telling you about the phosphorus mines. Everybody had a story about the phosphorus mines, a story that would always be offered in reply to a story about the forests. It was something to brag about, a competition—had you been in the woods and lived through it? Well, this one and that one had been in a phosphorus mine and lived through it! What were the woods? The woods were nothing!

But then you found out that it was not often one went into a phosphorus mine and came back out. The dust got your lungs and, all in good time, that would be that. So they only sent the weak ones there—because that was going to be that for them one way or the other. The strong ones? Here, take an ax and saw.

I was strong. And in the forest that enveloped Fosforitnaya there was a furor of pine to use my strength on.

The camp was only a few hundred yards from the station, and I could see it through the clearing that opened it to view—five big tents and three squat wooden structures—and as those of us that were unloaded got nearer, I could see the barbed wire, several depths of it, with guard dogs strutting along in between, and the usual four gun towers looking down on the whole affair. It seemed that those tents and low wooden buildings cringed beneath the tall eyes of the gun towers. But the forest beyond and to the sides did not cower. It pressed against the little outpost, a thick heave of pine that might have been a tidal wave of wood stalled for the moment.

The air was very cold—and already the ground was under feet of snow—and winter was yet to come.

I walked along with the others, head down, not thinking— once in a while looking up as we made our way to the camp, maybe thinking once in a while would my black quilts do, but mainly *not* thinking, *not* looking up, mainly just taking my time with whatever would come, but knowing it would not be good—that it would be the forest or the phosphorus and a new kind of cold.

The hunger in me was out of control as I kicked my way through the snow. It was the promise of food that set the hunger raging—that prospect that somewhere up ahead, there in among those tents and dwarfed buildings, there was something to eat.

Food? It's funny about food, funny finding out how long you can do without when you know there is no choice—and then how that ravening can seize you when a morsel is somewhere in sight.

I had not eaten since the bread portion handed out that last day at Vyatka. There had been no feeding along the long ride north —not for me, not for anyone in the Stolypin. There was water, but that was all—and when they let us out, there were not a few who could not move. And some who could move fell into the snow after a dozen or so steps.

I don't know what happened to the ones who fell down or to the ones who couldn't make it out of their wagon cells in the first place. I knew that many of them were women, but I don't know what happened to them. I just kept walking, pushing in the direc- tion of the camp, those five tents, those three buildings, the gun towers, the fancy-stepping dogs.

I was starving—and I knew it—and the only thing to do about it was to keep on walking.

I could see the gates now—and then I could see something that was like seeing my dead mother beckoning. Is it vile to liken your mother, the ghost of her love, to the prospect of food?

I say a starving man is sent back to nature's first lessons.

Two tables were set up in front of the camp gates, a large steaming pot atop each. I could *see* the steam, see it and smell it and taste it all the way from where I was, the vapors flashing briefly up and then vanishing against the bleak backdrop of the camp.

Those who could run, ran—and I with them, six or seven of us hurling ourselves along the last few yards. We formed a queue and waited for a signal, others in the long march behind us in staggering groups of two and three adding themselves to the line.

But there was no signal—nor were there any bowls or dishes or anything of the sort on either of the two tables. A man stood behind each pot, there to ladle up whatever was in there—and at last the fellow who waited at the front of the queue fell forward and placed himself before one of the tables, whereupon the man behind the table snatched off the waiting man's hat and ladled a serving of soup into it.

You could see how hot the soup was, how the man up front there was trying to get it down before it drained through his hat, how it must have been scorching his mouth to do it. I was fourth in line and I waited. I waited and watched that first man, his face buried in his hat now, a man made into a draught horse with his muzzle in the feed bag.

Now the two men dishing out the soup began to gesture to the queue, *You here, you there, hurry along,* and then there were guards stationed at the gate waving on those who had had their ration, *Get the soup into your mouth and do it fast and get in here!*

The second and third men had no hats, and neither did I. They took the scalding soup into their cupped hands, and tried to hold it and tried to get it down, while the guards at the gate called out for everyone to hurry or no one would get anything, and I started to move forward to one of the pots, and as I negotiated those few steps I could see that the first man and the second man were suddenly overrun by a mob of prisoners just inside the gates, and you could see that it was the food they were after, and the third man saw this too, and he was trying to get it all down and get his hands licked off before he stepped inside the gates, but the guards were shouting at him to get the * in there *now,* because if he didn't

get the　✶　in there *now* they were going to shut down the food
line, and I saw all this happening as I held out my cupped hands
and took into them a dipperful of blistering liquid and mashed my
face into it and sucked it all up, because what was the burning
alongside the starving?

I licked at my palms and then I wiped my palms hard on my
quilts, all the while looking at the third man, who was doing the
same, still standing just outside the gates—and that's what I did
too, and then, like him, I wiped my lips with my sleeve, and I
think everyone still in line saw the two of us do that and they must
have known to do the same. Like the third man, it was not until I
was sure I had all the food off me that I stepped inside the gates.
But I didn't turn around to see what those behind me were doing—
because what I saw once I got in there made me sick, and I just
kept on walking fast, not turning around and still wiping at my face
and my hands.

It was the second man that I saw, lying to the side just inside
the fence. He was lying on his back with both hands over his
mouth, and it wasn't until you looked where the hands didn't cover
that you saw the blood running along his jaws onto his neck.

They had bitten the man's lips to get at the smear of food still
on them.

We were starving, those of us that had made that six-day ride
north with nothing but a small measure of bread at the start and a
bit of water each day thereafter. But here in Fosforitnaya they were
also starving—and they'd been doing it for longer than six days.

Food was in shorter and shorter supply now, and for those
that did not work there was no food at all—except for what one
could scavenge or find on a man's lips.

It was not that those who were starving in Fosforitnaya did
not want to work—it was that they *could* not work—for these men
were the men that were choking and dying from the phosphorus,
men too weak to work but in their desperation made instantly powerful by the promise of food, whatever it would cost to get it.

What will starvation do to a man? It is a tyranny of the flesh
that must be seen to be known. Even then, it can only be witnessed,
not comprehended. It is too exceptional a spectacle, the human
form turned inside out into a mouth wide to anything that will go
into it. What can any of us understand of this until the screaming
tissue of the stomach knows? Men will kill for women and for

money and for power and for principle and for hatred, but never
with the savagery that they will kill for food. But it is like three,
four, five potatoes to speak of this now, here, at home, at home in
America, in the midst of a bounty that never fails to startle me.

I go with my daughters, here in Detroit I go with them to the
markets, and I am made dizzy and breathless by the array that leaps
from shelf to shelf. It is like a cataract drowning me in a delirium
of succulences, and my eyes see bags of crackers running with
juices.

Here, as in every *Gulag,* they domiciled you in accord with the
work force you'd been assigned to—Tent 1 for lumberjacks, Tent 2
for mechanics, Tent 3 for the ones who went to the phosphorus
mines, and in Tent 4 and Tent 5 there lived the ones who weren't
going to live very long, men and women who did not work and
therefore were not fed. If they ate, it was what they could gather
from foraging or from doing worse. Did they eat the bark off trees?
They did. And it was a diet that only hastened their dying.

But when you are starving, it only matters that you fill your
belly—and anything will do if anything must.

The work was in shifts here, and so was the sleeping—and
when I found Tent 1, I also found many men asleep inside. There
were two long tables in the place and between them a stove that
burned wood, and the sleeping setup was on decks, and I took a
bunk up on top—as near to the stove as I could manage. It was a
long military tent, Tent 1, two sets of shelves along either side, and
I figured to get myself up there on the upper deck no matter what
I had to do to do it—because this was as far north as I'd thus far
been and maybe there'd be a little more heat up high.

These were long solid shelves, these decks, no divisions between, and I just picked a spot as near to the stove as I could and
started climbing up. There were men up there from one end to the
other, and I just went up there and started pushing my way between
two men.

One of the men up there started kicking at me to keep me off,
but I pushed up and lay back and slammed the butt of my hand
into the muscle in his thigh. The man quit his kicking.

He didn't say anything. I didn't, either. I just pushed all the
way up there and forced my way between the two of them, and

once I was in there I shoved them both back enough to make a space for myself.

I stayed up there waiting for whatever was to come—work, food. About an hour later a work gang returned, men as rough and scabby as the trees they fought, and just as silent. I watched them sort themselves out to different places on the shelves, and I could see there was one that was heading my way because he was looking at me like a man that was coming, all right.

He was smart enough to stand away from the deck a little bit— to hold himself outside of kicking range. He stood there and called up to me, a fellow all woolly with great masses of black hair.

"You! That is my place!"

"You!" I called back. "It was."

"That is the good place," he called. "You ask the others here and they will tell you I get the good place."

"I ask no one," I said. "Speak to me again and I'll come down there and break your back for you."

He looked at me.

You would think the others would have been watching all this —but no one paid any attention. I kept checking the tent, to see if he had allies, to see if there would be more than one to fight— but no one was looking our way, or if anyone was, it was with indifference, the blank countenances of exhausted men.

Again the man called up to me. "I say come down!"

I didn't answer. I rolled forward and vaulted off the shelf, landed with my feet planted in front of him, and pumped my knee into his groin. When he staggered and dipped his head, I chopped him behind the ear, and then I let him have it a second time just before he went to the ground.

I looked around the tent.

Mostly no one was looking back—and the few that were quickly looked away when my attention came to them.

I climbed back up and waited, now and then leaning over to check on the man that was down. In a while he got up and moved away. He didn't look back at me. I'm glad he didn't. If he had, in reflex I might have said I was sorry—and that would have been a mistake.

In time the whole place began filling with men back from the woods—and as they came they roused the men that were sleeping— and it was then that I discovered the sleeping men were loaders, not lumberjacks, and that the loaders slept by day while the jacks worked the woods, and when the jacks slept the loaders went out to pull the logs out of the forest and get them up into the railroad wagons that waited to collect timber.

The loaders were called out for lineup, and the lumberjacks took their places. I stayed where I was while new men took the places of the two men I'd shoved aside. These new men looked at me with no great interest and then they looked away and slept.

That was okay with me. There was no one I wanted to talk to —and the less talking I did, the less chance anyone would find out I was an American. It's not that I worried so much about being found out—because for a long time now no one would have taken me for anything but a Russian. But there was no reason to risk discovery—because there was no telling how that might worsen things for me. Why take a chance?

I kept my mouth shut as much as I could. And what was there to talk about? Grunts were all you needed for the little exchange that was now and then necessary. Did I have questions to ask, things I needed to find out? What did it matter what I would ask? The facts would be the facts, and I would know them soon enough. What difference if now instead of later? What could it change?

Change? There was only one change that was worth notice. Freedom and return to America.

Anything less was all the same—a captive somewhere on Soviet soil—it was all the same.

You went to the woods before dawn. They called you out, and you formed up at the gates in rows of five, and guards with plywood boards double-checked the numbers as you left the camp, and as soon as your team stepped outside the wire, guards and dogs fell in all around you, and someone would shout out the rules:

"Head down, no talking! Keep walking in the same direction you're told! Stop walking or take one step to either side, you will be shot with no warning!"

My second day there, they shot two men who slipped in the snow and fell.

But wasn't this really a warning? Weren't the workers in such abundant supply you could kill off two just to give the others the right idea?

They shot two men that second day, one coming, one going, and on the third day going out and coming back the men went

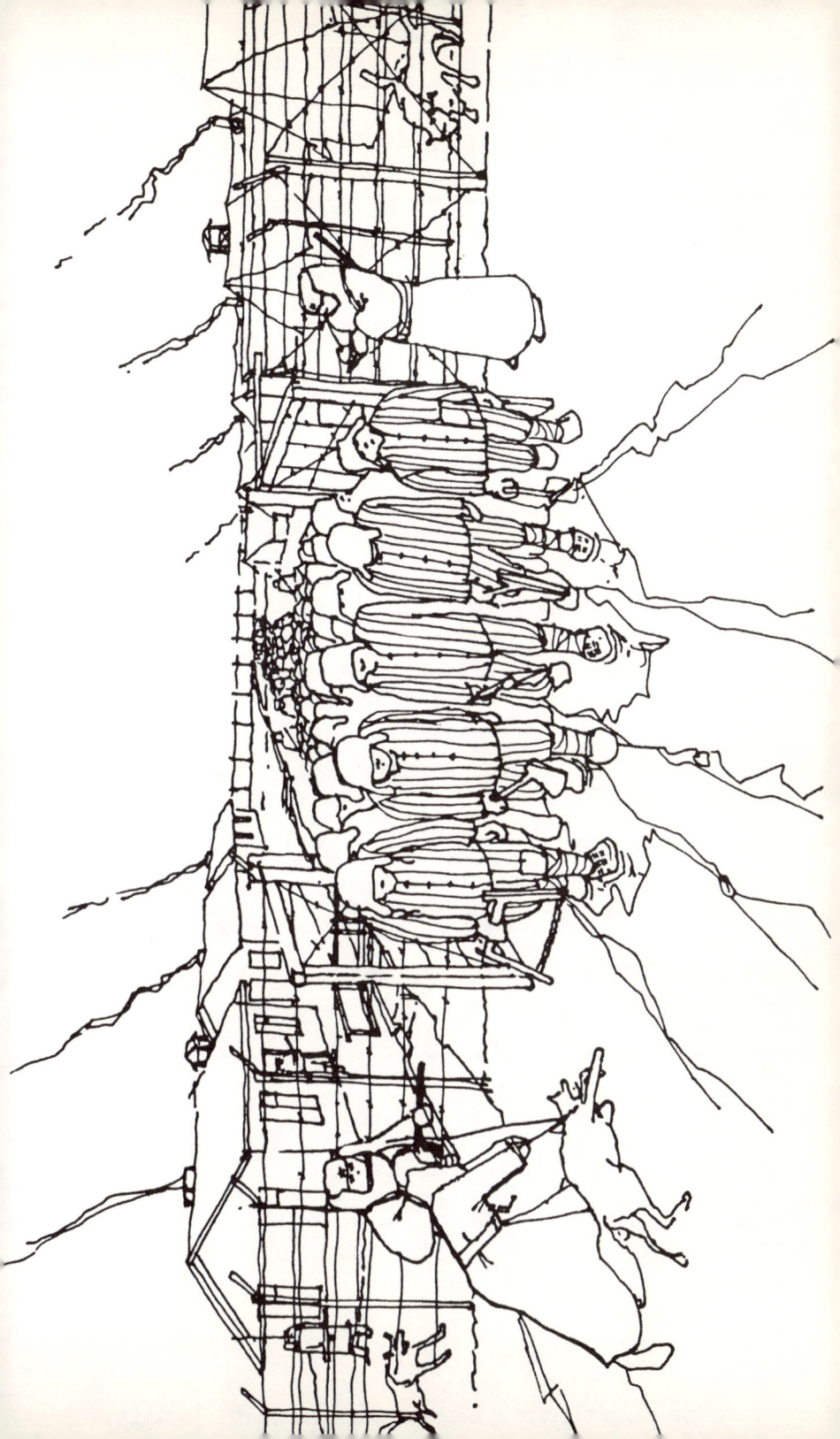

buddies on the long saws, two long saws to a line of five men, each man with a grip on the lifeline held out in front of his row, to give a man some check against bad footing in the snow. And if a man went down, you could feel it along the line of saws, and you yanked him up as fast as he fell.

For the rest of my time at Fosforitnaya, that's how we went to the woods and how we came back from them, holding saws between us. You didn't know another man's name—and you didn't care whether he lived or died, but your hands and his hands gripped the same thing—and if you were keeping him alive, it was only because that's what he was doing for you.

I went to the woods in Fosforitnaya, to work pine in the manner that I had worked birch in Nuksha 2. But I went to the mines there as well, each time wild with rage that there must have been some mistake, that I was not weak, that I was strong, that I belonged in the woods. But they sent me to the mines, anyway, and perhaps it was for punishment or perhaps to break me down. I don't know. They sent you—you went—and in my case it was only seven times, each time for two or three days in a row.

Was it worse in there, down there in a space you had to back out of because it was too cramped to turn around? Down there where the dust went into every opening in you no matter what tricks you tried to keep it out?

Is a phosphorus mine worse than a forest?

It is a crazy question, a question that could only entertain men already mad from deliberating between horrors. It is a question no more reasonable than a choice between cancer of the bowel and cancer of the brain.

It was bad in the phosphorus mine.

It was bad in the forest.

It was bad in the snow.

The dogs were bad, the fear was bad, the sickness was bad, the slop they fed you, the times they beat you—it was all bad—and after a point, what is the use to measure?

I had a piece of rag and I would fold snow into it, and then I would try to tie the thing over my nose and over my mouth, and to keep it tied, and I went down there and dug in that murderous cold and then I backed out with a sack in my hand, dumped it where they told me to, and then I went back down again, crept back down into that strange cold you have to get inside the earth to feel.

It is a different kind of cold down there, a cold that seems to have its source inside you and to billow out from there to the surface of your skin. It is not cold so much as it is chill, partly a thing the thermometer measures and partly a thing it can't—partly that thing we call dread.

For a while I coughed blood like the rest of them that went down there. But I always went back to the forest in time, and I was always glad to get there, and no matter what my norm was, I made sure I met it—because you only had to fall short once, at the most twice, and they sent you to the mines for good.

My plan down there was two sacks—dig out chunks enough, beat them into powder with a little ram they gave you, shovel it all into a sack, tie it, drag it out, and then go on back down to do another.

I couldn't keep the wet rag over my nose and mouth, the both —so I did a better job of it over just my nose and kept my mouth shut, and breathed through my nose and went for faster speed down there, trying to finish my two sacks as swiftly as I could manage and then get the * out of there. I couldn't have done it any faster than I did, but I would cough blood anyhow. Back in the woods, for days after I'd still be coughing blood.

Those that stayed, they never lasted very long.

Yes, I suppose the phosphorus was worse than the forest— unless of course you *chose* dying over the one alternative to it you had. It was a choice that many made—taking death over the weight of living, over the thing that endlessly slammed itself into your face when your little sleep was ended and you rose to do another day.

My norm in the woods was twenty cubic yards.

I met it.

I never missed it once.

We cut everything in our zone—and sometimes it was birch as well, and that made the quota harder. But the idea was for the work gang to clear it all, brush, pine, birch, whatever grew, burning what could not be used and sawing up the rest—and sometimes, when the loaders were shorthanded, loading, doing that too.

I think the idea was to clear out the forests of Siberia—an area larger than the United States. I think that really was what the Soviets had in mind, and they built the railroad tracks north as far as the men were cutting, and when that region was cleared, they laid tracks farther north. But when I was in Fosforitnaya, that was as far north as the tracks were laid, and I sometimes loaded those platform cars—and it was a good thing to do because when you'd been cutting and then went to loading, it gave you the notion you were getting somewhere. You weren't getting anywhere, but it was pleasant to make believe you were.

There was no getting anywhere against the forests of the north. There was no getting anywhere against anything in the north. Not really.

It is a place to be if you are ever dismayed by the opinion that man has made himself more powerful than nature. It is a place to restore your respect for nature, Siberia is. There is no beating it back. There isn't even any living with it. All you can do is smack at it and then run away and rest a while and then go back and smack at it again.

You can make little cuts in Siberia. But you could never make anything as considerable as a wound. If there was wounding, it was what Siberia did to *you*. Unless it just killed you. But if it didn't, then it left you with a lifelong wound, a hollow of cold that lay in your heart and never ceased freezing you from the inside out. That and a colossal crashing of wood rolling thunderously out from a corner of your brain in every sleep that comes to you for the rest of your days.

Yet even now I think of Siberia as a magic place—a place where marvels happened—Galina miraculously there in the snow, our infant child in her arms, and Loon, Red Loon, my friend, his wild impossible laughter a boisterous torch in the icy Arctic dark.

THIRTY-SEVEN ————————————————————

The place had a name, and I found it out because I sometimes saw it stenciled on an ax or a saw—on a new one, anyhow. The English for it was Hard Labor Camp Number 231/1—and I sometimes used to go out to the woods or come back from the woods trying the English for it and then the Russian for it over and over in my head. Was the effect more fearful in Russian—or in the language that was my own?

The name of a thing changes a thing—it's an effect that all of us know—and somehow the knowing that this place was called what it was made what it was worse. It was like being shot, on the one hand, or being executed, on the other. They came to the same thing, but you'd rather be shot than executed—and that's how I felt about that name, in any language—Hard Labor Camp Number 231/1, *Gulag* 231/1.

And I learned some other names in those first few weeks in 231/1—the names given to the two Commandants who more or less ran the place. One we called Krivoshivka because of the curious way he held his head, as if his neck were broken—or *had* been broken and then remarkably healed at an angle; the other fellow we gave the name Kuznets, forger—and why I don't know—but perhaps because it was thought that he'd alter the papers on you without going to a higher authority. But these were the names we used for those men, and I don't think I ever heard any others. It might have been better to call them Big   ✳   and Bigger   ✳   , although you could never be sure which one deserved the more venerable title—since each seemed to vie with the other to prove the crueler. Besides, they looked very alike, great hulking fellows, truly startling in their size. They occupied the Commandants' office, one of the five squat structures I'd seen from the station, and it must have been something to see them sitting there together in that little shack—but mainly they were not in there; mainly they were out and around the camp tormenting whomever they could find.

Sometimes, very late at night, when the jacks were all sleeping, Krivoshivka or Kuznets or the both of them would show at the flap of the tent I was in. One or the other or both would call a man out. There were two hundred men in that tent, sometimes more, sometimes less, but about two hundred, and the Commandant had plenty to pick from. Neither would step inside but instead just stand there at the flap and keep calling until the man waked up and went out. If you listened hard, you could hear one or both of the Commandants shouting for a while, a kind of teasing and challenging, the sort of thing we imagine boys do—*Who do you think you are, a lumberjack, eh, tough guy, eh, a real tough guy, huh? So if you're so tough, then how come I can beat the   ✳   out of you? Oh, you don't think I can beat the   ✳   out of you, is that what you think?*

After the first time, I never stayed awake to listen. I didn't want to hear it and to hear what was sure to come next. What did it matter? I would see enough of it the next morning, when I formed up at the gates with the jack who'd been out to see Krivoshivka or Kuznets or sometimes with the truly unlucky devil whose attitude or size had inspired both Commandants in equal measure.

But no one called for me in the night—and that was as far as my interest went. The first time and the second time, but the second time for only a moment or two, I listened to the banter and to the crescendo toward worse, but thereafter when the calling of a name would wake me in the night, I would just keep my head down on my log pillow and try to fall back off to sleep.

It was never very hard to do.

The bell was going to slam you awake at five in the morning, some metal they banged together in front of one of the two administration sheds. You were going to be getting up to labor that took you right into the night—and in six or seven hours there was going to be that metal banging again. So it was never very hard to fall back into sleep, whatever was going on right outside the tent. The morning bell would go off and one of the Commandants and some sixes would come rushing into the tent, heavy clubs in their hands, all of them yelling, "All out! All out!" And they would run around the long tent bashing those clubs on the tables and the sleeping shelves.

"All out! All out!"

And all turned out, shapeless bundles of men rolling out of their bunks, their quilts all bunched up from the tumult of sleep, each man now going to where he'd stashed his bowl or tin can or the spoon he might have managed to snatch and hold onto, and then, as if a live wire had been run under every single one of them, like a stream of animate rags you saw them moving in a fast hobble to the eating shed to get their morning *Balanda,* and you were moving with them—like them, a dead man with a living center somewhere down in there under your quilts, a place that was all ache and an unholy wanting for the hot trash soup that was your first feeding of the day.

You ate what you'd earned, and then you formed up five abreast at the gates and took the ax they gave you and the long saw if they gave you one of those, and then you gripped a place along the line of saws and waited for the signal, and then you moved out beyond the wire and heard the rule, every time registering the exact lift and fall of every single word: *"Head down! No talking! Keep walking in the direction you're told. Stop walking or take one step to either side and you will be shot!"* And then they were all around you with their old-fashioned tommy guns and their dogs, and you trudged behind the man in front of you, your *Lapti* squeaking in the fresh snow, and you walked and walked, holding your place on the line of saws, and it didn't matter where you were walking until you heard the command to halt, and that was your zone and you worked it and worked it until it was dark again, and then you turned yourself around and went back, only this time muddy all over and wet through, the wet freezing on you in the night air, and this time only one hand on the line of saws and the other holding the rope you'd cinched around one, two, three logs, wood no good for lumber but wood good enough for the stove back at the tent. You, like the rest of the swaddled creatures to your left and right, holding tight to the rope that secured the one gift the forest could give and tight to the saw that secured your life, the frigid air skimming up under your jacket now because the rope that had tied it down now tied logs—so that the logic of outflanking the cold *later* broke against the logic of deceiving the cold *now,* but it had to be one way or the other. You did what the men did, the other *Zks,* the thing they called you now, prisoners, and like them you took the rope from your waist and ran it around one, two, three logs, what you could find, what you could carry, and made a knot.

That was the routine you let settle over you—and the sameness of it was a kind of talisman that you rubbed every day to keep your faith that you were safe. You doted on that routine, and you wanted it to keep on going that way forever, because you knew that when it stopped, what it stopped for would be nothing you wanted —because you knew what every *Zk* knows. You know that a change is a change for the worse.

But one time it wasn't.

It happened this way—details that are to this day very clear in my mind. For some reason none of us knew, we were ordered out of the woods early—one or two hours earlier than usual. There was no way of telling time exactly, but the sky was still somewhat light —and the jacks were formed up, counted, and started back: *Head down. No talking. Keep walking in the direction* . . . the usual.

We got back to the wire, were counted, went to the tent, unloaded our logs, got our bowls or pails or tin cans, and started out for the food we had earned.

There was a creek that ran through the camp, and it divided the wooden sheds from the sleeping tents, and you of course had to cross the creek to get from your tent to the feeding shed, and there was a plank of wood over the creek even though it was frozen. But the plank was there because the creek ran along a deep gully, and when the creek was frozen the gully would fill with snow right up to the plank, and the plank was icy and treacherous and a fall off it was nothing you wanted, but you also didn't want to cross through that depth, either. So you used the plank and watched your footing.

The jacks were moving across the plank now, but moving in the other direction were the mechanics—because the mechanics worked and were fed according to a different shift, and this was their customary time for feeding and about an hour or two early for the jacks—so the two groups were going to collide there where the crossing was—the jacks going, the mechanics coming—and there was no way for them to do anything but collide, because no *Zk* ever got out of the way for another *Zk*. It wasn't something you'd do even if he worked the same team as you did or slept next to you or was the man beside you on the line of saws. You never gave ground to another prisoner—and if he was a prisoner you'd never seen before, a prisoner from another tent, not for anything would you step aside to let him go by.

I don't think it's necessary to call this the code of the wolf-bloods or even to say that it is a practice that arises out of the circumstance of captivity. I think it has more to do with exhaustion, with the saving of energy, with the conservation of whatever life is left in you for the doing of only what you must, for *work*—because strength meant work could be done, loss of strength meant that it couldn't, and if it couldn't, if your norm surpassed what strength you had left, then you were not fed, to begin with, and you were sent to pickax and powder the phosphorus, to end with.

So you never stepped aside—or made any other movement of arm or leg that was not a movement you *had* to make to eat and stay alive.

It is in this light that you must consider the collision of the mechanics and the lumberjacks on the plank that stretched across the little abyss the frozen creek created, jacks and mechanics cascading into each other like opposing columns of marching rags.

There was nothing comic about it. Men were hurt.

There was no fighting. Who had energy for fighting? But there was butting and shoulders heaving into chests and men falling heavily, and nothing at all comic in any of it, this silent commotion of dark husky shapes, some struggling to force their way forward without losing the food they carried in cans and in pails and in bowls, others trying to hit with empty pails or cut with tin cans, and all of this in *silence*. It was not comic—it was eerie.

I went piling forward, my tin can jammed under my arm, my hands out in front of me to handle whomever I'd have to handle, because one way or another I was going to have to ram my way through someone, and just as I stepped onto the plank a man stepped on in the opposite direction, and he was carrying a pail and he was holding it in a way to deal with me and keep his soup from spilling, and I felt lousy for him because I knew what I could do, knew the strength I had, and that man was going to lose his soup, and I would have stepped back or stepped aside, but if I did either of those things the jacks behind me would have mobbed me and killed me, and there was just no choice, it was going to be that man and his soup because it was not going to be me. But the man coming just kept coming, holding himself ready to walk right through me, and just as I got up close enough I dropped my shoulder and brought it up hard under his chin and pushed with my legs and shoved forward and he went off into the snow, into the ravine and all the way down into and under that snow. I stopped on the other side of the plank, to let the *Zks* pass in either direction because I'd done what I had to do but I was a long way from hard enough yet not to worry about the fellow down under the snow. I couldn't go down there and help him out, but I couldn't go on to the feeding shed without first seeing that the man was out of there and all right, and I could see the snow in a great flurry down there and in no time at all the man was scrambling up the bank on the other side, the pail still in his hand but for sure no soup in it anymore. He stood there glaring at me and shouting and calling me everything foul he could think of and he was doing all this in Finnish, and I knew enough of Finnish and especially Finnish swear words because I'd learned plenty of them as far back as Detroit, there were that many Finns in our neighborhood and among the worker friends my dad had, and there were even more among the people in the American Village—or, anyway, had been. So I swore right back at him, called him in Finnish all the things he was calling me and then some new ones, and then he started swearing at me in English, and I stood there and did the same to him, and then he went to German, standing there in the snow up to his waist and shaking his empty pail at me and cursing me in German, and so I cursed back in German. So he switched to English again and so did I, and suddenly he was laughing like a crazy man, and it was such a wonderful thing to hear, that man's laughter, a rich human booming noise, an eloquent music, the shared triumph of man over the clattering * of circumstance, an uproarious thing, something transcendent and downright gorgeous tearing a hole in the cruel, dismal opacity that lay like a lead shield over captives and captors alike, the pitiless gray-on-gray invention that was Hard Labor Camp Number 231/1.

I tried to laugh with him, but what came out of me was no better than a croak, a mean thin measly rattle of a thing, paltry alongside the fabulous wealth and volume that issued from the crazy man across the way. It astonished me to hear the small, stunted, scratchy eruption that now accounted for my effort at laughter. Is this what had been done to me, a slow surgery that had trimmed away the tissue so that there was no organ in me to laugh like a man?

When he heard the wretched sound I made, he laughed all the harder, that splendid lunatic who'd lost his supper in the snow.

"You poor, miserable bastard!" he called out to me in English.

"Yes," I called back. "That's what I am, I guess."

"Oh, you're a sad one, all right!" he called. "You American?"

"Yes, I'm American," I said.

"Me too! From Detroit!" he called. "Name's Albert Loon! But they call me Red Loon! Come see me in the mechanics' tent sometime, guy with hair to go with his name, hey?"

And with that he laughed again and turned away and struggled up the bank to gain a foothold on the boardwalk.

"Sorry about your soup!" I called to him, but he only waved his hand and called back, "I'll live!" laughing like a wild man as he moved into the grim, wan light of early evening.

We were still on the Stalin six-day week, the week with no day names, and it was on the one free day we had each month that fell on the eighteenth day that we went through the standard procedure of clipping and showering while our clothing was processed in the *Zharo Kamera* and the tents were hosed with carbolic acid, and it was on this free day that I got my first chance to visit with Red Loon. Like mine, his family had contracted out of Detroit, and they'd been sent to work at a paper mill in Karelia, a place near the Finnish border and not far from Leningrad. This big laughing man talked almost jovially about his arrest. He'd had no jail, no beatings, none of what I'd had—but he'd had no trial, either—they'd just arrested him back in Karelia and handed him a piece of paper that said *Very Dangerous Person* and had the number "3" marked on it, and then next thing he knew they'd shipped him here and that was that. But he'd been in 231/1 long enough to turn up quite a few Americans, all men from Detroit— Benny Murrto, Blackie Pessonen, Jim Domyano—those are the names I remember.

These men are all dead now, and Red Loon is dead now.

Even with the easier work the mechanics had and even with the better food they got, those men are all dead, and my friend Red Loon is also dead. They all died—just like that.

But when he lived, Red Loon was my friend—and every free day we would try to visit with each other—to talk, talk about Detroit, about our families, but never talking about the thing that had happened to us because it made no sense to talk about it, and it was no good to think about it because you had to live it and not think about it, so we would just talk about what it made us feel good to talk about, and we would play chess with one of the homemade sets the mechanics had fashioned up, and I don't suppose there's any saying the good it did me to find this man.

Our talks, his richly robust nature, his will to see all that happened to him and to others in terms that were colored by irony, it was an experience that began to restore me to myself, that helped me begin to retrieve the identity that had gradually slipped from me or been stripped from me the minute I stepped into that open touring car that sunny afternoon in Gorky.

If "spiritual" is not too strong a word, I suppose it is accurate to say that it is in this sense that Red Loon saved my life. But it is also accurate to say that he saved my life in the more evident sense, and you shall have the testimony on that score when the time comes.

It was Red who told me that Camp 231/1 was considered an extermination camp—not to the extent that they were going to go out of their way to kill you, but in that they didn't expect any of the *Zks* interned in 231/1 to survive—all were considered expendable, and *all* meant all *Zks* interned in all eight campsites—because that's what the numeral "1" after the slash stood for, the first of eight different campsites, another thing Red knew. I never found out how Red came to know so much about this and that; I expect it had something to do with his inveterately outgoing personality, a manner in sharp contrast to what passed for my personality in those days. In any case, it was from listening to Red that I learned what I learned about the circumstances that surrounded me—and I never tired of listening to him—it was like getting draughts of some powerful whiskey to be in his presence, so much high energy came radiating from him. Even when he talked about his wife and son—back in Karelia, he hoped—there was no detectable sadness in Red's voice. At worst, he'd get wistful for a moment or two, but then he'd abruptly brighten again, crack some sassy joke about what a lousy chess player I was, and in no time at all he'd be back, centered within his intrepid cheerfulness again and that unaccountable brio of his.

The man was nothing less than phenomenal in his indomitable capacity for optimism, always touched with just enough rueful irony to put him on this side of sane. There really was no killing a man like Red Loon. You could bring him to a stop, but you could not defeat what he incredibly was.

It was after about three months of 231 that I was convinced they were going to kill me. I was called out one night, very near midnight, it must have been. It was Kuznets.

I heard him. But for a time I did not move. I was awake, and I just kept my head down on the log pillow and listened—figuring maybe he'd go away. But he just kept calling—and I finally rolled out of my berth and jumped to the floor.

He was there at the flap, grinning, his expression ghoulish in the light the lantern that he carried gave. But he did not set down his lantern to start up some challenging exchange with me. Instead, he just told me to follow him. We crossed the plank to the other side of the camp, and he motioned me to follow him to the Commandant's office. We went inside. It was wonderful in there, the warmth of the big stove the first real warmth I'd had in a long time.

The little room was empty. Kuznets sat behind his desk and gestured for me to sit on the floor. I took a place near the stove, but I didn't get to sit there for very long. Three armed guards showed up, all bundled against the cold of the night. It was then that I thought that this was it, that they were going to take me out and shoot me.

They took me out, all right—but not for shooting. Instead, they marched me all the way back to the Fosforitnaya depot, and I slept in the little shack there until just before dawn, and then they waked me and loaded me into a Stolypin car, in a cell all by myself. So far as I could see, there were no more than a half dozen men in the entire car, aside from the four guards that kept parading up and down.

I waited. I waited hours for the motion of the thing to tell me which way it would be—farther north or south.

It was south!

My heart soared.

Had there been some action on my case? Had someone intervened? Had the error been discovered?

For the first time in a very long while I thought about Miriam and Leo and my dad. I can't tell you how very odd it was to find my thoughts embracing the people I loved. It was no good thinking about them when times were bad—it just made matters worse, is all. But now that I was moving south, their faces and their voices poked at me like fingers prodding for attention.

A chunk of black bread was thrown in to me after we'd been moving south for some hours—and that was all the food I had until the train pulled into Gorky and until I was loaded into a prison van, shoved into a locker, and then deposited right back where I had started—in *Spets Korpus,* the special building for politicals situated among the seven buildings that constituted the Gorky prison.

I was stripped, searched, fingerprinted, all of it there in the same receiving room where it had happened in the first place, and then I was taken up to the third floor—everything the same—the guards calling to one another as I was moved from level to level—the same instructions—*head down, no noise, hands behind back.* I was marched along the thickly padded walkway to Cell 77, a guard in front of me, a guard behind; the door was jerked open in that same sudden manner, as if to surprise those within.

But the scene inside was very different. The cell was painted and pretty clean, and there were only two other men in there, and instead of the steel shelves and boards, there were canvas rigs suspended from the walls, four of them, like bunks you'd expect to find on board a ship. But there was a *Namordnik* in place, and the only light you had was what came from the bulb that shone above the door.

It wasn't so bad in 77. There was a pot, but it wasn't so bad— and by the time the food came for the last feeding of the day, I'd found out talking was okay and you could sit around or lie around in any position you liked, and you could even send out a letter if you could get the stuff to write on and write with.

I did. At first I thought I was going to have to beat up one of the men in there to get those things. What did he have left? A few scraps of paper and a bit of a pencil and one envelope? I wasn't going to ask at first—at first I was just going to take what I needed— but something checked me, and I told him my story, told him I had been arrested two years ago and that this was my first chance to get word out to my family.

He gave me what I needed.

I wrote Sam—I wrote my father.

I can remember exactly what I said.

Dear Papa,

I am alive. I am in the Gorky prison, Cell 77. I love you. I love my sister and my brother, and you are not to worry about me. I am a man now and I am all right. I don't know why I'm here, but I am glad to be alive. I know in my heart that I will see you again. I think of Mama often, may she rest in peace. Please kiss Miriam and Leo for me—and here, dearest Papa, is a kiss for you.

Your loving son,
Vickie.

The year was 1940.

My father died in 1953.

He died before they set me free.

Did he ever get my letter?

I know exactly what it said.

I would have said more had there been room on the paper— a piece of scrap paper, really.

But I think that letter said enough. Its few sentences delivered my heart.

THIRTY-EIGHT _____

Not to this day do I know why they sent me back to the Gorky prison. Of course, at the time I thought it was to prepare to release me—or to execute me. But it was for neither of those reasons—and who can fathom what reason it was for?

They kept me in Cell 77 for a few weeks. And then once again I was moved—this time back to the white building on Vorobevka Street, the Gorky installation maintained by the NKVD.

I was moved by the usual means—the van, the locker—kept under heavy guard all the while—and then I was led to the basement of the white building and locked into a cell with three other men, a cell that proved even more agreeable than 77 was—this one with beds.

We could talk—and it took no time at all to discover that each of us was a political prisoner and that the authorities must have regarded me as a relatively significant prisoner of some kind, because each of the other men in there with me had been charged with a major political crime.

They were intellectuals—writers, teachers, one a scientist. And each was convinced that he was awaiting execution.

Meanwhile, nothing happened—the days just passed into weeks and then months—and then they stopped. With no explanation and to no seeming purpose, and for no reason I will ever know, I was packed off back to Hard Labor Camp Number 231/1 again —taken all the way back in a Stolypin wagon as if the months in Gorky were just some sort of holiday I had earned, and now that it was all used up, it was back to Hell for me.

I'd done a foolish thing back there in the NKVD cell. There was a man named Domensko in there, a teacher—and he was convinced he was either going to be shot or sent north—and he kept asking me questions about life in the north—what the work was like and what the camps were like and how cold was it really, was it really that cold? And I could see he was terrified, and I tried to make light of what I'd been through, but the more I tried to brush it all off, the more convinced he was of the magnitude of the thing. He kept on saying that I was a tough fellow, an outdoorsman, a sportsman, and the like, a fellow who could go up against the arduous life and make out all right, but that he, Domensko, was, after all, just a professor, not a man for that sort of thing—and he was very frightened, it was clear, perhaps more frightened of being sent to the north than he was of being taken out and given a bullet in the back of his head.

I don't think that's an overstatement. You have to understand that Russians are virtually raised on a fear of Siberia. I remember years ago, when I was a boy, how sometimes parents would reprimand you and then unwisely threaten you with the police. "Do that again, young man, and I will go out into the street and get the first policeman I see!" I believe it is in this connection that Russians first learn their terror of the north. "Do that again, spill your soup again, and it's off to Siberia with you."

Well, a mother, a father, you perturb them enough, even the best of them will say something foolish like that to a child—and make him, not meaning to, very afraid. It was like that with Domensko, I think—his fear of the north, it was unreasoning, utterly out of control.

In any event, he kept asking me how one kept warm in such impossible conditions, and he was always eyeing my quilts, the black ones I'd been issued at the work colony, and I still had all this stuff on—the quilts and the basket boots, they were all the clothing I had—and one day, shortly before I was moved back out to the Stolypin that took me north again, I gave Domensko my quilts and my *Lapti*—and in exchange I took his professor's suit and his shoes.

It seemed to me the thing to do—and besides, what would I need with the stuff anymore? Surely I was not going back to where I'd just been sent from, after all that trouble taken to transport me pretty much all by myself. And if Domensko was going to be shot, in fact, well, the fellow should have something that he wants first.

But it was I that went north—and I went in a fancy suit of clothes and city shoes. But things were in an uproar when I got back to 231/1—and there was so much activity going on and such a lot of commotion, you could have walked over to a man, broken his neck, stripped the quilts and boots off him, and not a single soul would have blinked an eye or even noticed.

I went to the mechanics' tent and found Red sitting on his bunk and tying together the few things he had, his make-do chess set and an extra pair of socks and a spoon he'd made and some other odds and ends.

He hugged me when he saw me, and I hugged him back—but I could not laugh the laugh that he did. I didn't even try.

"Going to a party?" he said. "A dance, perhaps?"

"Where are *you* going?" I said.

"Two thirty-one stroke five," he said. "All the mechanics are. They're sending every   *   one of us to Subcamp 5. So what the   *   are *you* doing back here? You just up and disappeared—how long now, four months?"

It was so good to see him again. He sat there on his bunk, fumbling with the little bundle he was tying, but I could see he was nervous and pleased about seeing me and didn't know what to do with his hands. He finished fooling with the knots he'd already made too many of, and now he took to pulling at the short bristles of his russet beard.

"Still use the same barber, I see," I said.

Red laughed.

"Me," I said, "Red, old chap, I don't believe you'd believe if I told you. But, anyhow, I was all the way back in Gorky living high on the hog."

He studied me hard. "Thought you'd come back here and look up an old buddy, is that it?"

"That's it," I said. "Had a little time on my hands. Why not? A fellow has to keep in touch, right?"

But the banter left off soon enough. Red wasn't up to it—and for me it was always a trial. He went back to playing with those knots again, and with his head down he told me that Benny Murrto had died, that Jim Domyano had vanished, and that Blackie had been sent off to Subcamp 6, and then Red just stood up, tucked his little bundle under his arm, and shook my hand.

I could see that he didn't want to talk anymore. He said good-bye and that he'd be seeing me around, just to keep an eye out for the best-looking *Zk* in Siberia, and then he walked to the flap of the tent.

He turned around when he got there.

"Vic!" he called. "You'd better get yourself some quilts and fast—and you better get your   *   over to where the jacks are.

They're going to start counting noses around here any minute now, and we don't want them to miss an ugly one like yours, now do we?"

He laughed there at the flap, standing there with his little bundle slung over his shoulder now.

I called out, "Sure!" and "Here's luck!" and gave him the thumbs-up sign, and he gave it back, turned quickly, and went out through the flap.

I was sent to Subcamp 8.

Of all the places I had so far been, Subcamp 8 was the worst.

In 231/8 the work was harder than any I'd been made to do— and the living conditions surpassed mere abomination.

It was foul—hellish and foul. Subcamp 8 *was* Hell. Not Hell, the metaphor—but Hell, the place.

It was a forty-mile train ride into Hell—and a twenty-mile walk after that. It's not that you have to go very far to get to the Hell that every man sometimes goes to. For some men, Hell is just a short jog to the interior of themselves. But I had to travel hard to get to mine —and now that it's long behind me, Hell for me too is just a short trip within.

There was no shelter in 231/8. No tents, no barracks— nothing. The *Zks* made igloos, dugouts, chop-outs, lean-tos—and the only way to warm yourself was a fire.

And some men weren't strong enough to build themselves anything—and that finished them off before we'd been there a week. The camp was right in the forest—and the idea was to clear timber off an area great enough to build a real camp there, so it was the jacks they sent to 231/8—and it was the jacks, plenty of them, that were dying in the snow.

I had my quilts, new ones I'd been issued at the Vyatka prison, a way station en route to Subcamp 8, the same place I'd been before —and I had an igloo, one big enough for me, and that was it. I had a fur coat too—and a hat—items I'd traded in Vyatka for the fancy suit I'd gotten in Gorky. The coat was short, but it was good.

They had horses here, Army horses no good for service anymore—and there were sleds, drag sleds. And that's what it was there in the woods—you and your ax and your saw and horse-drawn sleds to load once you'd cut and sawed your plan for the day.

But the horses were dying because the prisoners stole their food

—and then when a horse died, the prisoners ate the horse—and sometimes they didn't wait that long.

Food? There was scarcely any. It was the worst yet. They gave you what they gave you—and then you had to make do—and some *Zks* killed the horses to make do, and then the guards killed the *Zks* who did it.

I called them sleds. They weren't really that. They were affairs contrived from logs and chains and a harness—and I don't know how those horses did it—and some didn't. If they got food, it wasn't much—and some got no food because the men got it away from them—and everything was dying there in that labor and that cold—men, horses, and even guards and dogs.

It was hard. It was hard on everything that lived there.

I worked in a team of two, me chopping and sawing and another man handling the horse and loading—and one day there was no man to work with me, and I did it all, felled the trees, cut the wood up, loaded, and tried to manage the horse. Could he see those eyes of mine? Was that why he let me manage him? Because what did I know about horses? But everything went fine—and the Commandant was very pleased—after all, here's one man doing the work of two. So when the Commandant came by that day, and he saw how good things were going, he decided to kick up my plan for that day—and I said no, and anyway the horse couldn't take any more. The horse! Here was the *man* saying the *horse* couldn't take any more—and the Commandant flew into a rage and began slapping my face with a riding crop he carried—and he kept on doing it until I snatched it out of his hands.

I gave it back to him. With no threat in it, I said, "No more," and I handed him back that riding crop.

He walked away. He didn't say anything—he just walked away —but that night two guards beat me up and thereafter every free day I was sent to the isolator—a chop-out where they stood above you and poured water down on you every two hours or so.

After the first time, my toes froze. When I got out that next morning, my toes were frozen—and I went to the wood shack they had for the Commandant, to say that my toes were frozen and what should I do? He went outside and called someone—and a man came and the Commandant said, "This is a doctor."

He was a man I hadn't seen before—but that was unremarkable—in 231/8 you didn't look at faces much. Mainly they were covered against the cold, and even if they weren't, what was there to see? You didn't want to see it. It would be a face that would tell you what yours was—and you did not want to know.

The man said for me to take off my boots, and I did it—I undid the cords that bound the *Lapti* to me, got them off, and then the rags and paper that my feet were wrapped in. They didn't look good, those toes—white, lifeless-looking, gleaming like a nightmare's idea of jewels.

The man said to the Commandant—Andrevsky, that was his name, the Commandant—the man said, "Do you have scissors?"

Andrevsky went poking in the drawers of his little desk and produced a pair of scissors, and the man took them, gave them a fast look, then jerked up one of my legs behind me—because I was still standing—and held my foot up behind me the way you would if you were shoeing a horse—and I didn't feel anything much but I knew what he was doing—and then he did it to the toes on the other foot, the same way, my leg behind me like a horse being shod—and then he let that foot down and I could see what he'd done to both of them, the blood spreading around me on Andrevsky's floor, and all this time Andrevsky was chanting, "Good, good—this will fix it. Very good, much better, this will cure the poor fellow's problem."

It was awful to look at, what he'd done to them, trimming and cutting and getting rid of everything that was frozen, and the Commandant had some benzine there, and that's what the man put on them, where the flesh was open, and he said it was to stanch the bleeding, and that it would do it and not to worry, and then he told me to get back into my papers and rags and get my basket boots back on, and I did as he said. And when I had everything back together again and was standing there, I said I couldn't work that day —that I was going back to my igloo to get off my feet.

"No, no," the Commandant said. "It is much healthier to work." He turned to the man who'd done the cutting. "Isn't that right, doctor?"

"Oh, yes," the man said. "Better to stay on those feet and keep the blood circulating. Work will be good for him—it is what I prescribe."

"You heard the doctor," Andrevsky said and smiled. "It's in your own best interest, Comrade."

I worked a full shift that day—well into the dark, and the pain wasn't so bad at first—but after a few hours it was terrible, and I began to wonder how you got gangrene and what I could do not to get it—and I was even crazy enough to think maybe it was true, maybe work was the best medicine, keep walking and working—and I had to walk for miles those days, right after they'd amputated the tips and the tops of my toes, my work zone was so far from where my igloo was—and when I got back to my igloo at night, I would take off the basket boots and the rags and newspapers and just let the wounds bleed, figuring this was the best way to keep from getting gangrene, just let the bad blood bleed itself out.

And it was like the business with the gunshot wound in the liver, the time that bullet went all the way through me, and I just got better for no reason at all, and maybe the reason was that's what I wanted to do, to get better and not get worse—and everything went on the same, the same work with the pines and the birch and the heavy brush that was in there, and the same with the isolator, going there every free day—and they even kept pouring the water on me.

But I didn't get frostbitten again.

It was spring, suddenly—and the work was harder—because even though you didn't have the cold to contend with and the snow interfering with your work, the trees were tougher to cut and harder to saw. In winter it hadn't been so bad to get them down—because it was a severe winter, one of the worst, and trees just cut and saw easier when the cold is great—but now the trees fought you, they fought back as they came angrily to life—and the work was harder, and because of the weather, the norms were taken up a notch, and the forest was mud, and you fell all the time and you were always soaked through from mud and sweat—and with the change in weather, the water went bad. And the summer was worse—with the woods alive with every infestation—an unimaginable diversity of crawling and biting things—and the sweat on you drawing them in under your clothes.

Then the food fell off sharply as the season moved to autumn. The weather was okay, but where was the food?

Did we know the Soviet Union was at war? That what little food there was was going elsewhere? And that there was less and less of it, anyway, to go anywhere? No, we knew nothing of this—it was only by accident that we eventually found out about the Second World War.

Meanwhile, more horses were getting bashed in the head and dragged off to some bonfire where the branches and brush were discarded—and sometimes they weren't even getting the sort of half-cooking a bonfire could produce. And then there was an epidemic of something, people dying left and right from the bad water—because all through that winter you did your urinating and your defecating there in the snow, and it all ran off into the water hole, and when the thaw came, that was the only water there was to drink, and some drank it without boiling it—and people were dying from some kind of intestinal trouble—until there were only sixteen *Zks* left.

There was hardly any food now—even for the sixteen and for the guards and dogs there to watch them. Once a day we got *Balanda* and that was it—except for what you could turn up foraging. It was around this time that I began eating tree slugs. I ate them raw. They weren't so bad—I guess you could say they tasted like pork.

We were all kept in a sort of cell now, an affair that had been put together inside the one small barrack that had been built. It was too small for the sixteen of us, and there was no heat, and even though it was still autumn, it was already very cold. And the *Balanda* began to show up with less and less of anything of substance in it, maybe a fish bone now and then, but mainly just a few broken leaves, and sometimes some cabbage. I took to eating more and more tree slugs and to keeping my eye out for anything that moved. Others didn't have the stomach for that sort of thing—and they ate wood—and it wasn't too long before there were eleven of us, all told.

And still they kept us there and kept us working, working harder than ever row—and I suppose this was because of the war—and with the worsening of the food supply and the hysteria that began to set in, the guards were quicker to come at you. Tempers were a hair below the skin now, and you did all you could to keep from inflaming the wrong person.

But who wasn't the wrong person?

They wouldn't let us make a fire there in that barrack cell we were quartered in, and it was getting colder every night—and all they'd tell us was to keep on working—because the faster we did our work, the sooner we'd be sent to another campsite, and that one was going to be better than this one—so work! It was your only way out.

It was down to about forty, forty-five below at night now—and just when there didn't seem any way to stand it in that cell anymore, they moved me, marching me off to Subcamp 6.

I walked it. My feet weren't healed yet. But I walked the nineteen miles.

I walked nineteen miles to what I believed must be better than what I was walking from. But it wasn't.

Subcamp 6 was Hell's annex—a camp for punishment.

The *Zks* were there for special punishment.

Andrevsky? I suppose it was that thing about the horse—and the riding crop. I suppose he'd figured I wouldn't make it through the work those scissors did—or the isolator—or the epidemic. But I had—and what was there left for him to do but to transfer me to 231/6?

And here there were self-choppers—because the work was too hard to do—and no one was going to go to the forest anymore because you were convinced the work out there would kill you—and if the work didn't, then the starving men would—because there are men that will eat men before they will eat wood. So the prisoners were chopping off parts of themselves—toes, fingers, sometimes hands and feet, and a few had even done arms and legs from elbows and knees down. A finger or a toe, you could do it yourself, but for something bigger, you needed someone else—and it wasn't hard to get someone. You could trade with him—get him to do it to you if you promised to do it to him—and maybe there were some that were more than willing because they just needed to hurt *something*. But if you couldn't get someone to trade, then you gave him food if you had it—and the going rate was one ration of bread for a hand or a foot, and two rations of bread for something like an arm.

But as soon as the thing got well under way, the camp administration was on to it, and if you showed up with your hand cut off, they beat you instead of throwing benzine on where there used to be a hand—or they just sent you to the woods, anyway—and so you died out there just as you had feared. But it was crazy how some of them kept at it even so. Was the fear of the forest so great? Or was it that everyone here had gone mad, some kind of delight infesting the place, a contest to see who could cut off the most? And before it wore itself out, there was a *Zk* with both arms cut off and two others who'd arranged to have both legs chopped off.

Fear or insanity? Both, of course—but even something more,

perhaps, a morbidity beyond simple madness. Revenge—perhaps the kind that is inflicted upon the persecuted because the persecutor is out of reach.

But even in good times, mutilation was not exceptional—only the motives were different. You lost something, a nose or an ear or a hand or an arm or your life if you happened to be the stakes in a card game.

It was what the criminals played for, the stakes they saw as attractive—because if there's plenty of food, what good is that? And if there is no food, then, again, what good is that? So parts of bodies and better were the traditional stakes in the card games the *Urkas* were always playing—and you saw this in good times and bad times —and no matter how desperate the conditions of the camp, there'd always be enough wolfbloods who played cards. No matter how exhausted they were, there was still enthusiasm for a game of cards— and the ingenuity to contrive a deck of them out of something or other around.

And before each game started, the stakes would be fixed.

See that one there—the bald one? His nose.

The one with the scar over his eye and the limp. Him. His life.

I'd sometimes overhear them—and I knew who was going to get it from the loser. But I never said anything. I never did anything to stop it. And once I knew the fellow pretty well—maybe I had exchanged a few grunts with him—and I knew he was the stakes for that day, for the game that was played on that free day—because the men were playing it before I left for the forest that day—and when I got back that night, the man was pinned to his sleeping shelf with a crowbar speared straight down through his temple.

I knew that man was it for that day—but I had said nothing to him about it. What if I had? Could he have protected himself? Could he have fought them off? And where could he have run to? Who could he have run to?

That night, when I got back, he was stuck to the board he slept on, a crowbar perfectly perpendicular to the side of his head, going into it and into the board under it.

The other *Zks* were all in there—nobody saying anything or doing anything—and we all went to sleep that night with the man just like that, stuck to the board like that right up until the morning.

But he wasn't there when I got back the night after.

Yes, I was like ice, like wood, like the hard barren earth all around me.

I was a man who lived *here,* a man of *this place*—and I was nothing that was not a match for where I was.

Subcamp 6 was one barrack—and the feeding shack was about twenty-five yards distant—and between the door of the barrack and the door of the feeding shack there was a barbed-wire runway, a corridor created by running lengths of barbed wire from one door to the other, and the runway was a door's width, and inside that runway there were always three guard dogs, and there was a sort of ceremony to getting the little food there was, and perhaps they had that ceremony to keep you from wanting the food—because the shortages now were devastating. Yes, you'd earned your food by working your norm. But now you had to work for it again.

There'd be guards on either side of the runway, outside the barbed-wire fences—and each of them held a long pole. Inside the runway were the three dogs. Outside were eight, ten, maybe more, guards—with their long poles.

One *Zk* at a time did his eating—and this is how he did it. He opened the door on the barrack side, and the other *Zks* inside quickly slammed it shut behind him. Then he ran.

He ran to the feeding shack and through the open door and he was handed a bowl of *Balanda,* and the game was he had to get out of there as soon as he had that bowl in his hands, and as soon as he was out there, the guards would start jabbing with their poles, and the dogs would harass the man—not bite him, or anyhow not bite him badly, but nip at him, and bark, and jump at him to get the food, and so he had to run, or anyway keep moving fast, because of the poles and the dogs, and meanwhile he had to get down the soup, because if he just ran back to the barrack side, that door would open for him and the starving *Zks* inside would take away his food.

That was the game. But you only got to play it once a day—because in 231/6 there wasn't enough food for more than one game a day.

So the idea of the game was to eat that way.

It was like anything else.

You couldn't believe it at first.

Then you got good at it.

And then you prided yourself on your skill. That's what a prisoner is, in a way—a man who at first can't believe it, and then he gets good at it, and then proud of getting good at what he could not believe.

It was deep winter now—there in Subcamp 6. With the dwindling food and the terrible cold, matters came to a halt. The *Zks* refused to work. Why work? If you did, how much food would you get for it? And if you did get food, then the ones that wouldn't work and that weren't getting any food would take from you the little you got.

The *Atoman* issued an order to all the wolfbloods—no more work—force them to move us out of here to a better place! And then a rumor circulated, something to the effect that the little valley we were in was going to be flooded as soon as the thaw came—and that that was why they had us here—to drown us here, to drown us in the spring.

It was like Subcamp 8 now—a kind of panic all around you— hysteria overlaying the hysteria that had already been the condition of the place, and what control there was seemed to be coming apart. The prisoners were bolder—the guards crueler in reply.

And there was the cold, worsening every day—and at night it was indescribable. There was just the small wood stove, and men would kill to sleep near it. Those who slept against the walls had it worst—and in the morning they had to cut themselves away from the wood with axes if there had been any wet on their clothes. If you went to the pot and got yourself wet, or if you bled, or anything, had any moisture on you, it froze during the night—and you just hoped it only froze the wood to your clothes.

It was around this time, midwinter, that we got dogs. Just two of them—and I was one of the lucky few that got to eat them—and I never found out how the *Atoman* and his people had brought it off, but they had captured first one dog and then another, and for about five days we ate dogs, about ten of us, sort of half-cooking them on the embers in the wood stove, and doing it in the very early hours of the morning—because of the smell.

It drove the others crazy, that smell of cooking meat. But only the strong got it—and it was the *Atoman* who made the pick—and I was one of the ones he picked. How long had it been since I'd had meat? I don't know. Aside from the tree slugs? I don't know.

I loved eating those dogs.

The ringleaders were shot for it—the *Atoman* and one of his kings. They killed the *Atoman* and his king for turning those dogs into food, but I can't recall their ever killing anyone for eating men.

It used to happen the same way—mostly in the woods—a man falling down with some injury or illness or weariness, and then he wasn't there anymore, the bones and blood under the snow somewhere and clean snow scooped on top.

Is that five potatoes? It is infinite potatoes to those who have not starved—but to the starving men in 231/6 it was nothing but food.

We didn't know it, but there was a war going on, and it had been going on for some while. There were indications—the little food and bad food declining into less food and worse food, and increasingly there were more and more heavily armed troops in sight. There were these indications, but who could interpret them?

Interpret? It is a word that has no relation to the circumstances I am talking about. It connotes mind, an action of mind, the machinery of thought.

You did not think.

You moved here, you moved there—you picked this up, you put that down. You acted in precise accord with the actions expected of you—and that was all you did.

Thinking? It is absurd to consider it in connection with the elementary motions of life I am talking about.

I am talking about working to eat and eating to live—and the only thing loftier than that was sleep.

Sleep was your one spiritual instant—if you were lucky enough to dream.

They moved me to 231/5, *Lager* 5—to use the language of the time, the term *Gulag* really serving for the main-camp management, the administration that oversaw a series of subcamps, or *Lagers*. Anyway, they walked me to *Lager* 5, another subcamp of *Gulag* 231, a distance of about five miles from 231/6.

It was March now, 1942.

I worked the woods at 231/5—did my usual work as a lumberjack.

If *Lager* 6 was Hell's core, *Lager* 5 was the furnace that fired it. Not that the camp itself was so bad—because this was a big one and pretty well turned out. The *Zks* here numbered about five thousand, and Red was here, and how could it be bad where Red was? And 5 wasn't. It was the best-outfitted of the eight, then fifteen, then twenty *Lagers* that made up *Gulag* 231.

But for me it was the furnace, the engine that made Hell burn.

I found Red after about a week in *Lager* 5—I think I heard him laugh before I saw him. He was on his way to form up with a team of mechanics—and I heard his raucous laugh and turned and saw his violent hair.

I called out, "Loon, you   *   *   , will you quit all that noise!"

He wheeled around and saw me.

"Vic! Hey,   *   , where's my soup?"

"Get off my plank, Loon!" I hollered back, and he came running.

We embraced like brothers—because that's what I suppose he was to me, the brother Leo never was.

We only had an instant to talk—he had to form up with his detail. But it was in the course of that brief exchange that I found out there was a war on. Red had deduced as much—from all the military uniforms that had been replacing the standard camp-gear issue at 231/5—and especially from the blood that every one of those uniforms had somewhere on them. We didn't know who the Soviets were fighting—how could we?—but we knew they were in combat somewhere with someone.

Would this alter things for us?

Oh, yes—but not for the better.

On the contrary, more work was expected from the *Zks,* and there was less food to compensate for it—and with war there comes killing—it's what war is—and killing is a state of mind: it originates at the front, but it doesn't stop there, it permeates the condition of mind that prevails in the land—it is the patriotic fever flourishing into disease.

Anyway, I'd been there a week, in *Lager* 5 a week, when all the foreigners were rounded up. There were eighteen of us, and Red would have made a nineteenth, but for some reason he wasn't among us.

One morning, well before dawn, I was called out and told to present myself at the gate. When I got there, about six others were standing in the snow. I asked one of them if he'd eaten yet; he said no—and he didn't think the others had either. We stood around waiting, stamping our feet in that vicious cold, the clutch of us in a kind of huddle with eighteen guards and eighteen dogs in a similar huddle about ten yards away from us. In time our number also came to eighteen as we were joined by other *Zks,* and it was presently apparent to us all that we constituted the camp's entire population of foreigners—except for the absence of Red Loon.

When our number matched the number of guards that were grouped nearby, we were counted and marched through the gates, and then they kept us marching—*single file, head down, no talking, just keep walking in the direction you're told*—with the guards flanking us on all sides, some armed with those old-style tommy guns, the rest with rifles.

They were marching us in the direction of *Lager* 8, and it was a hard walk—because the snow was bad—and as dawn broke it was a terrible morning, the air heavy with a thick mist that chilled you right through whatever you wore. It was hard to tell, but I think three of our number were women. In the swaddled clothing we wore, and in the mist, and with our unwillingness to bother with each other, it was uncertain—but I had the idea at the time that there were three women among us—but I would never know for sure—because after we got where we were going, I never saw any of them again.

In time we came to a railroad track; I guessed we were somewhere in the outer zone of *Lager* 8. The tracks were temporary, it looked to me, and they were laid upon a high bed that had been pushed up to receive them, a ridge that I could see went from one edge of a vast clearing through to the other, the tracks vanishing into forest on either side.

The guard boss called a halt and told us to sit. He pointed.

Up there on the tracks there were eighteen railroad cars—not platform cars but huge coal cars—the kind we used to call sixty-tonners—because that's roughly the amount of cargo they could carry, that weight.

The guard was pointing—and we all looked at those wagons, spaced equidistant from each other, eighteen of them, spaced out in even intervals from one edge of that enormous open area to another.

"*Zks!*" he called to us. "You are swine, but you are working swine. You are the filth from capitalist nations, but you are good swine for us. We will not let you wallow in the mud. You are better swine than that. See those wagons? You will load them. Each one of you will load a wagon. When a *Zk* had loaded his wagon, he goes back to camp. When a *Zk* had loaded a wagon, he eats. Not until you have loaded a wagon, from the floor right up to the top, do you go back or do you eat. Now, swine, because we love you, we do not want you to be alone and frightened way out here in the snow with no warm place and no shelter and no food. So each *Zk* will have one of us for company, and to make it a complete family, there will also be a family dog. Now, *Zks,* get up and come get your axes and your saws—because you are going to load those wagons with logs, and when you have cut them just so and loaded your wagon, you and your guard and your dog go back to camp, a happy family, yes? Now, up, *Zks,* and come get these excellent tools. Stand up like the good oxen you are." He laughed. "Did I say oxen? Forgive me, dear *Zks*—swine—you are much better beasts than oxen. You are all excellent swine. Now, *Zks!* Begin! Because the longer it takes, the longer no shelter and no food, and your masters, we also want to hurry back and get out of the snow, yes?"

It could not be true!

I must have misheard the man!

Surely the man was not suggesting that we each load an entire sixty-tonner! That each of us cut enough trees and saw them into logs enough to fill a whole wagon that size? And did he say that you would have neither food nor shelter until you'd done a thing as colossal as that? And where were the trees? There were no trees around here. This was a marshland! Where were the trees?

The treeline was a mile or more away!

This must be a joke!

It is a joke, surely.

The bunch of us, the eighteen of us, stood gaping in stupefaction.

But no one said anything. Instead we took the tools they gave us, and then a guard took each *Zk* off with him to one of the eighteen wagons.

I stood speechless, there before the wagon I was told was mine. I was simply and absolutely struck dumb.

I sat down in the snow. I wanted to laugh. Should I cry? What could I do except one or the other? This was utterly preposterous. I looked up at that wagon, there up on that ridge where the tracks were laid, and it was awesome, the mere prospect of it, that huge iron thing seen through the mist against the iron sky.

Even if there were *no* snow and even if there were *sawed* logs stacked right here in front of the wagon, how in ✳ would you get them up there and into that thing?

No man could do this! No man would even try to do this!

I will not try, I said to myself. All right, I said, I will sit here and die, and I had no sooner voiced this thought to myself than I stood up, the will in me to do the task even larger and crazier than the task itself.

The guard with me jabbed me with his tommy gun, and when he did it, the dog with him snarled.

"Get moving, hero!" the guard said. "Let's go, Lindbergh of Russia, let's see what a hero you are!"

I knocked the barrel of his gun away. What did it matter?

I walked off. Would he shoot me now? What would it feel like, those bullets tearing into my back? Would the quilt slow them down? I tried to remember what it felt like when the bullet went through my liver. It felt like nothing, so far as I could remember. The noise hurt your ears, and there wasn't any pain until later.

But with what came out of a machine gun, there would not be any later.

I kept walking, about fifteen yards between me and the guard now. I began to circle, a gradual circle, so as not to put too much distance between me and the guard. Was he going to follow me all the way to the treeline each time I went there to cut a tree and drag it back? Surely he was not going to let me go that distance unattended. Did they plan to relieve the guards, or were these men going to stay out here right along with us the whole time?

Perhaps they expected none of us to try. Perhaps the idea was that we would lie down in the snow and die.

Perhaps there was no idea at all.

I kept walking in a wide circle, thinking—trying to think—calculating distance, weight, bulk, anything that would give me some notion of how long it would take to do it, how long I'd have to go without food and shelter.

Perhaps someone high up had lied, had said, *Look, I have eighteen wagons of timber out there,* and with the eighteen of us dead in the snow he'd have some sort of alibi.

I figured I could make ten round trips between the treeline and the wagon if I started at first light and worked until dark. I figured, given the maximum I could saw and carry in a day, it would take at least ten days to load the entire car—that is, if I could dope out a way to get the sawed logs up to that height, up into the wagon.

If I were lucky, I could do it in ten days. How could I go for ten days out here in this cold—with no food—and with no food, where would the stamina come from to do the work?

The wind was coming up. It was colder now—but the mist was blowing off. I couldn't see all of the others, but those I could see were just sitting down, a guard and a dog standing nearby.

I stopped and I sat down again. I kept trying to think, trying to figure something out. If I were lucky . . .

I was sitting on something! There was something there just under the snow.

I got up and kicked away the snow with my basket boots.

It was a log! A big log—thick!

I stood on it and walked to one end—and then I turned around and walked to the other end.

I stepped off to the other side—and stepped onto another log!

There was one jammed up right next to another—and then another one after that! I kept going. There was a whole line of logs—and I walked it off and it went for quite a distance, and when I saw that they were pretty much perpendicular to the tracks, I realized what they were—that they must have served as some kind of ramp for the logs that were rolled down from the forest. After all, this was marshland—they must have laid a bed of logs all along here so that the cut timber could be rolled down from the treeline. The plane from the verge of the woods down to here was an incline, and the jacks who had been working here must have laid this ramp to ease and speed their work.

I would need logs that were long and not too heavy. I uncovered three of them—and notched the end of each. I dragged one and then the other and then the other to the wagon, my heart booming, a kind of manic exultation overtaking me.

Was I not the Lindbergh of Russia? Was I not the American kid who'd knocked Russia on its * ? Was there a   *   thing these   *   could ask of me that I could not the   *   *   do?

The   *

I laid those long logs up against the bed of the wagon, fitting the notches just so. I made a gangway of them—and then I went back to where the cache of logs was and I started.

I worked all that day. I worked until it was dark and I couldn't work anymore.

The guard never said a word to me that whole first day. He saw where I was getting the wood from, but he never said a thing. I kept waiting for him to stop me, but he didn't—and when night came I dug into the snow and slept the sleep of the dead.

I cut up about thirty long logs that first day, cut them into equal lengths and dragged them up there and stacked them inside.

I slept.

I started in again at the crack of dawn.

The second day I began crisscrossing with spaces between. The guard wasn't paying any attention, and then I saw that it was a different guard, and that they'd relieved the first guard during the night, and this guard wasn't paying any attention, and unless he got in there with me he couldn't tell, and so I crisscrossed, and with crisscrossing, I had almost half of the wagon filled by nightfall of the second day.

I wasn't even hungry. Nor was I tired. There was only one thing in me—and it filled me up—the conviction that I would do it, I would do it,   *   *   _I am going to do it,_ and it was like an elixir that gave me food enough and strength enough to do the same   *   monumental task nine times over!

Again I slept. I dug into the snow near my cache of logs—and I slept—and the third day I began stacking logs on end, so that the interior of the stack would be hollow, but you wouldn't see it because all along the outside and the top I'd finish with a solid shell, and brace the whole thing up then, and by the end of the third day I'd filled all of the wagon except the doorway, and as I was walking back to dig in for the night again, I saw where there was a third guard with me now, and that he'd probably been with me all that day, but I hadn't even noticed. And what had _he_ noticed?

Nothing.

It was hard to sleep that night—because it was then that the hunger came. It felt as if my stomach were consuming itself.

All that night I lay awake, trying to fight back the hunger that was eating me up.

I will do it! I can do it! Lindbergh of Russia indeed! There is nothing on this   *   Russian soil or in that   Russian sky that a kid from Detroit cannot   *   *   _do!_

Toward first light I fell asleep, and then the guard was kicking me. It was not long after dawn, and I got up and tried to warm my-

self—and the hunger had somehow left me. For how long? I started —and as soon as I tried to hoist a new log and prop it up to begin sawing, I felt it, a hunger so wild it was like wire bands snapping all over my belly and chest. I scooped up snow and swallowed mouthfuls of it.

Inside myself I was screaming　　*　　*　　over and over— and I went to work.

I stacked the doorway solid. I was finished before noon. I came down the gangway and took another look at it.

Yes, it looked okay. And who was going to take the thing apart to check me?

The guard was sleeping.

I waked him and pointed.

"What do you want?" he said.

"Look," I said, and kept pointing. I was crouched over him and I could barely hold myself like that, my back bent in that position.

"Look," I said.

He stood up. His dog came to him and began nosing at his legs.

"Good," he said. "We go back. Get your tools, and we go back."

"Good," I said, and I did something incredible.

I slapped him on the back. As if he were a partner in my labors and an accomplice in my deception, I slapped the　　*　　on the back, and I said, "Good."

With the guard and his dog leading the way, I walked back to *Lager* 5. All that distance my heart roared with triumph. I thought of all the things I had ever done—of all the things I'd done that were hard things—and then I thought of *this*—the sixty-tonner, the logs, the gorgeous lunacy back there behind me in the snow.

That thing was the best.　　*　　it and　　*　　it, it was the best!

I was the only one of the eighteen to return. Of those others, had three been women? I think three were, but I am not certain. But I am certain of something else—most of the eighteen were old.

I don't know the names of any of those people. I only know they were all foreigners—and that Red Loon was not among them.

It's a hard thing to know—if I hated him for not being tested. But I know I didn't.

He might have failed. With all his exuberance, he might have failed. And *then* what? Who would I have *then?*

But Red Loon died, anyway. And those seventeen others, they died too.

I lived. I had done the greatest thing I have ever done—and I lived.

I like to believe I earned it—that there in that snow, looking up at that iron wagon, I earned life.

It's true. I had stood on the shoulders of luck, it's true. But I had to reach.

THIRTY-NINE

They came to get me about two weeks later.

It must have been easy to catch me, to figure out who did it. Had anyone else even tried to load his wagon?

When they got that wagon to where it was going and began unloading it and found all the hollows I'd contrived, they would have known right off it was me. But it was anyway good that I did it. It gave me life—punishment, but life—whereas not to have done what I did would have finished it for me. I would have made an eighteenth in the snow.

They came and got me and took me to the central isolator.

I'd really forgotten about what I'd done—and so when they came to get me, I was confused at first. Why me? Hadn't I just performed a miracle for them?

They took me to the central isolator in *Lager* 5, an arrangement of about a dozen outdoor cells, one next to the other. On one side of me there was a man who'd chopped off someone's head. We talked a little bit at first, and then I didn't want to talk to him anymore. He'd been playing *loser cuts* in a card game, and he lost—and the stakes were somebody's head.

He'd been in the isolator five days and had five more to go.

Me, I didn't know how many I was in for. They beat me up when they got me there, but they would not tell me how many days they were going to keep me.

There were three shifts of guards, and it was the early morning shift that beat me up and that also saw to Tanya, the girl locked in on the other side of me. They saw to Tanya, the early morning shift. She was only thirteen.

I didn't want to talk to the man who'd done the chopping, but I wanted to talk to the girl. She was female—and I wanted to talk to her. How long had it been since I had exchanged words with a female—of any age?

Tanya was thirteen—and they did it to her every morning—until they let her go.

She was from the Omsk region of Siberia, and she'd been working on a collective farm there, and she got ten years for stealing a handful of grain. These were the war years now, and Tanya said lots of kids had done it, stolen some oats or some corn—because they couldn't stand the hunger anymore—and the rule was harsh—and if they caught you, you got ten years—and she had been sentenced to ten years at hard labor, but she couldn't do the work, and so they put her in the isolator and they used her.

Tanya wasn't the first kid I'd run across in *Lager* 5. There was a kid we called Crab—because of the way he scrabbled around in a sort of crablike motion, his bottom half all twisted from how the bones had grown together cockeyed after they'd broken them for him, the police who'd caught him stealing a potato. You'd always see him around the feeding shack, spidering around across the ground with his head down and his attention fixed on the plot of ground between his legs. He ate by scavenging. He couldn't work and so he wasn't fed—and because there was a rule against sharing, the *Zks* wouldn't actually *give* Crab anything—but a few of them always spilled a little something where he could get at it.

Crab had been running away when they caught him with the potato in his pocket and broke his hips and thighs and legs and feet for him. He'd tell anybody who asked him—he'd tell them he had been running away to find his mother. She was working on a collective somewhere, but he didn't know where.

They broke his bones and gave him ten years—and the *Zks* gave him something too—the name Crab and whatever they figured they could afford to spill on the ground.

Crab couldn't do anything but scavenge. But Tanya could.

I could hear them in there with her.

Did I hate myself for listening? How could I not hear? Should I have clapped my hands over my ears?

Her screams were strange to me—strange in the quality of feeling that they were made of and strange in the feelings they set off in me. There was more to them than just pain.

It was an animal I heard in that cell next to mine in the central isolator of *Lager* 5—a female animal thrashing around in the grip of three male animals.

I saw it once before they let her go. Once I turned around and looked. I had never seen the coupling of human beings.

I don't know how to describe this very well, nor do I think it is necessary—except that it is necessary to think about the feeling that it all left me with.

I couldn't help it. I turned once. I could hear a kind of heavy grunting sound coming from her, a fast and regular cadence. *Hunnnh . . . hunnnh . . . hunnnh!*

I couldn't help myself. I turned around to see.

I did not want to look away.

I was a year in that central isolator.

I got regular beatings there—fists and sticks and clubs—and all I got to eat was the thin trash soup and once in a little while a bit of bread.

I was running down now—coming the closest I'd come to complete collapse.

It wasn't the food and the beatings and the vermin that rained down on me every night—it wasn't that so much as it was simply sitting and doing nothing and sleeping and doing nothing, day in and day out.

My vision started to go—I noticed that at dusk, especially, my vision would come and go, as if a window shade inside my head were being playfully lowered and raised—and it got harder and harder for me to stand in one spot for very long. A kind of vertigo would abruptly come sweeping over me, and I would sway to one side and then I would quickly have to squat or fall.

Sleep was impossible at night—the bedbugs were that bad. God knows where they came from, but every night they did—and so I did my sleeping during the day, dozing mainly, because days the lice would wake you from the deepest slumber. But they ate at you on and off, whereas the bedbugs never left off for an instant—and all you could do during the night was to keep moving and beating at yourself—because they literally rained down on you, a steady cascade of insect life showering down on you from the wooden framework over your head.

I think I was very near death when they let me out of there. My vision was worse, much worse—the world around me muted by a brown haze that I could not blink away—and walking, just walking, was a chore. The slightest bending would make me cough, and sometimes the coughing sent me into a convulsion of pain—I'd drop to my knees, gasping, my vision gone to black now.

When they let me out, two of them came to get me, and when they took me by the elbows to get me moving, my legs buckled under me and I fell crazily sideways and couldn't get up.

They raised me. And then one of them grabbed me hard around the waist and walked me like an invalid. He walked me to the outer door of the isolator and then he let me go.

I fainted dead away, and I don't know how much later it was that I came to, but when I did it was fairly dark, or else it was my vision going deeper into brown.

It was very cold, and I was just lying there, and it was clear they were just going to let me lie there and die if that's what I wanted—and so I started to crawl. I didn't have any objective exactly—except to move and keep moving. If I had an objective, it was to exhibit the motions of life, and to get as far from the isolator as I could while I was doing it.

I crawled about a hundred yards, and I came to one of the elevated wooden walkways that were the "sidewalks" you used in a camp. But for the life of me, I could not pull myself up onto it. The thing was about a foot above ground level, but it might as well have been a mile over my head—I just couldn't do it. And the more I strained to get myself up there, the more my vision went from brown to black. I quit trying and let myself down into the frozen mud.

I was still there the next morning—and I could only tell it was morning out of a little round window in my vision, because the rest of the scene before me was lit as if by some tiny light bulb, the kind of thing your parents might install for you if you're the sort of child who's fearful in the dark.

I tried getting up on the walkway again—there were people moving back and forth across it, work teams going this way and that —and they were all passing me and leaving me to lie there—and I wasn't even surprised by this, because wouldn't I have done the same? I kept at it for an hour or more, kept trying to get myself up there, people going by all the time, *Zks* and guards, all of them silent as they moved to their work. And then something happened to me that filled me with the most extraordinary feeling.

How do you talk about this when you are a grown man? I suppose it is a feeling we all of us have in infancy—and forget. And I suppose it mixes concepts of helplessness and security. We are clearly powerless, but in our powerlessness we enjoy a fabulous infolding, an enveloping that is total and totally safe. We are borne aloft, raised up, lifted, just a little thing—one moment dangerously athwart the wide world of a piece of floor, the next moment lifted, aloft, all our parts encompassed.

It was Red Loon who lifted me. He lifted me like that, as if I were an infant.

He took me up in his arms and held me and started moving— and I could hear him muttering as he went: *   *   *

 *   , look what they did to old Vic. Hey, old Vic, look what they did to you, lad. Why, I bet you don't weigh twenty-three pounds, and half of it's * , right?   * , look what they did to old Vic.   *
 *

He carried me to his barrack, but I didn't know that at the time. He stuffed me under his berth, but I didn't know that, either.

All this time I remember saying one thing and Red Loon answering.

I said, "I'm blind."

Red said,   *   . You're too mean to go blind, Herman. Herman, you are just the *meanest* galoot. Oh no, mister, you're just too, too mean to go blind."

I was under his berth when he waked me. He had food. Red kept me there for two or three days—and all I can remember of it was eating and drifting off into a stupor and Red's waking me and feeding me again.

I don't know where Red Loon got that food from. I don't know how he was able to get it to me. Nor do I know how he got away with keeping me there.

All I know is that the man nursed me. That's the only word that fits. He nursed me.

The morning I left Red's barrack, I left it before dawn. I left before the Commandants and their sixes would come to bring all the *Zks* crashing from sleep.

I stole out in the dark and made my way to the feeding shack.

I wanted food and I knew I wasn't going to get food unless I worked, and I didn't think I could work yet—I was stronger, but I wasn't strong enough for the woods yet—and I wanted to get to the feeding shack before any of the _Zks_ got there. I knew an old man who worked there. He was a Jew, and I figured he would break the rule and feed me—because I didn't want Red feeding me anymore—because maybe he was feeding me out of his own ration, and even if he wasn't, he was still breaking a rule, and what if he were caught on my account?

So I went to the feeding shack and there were already four workers there, the men who prepared the food. I took the old man aside—this old man Joseph—and I said to him, "Look, I'm a Jew, a _landsman,_ and I need food."

"Work," he said. "You work, you eat."

"I can't," I said. "I'm weak, I'm sick—I've been in solitary a year. Do you hear me? I've been in the isolator for a year."

He turned away from me. Over his shoulder he said to me, "Don't lie. No one goes there for a year. And you're no Jew. Don't lie to me."

I went after him. I was trying to keep my voice down, but I was very agitated.

"I _am,_" I said, and, like a madman, I started jabbering at him in Yiddish, and when I got to the end of some meaningless phrase, I said, in Yiddish, "How can you deny a fellow Jew?"

This old man Joseph jerked his arm away from my grip.

"Go eat in the   ✳   ," he said. "You heard me, liar—go eat in the   ✳   ."

I don't know. Perhaps I was still delirious—maybe I was raving. Because I actually walked out of there and began to make my way to the outhouse that was not very far away. I remember muttering to myself—"All right, you tell me to go there, I'll go there," and I kept thinking this would spite him, make him sorry he had refused me.

I was making my way to the outhouse, whispering to myself and then just whispering it in my head. No one ever used the outhouses in these camps—at least there was no one I ever knew that did. You just used the best place you could find—and for me that was always somewhere in the woods. You saved it for when you were out there—you trained yourself to hold it for then—and it got to be habit, and you never gave it another thought—once a day in the woods and that was it. It would never have occurred to me to go to the outhouses because of the filth—and the risk of contagion. Did anyone go?

Well, it would be something to see, I thought—and when I pushed back the door, it was! It was worse than anything the *Parasha* could deliver.

It took your breath away. The smell was a hand that took you by the throat.

And then I saw.

There were three dead men in there, and five rats, as big as small dogs, as big as dachshunds, chewing away at those bodies.

They came to attention when they saw me, their red eyes gleaming in the dim light that penetrated through the spaces in the boards.

I staggered back—as if struck—yanked open the door and flung myself back out of there.

My heart was heaving fearfully—and I tripped on the walkway and fell—got myself up and hobbled back toward Red's barrack, limping from the bad twist my ankle had taken.

My ankle. It's funny how the parts of the body are forgotten when it is in fact the body itself that your whole attention is centered on.

This was the ankle they'd burned.

And now it was twisted, maybe sprained a little, and it was a thing to think about. When you lived as I lived, *anything* could do you in—the slightest scratch giving way to massive infection, a simple head cold exploding into death.

You knew it would kill you to worry, and you tried not to worry, but you worried.

I got to the barrack and I got under Red's berth and I slept.

I waked up in the early afternoon, came awake with what seemed to me the most extraordinary idea since the invention of the wheel.

Now that I look back on this time, I know that I must have been half out of my mind. But at the time, the idea I had seemed to me a stroke of genius.

I would trap rats!

It was meat.

There was meat there, an endless supply of meat—and all I had to do was reach out and take it.

How hard could it be? It would be easy.

Rat. What would rat taste like, anyway?

I'd eaten slugs and dog and horse. I'd probably eaten human meat too—though I was never certain.

Rat. All the rat I wanted.

Hadn't I eaten bugs and snakes? And who really knew what they put in that *Balanda?*

I was tremendously excited to have a project—a problem that I could exercise my mind on, an ambition—a kind of contest between me and those giant rats.

I knew *Zks* died all the time—were shot, fell over, choked on their own bile, dropped dead from everything in sight, wheezed their last and that was that—but it never had occurred to me where they were put before they were taken away in the burial wagon that every day or so trundled to the gate of the camp where it would pause for a time while a guard with a long sharp rod of iron would pierce each heart to make sure. These dead, they were obviously collected and stored in the outhouse until the burial team came around with their wagon. What better place to store the dead until you could get rid of them—because who ever went to the outhouse except a man who'd been told to go there in jest and who went because in the trance he was in he'd go anywhere you told him to go?

My vision had improved some, but I was still periodically blind. Eating rat changed all that.

I ate it for six months—every day for six months, for maybe even longer than that.

I believe it was that interval where I ate rat that got me through all the hard years thereafter. Surely it was what got me over the hard time I had just been through.

It was rat that brought me back to life.

I liked rat. It was good. Does this seem expressive of what those years did to me? Of what you can do to a man if you only have time enough?

I suppose it does.

To this day I savor that taste on the tongue of my mind.

Red returned shortly after nightfall.

I stayed where I was, under the berth, and when he sat, I reached up and pulled at the cuff of his quilt trousers.

"What's up?" he said.

"I've been out," I said. "Went to the kitchen. I made a deal with Joseph. He'll give me food if I catch the rats that have been stealing grain from his closet. Can you make me a cage in your shop?"

"I can try," he said, and patted the berth to assure me.

If I dreamed, it was of what lay ahead. If I dreamed, it was of me in a wrestling match with a rat like a horse, the two of us skidding across a vast area of moldering boards.

When I waked the next day, Red was gone.

Again, I slept. I pushed myself all the way in under his berth, and slept.

That night Red brought the trap. It looked to me like an invention of unparalleled intelligence, a stupendous contrivance, a work of the highest mind.

He was sitting on the berth and he held it down to me and then he let it go into my hands.

"That do you?" he said.

I punched the underside of the berth. I hit it three times, hard. Already I was that boy running.

"Good," he said, "because, lad, I've got to move you out. One of the *Zks* in here said he was going to report me if you stayed. Vic, you've got to hustle up something else. Think you can make out now?"

I punched the bottom of that berth—three times again—and I said, "I'm okay. I'm good now. Just one thing. You got anything here at all—a bit of food—anything?"

"A fist of bread," I heard him say.

"Can you give me about a fourth of it?"

Then I heard him rustling around inside his clothes.

He reached down his hand. And opened it. There was about half a fist of bread in there. I took it and quickly ate half of it.

I punched the underside of his berth.

"That's okay," I heard him whisper.

I stayed under there until I thought about what to do about the cage. There was no hiding it under my clothes—it was too big for that. I'd just have to walk right out of there with it the same way Red had walked in with it.

I waited a little while longer. I was trying to calm my heart. How long had I been under there—how many days?

It was tough moving at first—but once I was out and up and had taken a few steps, I was okay. I turned quickly, to make a thumbs-up sign to him, but when I turned I could see that Red was fast asleep. I just kept going, not looking at the other men in there, just moving in a little trot to the door.

Outside it was twilight, and in the dim light my impaired vision fogged everything farther than a few yards off. But I stayed on the boardwalk and made for the outhouse.

Would the rats be there?

If there were bodies there, the rats would be there—but how would I get inside and set the trap?

I pushed open the door. It only took one glance to see a set of glittering eyes. I let the door swing back.

I wasn't going in there.

I worked fast. I put the bread inside the cage, set the release device, shoved the door open again and set the trap down just inside the door against the wall. I started to get out of there, and had gone several yards when the thought came to me that there would have to be a weight to hold the trap in place. As big as it was, the rats were big too, and strong, and if I actually caught one, he might drag the trap somewhere deep into the interior of the outhouse. How could I go any distance in there after it?

I went back, my eyes scanning the ground as I moved. I was looking for a rock. The light was failing fast, and with my vision it was hard just to tell where I was going. I couldn't see anything that would do—but when I was a yard or so from the outhouse, I saw a cinder block leaning up against the wall on the side I was approaching from.

I took it up. I needed two hands to do it—I was that weak still. I struggled with it to the door, bumped the door open with my knee, and lowered the cinder block onto the top of the cage. I wanted to make sure it was good and stable, but I wasn't going to take the chance.

I let the door swing closed and started away from there, for the first time wondering where I was going to go.

But why not go back to my barrack? Back to where the rest of the jacks were?

All right, I couldn't work yet—but all that meant was that I wouldn't be fed—and what did I need with the ration when I was going to be getting a feast?

I don't know how I made it to the barrack that housed the

lumberjacks. It was dark now, and my vision at night was no good to me at all—but I made it, and not anyone in there said a word to me, all those *Zks* who'd not seen me for a year—and *Zks* who were new to the place—not one of them said anything.

The light in there was enough for me to see by, and I just found a place and took it and lay down.

In the morning, when the Commandant and the sixes came to run everyone out, I just stayed where I was.

"Zk!" the Commandant screamed at me when all the others had vacated the place. "All out, *Zk!"*

"Can't work," I called to him. "Sick. Injured my ankle."

"No work, no food!" he shouted back.

"I can hardly walk," I said.

"Better to walk on your knees, *Zk,* than to starve! Do you hear me?"

"I'll work tomorrow," I said.

I heard him stomp out, and I could hardly keep myself there on that platform. It was like before I went up, knowing I was going to be coming down, the longest jumper from sky to earth. My belly lurched with anxiety, anticipating the succulence of rat.

I waited about two hours. I tried to doze off, so that the waiting would be easier, but I couldn't—and at last I got up and started for the outhouse.

It was like being on my way into the ring, like heading my plane down the runway and gaining speed. I was moving briskly along the boardwalk now, no pain in my ankle, my heart leaping in my chest.

Why had I lied to Red? Because I was ashamed to be seen as a man who would eat rat? Because if I had told him what I intended, he would have insisted that he keep sharing his food with me? Was it to spare him or to spare myself?

I don't know. My instinct told me not to tell him—that he would try to stop me, would not have made the trap.

It was 1943. The war was in full tilt. Food was the scarcest yet. Still, that a man would eat rat?

I knew it was better not to tell Red.

And I was right. Because after the first time and when I offered him half, Red wouldn't touch it. He said I was crazy and he wouldn't touch it. He said it would make me sick, make me crazier, and to get it away from him. No matter how much I assured him and no matter how reassuring my growing vigor must have been, he could not abide the notion of my eating rat—and it was unthinkable to him that he might eat it himself.

During the course of those six months I had rat to spare, but not any more than three men in all that time would take the share I pressed on them. Out of the scores I off and on offered some, every one but three said no—they'd sooner starve. And that's what they were doing.

The usual food supplies got down almost to zero, and even the forage was thinning out to where there wasn't much to be said for that—weeds like ivy and cypress, the favorites, had virtually vanished from all the work zones. Even so, of all those *Zks* I got the word to, no more than three would eat rat.

As for the rats, they had no such daintiness when it came to eating men. But in my daily visits to the outhouse, I learned that a rat is fussy in one respect. If a man is the least bit alive, the rat goes for his bowels and guts; whereas it's nothing but the soft exterior parts if the man is dead—chiefly the testicles and the penis and the buttocks, and the earlobes and the cheeks.

There were stories about rats killing people, people who were in pretty good shape but who maybe fainted in the outhouse or got themselves cornered somewhere. So I was more than a little scared on the way to the outhouse that first time. I suppose it's correct to say I stayed scared enough for a while to come. There's something about a rat—I imagine we all recognize what it is despite our knowing that he's really a thing of no immense size. But they can panic you, and when they're inflamed or see no way of escape, they can come at you with the ferocity and biting power of a bobcat.

That first time I reached in with one hand and grabbed and pulled the cinder block up and off and then, outside, let the door go back in place. I leaned the cinder block against the wall by the door, and I was starting to put my hand back in to pull out the cage when reason got control of my excitement and I stopped. I let the door close again and went looking for a stick or something with some sort of hooked affair on the end.

It took me about a quarter of an hour to find something right —a length of wood with three nails still stuck in it. I banged the nails on the cinder block, to make sure they were well set—and then I pushed open the door, squatted, and started fishing with my hook. I could hear him in there, his frantic squealing, but I didn't want to open the door any wider and look. Perhaps looking would have frightened me off—but this first time I just went fishing blind with my hook, reaching back against the wall, realizing I could do it better with my left hand than with my right and so changing hands and then trying again.

At last I got a purchase on the top of the cage, and as soon as I started to draw the thing toward me I knew I had something, the weight was so considerable. But I had expected to feel a terrific movement in there, and there wasn't. Whatever it was, it was inert—and I thought that maybe the thing had died. Did rats sleep?

I got the cage to the crack in the doorway—and *there it was,* just glaring at me and not moving. It was huge! It must have fought off every other rat in there to get at that nub of black bread.

I stood up, took a step or so back, leaned forward, pushed the door open just enough to get the cage through, and then I hooked it by the top again and yanked it on out.

The rat went wild!

Was it the motion? The daylight?

I had him out of there, but what now? How to kill him?

I looked around. The area was pretty much deserted, but I was anxious I might be caught. I dragged the cage around back, and then I sat down a little ways from it trying to figure out what to do, how to kill the rat without his biting me or getting away. I could already taste him. It was driving me crazy. I'd given no thought to this part of it—the killing and then how to cook my kill.

I would drown him! Was there anything safer and more effective? That way you'd know he was really dead—because you'd see the bubbles stop rising.

I knew there were rain barrels all over the place, oil drums that were set to hold rainwater for drinking or washing or whatever use you could make of it. They were spotted all over the place. I jumped up, thrilled to have a solution. I ran the stick through the top of the cage so that I could grip both ends. It wasn't easy to lift now that the rat was in a frenzy inside of there, but I got going with it, and less than a hundred feet away I came across one of those oil drums. I got the cage over the top of it and let it slide off the stick. He went right down through the skim of ice to the bottom.

I sat off to the side. I gave him plenty of time. I kept looking around to see if I was being watched.

Would it be safe to do this every day? Could I do this and still go to the woods? Now that I look back on it, at the time I am talking about, I was so utterly absorbed in eating rat I cared next to nothing for the risks I took. I think it's accurate to say that I was willing to be shot so long as I was getting that meat.

I got up and went over to the oil drum. I reached down with my stick and then I thought better of it and reached down with my hand.

I got it up out of there and set it gently on the ground.

I don't know what came over me. My belly was thinking too fast.

I undid the trapdoor and pulled him out of there and with my teeth I tore the fur off him and kept spitting it out and then used my fingertips to burrow under his skin and with my teeth and with my fingers I stripped him as best I could and then I just tore away and ate him.

I ate all of him. That first time I ate all there was—everything except the head and the guts and the bones and the tail.

I ate that first rat raw—and after that I ate most of them raw— only sometimes I was able to get one of them half-cooked in a bonfire in the forest, at least burned in certain parts.

I can't hazard a guess how much that first one weighed, but I think I ate about five or six pounds of meat off him. I don't really know. I know I just kept eating until I couldn't eat any more. I didn't move from the spot. I sat by that oil drum, in ecstasy. It was incredible—how I savored that rat—and I don't think there was that whole time another thought in my head except *meat, meat, meat.*

I thought long and hard before writing this part of my story. I thought long and hard about how much truth one can tell—and what it would mean to carry on life here in Detroit amid the history of events and feelings my words will make public. There are parts of my story that stop me—and I think: Tell *this*? Not even my daughters and wife know these things!

I think I will say that I want this book to be an even longer jump from sky to earth than was that which I made on the 6th of September in 1934. I want it to be the longest jump of my life, this book. I am thinking that this book must be the best jump, so that everything it is about may be vaulted to a place beyond.

And it is because I think this that I am telling it all and leaving nothing out, whatever it might mean to those who will read what I write.

I ate rat. I ate it raw. I did it many, many times—and I never felt in myself anything less than delight and great fortune for the food that it was.

Perhaps it is a small thing—to eat rat. Perhaps it is also a small thing to say that it pleased you, that you, in time, craved rat.

I was an animal in a fever to stay alive.

But I was a man then, too.

It was never easy, I tell you, to be both.

FORTY _____

My vision came back. It got again as good as it ever was—and I don't doubt for a minute that it was the meat that did it.

I was strong again—stronger than I'd been in years. But maybe where I was it wasn't a better thing to see clearly. Maybe you were better off when your vision was fuzzed, as if gauze had been laid over your eyes after it had been dipped in something brown.

I saw the life around me again—and I looked. It was like looking in that mirror while they worked on my liver.

I looked inside that outhouse. Every night when I set the trap and every morning when I went to retrieve its captive, I looked at the bodies in there and at the rats that were eating them.

The clothes were always off—because who threw away clothes on the dead? Or on someone almost dead? It was then that I noticed the habits of those rats, the meat they favored live and the meat they favored dead, and I gave them what they liked to catch them. I would bait my trap with a part of the rat that I'd eaten earlier that day, and it never failed me, that bait. There was not a day in all those days, from the spring on into the fall of that year, that I did not find my rat waiting for me, not a snippet of bait left in that cage.

I got bolder with the rats. For about a week I drowned my catch, but then I got a knife from Red—a hacksaw blade that he'd made an edge on and also a handle by wrapping one end with electrical tape. I asked him on a free day, and by that night he had me one—but he didn't want to talk about what I wanted it for.

Red Loon, he wouldn't eat rat. If he had, would he have lived?

But I had my knife and I used it to cut their heads off to kill them. I'd reach the other end of my stick in there and hold him down, and then I'd open the trapdoor and cut off his head. Then I'd take out the intestines I had hidden under my jacket, bait the trap, set the release device, shove the cage carefully against the wall inside, put the fresh rat under my jacket, and then call out to the guard on the tower nearest that I wanted to go back to my barrack.

They'd always make you go through the same routine, but they weren't so hard on me, really—because I think they all thought I was completely insane—this man who nightly insisted on the jeopardy of the outhouse just to move his bowels somewhere other than where everybody else did it.

Did they ever wonder how come the rats didn't bite me? They wondered nothing. I didn't know it, but I guessed it—they took me for a lunatic, that's all.

I was living in Barrack 12 now, the same place I'd been quartered when I first came to _Lager_ 5—it was where all the lumberjacks were.

I was working again, had gone back that next day, just as I had promised—and it was nothing to me now, now that I was getting meat. They could double my norm, and with the meat I was getting, I was okay. Every day I took my rat to the woods and always some time around midday I'd eat my rat, sometimes trying to cook him, sometimes not—and when the snows came, I'd sometimes chop him up with my ax and try to boil him in a pail. But mainly I ate my rat raw—and it was just as good that way. It was when the fall came and the weather turned that I had to use the bonfire—because the rat would freeze, there under my jacket, and I'd have to warm him up first.

It was around this time that Red died. He just wasn't there the free day I went looking for him. They said, the _Zks_ who knew him, that he'd died during the night—some kind of bleeding from his rectum, his trousers soaked with blood when they found him and took him out of there.

Had he been there in the outhouse that morning? When I'd gone to the outhouse that morning to collect my catch, was Red's body among the ones that were there? Had I looked?

I didn't remember.

He was dead. That was the end of it. There is not one thing more to be said about it.

Many died. Red Loon died too—just a man.

Men die. This is also what a man is—a thing that stops.

How does that happen to a man, bleeding that way, the blood suddenly pouring out of the rectum? It had poured through my mother's head, this same liquid that would not be contained.

I made sure I never missed my diet of rat—and I took to eating their livers just to make sure I was getting all the benefit I could.

Bleed like that? How does it start?

I went to the woods and I worked hard and I felt strength in all my body and I ate that meat with a vengeance, and the organs too—first the liver and then the heart.

The snow came early that year—1943—and since the dead rat would freeze under my clothes, anyway, I took to burying it under the snow until the time I could eat it. It was cold against me under there, the frozen rat under my quilts, and so I'd just stick it under the snow somewhere in my work zone.

But one day they moved the work zone before I'd eaten my rat. I'd cleared all the brush and timber out of that area, and so they'd moved me. But it happened before I could get my rat.

There were two guards with me that day—two guards and one dog—and it was eating time for them, around two o'clock, and they took a position in the snow and sat down facing each other, and I could tell they were getting ready to eat, and I wanted my rat —but it was back there under the snow.

I called to the guards.

"Permission to return to the old work zone!"

There was no reply, no movement of their heads. Then one of them idly turned and called back, "Why?"

"I dropped something there!"

It was a foolish statement, but what else might I have said? What if they asked what I'd dropped?

"What?" I heard him call.

"I dropped my spoon. I had a spoon."

"So, *Zk,* what will you do with a spoon?"

"For tonight," I said. "To eat my soup."

"*Zks* don't need a spoon for soup. You have a mouth, *Zk?* That is all you need."

They laughed at this, the two of them shaking their heads with mirth.

"Please, sir," I said, "I want my spoon."

It was the same guard who spoke.

"Then go get your spoon, fool!"

"Do I have permission?"

"Fool, I told you, go get it! But do you have permission? Go get your spoon and find out!" He had his tommy gun on his lap, and he raised and pointed it at me and waggled it back and forth. "Go, *Zk,* step across the work-zone line and see if you have permission or not!"

"Will you shoot me?" I called.

"I don't know, *Zk!*" He turned back to his partner. He said to the other guard, very loudly so that I would hear, "Will you shoot the idiot who says he must cross the line?"

The other guard shook his head and called out, *"Zk,* he asked me if I will shoot you if you break the rule. The answer is this, *Zk*— I also don't know!"

Now the first guard spoke again. "Go, *Zk,* and find out if you come back!"

Again, they both laughed and then, clearly bored with the teasing, they went back to their food.

I was ravenous. They were eating. My rat was back there— *meat.*

"All right," I called out. "I'm going! If you shoot me, then you shoot me!"

They said nothing.

I started toward the rat. It was under the snow about thirty yards distant. I walked past the guards and, as I passed them, I turned and started walking backwards, and when I turned, they did too, and the first one raised his machine gun again and waggled it at me. He made a shooting noise, a machine-gun sound, and then he laughed and then the other one joined in and I thought, all right, let them shoot me in the back then, and I turned around and walked on toward the rat.

What if the dog smelled it? What if he came after me or came jumping up at me on my way back? Would my eyes stop him? What foolishness! They were right. I was a fool—to think something so crazy, that my eyes could do that. But wouldn't the dog keep sniffing around the food the guards had? It was right where he was, and surely its aroma would hold him there.

I kept going, thinking, *Any moment the dog will come dashing by from behind me and nose out my rat or any moment it will be bullets that will come from behind me.* There were only a few yards left, and then I was there and I got down on my hands and knees and started casting about in the snow as if I were looking for something lost.

But I knew where my rat was—I knew the spot exactly, about one foot from a large rock I'd chosen as a marker. I made my way toward the spot, going gradually, beating away the snow as I went, putting up a great show of someone searching. Were they watching me? I did not want to look to see.

I had the rat uncovered now, and I snatched him up and stuffed him inside my jacket. The frozen fur felt like quills against me.

I was starting to stand up when I heard one of them call out, "Imbecile, did you find your spoon?"

"Just now!" I called back.

"Bravo, imbecile!" It was the first one, the first guard, the more aggressive of the two. "What a clever imbecile you are! Now, imbecile, are you asking for permission to return to the work zone?"

"Yes!" I said.

"Well, imbecile," he said, "you might and you might not have it. But come ahead and find out."

"I'm coming," I said. "Please don't shoot me—I only had to get my spoon."

"Wonderful, imbecile, wonderful. And you found it, yes? Very good. Now come show us your nice wood spoon so that my friend and I can admire what a clever fellow you are. Come, imbecile, hurry along. We are very eager to see."

I started trotting in their direction. They had their tommy guns trained on me, both of them did, but they were still seated, a few opened tin cans resting between them on the snow. It was all right to trot—my rat had lodged himself against the cinch my waist rope made, and you wouldn't notice the bulge in those bulky quilts.

I was within a few yards of them when the first one called out, "Halt!"

I stopped. I stood where I was. For some reason I was breathing hard—perhaps from excitement. Certainly it was not from exertion, and I wondered if they would notice.

"Down on your knees, *Zk*," the first one said, and then the second one said, "Now all the way down—face down in the snow!"

I did as they said.

I waited for something to happen. Nothing did. Minutes passed. I could hear them eating and muttering to each other. It was as if they had forgotten all about me. I was about to look up and say something when one of them, as if he'd read my mind, snapped, "Face down, horse! Keep your nose in the snow!"

I was lying on my rat, the tufts of frozen fur like little spikes in me.

They went back to their eating and their talking, and I must have lain like that for more than fifteen minutes, the hunger in me a creature with a hammer now, when the first one said, "All right, imbecile, we will look at your spoon. Come show us the wonderful spoon that you have."

I got up and brushed myself off.

I stood up just a few yards from them, and it was the first thing I saw.

I saw the tin cans that were sitting there on the snow between them, the lids of those cans flaring up and back as if the knives that had cut them loose and pried them up had inflicted pain. It was one of those autumn afternoons of tremendous clarity, the sun an orange not seen any other time of year. The air was brilliant with light, and the snow flashed with iridescences wherever you looked.

But I wasn't looking anywhere but at those tin cans. I did not move toward the guards. I did not make some sort of fraudulent motion to appear as if I were reaching for the phantom spoon. I did nothing but stand there and stare, my eyes unblinking—and then disbelieving—and then seeing that, yes, there was no mistaking what I was looking at, no question but that I was seeing what I was seeing, no chance in the world that it was my vision or a trick the light contrived or some distortion issuing from the bruised region of my brain.

It was the labels on those tin cans that I saw—those cans there between them on the snow. There were three of them and there was no error in this, no mistaking any of it.

The first guard was standing now. He had his tommy gun cradled in his right arm and he had his left hand out toward me, and I could dimly hear him saying, *"Zk,* show me your spoon."

I stood there motionless. I could not jerk my eyes away from what I saw.

Again he ordered me to produce my spoon.

"Give me your spoon or I use this!"

He raised the nose of the machine gun so that it lined up with my belly.

I remember thinking something utterly mad: *If the bullets hit the rat, will they ruin the taste?*

I actually thought that.

But only for an instant. My mind was too cluttered with the carnival of feelings that whirled in me as my eyes kept studying the labels on those three tin cans.

It was not possible!

I screamed. I think it was the first time and the only time in my life that a scream escaped from my lips.

I stood in that snow, staring and screaming.

I don't know what they thought of my screaming like that. I knew the other guard was standing up now, but I wasn't looking at either one of them. I was only looking at the labels on those tin cans, and I could hear myself screaming there in the forest, the two of them standing there and watching me do it.

"Stop that!" the first guard shouted.

I didn't stop. I just kept forcing them out of me, one long scream after another, until my voice broke and then cracked and all that came from me now was a kind of hoarse, watery honking, like a wild thing breathing his last, and then nothing came out of me at all except the whistling air my lungs gave while my mouth hung open in a gigantic effort to put my screaming back into the blackening space around me, and then that space swiftly drew itself together into a tight little shroud that went all around me, and when it was all the way around me and very tight, I let myself down onto the snow and cried.

I cried for myself and for what I had seen.

I cried for Red Loon—and for my mother and my father and for Rebecca and Miriam and Leo.

I cried for peasants that threw rocks at cows and peasants that were chased from their homes in the night.

I cried for Belov's lip and for my liver—and for Tanya and Crab and that woman with the black, black hair and the white, white skin, and for all the people in Moscow who sobbed when they touched a truck.

I cried for the sound of the word *Piccolino,* and for the taste of Vernors, and for the love of * , I cried and I cried.

I cried for everything I could think of, and for a world that is all irony, all joke.

Listen.

Listen to me.

The labels on those cans—there were three of them—*Franco-American Spaghetti, Campbell's Pork and Beans, Dinty Moore's Beef Stew.*

I sat there in that snow mutely sobbing, spikes of rat hair like a scrub brush on my chest, while those two men gazed at me, their mouths still smeared with—   *   *   *   *   *

Franco-American Spaghetti!

Campbell's Pork and Beans!

Dinty Moore's Beef Stew!

They let me sit like that. They did not touch me.

It's not that it mattered so much how they had that food—it was only that they had it at all! Were the Soviets at war with America? Had they captured that food? Or was America an ally who had given it? Either way, what did it matter to me there in that snow, willing to die for my rat meat while the men that would kill me ate Dinty Moore's Beef Stew? Later on, when I found out there was plenty of American food around, for the Russian army that was getting it, I never again saw anything with American labels. I mean, it would say it was from America, all right—but it never said who the maker was—like Dinty Moore's or Campbell's.

It was late in December of 1943 that I found out how they got that food. An Air Force colonel from the Red Army interviewed me in the Secret Service shack there at *Lager 5*. It was from him that I learned the Soviets were fighting the Germans and that the U.S. was in it on the Soviet side.

Would I fly for the U.S.S.R.? he wanted to know. They had come across my records, and flyers were desperately needed, so would I fly?

I said yes. I said of course. I said that I would do anything to get out of there. I said if my country was fighting alongside the Russians, then I would fight for the Russians.

He said he would arrange it.

Nothing happened.

On three different occasions the question came up, and each time I assured them I was willing to fly. But nothing ever came of it—and I stayed where I was and worked the woods.

But nothing was the same ever again—not after that day when I cried. I cried it all out that day, emptied myself of everything but a stupendous rage. I could not die with so much in me. I carried that rage in me like an iron heart.

I would live through this. I would see it all through. I would do it with the will that rage gave me.

It was when my cage disappeared from the outhouse that I stopped eating rat. But the food was somewhat better now—and there was no Red Loon to make me another trap.

It didn't matter. Nothing could finish me now—not anything they could come at me with. I did the work and I ate the food and whatever they gave me, it was enough, and if they gave me nothing, that too would be enough.

I went to the woods and chopped and sawed and dragged and loaded and I spoke to no one and no one spoke to me and the iron in my belly spread spokes into my arms and legs until I was a wheel of fury, turning in long slow cycles through the months and years— 1944, 1945, 1946, 1947, 1948.

I was doing time.

Take whatever you are, and add ten.

That's what they call it and that's what it is—*doing* time. You either do it or time does *you*.

They gave us a free day on VE day.

They gave us another one on VJ day.

But we none of us knew about the bomb—about Hiroshima and Nagasaki.

What *did* I know about when it was 1948 and it used to be 1938?

Did I know about the U.S. and the U.S.S.R.?

I did not. Listen—I did not even know if my father lived—if Miriam lived.

What did I know?

I knew I had done my time—that I was ten years older and a thousand years older than that.

The end of July came—July, 1948—but they would not let me go. They sent me to the woods. They said nothing when I said, "Ten years. Let me go." They just sent me to the woods.

But at the end of October, it was over—at least this part of it was over. They called for me. They told me to get my things. I had nothing. I didn't even have that spoon. I had the clothes that were on me, two arms and two legs.

I had my rage.

What did I know when they let me out of there? When I walked out of the gates of *Gulag* 231, what was I?

Think of it! In 1931 I was a boy from Detroit off to an adventure to capture tigers. In 1948 I was a man from the woods with a taste for rat.

That was the only capturing I had done, this boy who'd sought lions and tigers and bears in the dappled jungles of his father's fantasy. I'd captured about a hundred and eighty rats, and I had eaten every one of them and most of them raw.

What was I when they let me go?

I was a man who had done that.

PART 4

UNDER THE ICE

FORTY-ONE

No one told me anything—and I stopped asking.

A day came in October when they marched me out of there, out of *Gulag* 231. They marched me under guard to the depot, loaded me into a Stolypin, trained me south to Vyatka, unloaded me into a van, motored me to the prison, where they searched me and finger-printed me and did all the rest, and after five days they took me out of there and put me into another van, and the van carried me back to the station, but this time there was a cattle car waiting for me and for about forty more men, and when it moved, it moved north, back the same way I'd just come from, past all the places I'd just passed —only this time it kept right on going.

It kept on going past Molotov. Past Sverdlovsk.

And still that train kept on going.

And when we passed Omsk, I knew it—and the knowledge of it was like a jackhammer going off.

I was in Siberia now.

Was this the freedom I'd been purchasing tree by tree, log by log?

And still the train did not stop. It kept pushing east, east past Novosibirsk—and it kept on going, ten days now, and each day they put in a pail of water for the bunch of us, and to each man they gave a fist of bread—and after eleven days the train stopped, and when it stopped it was deep in Siberia that it stopped—and I was really there now, north of China, north of Mongolia, in a place whose name was like a snarl.

Krasnoyarsk.

They took us all out and marched us through the side streets to the city jail. We were searched. We were fingerprinted. And then they put us all into the same cell.

How was it I kept from screaming?

I suppose it was because I'd screamed my last that day in 1943. Three tin cans of American food there in that Russian snow, and I was never going to scream again.

Only now do I think that it must have been the same for my father in his time—that there in Czarist Russia, in some small village in the Ukraine, he'd done all the screaming he was ever going to do, and the man that I would know, the Sam Herman who sat in stony forbearance while his wife shrieked her agony in his ear, was a man like the son he had made.

I would never scream again. And I would ask them nothing.

I would sit if they told me or I would stand if they told me, but I would do it all in silence.

What difference would it make? Would asking tell you more than nothing?

It was then, waiting in that jail in Krasnoyarsk, that I came to know my father, not his ideals but the single principle that anchored him.

If it's the same whatever you do, then let it find you as indifferent to it as it is to you.

Was this my father's idea of dignity? Of manly grace amid the grief of the fugitive life?

I will never know if it was his.

I know it was—and still is—mine.

I was there two days when they took me down to the main floor to a little office where a man who fit it just right kept referring to the folder of papers he had in front of him as he reviewed my prospects with me.

He flattered me. I don't know why—but I was glad he did. I was happy he said the things he did—whatever it was that made him do it. It had been so long since anyone had noticed me as other than something in quilts that produced so many cubic yards of wood.

He said, "Ah, you are Victor Herman. You are a famous man."

"I was known for parachuting," I said.

He said, "I see, I see. And I see that you are a fine athlete too—yes?"

"It was all a long time ago," I said.

"Ten years, ten years—to be sure," he said.

"I liked to do those things," I said.

"Some people would say a great athlete," he said.

It was hard to keep my feeling down. I had to fight the tears. I had to grit my teeth to keep from sobbing.

"I loved those things," I said.

"Of course, of course," the man said, his bushy eyebrows making a great commotion on his tiny face as he concentrated his attention on the papers before him.

He said he was an investigator—NKVD.

Whatever he was, I think he felt sorry for me. I think he really did. I suppose he every day saw men with histories like mine. But I think this man felt sorry for them all.

He said, "You were attached to *Spartak,* yes?"

"I was," I said.

I suddenly wanted to tell this man everything. Did he remind me of my father? Not really. It was, rather, that he reminded me of people, of just anyone who was like anyone and not like what for ten years I'd been with, shapes that pushed or did not push.

I said, "My last day, that's where I was. I mean, when I was picked up, arrested, it was right from *Spartak.*"

I think this embarrassed him, my enthusiasm to talk. How difficult his job must have been for him, having to talk with people for whom talking was an extraordinary new way to pass the time.

"I did a lot of things with *Spartak,*" I said. "Boxing, track, riflery—I loved to do them all."

"I see, I see," the little man said, shifting uncomfortably in his seat. He closed the folder he had before him. "Would you do these things with *Dynamo,* Comrade Herman? If I could arrange it, would you?"

I knew what *Dynamo* was. There were two major sports organizations: *Spartak,* for civilians—and the other one, *Dynamo,* for those attached to the Secret Service or to the Secret Police or to the NKVD. They were rivals, these two—and think of the irony of it! After ten years of suffering at the hands of the Secret Service and the Secret Police and the NKVD, this man wanted me to get these people medals.

I could not have been happier.

"Then I will be free?" I said.

Again he moved uncomfortably in his seat, this small, kind man. He said, "No, Comrade, not exactly. You are exiled. You must remain here in Siberia—in Krasnoyarsk. That is, if all goes well. If not . . ." Here he looked away, as if discovering something of interest in the air above my head. "Well," he said at last, "there are worse places in Siberia, my friend—much worse. In the cities, it is not so bad. But in the villages and north of here . . . But there is no need to think about that. So long as you are willing to lend your energies to *Dynamo,* there is nothing to worry about."

I leaned forward.

"But listen," I said, "how long does this exile last?" And then, because I believed I had turned up a friend, at least a man of feelings, I said, "You understand that I am an American? I don't know what's happened to me, sir. For ten years crazy things have happened to me, and there is no way to explain it all. I don't understand. How long?" And I whispered this last: "Don't you see? I am an American."

Now he too leaned forward, his elbows propped awkwardly on his desk, his stature so diminutive that the confidential posture he tried to adopt seemed to give him huge discomfort.

"Comrade," he said, "let us not discuss these things. Do you understand?" He was whispering. He said, "It is better not to discuss these things."

He dismissed me, and I was taken back to my cell, but a few days later he again had me brought to his office. He told me that he had spoken with a man named Falk, and that this Falk was the chief of *Dynamo* for the Krasnoyarsk district, and that it was all okay, I was to report to this Falk's office in two days' time—and with that the little man put scrip for twenty rubles into my hand and said I was free to leave.

"I don't understand," I said.

"You are free to go," the little man said.

"Just go?"

"Precisely. In two days you report to Falk. He will exchange twenty rubles for the scrip you have. And now you may go."

"But go where?" I said. "Where do I go? Where do I sleep?"

"Wherever you choose," the little man said. "So long as you remain in Krasnoyarsk, you are free to go wherever you choose. Now, let me bid you good-bye," and he rose, came around his desk, and reached out his hand to clasp mine.

I shook his hand. I took it hard in mine and squeezed it, trying to make the pressure say the gigantic thing I felt.

"I know," that little man said—and again he seemed to find something interesting somewhere above my head. "I know," he repeated—and then he repeated the address of Falk's office. "Do not fail to report there in two days. Now take this, and good-bye." He pressed three rubles into my hand.

"All right," I said. I wanted to hug him. I wanted to lift him off the floor and hug him. But I just turned away and at the door I turned again and said good-bye.

There is no way to talk about the feeling that I had.

How do I tell you what was in me when I walked out into the streets of Krasnoyarsk? It was cold. I knew no one. I hadn't the faintest idea of where to go and what to say—or even of how a man walks when a man is free.

I don't know if I was inexpressibly frightened or inexpressibly happy.

I know I felt very alone.

And I am sure I was very frightened and very, very happy. I think I felt the way a man feels when he has been saved from drowning, but safety is a far-flung solitary beach some fortuitous wave has swept him on. I mean, I think every man in a case like that feels the same sort of thing—a kind of jittery alarm contesting with an uncontainable joy, both feelings racing along some continuum of heightening excitement.

I stopped the first person I saw and asked which way to the public bathhouse. How long had it been since I'd been clean? Did that man see the hysteria in me? Did he take me for a prisoner?

I wanted a steambath, as hot as I could stand it. I wanted to wash myself and wash myself—oh, how I wanted to get it all off, what ten years had caked me with, the vapors of ✳ that coated my eyes.

It was the 14th of October, 1948, and I walked the streets like any man. I had nothing but my hideous memories—and a kind of freedom to carry them around in.

I walked the four miles it took to get to the central bathhouse. The ticket to get inside cost one and a half rubles. I had no soap, no towel—but bits of soap I found inside, and as for drying off, I'd let the air do it. I steamed myself and scrubbed and then I did it all over again, and I guess I repeated this routine about ten times before getting back into my prison clothes, the black quilts I'd been wearing for longer than I could remember.

You had to exit through the barber shop—I suppose to encourage business for the three women that did the barbering there. One was a young woman, a redhead—I wish I could remember her name. She called to me as I was passing through, making some sort of joke about my trying to get away without a haircut and a shave. The other customers in there laughed, and she turned on them and told them to shut up.

"You need a haircut and a shave," she said, turning back to me.

"No money," I said, and started on my way again.

"Come here," she said. It was a command.

"What is it?" I said.

"You just out of prison?" she said.

I looked at the other barbers and at the men seated there, the ones that had laughed.

"How do you know?" I said.

"How do I know," she said. "Just look at you," she said.

"So what?" I said.

"Come on," she said. "I'll get you looking like a lady-killer again, and you can pay me some other time."

What was it in her speech that affected me so? I was not used to this sort of thing, yet I think I was right in taking it for a kind of sexual banter. She was pretty; just that one word, *lady-killer,* and my senses were crazily aroused.

I waited. I waited until she was through with her customer, and then I took my place in her chair.

It was extraordinary—the simple business of being shaved and barbered by a woman—her touching me, my hair, my face, turning my head this way and that.

It got me terribly excited—and I began to imagine all sorts of things about her and me, our being together in some kind of sexual way. Was she having the same kind of thoughts? How does one know such things? I knew nothing about the sort of signals you might search for—and even less how to express them.

I was remarkably excited—and nervous—and I think that much she could tell. I kept trying to catch a glance of her face in the mirror—and then I was suddenly ashamed of myself, thinking this way about her. Here she was, this cheerful woman, showing me such kindness—and there I was, possessed by these lewd feelings for her.

Maybe freedom had made me crazy. I was so ❋ *happy*—
and so sensitive to everything. Everything made me want to cry, the
charity of that little man who said, "I know," and now the generous
kindness of this pretty woman. It all made me want to cry—to do
something—to show the feeling that I had in me—but at the same
time I felt so terrifically *numb*.

I suppose I was transfixed by the human spectacle. It all
seemed so richly subtle and sweet—and sensual. My God, someone
was *touching* me, touching my hair and my face, and it all seemed
to me so tender and, yes, sexual.

When the other men had finished and left, she was still working
on me. It was then that she started teasing me, teasing me about
having been away from women and so on. I was glad she did it. It
was erotic, that teasing—and it sort of confirmed the thoughts I'd
been having about her.

When I could see that the other two barbers were out of ear-
shot, I began telling the redhead all about myself. I told her everything. It was wonderful to have her hear it, to hear myself telling it.

But when she began to cry a little bit, I felt ridiculous—and
evil—because I had made her feel something that had no real
feeling for me anymore. And also because I think I told her just to get
her to feel sorry for me. I admit it—I thought that if I got her to feel
sorry for me, she might grant me favors, her body to touch.

It worked. When it was finished and I stood up to go, she
followed me to the door, and as we neared it she said I could stay
with her a while if I wanted, that I could sleep at her place, and
when she said this last she squeezed my arm.

The prospect terrified me, as much as I wanted it. I began to
make some sort of lame excuse, and then I stopped myself. I said,
"I never have."

"Have what?" she said.

"You know," I said.

"Oh," she said. "Then, so much the better," she said.

"No," I said. "I can't. I want to, but I can't. But you are very
kind. I'll pay you back, I swear," I said.

"That's all right," she said. "Whenever you want, I'm always
here."

I opened the door and stepped outside, but she followed me
into the cold early evening air.

"Where are you going?" she said.

"That's okay," I said. "I have a place."

She came up to me and put her hands on the face her shaving had revealed.

I think she wanted me to kiss her—or that she was thinking of kissing me. But I couldn't. And yet I did something even bolder. I could not resist doing it. My hand seemed to move of its own accord, reaching for her breast quite independently of anything I might have willed. I touched her lightly there. It was the first time I had ever done a thing like that, and the doing of it made my senses reel, the softness, yet the weight of it, a kind of heavy softness unlike anything I'd ever felt.

"That's all right," she said, her hands still cupping my face.

My eyes welled up with tears.

"Thank you," I said, and then I walked away from her as fast as I could.

I spent a long time sitting on a bench. I kept thinking about touching her breast, what it had felt like. I knew I had better be thinking about how I was going to get through this night and the next one, that I'd better have some sort of plan until the time I could go see Falk. But all I could think about was touching that redheaded woman.

A street vendor came by—he was on his way home. He was selling watermelon and milk—little pieces of watermelon and milk. He said it was two rubles for a slice of watermelon, and I asked if he could cut me a slice worth a ruble and a half, and that's how I spent the last of my money.

I went back to my bench and sat there eating that watermelon as if it were the first food I had ever put into my mouth.

It was dark now—and very cold. I'd been wandering around for the last hour, and had finally made my way to the main street, which was Stalin Street. In those days, all the main streets in the cities were called Stalin Street, and in Krasnoyarsk, a city of 400,000 people, that's all there really was that earned it the reputation of a city—the main thoroughfare, Stalin Street. The place was really a huge village, shacks and hovels for the most part, spreading away in all directions from Stalin Street.

Anyway, once I was on Stalin Street, I'd seen all I wanted to see. I walked up and down a while, and when I got tired of doing that, I asked directions to the city stadium.

"Which one do you want?" said the old woman I'd stopped to ask.

"There's more than one?"

"There's two," she said.

"Which one's closer?"

"Locomotiv," she said.

I went the way she'd told me, but it wasn't much of a stadium. I went back out into the streets again, and got directions to the other stadium, the *Dynamo* stadium, and that's where I spent the night, in the bleachers under the benches.

It was cold that night—still October, but very, very cold. It didn't bother me much. I thought about the girl, her long red hair, the white smock she wore to do her work in. I thought about the body I had touched, the wider geography whose lessons I longed to learn. It put me to sleep, thinking about her. I want to say that it put me to sleep with a smile on my lips, but I am sure that would be made up.

In any case, I slept fitfully—but in the morning, it was like waking to the music of some ineffable symphony.

Imagine! In that bitter cold stadium, the morning mist in it so thick you could not see the turf, the wind angrily finding me even under the bench where I lay, I woke up ablaze with the delight a child knows when it is the first day after school's been let out and the world outside is radiant with the promise of renewal.

I think that grim morning when I unfolded myself from the fist I'd made of my body all through that frigid night, I think that morning in the *Dynamo* stadium in Krasnoyarsk I was the happiest man alive.

I climbed down out of the bleachers to watch when the athletes showed up for training that morning. I stood around watching all that morning, and it was just about noon that a man came over, one of the coaches, and he said he knew who I was. He said they'd heard I was going to be joining them, but that he knew me, anyway —from the time he'd been a starter when I'd run the 100-meter dash in the 1936 *Spartakiad.*

I didn't know him, of course, but we fell to talking about this and that, the old days mainly. He said he was also an exile—because he was married to a Frenchwoman and because her father had once operated a jewelry store in Leningrad.

He took me home with him that night. He fed me and gave me a place to sleep. He lived in a little house very close to the stadium, a place that belonged to *Dynamo*. Milk wasn't rationed in

Siberia, and I must have drunk at least two quarts of that man's milk
that night, gorging myself on everything his wife put in front of me
—bread and potatoes and cabbage and a glorious stew, the miracles
of ordinary life.

Emotion drove through me as if it were wind.

I felt so much! Everything made me feel something. All the
time I wanted to cry—to cry from the merest discovery. That
woman's curtains, thin rags of things that hung pathetically from
the one window the house had, they made me want to weep.

She and her husband made a place for me above the stove,
and it was then that I found out that's how Siberians sleep—on a
kind of shelf above the stove, and sometimes right on the stove.

It was wonderful, the warmth, the food in my belly, the charity
of these people. All of it made me dizzy with feeling.

It was a state of mind that was to stay with me for a very long
while. It was a kind of madness, surely—but I was happy to have it.

In the morning the man took me back to the *Dynamo* stadium
and got me clothes—a training suit like a ski suit, and heavy socks
and shoes and a coat of closely woven wool—and a cap that you
could fold down to cover your ears. He was giving me directions
to Falk's office when I realized I didn't even know the man's name.

I said, "Where I've been names don't count for much. But you
know mine. Please, I am sorry—what's yours?"

"My name is Alexander," he said. ·

I remember exactly what I said.

It will seem preposterously poetic to record it now, but at the
time there seemed to me no better thing to say. I said, "Dear
Alexander," and then I shook his hand.

I left Falk's office with twenty rubles cash in my pocket and a
whole new future laid out for me. The first thing I did was find
my way back to the bathhouse. The redhead wasn't there, and I
waited for her to show up, and when she did, I gave her ten rubles,
and when she tried to give the money back to me, I waved her away
and told her she'd be seeing me again the next time I needed the
best shave in all of Russia. I ran all the way back to the stadium,
and I made Alexander take the other ten rubles.

"What will you do for money?" he said.

"I have plenty," I said. "Falk gave me fifty, sixty—who knows,
I can't count, it's so much."

I went to the *Dynamo* gymnasium, a clubhouse right next to the stadium. The office was empty, and I went rummaging through the drawers of the desk that was there, and when I found pencil and paper, I sat down at that desk and I wrote.

Here is what I wrote:

Dearest Papa,

I am alive. I am in Krasnoyarsk, in exile. But I am fine. I was in prison and the camps for ten years, but I am fine. I have a good job here. I started it today. It is with Dynamo, *and I will be running the gymnasium where the athletes come for indoor exercises. I will also be coaching the boxing team. My pay is five hundred rubles a month. A Mr. Falk, a* landsman, *arranged it. I must stay here because I am in exile, but I don't know how long for. I think of you and Miriam and Leo. I know you are all fine and that we will all be together again one day. Please don't worry about me. There is nothing to worry about. I love you all very much.*

Your adoring son,
Vickie.

My father answered that letter. His letter came to me about two months later, addressed to the *Dynamo* office in Krasnoyarsk. His letter said:

Dear son, dear Vickie,

I cannot get permission to visit you. Miriam sends her love. So do Leo and I. My heart cries for you, my son.

Your father,
Samuel Herman.

FORTY-TWO ———————————————

Everything was new. But it took a while to see it. It took some while for the newness of things to make its way past your eyes and into your brain—small things, like a drink of water when you wanted it—big things, like women. Except at first, until you got used to it all, it was the women that seemed the minor matter and the glass of water that seemed important.

My father was alive—and my sister and my brother too—
—and I was alive, exiled to Siberia, but alive—and all that had really happened was ten years.

It was the best way to look at it—to see it all as a number of years, as nothing but time, an idea and nothing more, an interval lost but without event.

I went about my life as if this was what it was meant to be, that my role with *Dynamo* and my days in Krasnoyarsk had been or-dained from the time of my birth—but in one corner of my mind I planned. It was a plan I never had to think about; it did its own thinking, a ceaseless chant better than thought.

America, America, America.

Meanwhile, I made a life.

Of the five hundred rubles they paid me each month, I always sent three hundred by postal order back to my father in Gorky. I'd send letters too, but after that first letter all my father's replies said pretty much the same thing: *Work hard for Comrade Stalin, work hard for the U.S.S.R.*

I don't think he meant it. I think it's what he had to say. But I would never know the truth.

I would never see my father again.

The work was good and it gave me pleasure to do it. I coached the boxers and managed the clubhouse where the athletes worked at their indoor exercises and gymnastics. I slept there too—and all in all it was a pretty good life, not anything I am willing to complain about now.

Besides, the Siberians were natural fighters, fiercely aggressive and hard as bark, and it took only grace and know-how for them to make outstanding competitors in the ring. That was my job, and I loved doing it, loved feeling the shock in my shoulders when it was their fists that slammed bone. Let them hit for me, and let me teach them how to do it so that maximum damage is done. That is what I thought.

I admit it—every time those men hit, it was like another inch of revenge I exacted against everything I had been through.

I slept on an iron cot and I had a good stove to keep me warm

and my fighters to give me an interest in life, and life was all right
—and when I had my first woman, it was even better than that.

It happened this way.

The clubhouse often had women in it—but I suppose they
were really still girls. They'd come to play volleyball or basketball
or just to watch the men—but some came for serious work, and they
were mostly the gymnasts. At any rate, lots of girls and women were
always hanging around, and you saw them pretty much every day,
and when you saw them doing something athletic, bending and
stretching and jumping and running, you really saw them.

It drove me crazy with desire.

But I knew it wasn't going to be easy for me, women. They
frightened me. I didn't know how to talk to them, or how to be
with them. I felt clumsy and ridiculous and completely inept, and I
imagined my desire for them stood out all over me like some
monstrously obscene growth.

I wanted to look at them, those female things that danced in
and out of my corrosive vision, and at the same time I wanted to
hide.

One day there was a woman there—a gymnast. At first she
reminded me of that enraged woman in Moscow—because of the
black, black hair and skin that was whiter than I had ever seen.
This woman, too, had hair that fell about her head like black
water as she moved across the gymnasium floor, twisting her body
into a river of motion that seemed at once a violent energy and a
resplendent calm. I stood against the wall watching her. I could
not turn away. She was like no woman I had ever seen, this supple
masterpiece of arms and legs and buttocks and breasts, that black
hair like something heavy and wet, chasing her head in starts and
leaps, a long, glistening, capering animal of some kind.

The others, they always tied their hair up or bound it in some
way, but this one, she began showing up early every morning, not
ever talking to the others or joining in, but always out there bending
and stretching through a quiet place her presence seemed to create
around her, and her hair always dancing behind her, long and
loose, a rain of ebony.

She was a radiance, this beautiful woman, by turns a whirling
vibrancy vaulting through the space around her, the next instant, at
the end of an elegant sentence she had just inscribed in the air, a

breathtaking tranquility in serene repose. Every morning I watched her from that same station I took up against the wall, a towel around my neck and my hands gripping its ends as if to wring something from the dry terry cloth.

I knew she noticed me. How could she not? She must have known I wanted to stand there watching her until the end of my days, and I think the knowledge of this inspired her performance out there on the floor. I believed it was just for me that she moved with such erotic eloquence across the chill wooden boards, and I knew that if I were steadfast, never letting my attention waver, my eyes would do the talking that my tongue could not.

This went on for about two weeks, not a word passing between us, and I don't think she glanced at me once. One day she didn't show up in the morning, but came instead in the afternoon for a women's meet, a district-wide competition in gymnastics.

She was very good in competition, although she did not place among the winners. It was easy to see why—when you saw the others. She was much too voluptuous for this sort of thing, her breasts too womanly, her buttocks too much a feature of her body, her long legs slender and tapering, not muscled much at all. She seemed vulnerable, even a little ungainly, among the hard, abrupt bodies of the others. And that hair!

The effect was too much, impossible, too feminine, more a piece of sensual teasing than the brusque and strictly executed sequence of figures of the disciplined gymnast. I didn't feel bad for her. I could tell she knew what she looked like out there and that she would rather have that than the other.

She headed in my direction as she made her way off the floor, and when she got close enough, she spoke to me.

She said, "How was I?"

"You were beautiful," I said.

Had I spoken to her? Had I really said that? The words resounded in my head. *You were beautiful*. Was it something I said or had I just thought it?

She stood in front of me, not smiling, not moving, just looking at me as if I were expected to say more, her eyebrows vaguely lifted, her dark green eyes staring into mine.

There was something remarkably unflinching about her, something bold and full of force.

I wasn't sure if I'd said anything—or if she had—or if she'd already spoken paragraphs to me and it was a dream.

I said, "You are beautiful."

Still she did not move or smile or give any indication that she'd heard what I had said. Surely I had said something this time, but what?

"Why do you look at me like that?" I said.

"For the same reason you look at me," she said, her face expressionless, the incredibly white skin flushed from the heat in the place and from her strenuous motions on the floor. I remember thinking how straight this woman stands, and yet it seems effortless.

Her fine posture made her seem tall. Yet she was shorter than I.

"Will you escort me home?"

I didn't know if I'd heard her right. Was she asking me to walk home with her?

"Did you say, will I walk you home?"

"Yes," she said, even now no trace of anything more on her face, just that open, staring loveliness. It made me sleepy to look at her like this. It was as if we talked inside some sort of cottony chamber shut off from everything else. Everything seemed to me dreamy, muted, unreal.

"I will," I said, knowing as I said this that my speech was strange and yet somehow appropriate to the drowsy quality of the moment.

It really wasn't such an unlikely suggestion, that I walk her home. Once you were off Stalin Street and into the unlighted alleyways of Krasnoyarsk, the nights were never free of violence. Even my boxers came and went in groups after sundown.

We walked in snow. It was only four blocks away that she lived, but we walked very slowly and made it last. I didn't tell her much, only what my name was and that I'd been a sportsman and an athlete all my life. I think I was afraid to tell her more.

She spoke a little, not much. She said she was twenty-four, had been to university at Baku to study physical culture, and that what she loved was to teach—that she taught gymnastics in a secondary school here in the city.

I didn't know what to say to her. I wanted to say, *You were beautiful, you are beautiful, you will always be beautiful—please, please, be beautiful for me*—but I was capable of not much more than long painful silences and clumsy questions about things that did not matter.

I remember saying "Were you born in Siberia?" and her answering yes, that her father had been exiled, that he was a *Kulak,* that they had sent him here, and that she had been born in a village nearby, and when she used that term I suddenly wanted to blurt out everything—I wanted to begin the long tale all the way back to those rocks banging against the iron sides of that cattle car.

I was actually about to begin it, actually about to say, "I know about the *Kulaks.* Let me tell you about a time when some *Kulaks* threw rocks and it made my mother scream."

I said nothing. I walked her to her door, a house where she had a room.

We stood there in front of her place, our eyes fastened on each other the same way it had happened in the gym.

She said to me, "Why do you look at me like that?"

And I answered, "For the same reason you look at me."

Her face went very solemn when I said that—and then she gave a little smile, turned, and went inside.

It became a kind of invocation between us, an exchange that never failed to loft us into a kind of shared trance. One of us would say, "Why do you look at me like that?" and when the other responded, "For the same reason you look at me," it was suddenly as if a magical utterance had been declared and everything that would come after it would be different and charmed and special.

Her name was Galina. The whole of it was Galina Galaktionova.

She became my wife.

She *is* my wife—even though they made us divorce.

As I write this, she is in Russia. As I write this, she is coming here. I know she is.

It is because we looked at each other like that.

She took to coming later and later in the day, so that we were more and more alone in the *Dynamo* gymnasium, and every evening I would walk her home, neither of us talking very much, nor touching.

We did not need to. We only had to be with one another and we touched. It was exquisite, the way we touched each other with our eyes only.

And then for a long time she did not come to the gymnasium, and after she had been absent for two days I went to the boarding-house where she stayed and they said she had gone away to tour with the high-school kids she coached.

I thought, why did she not tell me, not warn me of her absence?

And then I thought, no need, no need—she is mine and I will never lose her.

It did not matter that she was gone. She would always be with me—if she never returned, that woman would be with me forever.

But the days became weeks and still Galina did not reappear, and meanwhile a woman hung around, one of those women who were always eyeing the athletes, a woman like that. She made a move for me, and I had the courage for it now, and I thought, yes, I would do it because I did not know about myself, and I wanted to know about myself before it came to that with Galina.

So I did it—I went with that woman—a very sad-eyed creature who had lost her husband in the war. She had short curly hair, blond, and I suppose she wasn't much to look at, but it was clear she wanted me, and just her wanting me was enough to make me deaf to everything else save the claims of desire.

All the while I was walking to her place with her, all that time I kept thinking how I was for the first time in my life going to see a naked woman—and yet I never saw her. It was night, and she wouldn't put the light on, and I was glad she wouldn't because I was so shy, and it wasn't until later that I realized the one thing I wanted most from her, the chance to study her body as you would some astonishing invention, that was something I'd not really had.

Her name was Elena.

She was my first, and I owe her so much. She was shy too. But she made it all easy for me. She helped me, and she helped me to herself, the small abundance she had to give.

I remember how she was always saying, before and all through it, "Okay." Everything was okay.

I had said, "Can I go to your room with you?" and she had answered, "Okay."

I had said, "Will you be with me when we get there?" and she had said, "Okay."

Elena.

I was thirty-four years old.

The room was very cold and the blanket was very thin and we were both shivering even with our clothes on.

I said, "Take off your clothes," and she said, "Okay."

She took off her clothes. I could hear her doing it, and then I could see her silhouette move to the bed and slip under the blanket.

I undressed.

I got under the blanket with her.

I said, "Are you cold?"

She said, "It's okay."

I lay on my back next to her, not touching.

My brain was racing for some way to go about it. What did I do? What was it you were supposed to do?

We didn't talk. We just lay there like that on our backs.

Then I thought to say, "You're cold—let me rub you," and in the darkness I heard her say, "Okay." But there was something different in it now, a sound I'd never heard before in anyone's voice.

I threw back the blanket and crouched over her and I started rubbing her feet. I tried to see her in the darkness, but she was just a shape. I kept rubbing her feet and then her calves, and I kept thinking, how long can I do this and what's next? I remember just before it happened I had said, "How do you like that?" and her answering, in that same oddly different quality of voice, "It's okay." But it was right after that, right after she had answered, that I felt her cool fingers on me, at first touching me lightly and then firmly, touching me unbelievably.

I was trembling, and then, very quickly, with her touching me there, the trembling graduated to a kind of dazed feeling, an itching that seemed both unbearable torment and the scratching that powerfully answered it, so that it was like two feelings that never go together happening at once, and I could hear myself groaning her name and thinking *My* * , *Galina* as everything came out of me in a rush.

I collapsed on top of her, the feelings in me swimming in a kind of glorious confusion, and I remember that before I fell into the towering sleep that would hold me locked into myself until morning, I hugged this woman and said her name—with love, I think, and with love, for the first time, I kissed her. I kissed her lips and then I kissed her hand and that is the last thing I remember before sleep sealed me off from everything except the sensation of her skin fused with the fragrance that rose from it, so that, just before I slept, I thought: That is what a woman is, a thing that can make of her body something ghostly, an ether, a liquid, a perfumed water if she likes.

All I know is that her name was Elena, and that she said okay to everything, and that I owe her eternally for the willing place she made of her body, so that in my fear I could step toward her and enter.

In the morning I proved rather more able than I had the night before, yet I knew next to nothing about women—and though I'm sure I really wasn't, Elena kept telling me how okay I was, that everything was absolutely okay.

I knew better—or guessed as much—and it was important to me—because of Galina. I wanted so much to be everything she'd ever dreamed, just as she was that for me.

I worried a lot, and I kept trying to reassure myself that nature provides, that love cures all—but I still worried a lot.

I was immensely shy about these things. Even in the morning, when there was light in the room, I was unable to look frankly at Elena, and I hid myself from her. Would it be the same with Galina—this foul awkwardness that spoiled everything, that made you weak with shame and emptied the situation of all the feeling you wanted it to have?

It was wonderful—but it was agony.

I was with Elena the next night—and it was better—and then the night after that—and that was better still—for both of us, I think.

And I saw her, too. I saw that woman. My * , the thing of her, that tremendous gift she was! It was wondrous, what a woman was! And then when I thought of Galina, a true beauty among women, my heart stopped.

Is it ugly that I confess these things? That while with one woman, I thought of another—that it was this other that I loved? But did I not love Elena too? How could I not love her, that good woman who kept saying to me everything was okay?

I think in those first weeks and months in Siberia I loved anyone who showed me the least charity. There was Red Loon, his kindness, and when he died, that was all there was. But there in Krasnoyarsk there was so much of it—the little man who'd interviewed me at the jail, and the woman in the bathhouse, and Alexander and his wife, and this Elena who said everything was okay—and *Galina!*

I longed for her as I had never longed for anyone. It was an ache that I carried with me all those days that she was gone, a hunger just like any other, except that it ate at your heart—and when her absence stretched from two weeks to three, I made up my mind.

The very morning she reappeared, I asked her.

I was standing against the wall, watching a few of the athletes warm up. I remember thinking when enough of them show up, I'll organize a volleyball game. I was just having that thought when I saw her. I could see her hair first, combed straight down and parted in the middle; she was standing out there on the other side of the saloon-style doors that swung open to give access to the gymnasium floor. I could tell she wasn't moving out there, but was just standing there in the entryway—was she thinking of going away? I tried to contain myself. What I wanted to do was to go quickly out there before she decided to go away—but I checked myself and waited, my heart jumping in my chest. Would my legs even carry me to her?

And then she pushed her way through, and I saw her—not very tall, but very stately, that austerity that announced her beauty like the single report of a bell. She was wearing a long black coat; I remember noticing that it buttoned all the way to the throat, and somehow that made her seem abidingly feminine, and when she took it off and laid it carefully on the bench that stood against the same wall I was leaning on, I could see the homemade dress she always wore, long and gray, a kind of muslin material that also buttoned all the way up and down. This too she took off, her pale hands, those long slim fingers working at the buttons while her head was averted to the line of men executing their calisthenics on the floor.

Her face, it was the face of all my dreams. Is this not something every lover knows? He sees this face, and he knows that he has always seen it. It was that way for me with Galina—it has always been.

Her slightest movements, her every gesture, merely the way she turned her head and exposed the long elegant stalk of her neck, there never had been anything like this on earth in all its millions of years.

She folded her dress very carefully and laid it on top of her coat, and then she stepped out of the black shoes that she wore, and in her black tights and on those narrow pale feet, their nakedness on those dark wooden boards a statement of everything most sensually female, she came toward me, in that same restrained yet purposeful stride that made her walk a thing to see.

She came right up to me. She stood before me, nothing on her face betraying anything of her thoughts.

She said, "Hello."

"You were away," I said. "With your students."

"Yes," she said.

"I missed you very much," I said.

"Yes," she said.

"You didn't tell me that you'd be going."

"Yes," she said.

I said, "I love you very much."

She stood there looking at me, her expression unchanged, just that serene, open aspect she always turned to the world.

I said, "Marry me, Galina. Marry me."

"I will," she said, still looking at me with those eyes that said more than speech could.

I reached out my hand to her and she raised her hand and caught mine. We held each other's hand like that for what seemed a very long time. We didn't say anything. We just gazed at each other.

"I will," she said again, and still we just stood like that.

FORTY-THREE _____

Galina moved in with me that night. I went with her to her place and we collected her things, just a little bundle of this and that, and on the way back to my room I bought a bottle of champagne and some potatoes—fresh ones, not frozen ones.

It was the 5th of December, 1949.

I fried those potatoes in cod liver oil—it was all you could get for frying—and I suppose they tasted awful, but we didn't mind it. We drank that champagne, and we didn't mind anything.

She sat there in my room on the edge of the bed in that long gray muslin dress, and I sat across from her on a log. The room was warm, but the walls and the floor were in frost, and we sat there looking at each other and not talking.

What was there to talk about? What could we say that our hearts hadn't said? There was nothing else we wanted to hear.

We ate those terrible potatoes and drank our champagne and then she undid all those buttons up and down her dress and then I stood up and came to her and took the glass from her hand and set it down on the floor.

I said, "Galya, my wife, I love you."

And she said, "Vitya, my husband—love, love, love."

About three weeks later they told Galina she had to move out. It was the NKVD that told her. They said she was in trouble, living with an exile, and that if she wanted to get out of trouble, she had better move out.

She was crying when she told me. But it wasn't for herself, I think—I think it was for me. They'd told her she'd lose her job and they also told her she'd be expelled from Komsomol, the Communist youth organization, but she said she didn't care about any of that—she cared only that they not make her leave me.

"What do we do?" I said.

"Do?" she said. "We do nothing. I told them no."

They did what they promised—fired Galina out of her job, out of Komsomol, and then they told her she couldn't compete in gymnastics anymore.

She told me all these things flatly, without any feelings of regret. It was only for me that she worried—that they might make things bad for me.

But nothing was ever said to me. I waited. But no one said anything to me. And when Galina stayed on with me, and no action had been taken against me, I went ahead and made my first move as if I really were a free man. One day I didn't show up at *Dynamo* and I went over to *Spartak* instead, and I told them who I was and where I'd been working, and I said I didn't want to work for those people anymore—because of what they'd done to me and what they were doing to my wife now, and that it wasn't fair, that I insisted on simple justice—that I was willing to work, but that I would do my work for *Spartak,* do anything they wanted.

They took me. It was incredible. It worked, and I thought it was incredible that it worked—and it was a man named Antonov that said it was okay, just to stay right where I was and he'd take care of it.

That afternoon I found a new place for Galina and me—it wasn't much, half a room, actually, but we hung a sheet up, and that divided us from the old woman who lived in the other half.

I started working for *Spartak,* doing much the same kind of thing, and getting pretty good pay for it, and no one bothered me, no one said one word to me.

I couldn't believe it. I started thinking, how far can I push this thing, how far can I go? Could I go all the way to America?

We lived on Communist Street, Galina and I, and *Spartak* gave Galina work, coaching girls in gymnastics, and things just went along like that, a life, and no one telling us otherwise.

I think that chant in me started intensifying around then—*America, America, America.*

Could I do it?

Six months later my *Spartak* boxing team won the district-wide competition. They had to beat my old *Dynamo* team to do it—and when they did that, *Dynamo* called me back. I received instructions from Falk to report to his office.

Dynamo wanted me back. I would return to *Dynamo* or there would be trouble—I could count on it.

I begged him to let me alone.

He said no.

I also said no.

I don't know what made me do it. I just did it. I knew better, but I did it. I said no.

I went back to *Spartak* as if nothing had happened. And still nothing had *really* happened—there was just that talk with Falk. He had stated his position, and I had stated mine, and nothing had come of it.

Life moved along like that for years—threats were made, but I'd stand pat, and then nothing would come of it—until the summer of 1951.

It happened the night of the morning Galina had told me she was pregnant.

That night I was arrested.

I was pretty widely known by now—because of my team. They'd won the All-Siberian competition and also the Far-Eastern competition, and by now I was too well known to just slip away and vanish. Besides, there was Galina—just as years before there had been Miriam.

It was always my will to compete that drew attention to me. But what was I to do? Not be the man it was in me to be?

In any event, I couldn't get away—and once again they caught up with me before I'd gotten away. Only this time it was worse—I had a wife, a wife and a child on the way.

They came at night. They took me to the city jail. Three of them came—right to the room where we were living, and they took me out that night. Galina did not cry. She just took my hand and held it for as long as they would let her, and I said, "Why do you look at me like that?" and she said, "For the same reason you look at me."

We parted like that.

I loved her so for the way she let it happen.

They kept me there four nights, and then they let me go. Nothing was said, nothing explained—they just held me for a time and then they let me go.

It was unnerving, but you had to try not to let it get to you. It was the way they did things, always that element of the unsettled, the vague—everything sort of weirdly inconclusive, as if whatever it was, it was a touch random, an accident, half mistake, half plan.

But they worked things out more than you thought—you could always count on their being a little smarter than you thought.

They took me home, the same three men. They drove me all the way there, and they followed me upstairs and one of them knocked on the door.

I stood there with them, not knowing if it was okay to enter yet, and while I was standing there and Galina was in the doorway looking at me, that same bearing even in her pregnancy, so tall, so stately, that austere serenity of hers, one of them said, "Comrade, do you know that this man is a Jew? An exile and a Jew? You cannot marry him, but you have his baby? Do you know that you live with an American and a Jew?"

Galina said, "I know," and she took my hand and drew me inside, and as if these men had come to pay a pleasant call, she said good night to them and closed the door.

She hadn't known either of those things.

What she knew about Jews is what we both knew by that time —that it was now government policy to act against them. And what Galina knew about Americans was even less.

That night I told my wife as much as I felt I had to. I did not tell her everything. I did not want her to know those things. What good would it do her to know?

It was enough that she knew I was an American and a Jew— but knowing it changed nothing between us. On the contrary, I think the knowledge of it strengthened the bonds between us.

Galina, my wife, she is a fearless woman. It is the calm that is in her, her unfathomable stillness. It is like a passion in tranquility, a thing apart from this world.

There was nothing that man might have said to her that would have moved that woman from where she stood. It is the way Galina is, and it is a great blessing to know such a quality resides in the one you love. A marriage is at peace when this is in it—whereas in most cases, I think, the marriage says: *This far, and no farther.*

For Galina and me, there was nothing like that—for us, no line was ever drawn. And yet I was not willing to tell her everything. I think it was because I did not want her to hurt for me. I had had a certain life, ten years of it. It was enough that I had had it—what use to make Galina have it too?

I went back to the life I had made for myself. But the chant got stronger. More and more I began to think how I might pull it off— escape with Galina and the baby that was coming. I guess I thought of every crazy scheme imaginable. But everything I came up with called for help—one, two, three, four people who would be willing to help you—but after my wife, who could I trust, especially now that Jews everywhere were under suspicion and the Secret Police scrutinized everything you did?

You heard about it, little pogroms that were breaking out all over Russia. It started on account of what was called the Doctors' Plot, ten doctors who were accused of plotting against the life of Stalin, and four of those doctors were Jews. Weren't the Jews the ones who had used their Jewish tricks to convert the others? Weren't these Jews, wherever they were and whoever they were, connivers and conspirators from the day they were born?

How could I do it—a man with a woman and a child? How could I get out of there and home?

I was obsessed with the invention of schemes to escape—convinced that if I just kept concentrating on the thing hard enough and long enough, something miraculous would reveal itself.

And then the baby was born, my firstborn, a girl, raven-haired just like her mother.

We called that child Svetlana, which means brightness or light, and in all the world she was all we had—our bottomless love for each other and for the child who was the issue of that love.

But they came again, nine months later. This time there was a truck downstairs. But neither of us knew it. It was there waiting for me when I got outside, and I didn't let Galina go down with me.

I said it would be just like before—a few days and I'd be home. She said, of course, that's all it is, so why do you look at me like that?

"Because I love you," I said.

"Yes," my wife said.

"Kiss the baby for me," I said.

"Oh, yes," Galina said.

"A few days. Nothing more."

"Of course," she said.

But when I got downstairs, I saw that this time it was a truck they had for me there and not a car like the last time.

That night they took me north. They took me north by truck, the same truck, two men in the cab, two more with me in the back.

Nobody said anything, and I asked nothing. It astonished me to find how readily I fell back into the temper of a *Zk,* unresisting, a man willing to go along. Surely this is not instinct but training, the conditioning that comes over the veteran prisoner, so that he knows without thinking when to shut up because nothing else will do any good. It is a kind of intuition you develop when you've been behind the wire long enough, a sense of boundaries, of your place in things, of how much you can push and when you can't push at all.

I kept my mouth shut and let them do what they wished to do.

The truck went north, and I went with it, my wife and infant falling away from me, farther and farther behind. I knew I was going somewhere, somewhere no good to go, and that was all I knew —and as for Galina, she knew even less. After a time, she would go looking for me at the jail in Krasnoyarsk, and I would not be there, and it agonized me to think of the terror that would seize her then. All that distance north, that was all that was in my mind—what Galina would feel when she could not find me, how she would manage to care for herself and for the baby.

The truck went north until the road gave out—a place called Maklokova. When there was no going any farther, that's when the truck stopped, about twenty hours after we'd started.

"You! Out!" one of the men in the back with me said.

I jumped down and they followed me.

"Citizen Herman," the other one said, a tall man in a heavy fur coat and fur hat, "do you hear me?"

"Yes," I said, somewhat startled at this strangely formal style.

"I am going to give you certain instructions," he said. "You will carry them out to the letter. I remind you that your woman and child are known to us. That point should be sufficient. Do you understand?"

"Yes," I said.

The three of us stood there in the road at the rear of the truck. It was just after sundown, and I could see off to either side that the snow was waist-high or better in the fields. It was monstrously cold, but I was warm—all except my feet. Just standing there in the road, my feet were already cold.

"Citizen Herman, you have been found guilty of certain infractions of the conditions of your exile. Accordingly, new conditions have been arranged for you. Do you understand me so far?"

"Yes," I said.

"All right," the tall man said. "You are to report to the village of Yeniseysk. You will find this village approximately forty miles north of here. If you walk due north, you will find it. If you lose your way, I tell you that it is along the Yenisey River. Have I made myself clear?"

"Yes," I said. "But to whom do I report there?"

"NKVD. You register there. Ask anyone, they'll tell you. Understood?"

"My wife and baby," I said.

The man said, "Understood, Citizen Herman?"

"Yes," I said.

"All right," he said, and the two of them climbed back into the truck.

I stood off to the side as the truck turned around in the narrow road. It took a long time for it to accomplish the maneuver, and I just stood there watching it, letting the illumination the headlights gave onto the fields do whatever good it could to convey some sense of the terrain. But this was ridiculous. It was a wilderness and deep in snow.

What more did I need to know?

At last the truck negotiated its turn, and began heading off back down the road, and I stood there watching it go until I could not see its lights anymore, and then I just stood there in the road waiting for my vision to adjust to the moonlight.

It was mid-December, 1952. I don't think ever in my whole life have I felt so abandoned and forsaken and crushingly alone as I did that night. But that was just for an instant, really. Because I put my hands in my coat pockets and discovered in each a little bag, rusks in one pocket, sugar in the other. And a knife where the sugar was.

Galina! It was she who had fetched my coat.

I had food, then—and something that might come in handy, the small knife Galina had put in with the sugar. And since I'd been skiing late in the afternoon of the previous day, my clothes were all right too. I still had on that ski suit and a sweater, and over that a coat. I had gloves and a hat. It was only my feet that were cold, my ski boots never having been especially good for warmth.

Anyway, I was all right. And I would continue to be all right. What was it—forty miles? I could do it—even in the snow, even starting out in the dark. I had food—the sugar alone was plenty. I had only to find the river and walk north along the ice. That was the way to do it!

But which way was the river—to the left or the right?

I stepped off the road into the field to my right. I found a tree and with my little knife I cut a fairly stout branch, and from this I fashioned a walking stick, something to use to poke the ground ahead of me to make sure it was okay. And since I'd already struck off to the right, I figured I'd just keep on going and try it out.

I found it. It was to the right, frozen solid, of course—and so what if the river meandered and forty miles might be sixty miles? At least I wouldn't get lost, and besides, I'd be safer from animals out there on the ice.

I turned left and started walking.

It wasn't so bad—except for my feet. They were cold when I'd started and they got worse and worse. But I just figured if I kept walking on them, it would be all right. I thought of the way they'd looked just before that man went to work on them with his scissors, how my toes had looked that time before he cut them.

I just kept going.

I don't think there was anything that could have made me stop.

It took me about two days to do it.

It was dark when I got there, but you knew you were there—because there was nothing else. All that distance from Maklokova, there was nothing else along the river. But when I saw a light, I guessed that was it—and I made my way toward it. A hovel was all it was, and I just kept banging on the door until someone inside opened it.

"What do you want?" a man inside called out.

"Open the door!" I said.

"What do you want?"

"Open, please!"

"Is it the police?" the voice called.

"It is an exile!" I shouted back.

"What do you want?" he called again.

"The way to the NKVD! Show me! I'm nearly frozen."

"Swear it!" the man called.

"I swear!" I shouted back. "Please open!"

When the door fell open, he stuck his hand against my chest. He held me like that, straight-arming me.

"I'm an exile," I said. "I swear it."

"Don't come inside," he said. "Not yet."

"What's the matter?" I said. "I swear, all I am is an exile. Is this Yeniseysk?"

"Yes, it is Yeniseysk," the man said. "Put some snow in your mouth, and then come inside."

"Snow?" I said.

"The teeth, the teeth!" he screamed at me. "Otherwise, you break the teeth!"

I did what he told me. I put a handful of snow in my mouth, and then I stepped inside. The man slammed the door and stood against it.

"The way to the NKVD?" I tried to say, not able to make myself very clear with my mouth full of snow. "Register," I tried to say —but all this time he was nodding. He understood.

He motioned me to keep my mouth shut, and then he gave me directions. When I nodded that I understood, he took me by the elbow and steered me to the door, opened it quickly, pushed me outside, and then slammed it closed.

When I got to the NKVD building, a fairly good-sized structure made out of wood, everything was shut down. I don't know how long I had to pound on the door to raise someone inside, but at long last a watchman came to the door and let me in. This time I knew about the mouthful of snow—a bit of luck because that watchman certainly wasn't going to tell me.

He let me in, but he didn't want to let me get very far from the door. It was hard to see what was in there—because there was no fire going and the watchman's lantern hardly gave much light. There was no electricity in these parts—I knew if there was none in the NKVD building, there certainly wasn't going to be any anywhere else around here.

The watchman kept saying to me, "What do you want?" and I kept replying that I was there to report to the Commandant, so that I would be registered, and the watchman kept saying that the Commandant was asleep and he wasn't going to wake him and that I should go away until morning, and then I'd just repeat my part all over again, and he his, until we'd gone through this contest several times, and he just gave up and went away, and when he did, I lay down right there where I stood—and for a long time sleep would not come because my feet hurt and because with my eyes closed I saw my ski boots moving across the ice, this boot, then that boot, again, and again, as if the whole earth were ice and I was the one man on it and, for a reason I seemed vaguely to know, it was immensely important that I circle the globe, this boot, that boot.

All that night I walked it off in my dreams—from Maklokova to Yeniseysk to Leningrad and London and from there to New York and Detroit, the earth in ice wherever I stepped, and not a soul on it anywhere, all of it deserted, even all the houses on Ironwood.

It was in that dream that I thought of it—a thought so powerful it waked me and kept me awake until dawn.

Ironwood Street. How was it that it had never occurred to me —all those years working the forest, those centuries of birch and pine?

Ironwood Street. Of all the conceivable names of streets and of all the streets I might have lived on, how odd that twenty-one years ago it was Ironwood that I had left to follow my father to Russia.

Of course these things are nonsense, really—the signs that foolish people insist we have—omens, foreshadowings, and the like. Yet it has occurred to me to consider that in my case there was Ironwood and then the vessel from London to Leningrad—the *Siberia*. I make nothing of these things—to me, they are mere coincidences, nothing more. And yet, *there* they are, if one wants to make something of them—but to such persons I would say, and so? Of what earthly good is a sign? What man ever really alters the course of his life by a step sideways taken in precaution?

Oh, yes, you can take that step—and the only difference it will make is that the path to the same end will take a little longer—until the frozen river every one of us walks comes to the bend that turns you back to what's inevitably ahead.

This is not fatalism, what I am saying.

It is common sense, the destinies our own inevitable choices decide.

At least it is better to think this way—because to think otherwise, to place the burden for it all upon the random turnings of chance, to think that way is to think yourself into the abyss of bitterness and madness.

One begins by thinking: *Why me?* And ends by never knowing.

It is better, I think, to believe it all destined, whatever the truth may be. One begins: *Me?* And ends with: *Of course.*

It is easier this way—it is easier to accept what comes when it comes.

This is a small and perhaps false philosophy. But it helps. At least in my case it did. There on that road in Maklokova, and later along the Yenisey and the ice going north, it was all easier to accept so long as I kept telling myself:

Of course.

FORTY-FOUR ————————————————————

I never saw the man who ordered me out into the frost. He was the man who sent me into the forest and the snow north of Yeniseysk. But I never saw him.

He said he was sorry, that he was simply carrying out instructions. It was from behind a partition that he said this, an arrangement not unlike that which we see in the confession box.

This Commandant who gave me my orders sat behind a partition in an unlighted cubicle, a sort of shutter between us.

He said he was sorry.

He told me to head north to the outskirts of the village. He said it was there in the forest that I must live. As for my making do, he counseled me on this score—he said that if I cut timber, the villagers out there would buy the wood from me, or anyhow, trade me food and clothing and other necessary provisions for whatever I cut. He said his orders were very clear on one point—that if I set foot in Yeniseysk, the penalty would be twenty years hard labor or twenty years prison, one or the other.

This man spoke in something like a whisper. I sat on one side, in the outer room where I had slept, while this man I could not see spoke to me softly that morning from behind a grid, no light showing through it from the other side.

I listened to him very carefully. I think his voice was more than a trace sympathetic. And twice he offered the sentiment that it saddened him to tell me these things.

He said his name was Commandant Guschin.

I think he meant what he said, about his being sorry.

I said, "But for how long am I exiled to this place?"

There was no reply. I knew he had heard me very clearly. I did not repeat the question.

I said, "Thank you," and left. I am glad I said it.

I stole both an ax and a saw on my way out of the village. I had that little knife—and rusks and sugar enough for at least another day.

I went due north—and kept going until I had passed the last dwelling and had achieved the edge of the forest, and there I quickly set about building an igloo. By noon I had it finished, and I had just begun felling my first tree, a big dry one, when an old man came by with a sled drawn by a reindeer.

He stopped a little way off and clucked his tongue at me. I just kept on working—it was tough going—thinking the noise he made was some kind of sarcasm. What did it mean? That I was some kind of fool, believing I could cut a tree so large and in such an extreme of cold?

The man kept up this clucking of his tongue, but I paid him no mind—or anyhow tried not to—but it was no good. How much docility must there be in a man because you hold his wife and his child in your grasp? Of course the rage in me was gigantic, but even that I could contain if it meant the safety of Galina and Svetlana. Yet must I suffer the sneering of every   *   Russian bully in sight? Like milk boiling over in a sudden rush, I'd had enough of that old man's ridicule, and with my ax gripped to chop bone, I turned on him and started across the snow. I could hear myself screaming as I closed on him, "Shut up! Shut up!" but he was waving his arms in some kind of signal, and I could see he was too terrified to whip his reindeer into motion, and I kept closing on him, screaming, and now he was screaming too, and he was saying, "Friend, friend, I just wanted your attention! Please, please, stop!"

I don't know. In some kind of release of feeling I sat down in the snow and groaned. I could hear him chattering away.

"Friend, friend, it is how we call attention here. Please, please, don't you understand? I meant no harm. Please, please. It is too cold to whistle, so one clucks the tongue. It is customary. Do you understand? Friend? Friend?"

I laughed. I laughed at my wretchedness because it was not in me to cry anymore. "I'm sorry," I said. "Please," I said, "please forgive me. You cluck the tongue. I'm sorry—I did not know. All right. Please forgive me."

"You frightened me," the old fellow said, how old I couldn't tell, he was so enfolded in his heavy furs. "Such a powerful young man, so good with an ax, trying to chop down a tree of such size and in winter, well, I tell you, friend, you frightened me good. I only wanted to trade for a little wood, eh? Do you hear me, friend? Young fellow, do you understand? Please, please, you frightened me so. My heart, do you understand?"

"I'm sorry," I said. "It's just that I didn't know. I am newly exiled here—I don't know the ways. All right?"

"An exile?" the old man said.

"An exile," I said.

"Ahhh," the old man said—with that he took me in hand.

I never learned that old man's name, though we traded together all that winter and through the late spring, and then he didn't come around anymore, and it was clear that it was death that kept him away. But he taught me many things. In those first few days in the forest north of Yeniseysk, it was that old man who showed me how to get by. Without him I would not have come through—and he was company too. It got so I couldn't wait for him to come around to pick up the logs I had for him and to drop off in exchange whatever it was he knew I would need—first a shovel, to make a chop-out— because he said a chop-out would give better shelter than an igloo would. And he told me how to build the chop-out and where, always at the base of a tree, so that when you had to dig your way out, you could tell which direction was straight up. And right from the start that old man traded me food, frozen potatoes and frozen cabbage, bringing his good company with him whenever he came to collect wood. He passed the word too, and I was thankful for that, thankful for the other villagers there on the outskirts who also came to trade for and sometimes even buy some wood.

I was still living in the igloo—because the chop-out was taking some time to get done. The work on it was hard, trying to cut down into that frozen earth, clear the snow, and then chop into the permafrost. And it was almost as hard to get the trees down, and I wanted to do plenty of that so I'd have wood enough for myself and a large enough surplus to trade and carry me over through the colder months to come. I'd been there a week now, a day or so more, trying to organize my situation, set myself up for the physical trial that was just weeks away and at the same time prepare myself psychologically for what I supposed was going to be the most awesome test of my life.

I was jittery. I just didn't know what was ahead—and I'd heard so many stories, tales of the appalling work the high Siberian winter could do on you, even if you were in a village up there—and here I was with only the most rudimentary shelter and means. The worst of it was not knowing—not knowing what that cold could really do. It wasn't the not knowing about the new sentence, what it would mean in months or years and days and nights without the ones I loved. I guess it was because I'd had practice at that sort of thing, practice at not letting time, an unknowably large block of it, crush me with its weight. There was nothing new for me in that part of it —but cold and snow, these were two adversaries whose most formidable power I'd not yet seen the full fury of.

I tried not to think about it.

I would think about it when it came. And it was going to come —that much I knew.

Meanwhile, a little more than a week had passed, and I filled the time chopping and sawing as best I could and working steadily away at the chop-out.

Already I was hurting all over from the strain—and the air seemed thin—it seemed as if there wasn't enough oxygen in it, and that made it hard to breathe, and the razor teeth of that cold relishing your lungs, that made breathing harder still—and I seemed to ache all over now, and the slightest exertion began to rise up before me as an insuperable task. Everything began to slow down—my movements, my thoughts, time itself. It all took on a kind of strangely slow yet bizarrely overlit quality, like the sluggish response of your body when in a nightmare you're trying to escape something unthinkably awful—you can barely move—but at the same time the few things I saw around me—the ax, the shovel, the saw, the igloo, my boots—these all seemed so powerfully bright, as if lit by small inner suns.

I began to think I was losing my sense of myself and the place where I was, that my grip on reality was getting pried loose, that each of those eight or nine days had worked a little more hypnosis on me—and sometimes I was convinced of it, convinced that I was in an unbreakable trance.

At intervals I tried to remind myself to wake myself up. I'd be chopping on a tree, and the voice in me would be chanting with the strokes, *America, America, America,* and then in a flash of absolute terror I'd think, I'm sleeping! And I would get dizzy with the fear of it, and I'd scream at myself to stop that chanting, and I'd try to concentrate on the strokes of the ax and keep the chanting out of it, but it would come slipping back at me, *America, America,* and I'd get scared all over again, and I'd think, *Maybe I really am sleeping and the fear is all just a dream,* and it would go back and forth like this for hours, until I'd crawl inside the igloo and really sleep. But in the morning it would happen again; once I'd started up working again, doing some sort of repetitive action—and all day long it was like a battle, and I never was entirely convinced which side I was on in this contest between trusting and distrusting the waking world. And on the eighth or ninth day there—out there how long now? Out there chopping at a tree? Chopping at the chop-out? What was I chopping at? Or was I chopping at all? But it was the eighth or ninth day and I was doing something and I was chanting and I think I looked up and saw something and then I was chopping or doing something again and I was screaming to myself *wake up, wake up,* but it was all so drowsily rhythmic, what I was doing and *America, America, America,* and it was wonderful to just look up whenever I wanted and see them, but even so I was screaming *wake up,* and I was truly terrified now, I was absolutely sure I was truly terrified because I could see them whenever I looked up, but I could not wake up, and the rhythm was so pleasant to have, and it carried you all the way into itself, and all I had to do was look up from the chopping I was doing or from whatever it was I was doing and I would *see* them *standing there,* over *there,* the *two* of them, my wife and my child, my firstborn, my *love,* so why wake up when it is better to sleep and see them and the chanting keeps you sleeping?

America, America, America, America . . .

"Vitya!"

Ahhhh, I remember thinking: *Vitya.* Galina's love name for me, what an excellent idea—and I set to chanting it, *Vitya, Vitya, Vitya*—and that was even better because then when I looked up and saw them standing there, Galya and my Sveta in her arms, I would also hear her calling *Vitya, Vitya, Vitya, Vitya . . .*

"Vitya!"

There was no torpor in me then. All that ache and languor, they were gone from me. If I was sleeping, it would not slow me down. Even in sleep I would run like a man racing. So what if I was sleeping and so what if sleep could conjure up such tricks? I would run and press those illusions to my body, throw my arms all about them and hold them and hold them and lift them up, up and into the air and carry them all around.

I ran—my arms out wide.

"Vitya!"

And I was thinking, *Victor, Victor, don't wake up!*

"Vitya!"

I closed my arms on them, ghosts that hugged me back. I lifted them.

I could hear myself. I was saying, *My darlings, my darlings!*

I walked all around with them like that, just saying what I was saying, carrying those ghosts in a circle in the snow.

I thought: *Madness, it is a miracle—it is God's best gift to man.*

I heard: *Why do you look at me like that?*

And in my dream, I answered: *For the same reason you look at me.*

And I just kept walking in that circle with them up there in my arms—until I could not do it anymore and I could not even stand anymore and there was no air to breathe anymore and slowly, gently, softly, I went down with them onto the snow, my back gently, softly floating onto the billowing snow, my burden hugged to my chest.

"Vitya, my darling, love, love," I heard Galina say, and I said, "Love, love, my darlings," and amazingly knew it was real.

It was as if I had always known—as if it were the most ordinary and expectable of miracles.

I was not sleeping. These were not ghosts.

I held them like that there in the snow. I held the two of them. I could not let them go.

"Love," I said, kissing each of their heads. "Oh, my loves," I said.

We did it together, the three of us, the high Siberian winter, my daughter following me into the furnace just as I, in my time, had followed my father.

But it took Galina to get her there—and how Galina did it, I will never know. Not *how* she did it, but *that* she did it, and that she *could* do it.

"It was crazy," I said to her, and hardly heard a word she said.

"I came down after you, and I saw the truck as you drove away —and in the morning I went to the jail and asked and they said you weren't there, and I guessed they'd taken you north," Galina said, "and so I got the baby and we got rides north as far as the road would go, because I just knew that's what they'd do to you, and then I started asking questions and that's how I got here."

She was breathless as she told me, exhilarated from the impossible proof of her intuition.

"Yes," I said, "but how did you *do* it? With the baby? How in the world did you manage?"

"I walked," my wife said, and more than this she never told me.

It was enough. That she was here—that they were here—it was enough, and although I knew it was enough, knew that it was an abundance so plenteous as to fill me to overflowing, the practical man in me didn't know whether to be joyful or angry. Here were circumstances so pitiless that I did not know if *I* could survive them—but a woman and an infant?

It was foolhardy, what my wife had done, foolhardy and brazenly irresponsible—and I loved her for it. In that moment when the reality of her daring and endurance was fully visited on me, I loved that woman with a love beyond all imagining.

It was so wonderful, to love like that, to be loved like that.

I said to her, "Why do you look at me like that?"

And she said, "For the same reason you look at me," and with the two of them still locked in my arms, I rolled over and over in the snow—until I heard Galina cautioning, "The baby—Vitya, the baby, you'll hurt her!"

I said, "Hurt her? There is nothing that can hurt this child! A child that has made its way through hell to live in a hole with her papa? Nothing can hurt such a child! Such a child is a champion among children and the pulse of her papa's heart!"

We were so happy then. It did not matter what lay ahead. It only mattered that it was the three of us to live through it—and live and live and live.

But that afternoon a villager came by to trade for some wood, and I made Galina take the baby and go with him. I told her it would only be for as long as it took to finish the chop-out. I promised. And as soon as they were out of sight on his sled, I set to work again, with a fever of industry that was enormous, and I chanted with each stroke of the ax, *Galya, Galya, Galya,* and with each shovelful of frozen earth I was able to pry loose, my heart sang *Sveta, Sveta, Sveta,* and there was nothing in this that was trance-like at all, no fearful slumbering, but a clarity of mind that was immense.

When I had a hole about five by five and about three feet deep, I started a fire up. It was easy getting a good fire going, easy because of the crackling cold air. I made a fire in the hole, and as it softened the walls of permafrost, the chopping and digging went better, and in two days, working steadily, I had a cavity about ten by ten and five and a half feet deep, and I laid branches over the top, a whole criss-crossing thick network of branches, and this I covered over with snow. My entrance was at the base of a tree, just the way the old man had advised me, and you had to hunker down and crawl a bit to get inside, but once you were inside, it was okay.

I worked out a little area in the center, and I had the firestones that I'd traded for wood, and I formed them into a circle around that scooped-out area in the center, and I figured I was ready. The old man had told me you had to be careful about your fire once the heavy snows came—because when you got snowed in, when the entrance got shut down with snow, you couldn't take a chance ex-hausting the oxygen content of the air trapped inside the chop-out. But it was all right to let the fire go full force now, and I built it way up, and then I moved in a supply of split wood and stacked it all along one wall.

That night, it was a good and a happy sleep that I had, and the next day when the first villager showed up around noon to trade, I asked him to get word to my wife that it was all right to come back now—to come back and bring back the child.

So be it. Let her follow her father into the furnace. It was what her father had done for his father, and although it will seem incredi-ble to you, not in the least believable at all, I never regretted a day of the ordeal I had for having done it, for having followed that man.

Does that not seem incredible to you?

But it is not you who is the man's son.

Svetlana was ten months old when she came to the chop-out.

It was in the chop-out that she learned to walk—and then to talk.

We tried to teach her what we could in the poverty of our circumstance.

We made snow figures for her—and told her stories. We told her the fairy tales that we knew—and when the pleasure of these seemed at long last too thin, I told her stories of America, whatever I could think of. I told my daughter about America, about Detroit—and to her it was a fairy tale, of course, one that was harder to be-lieve than Cinderella, more miraculous than two potatoes.

I made her a little sled and Galya and I would pull her around on it, and when she could, Sveta would laugh, but mostly she couldn't, mostly the hunger and the cold would not let her laugh.

Sometimes the villagers would bring us a chunk of frozen milk for her, but mostly what she had was the frozen cabbage and potatoes that we traded for. When there was a chunk of milk, Galya would crack off a piece and Sveta would suck on it, and you could see how it made her feel when she had it—because mostly she didn't.

She was all right then, Sveta was, and we did our best to keep on getting her the ice milk, but when the frost was truly furious, the villagers wouldn't come, and I was afraid to go to them, afraid I would get caught.

But a few times I did, anyway—I went, anyway—rubbing powdered dry mustard in my socks, and putting hot potatoes inside my mittens before going out through the entranceway I'd already dug clear. These were tricks the old man had taught me, ways to cope with the demonic cold, cold that got down to eighty below, and when the wind blew, you went in the direction it blew, you never tried to fight it, and the wind was always blowing that winter by mid-January, and you would not try to make your way to the village unless the wind was blowing in that direction, and then, when you got there and had the thing that you had gone for, you prayed the wind would stop or reverse its direction.

Days like that, and sometimes the nights you had to go out, you could hear trees explode and rocks crack and see birds drop like feathered stones, and you had to try to warm the air a little in your mouth before you dared let it get down into your lungs, and you tried to remind yourself always to breathe through your nose, and all through that January and February and most of that March we could not take Svetlana outside. For almost three months that child lived down in there in that black hole, her light the light the fire gave.

In it you could see the hunger and vacancy in her face. It is a thing that expresses itself in the region of a child's eyes.

I went out every day.

Even if I knew there would be no one coming to trade because no one would try the frost that day, still I went out to chop each day.

It was from fear of what worse might come—and from wanting to have plenty of wood for our fire and plenty to trade for food for the fires of the villagers who promised they would come. I trusted them —and I think they always came when they could.

It got so that I loved Siberians. They seemed to me such a benevolent people, dauntless and so willing to help. And I missed that old man when his visits ended, when the spring came and he did not.

We were in that chop-out all through that spring and summer and through the following fall and back into winter again, and it was in late October and November of that year that food was even harder to get. Sveta was almost one year older now, more body to her and more knowing in her, and with this change in her, the pain of her hunger enlarged, until it was a constant cry in her, and I begged Galina to leave, to take the baby and go to the village, but she would not do it.

We were frantic about Sveta, and frantic in our efforts to console her. We did everything to distract her from the hollow center we knew her appalled eyes stared at—we literally rolled on the frozen floor and capered hysterically to divert her attention to something other than her hunger, a beast that we knew never left off his chewing inside her.

Always, I told her stories about America and always, confoundingly, they seemed to weave their way back to the mystery of food.

"Papa, tell about the food in America."

How could I tell her? What would she understand? A child who knew of food only the chips of frozen milk that she sucked, a bit of potato, a bit of cabbage?

She would say, "Tell about the food in America. Does everyone have a whole potato?"

And I would say, "Sveta, darling, in America each person has two potatoes."

It was to make her understand.

Even now, when I write this, my daughters safe in this house and well fed from the bounty all around us, I want to weep when I think of that question.

Does everyone have a whole potato?

All the rest of her life, my firstborn will rise in the night as I do, gasping for a bite of anything, her mind forever captured by the specter of a morning without food. For the rest of her life my Sveta will be like me in this way.

I know it is because she followed me.

Is that something I say with pride?

Yes. But like me, she had no choice.

Life chose *for* her.

It got bad. It got much worse. But when a year was up, almost a year to that day in December when I had first reported to the NKVD in Yeniseysk, they came and told me I could get out of there —that I could leave and my family could leave with me.

I was free to live in Yeniseysk—but nowhere else. They gave us a little house in the village and they gave me a job as a local coach, and that was it—that was life as they gave it.

All right. It was a life. And it was better than we had—and therefore, it was good enough.

In time I made it better than that, my will to compete reordering my existence again.

I put together a team of local boxers. They hadn't done that sort of thing up there, but I got them doing it. I got together a team, filled out all the weight divisions with those hardy high Siberians, as rugged a collection of men as you would want.

I trained them—I worked them day in and day out—and I gave them the will to win—to hurt and to win.

They did. Our first year out, they beat the two major teams in Krasnoyarsk, the *Dynamo* and the *Spartak* teams that represented the city. They also took the championship for the entire Krasnoyarsk region.

I had a house. I had a place. I had a wife and a child and good work. And I was winning again, carrying off medals—and for me this was an acceptable life.

You forgot. You stayed busy and forgot—you forgot everything but one thing, the only thing in your past you wanted in your future.

America.

FORTY-FIVE ————————————————————————

I was called back to Krasnoyarsk. It was *Spartak* that called me back, and it was right after my Yeniseysk team won the regionals. *Spartak* wanted me back at my old job—win medals for them, they said, and I said that was okay with me.

I rented a room in Krasnoyarsk—on Perenson Street—and the three of us moved in—and I went to work for *Spartak* again.

There was a letter waiting for me there. The date on it was about nine months old.

This is what the letter said:

Dear Brother,

I am sorry to bring the sad news of our father's death. There is no need to discuss the details. He lived his life and now he is dead. It happened a few days ago. For the record, the remains are interred in the cemetery just outside the American Village, where, as you know, our mother is also buried. I must add the distressing news that our brother Leo is extremely despondent, although I am not at all certain that his state of mind is a result of our father's death. At any rate, I do my best to look after him, as does his wife. As for myself, I do not know if you knew that I was licensed as a physician specializing in pediatrics. I have, however, since changed my specialty to pathology. I will say only one thing on this score—it is what has happened to you, my dear beloved brother, that persuaded me to shift my attentions from one field to the other. I trust you will understand my reasoning—and, further, that you will see it as the least a sister can do to express her grief over her brother's life. Leo and I think of you always, and always hope for your swift and safe return from exile. We know that you join us in mourning the passing of our father. His ideals were of the highest, and he was a man unwilling to live for other than his ideals. He did his best. Please believe that.

Your loving sister,
Miriam.

It ended nothing, my father's death—his dying did not stop the walking we would always do together. But it would be different from that point forward—from that point forward, it would be side by side that we walked, one man next to the other, shoulders almost touching, but never quite, never quite doing that.

Stalin had died too—and unlike my father's death, the death of this other man ended a great deal. All of the U.S.S.R. would change as a result, and life for Svetlana and Galina and me, it would get substantially better for a time.

I stayed with my work at *Spartak*—and I let it absorb all my energies—and I tried to live a normal life, tried to see to it that life for my family would be as normal as I could make it—and I waited.

I knew what I was waiting for—and it wasn't just a chant anymore—I talked about it openly now, at least with Galina. Almost every night, we talked about it—about getting out, about getting to America.

It was in late December, 1955, nearly two years after my return to Krasnoyarsk, that a letter came from the Chief Prosecutor in Moscow. It said that my case had been brought before the Moscow Military Tribunal, that my case had been reviewed, had been judged to be a case of espionage, and that therefore it was the business of the Moscow Military Tribunal and not the Secret Service.

Two weeks later I received a second letter.

The letter read:

Dear Citizen Herman:

This Tribunal has reviewed your case, and finds that no case exists. As of the date of this letter, you are exonerated of all charges and are hereby informed that you are free of any and all restraint upon your person.

Cordially,
The Moscow Military Tribunal.

The letter was dated 10 December 1955.

I thought back to where I'd been on the date when I had officially become a free man. It somehow seemed to me apt that I had been where I was—a city called Noril'sk—the most northerly city in the world, a place virtually on the seventieth parallel. I'd gone there with my *Spartak* team for an exhibition match, and it was up there, near where the earth ends in absolute ice, that the tether had finally been taken from me.

How long had it all been? And what was it, every day of it since that day when I had stepped into that touring car and been driven through sunshine across the Gorky bridge to Vorobevka Street? And for what? To what purpose? And on what account?

This Tribunal has reviewed your case, and finds that no case exists.

Consider the huge insanity of that statement—the examination of something nonexistent proving its nonexistence!

And I, the beneficiary of this elegant exercise in the absurd, I was doing my part as well—situating myself very near the Arctic Circle to receive the good news.

But had I not been an active partner in their madness right from the very start? It seemed to me that I had—right from the very moment I'd shot those bull's-eyes there in the little stadium behind the American Village, and then offered, in reply to the question "How many times can you do that?" the wisecrack "How many bullets do you have?"

Where else would I be on the day that my freedom had been proclaimed? In the region of ice—that is where I would be!

Freedom. The very word!

There was only one condition of freedom that meant anything to me.

America!

Would Russia give me that?

Russia gave me eighteen years in the region of ice—eighteen years for what?

This Tribunal has reviewed your case, and finds that no case exists.

He lived his life and now he is dead.

You are free of any and all restraint upon your person.

His ideals were of the highest.

No case exists.

He was a man unwilling to live for other than his ideals.

Cordially, the Moscow Military Tribunal.

He did his best. Please believe that.

Eighteen years and for what?

Then let it be for the blessing of America again!

We drank a bottle of champagne, Galina and I—and we fried up some sweet potatoes in cod liver oil, and we laughed like two people utterly bereft of their senses.

I went to the NKVD the next day—to secure an American passport.

They said they had a passport for me—a Soviet passport.

I said no, that was a mistake, it was an American passport that I wanted, that I was entitled to, and that I was going to get.

The man was a colonel, the Chief of Police, NKVD—and I said to him, "No, I am an American citizen, and I want an American passport."

He said, "Shhh, please. Comrade Herman, I beg you, for your own good, please lower your voice and listen to reason. We offer you a Soviet passport. It is the only passport we are empowered to give you. If it becomes known that you do not accept it, I warn you, you will be sent back and you will *never* be released. I tell you this is exactly what will happen. I am warning you, for your own good, do not refuse. It is neither here nor there what your true citizenship is. I am giving you my best advice, and I beg you, for your own sake and the sake of your family, do as I say."

I did as he said. It seemed that I had had a lifetime of doing as they said, and again I did it. But I refused to sign any papers.

I accepted that Russian passport—without it movement around the country, and to a place from which I might be able to escape, was impossible. Without a passport, I'd be confined to the Krasnoyarsk region, to Siberia—with it, there was a chance I could get somewhere that would put me within range of the States.

I took it.

When I'd come to Krasnoyarsk, the NKVD headquarters was on Stalin Street—and now the NKVD, the People's Commissariat of Internal Affairs, had been broken up into the MVD and the KGB, the Ministry of Internal Affairs and the Committee of Government Security, respectively, and they were still together there on Stalin Street, only they called it Peace Street now.

So much for change. So much for the death of Stalin, for the ascendancy of Khrushchev, and for the truth about governments— you change a name.

Change a name, you change the reality. Review a case that does not exist, and then deliver your findings in the difficult matter: *Nothing exists.*

Eighteen years, they do not exist.

We have reviewed the matter and find that although you are an American citizen you are not an American citizen.

As an American citizen, you do not exist.

As a Russian citizen, you do.

Here, take this Russian passport.

I took it.

I walked out of that office on Peace Street with their Russian passport in my hand.

The names of everything were different. But the reality was the same.

I have, however, changed my specialty to pathology.

Galina and I drank a second bottle of champagne, and again we tried those lousy sweet potatoes fried in cod liver oil.

We ate every single one.

It was a celebration—of our legal marriage—a freedom that Russian passport granted me.

With it, we were able to register as husband and wife, and I was able to adopt Svetlana. And as for the second baby that was on the way, this one would be born into a legitimacy sanctified by the State.

So. The Russian passport. It had its uses.

We drank our champagne and ate all those potatoes and we got filthy sick to the stomach from them, and all in all it was a celebration to remember.

We vomited it all up, and it seems to me fitting that we did.

Something awful seemed to be over—something indigestible had been crammed down into us—something bilious and rotten and foul.

We got it out. We got it all out.

We threw up all that crap—and laughed like * about it.

But the laugh was on us.

They would not let me leave Krasnoyarsk.

When I tried to, they said I couldn't. They said that at the time of my rehabilitation I had agreed to make Krasnoyarsk the place of my settlement. They said I was free to do as I chose, so long as I stayed in Krasnoyarsk.

Had anything really changed?

Not much.

Janna was born. In 1957, my second child was born.

Aside from that, had anything really changed? Was I any closer to America?

It was a question I did not want to ask.

We made a life the best we could, and as for the one question that mattered, it would have to keep. Hadn't I had plenty of practice at that?

All that year I toured through the U.S.S.R. with my team. We boxed in the twenty largest cities, and in every one of them we came out on top. Even in Moscow, out of ten weight divisions, we won 7 to 3.

It was when we were competing in Kishinev, a city in the little republic of Moldavia and near the Rumanian border and not far from Odessa and the Black Sea, that something critical happened.

I was offered a job there—the position as head boxing coach for the entire Republic of Moldavia—and the officials there said they would arrange everything with the authorities in Krasnoyarsk. It would all be taken care of—I had only to agree and to send word to my family—and everything would be arranged, a house, relocation papers, the works.

I tried to act as if I were relatively indifferent to the thing one way or the other, and after a little pretense of this kind, I gave my assent.

In 1959 Galina made the trip with the girls—three thousand miles. We hadn't much in the way of possessions, really—it was just a matter of picking yourself up and going. And although she was Siberian by birth and although I had come to have such a great affection for the Siberian people, it was wonderful to put that cold three thousand miles behind us.

Here was life near the Black Sea, a very different proposition altogether. But the house that they had promised us turned out to be a hallway in someone else's house, and we had to sleep on the floor there (for three hundred rubles a month), and there were two other families living in that house, and they were always stepping over us to get outside to the outhouse, and Galina tried to put a good face on it, but I knew how I had disappointed her—and then it turned out that my pay was only nine hundred rubles a month, whereas back in Krasnoyarsk I'd been making fifteen hundred a month with *Spartak,* which is about a hundred fifty to two hundred dollars in the equivalent American money of the time.

This lasted until 1960, and in 1960 they offered me a choice. They said I could take my family to a collective farm about a hundred miles away and have a house, or stay on in Kishinev living the way I was. If I chose the farm, that's the work I'd be doing, but my family could live in a house.

I didn't even bother talking it over with Galina.

I chose the farm.

We would move to the village of Chenesheutsi, the four of us.

My wife and my daughters, let them have a house.

I signed the papers. Let my family have a house. So I signed a contract agreeing to work on that farm for a period of one year, and at the end of that time the promise was they would have an apartment for me in Kishinev.

We moved to Chenesheutsi.

But there was no house.

And the farm was a slave farm.

And once again my life seemed a comic penalty in a parlor game played by other people, people who hadn't the least interest in the outcome of the game.

I went to everyone in authority in Chenesheutsi, dragging my family with me. I said I'd been tricked, been duped, and I pleaded and showed them the letter from the Moscow Military Tribunal, and I got absolutely nowhere.

With my family gathered around me, I stood before the desk of one official after another, and the vision in my head was of those women who had been herded out of that boxcar to stand in the forest snow in their summer dresses, a traveling sideshow, sad, wandering, road-weary clowns whose sadness was the very word of hilarity. We were those women.

I got nowhere.

We worked the year out, Galina and I, and at the end of that year they let us go.

We returned to Kishinev—and I was given my old job back— and it was as if nothing had happened in the interim, as if I and my family had simply been absent for a long and pleasant holiday on the beach of the Black Sea. More remarkable still, they gave us an apartment, an apartment with three rooms, and we had the place all to ourselves, this wonderful apartment on Zilinski Street.

Someone had flipped over a card in that parlor game those people were playing, and to everyone's amusement and surprise, the instructions called for a reward. Me, I'd learned long ago not to bother trying to figure out anything Russian and official, and as for Galina, she was a native and never thought two ways about it. You took what came, and gave up wondering what brought it, and if you could live with whatever it was, so much the better—and if you couldn't, then you learned to.

It was 1961, and I had one plan—get by until I could get away —do anything to get by and anything to get away.

And so when they asked me to teach English, I was more than willing, more than willing to cooperate in any way that might improve my mobility and assure them that I was entirely trustworthy. Besides, the opportunity spoke to my great fondness for children— the younger, the better—and this was a position teaching English to kindergartners.

I was delighted. I was genuinely happy to have the chance— because it meant working with children and teaching them something—and because for the first time in thirty years I could speak openly in English with no fear of trouble or reprisal. It was extraordinary, the feeling this gave me, to be able to speak my native language whenever I wanted.

It was not until I began that work that I realized how profoundly bound we are to a concept of ourselves in relation to this or that language—as if the soul expresses itself in a particular tongue, as if the particular language you first hear issuing from your mother marks off something more than a linguistic province, that what it actually describes is a country of free response.

I talked in English to those children. I talked and talked and talked. There was no getting enough of it. You take away a man's language, you take more than a system of syntax and a store of vocabulary from him. You take away a man's language and you deny him that indelible sense of himself that writes him into the earth.

I talked in English to those little children, and whatever I recited—nonsense rhymes, the names of animals, the twenty-six letters of the alphabet—it was like a reinstatement of who I'd long ago been and lost.

Lion. Tiger. Bear. Repeat after me—lion, tiger, bear. Once more—lion, tiger, bear. Very good, thank you—now again, everyone, again! Lion! Tiger! Bear!

I recited, and the sound of my voice carried me and the years forward. It was astounding—I was happy in Russia.

Thank you—now again, everyone, and let me really hear you this time—Lion! Tiger! Bear!

PART 5

THE MAN WHO CAME BACK

FORTY-SIX

Teaching English and speaking English, these things heartened me hugely—restoring me to my sense of myself and enlarging the circle of freedom I felt widening around me.

It was after I had been teaching for a time that I went to the Foreign Ministry in Moldavia and applied for repatriation.

They laughed in my face.

I went through it all, step by maddening step—explaining how I had come to be in the U.S.S.R., the accident of my arrest, the years and years of imprisonment and hard labor, all falsely administered, the findings of the Tribunal, the lifting of all charges and suspicions, my innocence, and the insistent fact that I had never abandoned my American citizenship.

They laughed in my face. They said all those years of incarceration must have made me crazy. Who in the world would take me for an American citizen, a fellow who had been so many years in the Soviet Union and who—and here they actually *laughed*—had undergone experiences that so deeply involved him in things Russian?

They told me to go away, to stop bothering them, to give it up, this ridiculous fiction that I was still an American. They said that as far as they were concerned and as far as anyone else would be concerned, from the President of the United States to Donald Duck himself, I was a Russian, a citizen of the Union of Soviet Socialist Republics, and that, forever and a day, was that!

Later that week I wrote Rebecca. Would she still be at the same address? It was possible. It had been a good house, our father's house. Why should she and Bob not still be there?

I wrote her.

I also wrote my cousin Dave—another long shot.

I knew he was an attorney and I knew he was living in New

Orleans when we were living in Detroit. Was it possible the man still lived there?

I wrote him too.

I addressed the letter to: *David Herman, Esq., Attorney at Law, New Orleans, Louisiana, United States of America.*

I said the same thing to both of them.

I said:

This is Victor, Victor Herman. I live in the city of Kishinev, in the Republic of Moldavia, in the U.S.S.R. I have a wife and two daughters. I am an American citizen, and want with all my heart to return to America. Can you please help me? I beg you, please help me and my family.

With love and prayer,
Victor Herman.

At the bottom I wrote my address on Zilinski Street and I added a thumbprint from some oily soot that Galina made up for me.

What happened after that I know from Dave, from the first time he saw me in the U.S.S.R.

My letter to Rebecca had gone undelivered—this because she'd been divorced and no longer used the name Laing, and, moreover, she'd moved from the family house. But the letter to Dave Herman was delivered—because, as it turned out, he was a pretty prominent attorney by that time, at least conspicuous enough in those parts to be known to the post office people. However it happened, the letter got to him, and he, in turn, got to Rebecca and brought her up to date.

We passed several letters back and forth, Dave and I, and after that first letter, I expressed myself with greater caution. I couldn't believe that first letter had gotten through to someone, and after that I wasn't taking any chances—and as for Dave's letters, they were oblique from the very start—I suppose because of the notion Americans have about Russia, the censoring of the mails and so on—and I guess you could add to this a lawyer's conditioned circumspection.

But in any event, we arranged to meet in Moscow—we appointed a day, a time, a place—and it actually happened!

It seemed to me, when I saw him standing there in Sheremetyevo

Airport, that I had engineered the most masterful achievement of my life.

I kept saying to him, "Dave? Dave? Cousin David?" as if any minute he would say, "No, just a trick—no, no, fool, I am not your cousin David," and I kept studying his face and his manner, hoping to detect evidence that would reassure me, to see in his face and the way he carried himself the familiar motifs of my family.

All that time we had together I tried hard not to tell him anything of what my life had been like. I tried to keep it to the future, to the one subject that mattered to me, and I suppose if he had not been a lawyer and a massively grave and practical man, it would have been hopeless, my wanting to steer the discussion always on a course toward repatriation.

But very quickly Dave let me summarize what I knew of Miriam and Leo's lives and the deaths of my mother and father, and then we spent our time devising a plan. I pinned all my hopes on him, and he said not to worry, he would handle it all, just to be patient, and he would never give up trying.

It was strange, talking to that man like that, there in Moscow, in that drab airport—he was a person I did not know, except in childhood, and here he was, all that distance from New Orleans to Moscow, my only tie with home, my one good chance, and he said to me not to worry, it was in his hands now, and he would handle it all.

Had there been the tears left in me, I would have wept with relief.

He said to me that one thing was essential, that no matter what happened, that no matter how they threatened me or whatever they did, always to insist I was an American citizen and that it was my deepest desire to return to America.

I wanted to laugh when he said that. I think he saw that look in my face.

He said, "Yes, Vickie, I understand. But I must say this to you, anyway. No matter what, just keep repeating the same flat statement, 'I am an American citizen and I want to return to America,' and never say anything other than that."

"Of course," I said.

When we parted, I reached out to shake his hand. But he stepped forward and hugged me—and it was then that I wept, calling up tears and feelings that I did not believe were still in me.

"Good-bye, Vickie," my cousin said.

I was too overcome with emotion to talk.

I gave him the thumbs-up sign. It was how I used to say good-bye to Red Loon.

It was 1968 when that meeting took place.

FORTY-SEVEN _____

What do I tell you now?

Do I tell you about the eight years it took before I hugged my cousin on American soil—hugged him and hugged the son that came with him to the airport in New York to greet me? Do I tell you about the endless filing of papers, the endless refiling of papers, the endless corrections and revisions and refusals and apologies and reassessments and excuses and reviews and reappraisals and refusals and reconsiderations and boards and panels and committees and documents and certificates and endorsements and references and recommendations and refusals that were reviewed and reconsidered and reassessed and then revised and contradicted and returned for refiling, which then required further review and further study by this panel, that board, this official, that commissar, who was temporarily on leave, and *It is therefore with regret, Mr. Herman, that we ask you to exercise due patience, merely a matter of days, of weeks, of months, of years of time, but all in good time, everything in its course, please be patient, please excuse, please understand, please know that the committee will meet at their very earliest convenience, please know that a key member of the committee was regrettably absent, further notice will be tendered presently, in a matter of days, of weeks, of months, of years*—and all that time my cousin stood by me, never yielding an inch from his promise, and all that time I filled out their papers and entered the information in all of the blanks and copied the documents out in triplicate and waited and waited and said, *I am an American and I want to go back to America,* and I stood in line and I stood before desks and I stood in front of closed doors and I sat and I sat in their waiting rooms and I heard them say, *Our apologies, Mr. Herman, but we observe where you have committed a slight but crucial error in the completion of this form, and for safety's sake we recommend you do it all over again, and don't forget to do it in triplicate, and we'll be here and waiting when you come back in a day, a week, a month, a year, all in good time, everything in due course, these things, please believe us, take time, time, time, TIME!* And then a little more time after that.

Do I tell you about those years?

I lived them shrieking. I lived them loathing. I lived them despising the evil work a gargantuan and bottomless bureaucracy can do.

I filled in the blanks. I did what they said to do—and no matter how many times they sent me back to do it all over again, I did it—and if they thought that sending me back to do it all over again was going to get me to quit coming back with those papers in my hand, all filled out, every single blank, in triplicate, then they did not know that I had also once stood before a great iron wagon on rails with the snow up to my knees and my belly on fire for food and a man had said, "Load it—load it all!" and I *had*.

I filled in the blanks—every   *   one—for all those years. And I wrote to Dave and I wrote to Rebecca and to the Department of State and to every conceivable agency in America, and they all wrote to me, and my determination never wavered, and I just kept on saying it over and over again: *My name is Victor Herman. I am an American. I want to come home!*

The Department of State said fine, you can emigrate to the U.S. as a Russian; I wrote back, no, I will be repatriated to the U.S. as an American—and I sent a copy of both letters to Dave.

Meanwhile, the U.S.S.R. kept me swimming upstream against a torrent of red tape; when it comes to dodges and runarounds and equivocations and double-talk, the Soviet bureaucracy can give cards and spades to any state on earth. But in 1968 I was awarded a state pension—and the letter announcing it declared that the dole was in recognition of my mistaken imprisonment and the suffering I had endured all those years. Was this to dissuade me from my effort to be repatriated? I think so.

Anyway, the amount came to one hundred rubles a month, and I was glad to have it. Then they sent along a bonus of five thousand rubles. I was even gladder to have that.

I bought a car with that bonus, a 40-horsepower Muscovich, canary yellow, and we drove all around in the thing, Galya and me and the girls. They let us go where we wanted now, a sort of new mobility coming along with that pension, which I later found out was really a pretty high honor, something rarely awarded except to Party bigwigs. And that happened too—an invitation to join the Party, and I of course refused—said I was honored to be asked, but politely refused. And all this time my combat with paperwork continued—I never let up for an instant, but neither did they—and always, inevitably, in the end, it was the same, a delay for this reason, a delay for that reason, postponements, reconsiderations, further study, reviews, a procedural change, some formality over-looked, a blank left blank, a response smudged, a document mis-filed, a change of address, a this or a that, and then all over again, until you'd go mad if you already weren't, already so maniacally obsessed with the pursuit of what you wanted that nothing less than death could divert you from your course.

But meanwhile, in all other respects, they were making things attractive for us. Galina had good work as a girls' gymnastic in-structor, and I had my pension and two jobs now, giving refresher courses to teachers of English and also giving classes at the Foreign Languages Institute. In contrast to what had been, life was now pretty much splendid.

Except that it was life in Russia.

They wanted me to stay. Weren't they making that eminently clear? My life was entirely tolerable—it's fair to say that at this point it was not inconsiderably better than that. And while I was happy to have the comfort for the four of us, I never once relaxed my efforts to get out.

But year after year those efforts got me nowhere—not any-where could I see that one jot of progress had been made. I was still right back where I'd started. But not for anything would I quit trying.

Not that I ever thought for a minute I could wear them down. But I don't think they gave me the same benefit of the doubt.

Quit trying? Why should I?

Was I to die on soil where there thrived a system that murdered my youth? Was I to live in a land that put men into uniform in order that they be invested with the authority to turn a boy into a crab?

Like * I'd quit trying, regardless of the things they did to create reasons to stay!

And then they told me that every single paper and form and document and certificate and reference and endorsement and petition and affidavit, all of it, everything that bore either my father's name or mine, every bit of it had to be revised and newly stamped and resubmitted because my father's legal name was *Samuel* not *Sam*.

I did it.

It was as if that guard had said, "All right, now take out every single log and do it all over again!"

It took two years to get it all done—two years to go from *Sam* to *Samuel*—two years of sitting and waiting and standing in line and then the window closes and *regrettable, yes, a pity, we understand, quite insufferable, to be sure, but do come back tomorrow,* and I *did.*

The KGB impounded my car the day before Nixon flew in to Moscow for that famous visit with Brezhnev—they impounded my car and gave me orders to report every day to their office until notice to do otherwise.

Notice to do otherwise came the day after Nixon returned to the U.S.

It was crazy. Did they think I was going to drive my car to Moscow, stroll into the Kremlin, ask Brezhnev to shut up for a minute while I put my situation before my compatriot?

It was no crazier than anything else I'd been staring at for—what was it at that point?—forty-five years in Russia?

I reported every day at twelve o'clock.

The day after Nixon left, they said, don't bother to report anymore, here are the keys to your car.

It was like living in a comic strip, but there was nothing funny about it. To see it now, yes—but to live it then? I don't think so.

In 1974 I got a letter.

It said:

Dear Brother Vic,

Leo hanged himself. His depression steadily worsened from the

time of our father's passing. Our brother is at peace now. I am well.
I hope this unhappy letter finds you and your family in good health.
    Your loving sister,
    Miriam.

My brother Leo—I had hardly thought about him all that much. It's true, we had never been close—there had always been that tension between us, and I think it's correct to say it owed to our feelings for our father, how they differed in their expression. I had always felt that I loved him the more, and understood him the more deeply. But I'd always known that Leo's need was greater than mine—at least in the more apparent sense. He relied on my father in a day-to-day sort of way that I did not, and I think he was fearful when Papa was not around. Is it fair to say that I resented the extent to which Leo occupied my father's attention?

It is fair to say that I had never really known my brother—that Red Loon was more a brother to me than Leo was. But that may not be Leo's fault. Surely it was largely circumstance's fault. The years of my manhood were not where Leo was.

I think I must say that I had often thought of Leo those years when I was in prison and the years thereafter when I was in the camps. Did I never once think why is Leo not here? Why me and not Leo?

It would be a lie to say I did not. It would be a lie to say that I never once thought: Could my brother take this? And *this?*

But we never had a chance as brothers. Yet it is strange, this feeling that I have that until all my days are ended I will walk side by side with my father—why do I not feel something kindred for my brother?

I don't know.

My mother is always in my heart—and my father strides with me at my side. Why, then, this absence of feeling for my brother? He'd been such a carefree boy—full of high spirits and so sweetly dispositioned. I know that. I even know that I love him, and loved him when he lived—and yet he is a stranger to me, a presence I do not feel.

Perhaps it is a strangeness that not infrequently happens between brothers. Perhaps this happens when the father is a strong man and the sons love him so very much.

Red Loon? I would always mourn him, always hold in me a vision of his face. My brother Leo? When I looked inside myself to find him, I saw a tall boy chasing me, and then me, sick at heart, eluding him.

In 1974 a hammer hit me in the chest, a weight like all the heavens pounding.

I was home when it happened. Galina was away for a conference of gymnastics instructors, and the girls were in school.

It was a massive attack, a giant fist seizing my heart and squeezing.

I don't know how I did it, but I drove myself to the hospital. We were still on Zilinski Street, Apartment 93, on the second floor of 35 Zilinski, and I got to the hospital in time.

A stroke came with it—the both of them, a heart attack and a stroke.

Would I live?

I would live.

I would not die!

Not here.

No, no, no. Not anywhere. I would live through this too— and fight like * to do it. All that time willing myself to live, I thought of those weeks and months when they guessed they were going to lose me on account of that bullet going through my liver. I kept trying to run through my mind myself walking in that crouch, entering my house with my mother, my dog jumping up on me, my mother smacking him down and putting me to bed, and then Mama saying she would have to go out to get the medicine the doctor wanted me to have. I kept trying to run through my mind how I'd gotten up out of that bed, how I'd gotten back into my clothes, and with the dog with me and me walking in that crouch, I'd gone outside and stayed outside and didn't go back to bed.

They kept me there seventy-five days.

It didn't matter how many—it only mattered that I was out— and I wasn't going back to bed.

It was May when I got out, May, 1974, and in June I talked long and hard with Galina. It couldn't wait—we had to get it straight between us, settle questions, know where we were going. At least that's what I thought—and I should have known better— I should have known that with what was between Galina and me, thinking wasn't necessary. What questions should a man have when his woman will come to him through all that agony of snow?

"Sit, please," I said.

"All right," Galina said.

"I'm troubled, I'm thinking," I said. "Give me a minute."

"All right," Galina said.

"It's this," I said. "No matter what it looks like now, I'm going to get out. I mean, eventually, I know it will happen."

"So?"

"You signed certain papers, remember? And the girls did."

"Which papers?" Galina said. "Ah, yes, I know which ones—the ones about—"

I interrupted her. I did not want her to say it. I said, "The ones about your being entirely willing for me to leave the country, and the girls signed too."

"Yes, of course," this good woman said, "and it is true. We want you to have what you must have—at any cost, that is what we want."

"I know," I said, "and I am bothered by it—it's nagging at me, this whole thing. My thoughts aren't clear yet. This heart business—and the stroke—am I thinking clearly?"

"Yes, my darling," my wife said. "Perfectly. Please believe that."

"It's just that I've been thinking what will happen once I'm gone—and before it is possible for you and the girls to follow me. It will take time—who knows how long? And what will they do to you once I'm gone? I mean, what about work? Will you be able to get work? And the girls. Sveta's schooling—and Janna's work and school. There will be reprisals—I am certain of it."

"So? Are we not strong? Have we not already endured so much? It will be a small thing—and in time we will follow you and it will all be over."

"Yes, yes," I said, "but in the *meanwhile*. I mean, I just don't know—it troubles me terribly—but with the heart, I feel I must—I feel I must go as soon as I *can* go. But how can I go with a clear mind?"

"Because you must," my wife said. "Because you have paid for it a thousand times over. Because there is nothing to worry about. And because it is the only way—you first, then the girls, then me. It is the only way. We have discussed this, Vitya. Before the heart, before the stroke—and now more than ever, it is the only way, the only decision. We decided this years ago. Nothing has changed. Please, my husband, clear your mind."

"Yes," I said. "I know. But I cannot."

"My husband," she said, "listen to me—it is very simple. Unless you go, we cannot follow, and is it not true that you want America for us? So! There is no other way—you first, then the girls, then me. And did I not follow you through worse than this? Is it not because of the way you look at me and I look at you? Please," she said, "I do not want to discuss this anymore. It is settled. Please, my darling, clear your mind."

I said to my wife, "You are a good woman." I said to her, "I love you so."

"Love, love, love," she said to me, and touched my hair.

And so, as required and as planned by us some while previous to that time, we divorced, my beloved wife and I, registering the papers that were necessary, and thus taking one of the last steps toward the goal we'd so long and so arduously been working for. We had put this step off for a time when we felt we might be nearing our objective—and somehow the heart attack and the stroke, they somehow conveyed to me the hunch that it was going to happen, that America was not that far off anymore, that I would incredibly, unimaginably—great ✶ !—I would be *going home.*

Galina had to move to Moscow to prove we were not living together. She went there with the girls because that was where there was work for her, a job that had been arranged. I didn't want to talk about how it was when we said good-bye. It was very bad for us all—perhaps worst for me—because of the guilt I felt and could not shake off, no matter what they said to me to make it all right for me.

We tried to put a good face on it—but it was no good trying.

We just did it, and that is the end of it—untried surgeons operating with crude instruments.

It was terrible for me when they left. I could not keep my spirits up. What did I have? I had no one but my family—in all of this alien land, I had nothing, no one save those three that were mine and that I loved so desperately.

And then everything got immediately worse—and it was hard to find the strength to fight it.

My heart, the stroke, the loss of my family—these things left me with little in the way of reserves to fight what came next. I was fired from my teaching jobs—and then I was blacklisted and unable to get work, anywhere, at anything. And then they started taxing me, saying that I had earned money I had not earned and forcing me to pay taxes on this phantom income. I sold the family car to pay those taxes. It helped.

But the next thing was they came to the apartment. They said they had to search the place. They confiscated every document and photograph they could lay their hands on—books, papers, records, documents, even clothing. Those KGB men just came in there and started going through everything, and they threw everything into cartons and took it out of there.

They left me some clothing—and those other things—but even photographs, they took even those.

I just sat there watching.

I was too exhausted to protest—and what good would it do? Besides, insofar as anything really important went, I had all that somewhere else. Years back I'd started hiding things, documents and the diaries I'd kept and so forth—in fact I had three places where I kept things in hiding, and even to this day I cannot say what those places were. Even when Galina comes, I still cannot tell. Nor can I tell about the methods I found to get things out by mail and by courier.

It is nothing I would keep secret unless I had to—for those still there who use the same places and the same methods.

It does not matter. There are ways. We all know this. In any situation, there are ways. In the worst of conditions, people find a way. There is never any policing such human resourcefulness—and the more you try to crush it, the more elaborate are its devices.

But their coming there to my place and searching and taking, it was a violence against my home that seemed to me curiously ugly. I don't know why. There is something about people coming into your place—especially when it is the intimate place of your wife and your children. It is ugly in a way that goes very deep into something primal in a man, into his instinct to protect, I suppose. I sometimes thought about it in relation to the invasion of my person in those prisons and in the camps, how picking through the objects in my home seemed to me a greater indecency than their forcing their fingers into my rectum to probe and search.

Perhaps I am unusual in this way—but I don't think so. My guess is that other people feel the same thing, and it is strange that we feel it, this violation of something, just the corners of a room. It is obscene. The place is dirty after that.

They came to do that in 1975.

I made my annual application in 1976. It was just after the Helsinki Accords.

I waited as I had waited every year. I waited to be told, *Ah, no, a pertinent item has not been filled in, a pertinent document was not attached, a pertinent signature was left off, a pertinent this or pertinent that has been omitted, and anyway, with regrets, with apologies, with all due sympathies, petition denied!*

It was approved! Notice came. My application had been approved!

I had to sit down when I saw it there! I cannot tell you the feelings that rushed up in me—the years of waiting, the inferno of years before that. I sat there bewildered, disbelieving, and so elated I wanted to howl aloud. And then I did it—like a boy, letting out great whoops of uncontainable joy. I yelled and laughed and then I wept and got down on the floor and spread my arms against it and tried to stop the world from turning me over and over.

A few days later, a letter from Dave came.

Dear Victor:

It is my understanding from the State Department that your application to return to your homeland has been approved by both the government of the U.S.S.R. and of the U.S., and in fact you may already have had word of this wonderful news. Let me congratulate you on the success of your efforts and extend my sincere wish that you do everything you can to take good care of yourself during this difficult period. I know that your heart condition was a grave blow, but I want you to take special pains to look after your general health.

My most affectionate regards,
David Herman.

As always, I read between the lines well enough. Correspondence between me and Dave had been going on for years now, and I guess we'd both gotten very good at deciphering what the other one actually meant to say. Did I think they would actually try to kill me? Surely Dave thought so. In any event, real threat or no, I allotted a certain amount of money to pay for the services of a bodyguard—and it was easy enough for me to get a first-class one, what with my connections in boxing. Moreover, since the fellow was a boxer, perhaps his hanging around me so much was a little less suspect than it might otherwise have been. But what did it matter if they were suspicious? Wasn't it better that way? Wouldn't I be safer if they were on notice that I was wary, that I expected something?

Anyhow, I got a young middleweight from a neighboring town, a very trustworthy boy who respected me for what I'd taught him, and I think he was fond of me too. He was willing to look after me in a sort of informal way—and he said he didn't want any money for doing it—but I pressed it on him, not all that much, but enough to be fair to the both of us. The fact was, after the special tax assessment and the loss of both of my jobs, there wasn't that much from which to give him—but I wanted him to have something.

I'd had instructions that I was to report to the Passport Department on the 9th of February, that I was to appear there in Kishinev on the 9th, and that I would be able to fly to the States from Moscow on the 10th. It was mid-January when word came, and I immediately got word to Galina. It was arranged that she would return to Kishinev to our apartment—we would see each other in Moscow, and then she would take up residence in the apartment once I'd gone. We decided that the girls should return to Kishinev immediately, to be with me until it was time for me to go.

On the 8th of February I bought three plane tickets for Moscow—but I did this through a friend. The tickets were in his name. The KGB reviews lists of all persons purchasing air passage, and I wasn't taking any chances. I even went so far as to make it a six A.M. flight, just because I felt that was the safest time to go. I don't know why. Maybe I thought people are just a little less alert at that hour of the day. Anyway, that's what I did.

The night of the 9th I went to the passport office—around six o'clock, and by seven o'clock I had my release papers. That friend drove us straight to the airport and we got on that plane and we got to Moscow and registered at a small out-of-the-way hotel.

I went back to the hotel.

On the way to the hotel, I thought of the exchange I'd had with the man I had to deal with to get my papers.

"Oh, yes, Herman, we have been waiting for you."

"Thank you very much," I said.

"How excellent," he said, this bland man who worried me for the very reason of his blandness, "that you are to be reunited with your family in your motherland."

"I am very happy," I said.

"Good, good," he said, "and we have arranged passage for you tomorrow."

"Well," I said, "that was very kind, but I'm not sure yet if I'll be using that ticket. I think I'm going to stick around Moscow for a while, maybe as much as a month."

"Oh, yes?" he said, his manner showing not the least curiosity. "And why is that, may I ask? One would think you were in a great haste to return to your family in your motherland."

"Oh, I am," I said, "except I've got a lot of friends here in Moscow, and I want to say good-bye to them all. You know how it is—it takes time, and now that I'm going, what's the rush? That's the way it is, I guess—you hurry up, and then, when you get there, you're not in such a hurry anymore."

"Yes, of course," the man said, shuffling papers and then taking a hard look at me. "So, you do not believe you will be going to-morrow?"

"Doubtful," I said. "Very doubtful. I'll call and cancel the reservation—make a new one. About a month, I think, maybe three weeks, sometime in there."

"Excellent, excellent," the fellow said, and that seemed to conclude our business. He did some more shuffling of papers and rubber-stamped this and that, had me sign a receipt, and by nine o'clock I was out of there and on my way back home.

In Moscow we all met the next night—Galina, the children, me —in the streets at a place we worked out well beforehand. I kissed my wife and kissed my wife and kept on kissing her. The girls stood around, and I think we knew they were crying. We kissed hello and kissed good-bye and made our plans for the morning, and then the girls and I went back to the hotel and Galina someplace else.

I had the schedule worked out to the minute.

We all knew it—the girls, Galina—knew exactly what was going to take place and where each of us would be and when and what we would do if anything went wrong.

At six o'clock the following morning, I took a taxi from the hotel. The girls had left five minutes before me. I stayed in the lobby while they got into their taxi and gave the driver instructions. They were to take that taxi to within three blocks of the American embassy, and then walk the rest of the way until they were stationed, out of view, across the street from the embassy building. Galina would arrive shortly thereafter and take up a position about fifty yards from the girls.

Had Galina made the telephone call the night before?

There is a special number to call—a line to the embassy. It is a safe line—and those who need to know about it find out about it, no matter how regularly the number is changed. The word goes out to the people whose job it is to pass it along.

Even before I'd left Kishinev, I had the number.

And when I was with Galina the night before, she confirmed it through the sources she had in Moscow. She said it was the right number—and she would not forget. Forget? Impossible!

She was to have made the call—and of course she made it. How think that she would not!

That telephone call would tell someone at the embassy the precise minute I would present myself at the embassy doors—and if not, then they would know inside there that something had gone wrong.

There was more to this—a code number that Galina was to recite into the phone, a number passed to her by certain people in Moscow who had it from the person who would answer the embassy phone, and that number would mean my name, because my name was not to be used on the telephone.

I make it all sound easy, but it wasn't. From the time I'd had word I was getting out to actually getting out, things got theatrically complicated, and you needed a lot of help to manage all the complications, and there were people to help you, people whose business it was to help lots of people in these circumstances, and you can't really talk about it very much because then the whole thing wouldn't work anymore, because there remain in the Soviet Union so many people for whom this network of "friends" that suddenly reveals itself must do its work. Maybe the things I think are so secret are not really so secret. But I will not be the one to talk about them. No one binds you to secrecy, but common sense tells you what you should say and what you shouldn't say, and I will not be the one to say more than is necessary. It is enough to know that one does not do these things alone, that one must have help, that there are people who will give it when the time comes. It is enough to say that one is grateful for that, and that is all one should be saying on the subject.

Soviet KGB guard the embassy. They were all around there when I showed up, even at that hour. I arrived exactly when I was supposed to. I got out of the taxi, I paid the driver, and I walked right in. The guards did not challenge me. I walked right past them and the door opened for me without my even signaling.

I'd been told they could see outside from inside, and that twenty-four hours a day they were looking outside, monitoring the area, and that if the guards tried to stop me, they'd come outside and get me once I was on U.S. ground. But no one tried to stop me, and the door opened up for me as if my body had interrupted a beam and an electric eye had gone into operation, and it was all just as automatic as that.

Two of them inside laughed when I did what I did. It just happened. It just came out of me. I called out, "Hot dog. Hurray!" when I stepped through that door.

They smiled at me with the grandest smiles I'd seen in more than four decades, and maybe they were just ordinary American smiles, but they seemed to me to be wonderful smiles, real smiles, smiles that let go more than anything you ever saw in Russia, and I would be lying if I said that there was something else I noticed more than those smiles when I got inside.

One of the fellows inside called back, "Hot dog is right!" and I looked at him, and he was smiling at me, and you knew you were home when you saw that kind of smile. I just grinned that whole time in there. All that time I felt as if I had the most ridiculous grin on my face. But I couldn't stop doing it. How long had my face been grave, stern, sullen? It is the normal look, is it not? You thought so until you got inside and suddenly knew all over again all you'd been away from and how much it had changed you to be gone from it.

I grinned and nodded my head and smiled at everyone and everyone smiled back, and I felt like giggling. I felt sublimely happy —and boyish and weepy and silly and goofy and dreamy and crazy, and I just wanted to lie down on their carpeting and sleep or roll over and over or look at them all and hug them all and keep shouting "Hot dog!" at every one of them.

But I just grinned until my face hurt and stood there grinning while they all came up to me and shook my hand and some of them slapped me on the back and they all said hello and congratulations and welcome home and things like that, pumping my hand and smiling at me.

I don't think I said six words all that time I was in there, I was so busy grinning and nodding my head. I'm glad I didn't have to talk. I don't think I could have.

They gave me a passport, my passport, an American passport, and when I looked at it and saw what was special about it, I shouted "Hot dog!" again and some of them laughed and the fellow standing near me slapped me on the back again.

It was a Bicentennial passport.

I was in there for over two hours.

They told me to stay at the Dawn Hotel until the time I was to go to the airport. They said that was the only place I was allowed to stay because of the legal status of my situation—I think it was because I now had an American passport but was not registered as a tourist. We all shook hands again, and with that grin still on my face and that Bicentennial passport in my pocket, I walked out of there, and when I crossed the street Galina and the girls ran up to me and we all kissed like mad, and we hailed down a taxi and drove to the Dawn. But I didn't like the way things looked at the Dawn—it just didn't look right to me. They said at the desk that they couldn't give us a room until three in the afternoon and we waited there a little while, and I kept thinking people were watching us, and I got very jumpy. I gathered us all up and took a taxi away from there, and I told the driver to take us to a dump I knew about, a real dive of a hotel I knew about from the times I'd been in Moscow. I got to the manager there and gave him some cock-and-bull story about having left my passport at home, and then I bribed him to get a room. I paid him a hundred rubles cash for a room that went for ten—and then he wanted a second hundred for his trouble —and then he still wasn't sure he was going to cooperate, so I promised him I'd give him a third hundred extra when I checked out.

We went up to room number 10 on the third floor, and we talked for about an hour or so, and then the girls went off with Galina to the room where Galina had been staying. I wasn't smiling anymore. I could not smile at my family like that. It was awful, feeling so good and feeling so bad. It was not good at all, and the girls cried—but Galya was all right. I knew she would always be all right. That woman could take anything I could take—and then take it all over again.

We worked out a schedule for the next five days—where, when, how to meet, and all sorts of contingency plans if this or that did not work out. Were all these precautions necessary?

I will never know.

I know that's what we did. It seemed the smart thing to do. I wasn't going to let down my guard for a minute, and I didn't.

I can't tell you the name of that dumpy hotel. The manager made me sweat, but still he let me have that room—and I will not pay him back by giving the name of his place.

The next day I picked up the money Dave wired me—a thousand dollars, and later that day I got my ticket.

Pan Am.

Pan *American*.

The very name, it gave me chills to say it to myself.

I mainly bought the girls clothes with that money. I used up most of it on clothes for them—and I got something special for Galya—and when I gave it to her, I said, "This is because you look at me," and I should not have said that because it made her cry, and it was hard for her to get control of herself after that.

I didn't need all that money. Who starves in America? Please God I should only get to America, and whatever was what, I would manage. Worry in America? Those who do, it is a sadness—but for us who've been in other places, for us there is nothing to worry about in America.

We said good-bye. How many times had we said good-bye? We said good-bye very fast—because this time it was the worst.

"In America," I said to each one of them.

"In America," Janna answered, kissing me.

"In America, Papa," my Sveta said.

"Two potatoes," I said to her, kissing my firstborn again.

And to Galya I said, "Love, love, love."

I went away from them.

It was the 15th of February. The year was 1976.

The rest happened as in a dream.

The taxi ride to the airport, to Sheremetyevo, the business of checking in and going through customs, all those large and small motions of travel, they happened as in a dream, and I did not wake up from it until that Boeing 707 had jerked free from inertia and rolled the long way into position, nose to the wind. They revved the engines full-blast, all the way up, then all the way down, then up again, and the great lumbering thing started slowly, roughly forward, and you could feel the magnificent power in the thing, but there was no speed yet, as if all over this giant little brakes held it back, and then those little brakes one by one gave up their puny purchase, and the force and rush were terrific, and I didn't know where I was sitting and who I was sitting next to, because in my mind I was alone in that cockpit, and it was my hand that was on the stick and the plane was not a plane like this, a thing huge and with a complexity of instruments, but was a little thing instead, my shivering, creaking U–2, that crude U–2 I used to wheel through the crazy Gorky sky. But its power was fire and gigantic, a hundred monstrous engines arrayed in banks that hugged the mile-long wings that swept back from me on either side and were silver and polished granite and platinum and diamond, and I let the throttle out and eased back the wooden stick, and it blazed cold, a bolt of ice. I could feel the great ramming force all around me and then feel me and all that was around me going up into that leaping clarity, nothing but blue all around me and a detonation behind, my wings gleaming and sweeping back from my sides, long and glittering and jeweled in the light, my face turned up to the colossal glaze above me, *that light, that light,* and there is no noise, and no wind, and no language, though my mouth is wide and singing, and then everything that is me and around me, this machine and its glistening impulse and all the surface of skin that enfolds me, it fuses and flashes and opens into something, unfurls itself, races away from itself at infinite speed, these needles of light going up and out, a disk of hard gas skimming, my mind the long line of its diameter, all force gone now and in its place the achievement of silence, perfect and stunning, and only the sun's gliding eye keeping the secret that you have vanished into motion, are possessed of no dimension but the idea of the vector, and up ahead of you it is all escape, a radiance of bright soaring.

Wasn't earth my first prison? At the beginning of things, wasn't earth that which prepared me for the rest? Was not everything *not up here* not free?

I had looked up long ago and had seen those white letters, and after that it was all a prison. There was love down there— my daughters and Galya, Papa, Mama, dead Leo, Miriam, and Rebecca, and David, good David, and dear, gone Red Loon—and there was also the other down there, the face of every Belov, all that ruin of flesh, haggard and gaping, the furious death of astonished rats, a suffocation of ponderous snow.

I sat in that plane like any other, a man like all the rest, gray suit, brown shoes, seatbelt fastened, going from, going to. To what? Woodward Avenue? The Fisher Building? Seven-Mile, Nine-Mile, the spokes of Detroit? My home? I would taste Vernors and see Ironwood and I would tell myself I was home, and there would be nothing to tell me it was not true. Yet what was it that I left behind me? Trees cracked open in a black sprawl of rage, wood that showed its dripping organs to you and came at you to kill? That wood will follow me, and so will the mist pooled into blisters everywhere on the concrete that formed that devil cell. We sat there, sixteen men, all staring at a circle whose fierce circumference encompassed sixteen separate visions, each limitless and utterly alone.

And sometimes we saw each other and did not know a name.

Who knows another man? My father and the son he made? I write this knowing that it happened, that I am this Victor Herman I tell about, a boy who went out, a man who came back—my name is Victor Herman, but who is the man with that name? He is no more in place for me than was the shadow of my little plane rippling across the tumultuous snow. I feel I am somewhere *outside* of these things, beyond events and the flesh they are inscribed on. I feel I am a point without dimension, a velocity coursing first here and then there, a motion through the waters of time.

It is chalk, everything I have told you, a smoke making letters in the sky. The earth turns, the air splashes, and what is written disperses. But for a little while the eye can still decipher something. Then, all at once, it is a cloud.

And the next time you look, even that is gone.

EPILOGUE ⸻

The girls are with me now, Svetlana and Janna—both safe here with me in Detroit. My flight over was uneventful, although that hardly seems the way to talk about one's passage out of Hell.

I suppose I mean in contrast to the girls, their flight. For they came to me fifteen months later, freed at last. But the crossing for them was not so easy. It was anything but uneventful.

They, like me, had Kennedy as their destination, but the routing called for a change of airplanes in Montreal. Meanwhile, all the arrangements had been made—that is, I would fly in from Detroit to meet them, and they were not to stray, not do anything, until what they could do was walk into my arms.

It happened that in Montreal a helpful flight agent presented himself. *Ah,* said he, *and where are you young ladies headed? To our father, in America,* they said. *Oh,* said he, *and have you been away from him for long? Oh, yes,* they said, *for very long.*

The Montreal change of aircraft called for a stopover of about three hours. But since the helpful flight agent wished very much to be helpful, and since he could see how eager the girls were to be on their way to me, he suggested that they revise their plans and take an earlier flight from Montreal to New York. *You can save at least an hour and a half,* said he, and then he quite helpfully made the arrangements, the altering of their tickets and so on. *Why wait?* he said. *Why not be off to your father straightaway?*

The girls were delighted. The arrangements were made. And they boarded a Royal Air Maroc plane.

I, of course, had taken up my station to meet them. At the Pan American terminal.

Well, the girls had flown before—in Russia. In Russia an airport has one terminal. At Kennedy there are many—and at which one you will be found depends on which airline you fly.

I was at the Pan Am gate—waiting. My friend and lawyer Bob Greenstein was with me. We were there hours sooner than we had to be—waiting.

But the girls were meanwhile waiting too.

They had landed—all safe and sound—all the way from Moscow. They had of course landed in an Air Maroc plane. And there they waited for me, at the Air Maroc terminal, thinking, *We are here!*

But of course they weren't. And like the good girls they are, they waited—not straying, not moving from the spot, just doing as their father had instructed.

Meanwhile, I waited at my post at the Pan Am gate, and when their plane set down and had made its way to the gate, my arms trembled with the wanting of what I'd been promised to have.

We all stood there waiting—and then the passengers began streaming in, all that motion of arrival erupting all around me. My arms trembled. I craned to see. This one? No? Then *this* one! Ah, no. All right, the next? The next?

All those people moved into my burning vision, but not any of them was Svetlana or Janna.

When it was clear that they had not been among the arriving passengers, that it was not possible they might have slipped un-recognized (and unrecognizing) past us, I vaulted over the re-straining rope and started to make my way into the aircraft. But a member of the crew blocked my passage.

"You can't go in there!" he said.

"I must," I said. "My daughters. They're on that airplane! There must be something wrong—perhaps they're sick."

"No," he said, "there's no one on there but crew," he said. "Believe me, mister, the plane's empty. Everybody's out."

I came close to fainting.

But I did not faint.

We went to the Security Office. We called Moscow; we called Kishinev; we called Pan Am and Montreal and the State Depart-ment. We called everywhere.

Meanwhile, in the Royal Air Maroc terminal, the girls waited.

They waited three hours—and when they'd waited four hours, they began to cry.

It was only when they cried that the mishap was uncovered. Another flight agent—also helpful. It took an hour and a half for him to get the story straight and sort it all out.

I could have kissed him. I could have strangled his fellow flight agent in Montreal.

But I used up all my kissing on Sveta and Janna.

All the way back to Detroit, I could not keep myself from kissing them.

They are in school here now. They are learning how to program computers.

It's hard for them, the life, how different everything is. They're shy, and the differences make them shyer. But now and then they do a bit more than go to school and make meals for me. More and more they do a bit more, and by the time Galina joins us, I imagine she'll say, "Oh, Vitya, how *American* they are!"

Perhaps she'll say that. It will make us all laugh.

But I know there is something else that she will say first.

She will say, "Why do you look at me?"

I know how I will answer.

I began setting down this record about a month after I had made my way home, the only survivor of all those men and women and children who had gone from Detroit to Gorky and ended in Siberian camps all those many years ago. I am the one, the only one, who got back, who lived through it all.

The girls sleep in the next room—while I sit at my typewriter night after night after night—and all day long. There was nothing in me save the will to set it all down.

It's written now—all those days and nights yielding what I've put before you.

It's finished now—this account—and the girls are right next door. It's all done, all that bad time ended and behind me now—but still, as I write this last of it, I am here and my beloved is there.

They promised.

They said, just wait until the first day of 1978. The date, they said, was firm.

They said the same for the last day of last January. And then the same for the end of February. And now it is the end of March—and still—still—that woman who danced across the chill floor in that Krasnoyarsk gymnasium, pale feet, black hair, that woman, my beloved Galina, is *there,* and I am here.

This room that I write in is bare. Typewriter, paper, this table, the bed, a chair. Sometimes I look out the window. When I can write no longer, I sometimes do that—or I turn in my chair and gaze at that bed.

Galina will come.

I will shoo the girls away from the little kitchen. As to the cooking, I will do all of that. A simple meal. Just potatoes, cut thick and fried in cod liver oil.

There is a bottle of champagne cooling already—I've had it in the refrigerator since the first of the year.

It cools there—and once a week the girls buy two fresh potatoes and throw the old ones out.

I gaze at that bed. It is a small room, and I only need lean a little bit in my chair to touch the blanket that covers that bed.

I will sit here—eating, forking those terrible potatoes into my mouth—and she will sit across from me—*there*—on that blanket—a plate of those potatoes held in her white, white hands.

I will pour and then place the bottle of champagne on the floor between us.

Here, my darling, darling wife, your glass.

I don't think either of us will smile very much—or finish the meal that I have made.

Perhaps one glass. Perhaps we will drink one glass.

She will touch her lips and then set the goblet down. I imagine she will put it there, on the floor, very near the bed. She will touch her lips and raise her eyes to mine.

Will she speak?

No, I don't think so.

Nor will I.

Except to say, "Because you look at me."

Detroit
March, 1978

PART 6

ADDENDA

PREPARE FIELD FOR PACIFIC CLIPPER RUN

Universal Service Wire

SAN FRANCISCO, Feb. 18.—With the first of Pan-American multi-motored transpacific clippers, Col. Charles A. Lindbergh at the controls, expected to roar in over the Golden Gate within two weeks, work was under way today to get Alameda Airport ready to receive the flying boat.

The yacht basin at the airport, leased by Pan-American as the west coast base for its Hawaii-Philippines-China line, was being cleared out to serve as a landing harbor for the new planes.

"Clipper No. 7," a Sikorsky ship capable of carrying 46 passengers and a crew of six 190 miles an hour, is at Miami, where picked crews from Pan-American's Caribbean service have been testing the 'b in long experimental flights

The sea—some of them 3,000 long, or 600 miles beyond .ongest trek in the transparun.

.ionel Lindbergh is expected to the clipper west late this th, by way of the Panama .nal. With him is scheduled to fly Col. Clarence Young, the air line's operations chief. Fred G. Athearn, attorney for the air line, said:

"The plan is for Colonel Lindbergh to reach here with the first ship on or about the first of March, and to take her out on the inaugural flight shortly 'fter that. Regular service will not be instituted for some time, however, as intermediate bases are not completed."

After a few days of testing and tuning up, the "Lone Eagle" will take off for Canton, by way of Honolulu, the Midway Islands, Wake Island, Guam and Manila. On results of that inaugural flight will depend the schedule put into effect by Pan-American when passenger and mail flights are begun this Summer.

The clippers are designated to .aintain a 16-hour schedule between San Francisco and Hawaii, their longest nonstop hop over the ocean. Amelia Earhart flew the 2,400-mile distance in 18 hours.

GREEN ATTACKS AUTO BOARD

Universal Service Wire

TOLEDO, Feb. 18. — William Green, president of the American Federation of Labor, today had declared in an address that "the so-called National Automobile Labor Board must go."

While organized labor is desirous of obtaining collective bargaining in the automobile industry through peaceful methods, Green said, if necessary it will utilize other methods, including strikes, to obtain labor's ends.

Effect 2 Changes At Liquor Store

JACKSON, Mich., Feb. 18.—Lyle D. Hunt, member of the Jackson Board of Education and former athletic director of St. John's High School, has replaced Benjamin Sweeti as manager of the liquor store here. C. Forrest Braund replaces Lester Grindall as cashier.

Detroit Boy Wins Fame As 'Lindy of Russia'

Ex-Northwestern High Student May Soon Fly Atlantic

Comrade Victor Herman, former Detroit schoolboy, today is hailed in the Soviet Union as "the Lindbergh of Russia."

Only 19 years old, he is a daredevil flier a parachute jump record breaker, medal winning marksman and excellent all around athlete. Soon he may fly the Atlantic.

Today the Times discovered Comrade Victor Herman, "the Lindbergh of Russia," is Victor Herman, late of Northwestern High School. Victor Herman, in fact, American citizen, recently of 6094 Ironwood avenue, Detroit.

"Vickie never went in for athletics or anything like that while going through Northwestern High as far as the tenth grade," smiled his pretty sister, Mrs. Rebecca Laing, 21, of 8581 Bryden avenue.

'ALWAYS A DAREDEVIL'

"He was always a daredevil, crazy enough to do anything, and was greatly interested in mechanics. He was always pulling old cars apart. Otherwise, I guess he was just an ordinary boy.

"Then in September, 1931, my father, Samuel Herman, was out of work and he accepted an offer to go to Russia to become an executive in an auto plant there.

"Vic, then 15, and Leo my other brother, then 13; little Miriam, only 4, and my mother, who since has died there, all went with him. I could have gone, too, and taught school there, but preferred to stay here.

"Vic continued his high school education there and then went into flying school. It was while he was in high school he went out for a track team. In 1933, he wrote us, he won 12 medals for athletics and marksmanship.

PLACES IN 9 EVENTS

"In the 1933 Soviet Sportacide, representing Gorki, Autozavod, where the family lives, he placed second, third or fourth in nine events — various races, high and broad jump, swimming and shooting.

"However, I guess it was when he broke the world record for the parachute jump they began calling Vic 'the Lindbergh of Russia.'"

A friend of Victor, John Smith, another American living in Russia, who describes Herman as the Soviet Union's best all around athlete, described the event for the Times:

"Thirty thousand people gathered September 6 at the flying field to see the parachute contest. After some stunt flying the jumpers came out, some jumping while looping, or doing a spin. Then Victor came out.

JUMPS, EATING APPLE

"I watched his plane soar out of sight above the clouds. Then came a radiogram saying he was 24,800 feet up and jumping. After a little I saw him through my glasses, hurtling down with the speed of lightning.

"I could see him turning and over heels and spinning toward us. 'Why doesn't the parachute open?' the crowd murmured. It didn't open until he was 1100 feet above the ground. Through my glasses I could see him doing something.

"When he came down I found he was eating an apple. 'I found it in my pocket when I pulled the rip cord,' he said, 'and there

VICTOR HERMAN, 19, "Russian Lindbergh," in his Winter uniform as cadet air commander. Until four years ago Herman was one of Northwestern High School's hundreds of pupils here in Detroit.

was nothing else to do, so I ate it.' It was the best example of nerve I ever saw."

WANTS TO FLY SEA

"Vic graduated from flying school last September and now is going to the flying academy," said his sister. "His parachute record has since been broken, but he writes he is going to try for a new record soon.

"He loves it there—you couldn't pay him to come back here, although he is still an American citizen, and is not a Communist.' Nevertheless, 'he "Russian Lindbergh" may return to his native Detroit, she added.

"He has asked for a plane to try to fly the Atlantic, and has been promised one by officials," said Mrs. Laing. "He's very anxious to do that."

AIRMEN TO AID ABYSSINIA

By Karl H. von Wiegand
Copyright, 1935, by Universal Service, Inc.

LONDON, Feb. 18. —Adventurous American, British and German airmen, as well as White Russian officers, are offering their services to Emperor Hailie Selassie of Abyssinia, lion of Judah and king of the kings, in the threatened war between the descendant of King Solomon and Queen Sheba and Italy, it became known here today.

Public enthusiasm in Italy is being stirred and imagination fired by legends about the gold mines of Solomon and Sheba and the idea of a crusading conquest of the Ethiopian empire, unconquered in 3,000 years—and excepting Japan—the oldest unconquered country on the globe.

Although Premier Mussolini this week officially said he had "no aggressive plans," fears actually starting for Abyssinia came somewhat as a shock here and in Geneva.

Ras Tafari, now Emperor Selassie, is successor to Menelik, Abyssinia's great national hero, who annihilated an Italian army of 14,000 in the battle of Adowah attempted

SENATOR CALLS NRA SHELTER FOR CRIME

Universal Service Wire

WASHINGTON, Feb. 18.—President Roosevelt today had completed his message to Congress asking extension of NRA for two years.

Meanwhile Senator Pat McCarran (D) of Nevada loosed a blistering attack on NRA code authorities, charging them with being a "shelter for organized crime."

McCarran, jointly sponsoring with Senator Nye, North Dakota insurgent Republican, a resolution calling for senatorial investigation of NRA and its codes, is preparing a battle that may rock the Senate.

MANY TELEGRAMS

In a statement McCarran said he had received 1,500 telegrams since the resolution was introduced Thursday. He added:

"The charges include not only oppression of small industry, gross discrimination, monopoly, arbitrary misuse of power and hindrance of recovery, but also the direct charge that the codes have become a shelter for organized crime."

Declaring all but 5 per cent of the persons communicating with him were willing to reveal their names, McCarran said:

"The source of these complaints renders them all the more grave and I sincerely believe we would be derelict in our duty if we ignored or permitted to without examination what amounts to a wholesale indictment on a nation-wide scale of conditions which have arisen under NRA."

NOT ATTACKING NRA

McCarran declared he was not attacking NRA so much as he was seeking to find "what evils arose under it." He added:

"The NRA still is an experimental agency. If it is to become an integral part of our government, it is a fundamental duty of Congress to scrutinize what has been accomplished, what needs correction and what must be remedied, to ascertain and eliminate evils if they exist and to satisfy the people of the United States this institution, if approved, is worthy of approval."

Back Door Burglar Hunted in Dearborn

A back door burglar was hunted by Dearborn police today following robberies of homes at 5515 and 5525 Mead street, Dearborn. From the former house, occupied by Abraham Smith and family, jewelry and clothing valued at $65 was stolen; from the latter, occupied by Andrew Scott, the burglar took watches and other jewelry valued by Scott at $500.

Cuticura Soap

For the Daily Care of Your Hands

Prolong the youthful appearance of your hands by giving them the same care you give your face. Use Cuticura Soap every time you wash your hands; it will do much to prevent redness and roughness, caused by daily tasks, and to keep the hands soft, smooth and lovely.

Price 25c.

ADVERTISEMENT

WEAK WOMEN

MANY women both young and middle-aged suffer from periodic pain in side or back from headache, "heat flashes," should be kethod

Dionnes View Latest Pictures of Babies

Cott betw mod sug; fres styl PA and

Sh

Fre lace the

ADDENDUM A

A few years after Victor Herman left America with his family, his home town read about his acclaim as "The Lindbergh of Russia."

ADDENDUM B _____

JAIL TAP LANGUAGE

	1	2	3	4	5
1	A	F	K	P	U
2	B	G	L	Q	V
3	C	H	M	R	W
4	D	I	N	S or Z	X
5	E	J	O	T	Y

The English translation of the Russian jail tap language appearing above shows its division of the alphabet into five columns of five letters. To spell the word "dog," for example, one tap indicates the column beginning with "a," followed by four taps for the fourth letter of that column, "d." The next letter is derived by three taps followed by five taps, "o," and finally, two taps and then two more would spell "g." Numerals were tapped out as words: 101, "one-o-one."

After each word was completed, the sender would tap fast several times and the receiver of the message would also tap fast to show he understood and the message would continue. If a mistake was made or a message was unclear, a rubbing, erasing sound would be heard. Prisoners became adept at using a brief, telegraphic style.

OTHER BOOKS AND TAPES BY THIS AUTHOR

SEND A SELF ADDRESSED ENVELOPE, STAMPED

TO   FREEDOM PRESS, LTD.
     TWO WOMPROP PLAZA
     5823 MOSTELLER DR.
     OKLAHOMA CITY, OK 73112

FOR FULL INFORMATION AND PRICE LIST